aspects of
modern
communism

Aspects of Modern Communism

Edited with a Preface by RICHARD F. STAAR

*Published on behalf of The Institute of International Studies of the
University of South Carolina*

UNIVERSITY OF SOUTH CAROLINA PRESS
COLUMBIA, SOUTH CAROLINA

First Edition
Copyright © 1968 by The University of South Carolina Press
Published in Columbia, S.C.,
by the University of South Carolina Press, 1968
Standard Book Number: 87249–136–6
Library of Congress Catalog Card Number: 68-9362
Manufactured in the United States of America

FOR MARIE AND BARBARA

acknowledgments

This volume comprises the edited papers as well as remarks made by the discussants at a closed conference on the communist-ruled states of the world which was held near the campus of Emory University in Atlanta, Georgia. It is hoped that the analyses will prove helpful in understanding the different aspects of modern communism within the foregoing context, i.e., within an operational framework. The organization of the book follows the schematic program of the conference.

Because of their size and importance to world communism, the U.S.S.R. and mainland China are given three chapters each. All eight countries in Eastern Europe have been treated as a single geographic area, even though it is recognized that they are indeed dissimilar, beginning with Chinese-influenced Albania at one extreme and the Soviet Zone of Occupation in East Germany at the other. The smaller Asian states of Mongolia, North Korea, and North Vietnam are analyzed individually; the same applies to Cuba.

All five parts of this book have been edited by this writer. Professor Jerzy Hauptmann, who served as rapporteur for the entire conference, provided a most perceptive analysis by skillfully extracting the common themes and posing many questions for further study. His accomplishment, perhaps the most difficult to attain, represents a fitting introduction to the book. Thanks also go to the Relm Foundation of Ann Arbor, Michigan, for financing the meeting itself.

The Honorable Kenneth B. A. Scott, First Secretary (Politico-Military Affairs) at the British Embassy in Washington, D.C., discussed Dr. Kintner's paper. Unfortunately, his brilliant comments have not been incorporated into this book because of his official position in Her Majesty's diplomatic service. I am also grateful to Professor Robert H. Brisbane, Jr., of Morehouse College; Professor Jack W. Hopkins, at the time of Georgia State College but now at Emory University; and Professor N. J. D. Versluys, of Morris Brown College, for presiding over individual sessions. Mrs. Louise Crawley and Mrs. Charlotte Harris, secretaries in the Department of Political Science at Emory University, typed the edited manuscript.

preface

Just before the outbreak of the World War II in 1939, there existed sixty-five communist parties in as many countries with a total membership of 1.2 million. Only two of these actually ruled states (the U.S.S.R. and its satellite Mongolia). By 1968, the numbers had increased to eighty-seven parties and 44.6 million members. Fourteen, comprising 41.8 million or 93.7 per cent of the total membership, now rule their own states and encompass one-fourth of the world. The Communist Party of China with seventeen million (38.1 per cènt) and the Communist Party of the Soviet Union with 12.9 million (28.9 per cent) members are the largest and follow a policy of expanding growth.[1] Superficially, these statistics might provide the impression of a monolithic edifice which has been spreading at an alarming rate ever since becoming anchored in Russia just over fifty years ago.

In actual fact, the fourteen communist-ruled states are torn by domestic contradictions as well as serious problems in relations among one another. Only two more or less successful conferences have been held over the past decade in attempts to settle differences within the Bloc. During the period from November 14 to 16, 1957, the thirteen then-ruling communist parties met at Moscow following the fortieth anniversary celebration of the Russian Revolution. These leaders signed a compromise Declaration which stated that the socialist camp was "headed" by the Soviet Union. The original formula had included the term "leader" and was supported by Chinese but opposed by Hungarian, Polish, and Yugoslav delegates. The Declaration warned against nationalism and revisionism (rightist deviation), a clear reference to Belgrade's "national communism." Representatives from Yugoslavia refused to sign.

Just three years later, it was dogmatism and leftist deviation which threatened the unity of the socialist "Commonwealth of Nations." A world conference met behind closed doors at Moscow in November and December 1960 in an attempt to settle differences with China. The compromise statement only papered over the cracks in Sino-Soviet relations. The Russians apparently attacked the Chinese, and the latter responded with a claim to their own "general line" although it was not enunciated in public until 1963. The dispute with China has led to closer relations between

1. U.S. Department of State, Bureau of Intelligence and Research, *World Strength of the Communist Party Organizations*, Publication No. 8375 (Washington, D.C., April 1968), pp. 1–8. Note that *Pravda*, January 20, 1967, claimed a world membership of 50 million.

Yugoslavia and the U.S.S.R. as well as other East European regimes. In 1961, already Nikita S. Khrushchev acknowledged that the former "right-wing deviationist" represented a full-fledged socialist country. This rapprochement has continued under Khrushchev's successors. In mid-1967, Josip Broz-Tito flew to Moscow where he joined Soviet and five other East European leaders in signing a joint declaration attacking Israel and the West. Three months later, Belgrade hosted a similar conference at the deputy premier level on economic assistance to the Arab countries. The end of that year, the Yugoslavs were represented at foreign minister talks on the Middle East situation, held at Warsaw. There seems to be no doubt that Yugoslavia again is regarded as a member of the Bloc and even sent a military delegation to observe Warsaw Pact maneuvers, conducted during the fall of 1967 in Bulgaria, although it is not a member of that military alliance system.

Interestingly enough, it is this regime at Belgrade which probably will contribute most to change in Eastern Europe. At the fifth plenum of the Yugoslav Communist League in October 1966, Tito declared that his party must guide and not rule. However, the Theses on reorganization of the League merely altered the structure but not the authority of the Party. The forthcoming congress toward the end of 1968 will have to face this issue and resolve it.[2] Another innovation occurred in February 1967, when the Yugoslav regime allowed foreign capital to be imported. This coincides with attempts to attain convertibility for the dinar and perhaps ultimately a free-market economy. Such non-Marxist developments may have an impact within the other communist-ruled states of the area.

These measures are being watched by the East European communist leaders themselves with a great deal of uneasiness. They would regard any change from the monopoly position of the Party as a threat to their own power positions. All have followed the foreign policy of the U.S.S.R. without deviation, except for Albania and Romania. The latter refuses to consider attendance at Bloc conferences as compulsory. Party secretary-general Nicolae Ceausescu protested in an article[3] against foreign contacts with Romanian communists which had taken place outside of prescribed channels and may have been designed by Soviet leaders to block the exchange of ambassadors between Bucharest and Bonn. If this indeed had been the objective, it was frustrated. Otherwise, West Germany maintains only trade missions in four other East European countries: Poland, Hungary, Bulgaria, and, since August 1967, Czechoslovakia. Diplomatic relations, broken off in October 1957, were re-established in January 1968 between Bonn and Belgrade.

2. The Soviet Union has warned against "any narrowing of the role of the Party," an obvious reference to the Yugoslav communists. *Pravda,* February 20, 1967.
3. *Scinteia,* May 7, 1967.

In general, the U.S.S.R. has attempted to project the image of close and fraternal relations with all of its East European "allies." Bilateral consultations have been stepped up, and one multilateral conference has taken place outside the framework of the Council for Mutual Economic Assistance or the Warsaw Treaty Organization (WTO). Held at Karlovy Vary, Czechoslovakia, during late April 1967, it attempted to present a united front on the subject of European peace and security which should not have been a controversial issue. Albania, Romania, and Yugoslavia did not send representatives to this meeting of East and West European communists because they all refuse to allow the Communist Party of the Soviet Union to coordinate policies for the Bloc as a whole. Albania, of course, has not attended any meetings since October 1961.

The Karlovy Vary Declaration specifically attacked the United States and the (West) German Federal Republic. It called for a united front of all parties and workers, farmers, intelligentsia, Social Democrats, trade unionists, youth, women, Christians, and even the bourgeoisie to achieve "new relations" in Europe. These are to include diplomatic recognition of both Germanys, a ban on nuclear weapons for the Bonn government, and a simultaneous dissolution of NATO and WTO.[4] Agitation for this last objective will increase, as the year 1969 and time to renew the Atlantic Alliance approach. In view of this circumstance, the broad appeal for a world-wide "peace" campaign that would unite public opinion against the United States becomes understandable.

As a matter of fact, however, even if the two military blocs were dissolved, the system of bilateral pacts in Eastern Europe would remain. These treaties, originally signed for periods of twenty years, are being extended currently for a similar length of time. It was interesting to note that the Soviet-Romanian agreement, due to expire in February 1968, could not be renegotiated but was automatically extended another five years. Between March and September 1967, additional series of bilateral treaties have been entered into by the so-called (East) German Democratic Republic (GDR) on the one hand and Poland, Czechoslovakia, Hungary, and Bulgaria on the other. This brings the GDR into the network with all East European states except Albania, Romania, and Yugoslavia.

It should also be noted that recent maneuvers have been held in four separate exercises as follows: (1) June 14–19, 1967, in Hungary and Czechoslovakia under the direction of Ivan I. Yakubovsky, Marshal of the Soviet Union as well as first deputy defense minister and currently the new WTO commander-in-chief, with U.S.S.R. troops in addition to those of the host states; (2) August 14–18, 1967, East German and Soviet occupation

---

4. Text in *Krasnaya zvezda*, April 27, 1967.

troops held combined exercises in the Potsdam and Magdeburg districts with Yakubovsky and GDR defense minister Army General Karl Hoffmann; (3) August 20–27, 1967, on the territory of Bulgaria and in the western part of the Black Sea under command of Bulgarian defense minister General of the Army Dobri Dzhurov, with participation of Soviet, Bulgarian, and, significantly, Romanian troops; and (4) during the last days of August 1967 in northwestern Poland under command of Polish defense minister Marshal Marian Spychalski, with troops from East Germany and the Soviet Union in addition to those from the host country.[5] These war games tested operational problems at the staff level and probably represented substitute exercises for the large-scale maneuvers, held since 1961 every autumn. There is no hard information available to indicate that the Soviet Union has cut back its garrisons stationed in the GDR, Hungary, or Poland.

Apart from the threat of massive military intervention, which could be applied in an extreme case, the U.S.S.R. also can exert pressure on its East European client states through the Council for Mutual Economic Assistance (CMEA). Economic planning has been synchronized, so that all plans now coincide at least during the current five-year period from 1966 through 1970. Trade agreements were signed for this length of time, and these all foresee substantial increases which bind the partners even more closely to the Soviet Union. Many of the postwar industrial complexes throughout the Bloc are dependent upon deliveries from the U.S.S.R. of raw materials such as iron ore, coking coal, petroleum, and cotton. Trade has become reoriented, perhaps permanently, toward the East. Certainly, even the new leadership of Czechoslovakia in 1968 must take this into consideration.

The only exception and the sole country definitely committed against the Soviet Union is Albania. Its latest communist party congress in November 1966 boasted the largest congregation of pro-Chinese splinter groups ever to have gathered in one place. Tirana is following in the footsteps of its ideological mentor by introducing a cultural revolution, although of a milder variety than that of Peking. Government bureaucrats and party officials are being dispatched to work directly in production. Wall posters and Red Guards have been copied from their Chinese counterparts, but the ruling Albanian Party of Labor maintains strict control over these developments.

The cultural revolution in China, on the other hand, has intensified since the August 13, 1966, resolution passed by the Central Committee. It quickly expanded to envelop the party in a country-wide purge which has met considerable resistance from the apparatus. High school and university

5. *Ibid.*, June 21, 1967; August 20 and 29, 1967; and September 2, 1967.

students, comprising the Red Guard movement, have precipitated severe dislocations throughout the country. Mao Tse-tung in early 1967 found himself forced to rely upon the army. Even it could not control the rioting, and hence a new attempt at re-establishing order is now in process by means of a "three-way alliance": so-called revolutionary forces, cadres of party and government officials who support Mao, and the military. Behind this upheaval and turmoil, there is taking place the inevitable struggle for succession.

Despite this concentration on domestic affairs, the Chinese Communist leadership has continued its campaign of vituperation against the U.S.S.R. The latter has interpreted events in China as being anti-Marxist, based on a policy of transferring to the armed forces the leading role traditionally exercised by the party. An editorial[6] appearing in the main daily newspaper, published by the Communist Party of the Soviet Union, even called upon the Chinese in Aesopian language to overthrow Mao Tse-tung. Relations between the two countries reached an all-time low, when the U.S.S.R. embassy in Peking withstood a veritable siege by mobs during early 1967 for nineteen days. In mid-August, a Soviet ship was allowed to leave Dairen only after premier Aleksei N. Kosygin had threatened to curtail trade with China which totals about 311 million dollars.

As could be expected, the meeting between President Lyndon B. Johnson and premier Kosygin at Glassboro, New Jersey, was denounced by the official Chinese communist news agency Hsinhua as a "global American-Soviet deal . . . to intensify the suppression of the surging revolutionary struggle of the people of the world." The U.S.S.R. itself has insinuated that talks in Warsaw, Poland, between the United States and Chinese ambassadors (the 134th session convened on January 8, 1968 with the chargé d'affaires of China) have had as one of their objectives to make more difficult Soviet assistance for the "heroic Vietnamese people" and the strengthening of aggressive circles in Washington, D.C., which pressure for a further escalation of the "dirty war" in South-East Asia.[7] Neither Peking nor Tirana sent delegations to the fiftieth Bolshevik Revolution anniversary in Moscow.

Turning to the ruling parties in Asia, the oldest Soviet satellite, Mongolia, probably has no choice but to remain in the position of close ally to the U.S.S.R., due to physical proximity and the fact that Russian troops are stationed in that country. North Korea and North Vietnam, at one time within the Communist Chinese sphere of influence, today remain officially neutral in the dispute between the two giants. This shift in attitudes can be attributed to the abortive Peking-inspired *coup d'état* by the

6. *Pravda,* November 27, 1966.
7. Vl. Zhukov's article on "What Happens at the American-Chinese Meetings," *Krasnaya zvezda,* June 20, 1967.

Communist Party of Indonesia on September 30, 1965, which resulted in almost total elimination of that movement and the adamant Chinese stand on refusing to participate in any joint effort with the Soviets to aid Hanoi.

Mongolia's leaders have proved their devotion to the Soviet Union by engaging in acrimonious attacks on Communist China. In addition to this kind of support, Moscow apparently considers Ulan Bator useful as a model for the uncommitted and underdeveloped countries of Asia. This can be seen from announcements that during the current Five-Year-Plan (1966–70), the U.S.S.R. will provide 660 million rubles in aid and absorb 60 per cent of Mongolia's foreign trade, 30 per cent more going to Eastern Europe. Ulan Bator also hosted the ninth congress of the communist-front International Union of Students in 1967. However, even this isolated country has manifested signs of dissension in its domestic affairs. Almost half of the members and more than half of the candidates on the Central Committee were replaced at the party's most recent 15th Congress. These proponents of the "reactionary ideology of nationalism" appeared to desire neutrality in the Sino-Soviet dispute rather than a pro-Chinese policy.

After anti-Soviet demonstrations by Chinese both in Ulan Bator and in front of the Mongolian embassy in Peking, where officials from Mongolia were handled roughly by Red Guards, the chairman of the Mongolian Jurists' Union suggested that Mao Tse-tung should be overthrown by the Chinese people. A few days later, Ulan Bator abrogated the visa abolition agreement with Peking. The Chinese in response have labeled Mongolian leaders as fools and liars who demonstrate their subservience to the "Soviet revisionist clique." The U.S.S.R. is no doubt gratified by these recent developments which serve to bind its oldest (since 1921) satellite even closer than before.

On the other hand, even hosting international communist front organization meetings serves to break down the isolation of the Mongolian People's Republic which, until 1949, was called "sovereign" only by the Soviet Union. Other communist-ruled states extended diplomatic recognition during the ensuing six years, but it was 1955 before the first non-Communist country (India) did the same. After being admitted to the United Nations in 1961, the regime at Ulan Bator has slowly extended its relations until, by 1968, it has reached a total of about forty states. The only international conference not under communist sponsorship was held at Ulan Bator under United Nations auspices and discussed the participation of women in public life. More contact with the world outside the Soviet Bloc may assist in the attainment of some degree of independence for Mongolia. A UPI dispatch, published on January 21, 1968, reported a cultural mission from "Outer Mongolia" on an eight-day tour of France.

The leaders of North Korea, on the other hand, do not seem interested in extending contacts with the non-Communist world. A series of provocations and incidents in the demilitarized zone as well as attempts at infiltration from the sea into South Korea apparently had as their objective the creation of turmoil to affect the 1967 presidential and national assembly elections in that country. Broadcasts from a clandestine station, called Radio of the Democratic Union for Liberation of South Korea, appealed to the population for a united front to drive President Pak Chung-hui from power. Although this campaign failed, North Korean leader Kim Il-sung hopes that border tension will assist the Vietcong in South Vietnam. A plan is now being implemented to infiltrate small guerrilla units across the 38th parallel to harrass the Seoul government from the mountains. They presumably are testing the feasibility of full-scale partisan warfare in South Korea. In mid-January 1968, a thirty-five-man guerrilla unit penetrated across the DMZ and entered Seoul.

Defense expenditures were raised to 30.2 per cent of the total budget for 1968, in order to "remain fully prepared to wipe out the aggressor for good and reunify the country," according to North Korea's finance minister. The U.S. Navy ship *Pueblo* and crew, seized on the high seas and forcibly taken to Wonsan, had not been released by late June 1968. Perhaps much of this belligerence can be attributed to difficulties in the economy. In the fall of 1966, the regime at Pyongyang postponed completion of its Seven-Year Plan for an additional three-year period. First-hand information on the harsh conditions in North Korea has come from Lee Sukeun, deputy director of the Central News Agency, who defected in the spring of 1967. Apparently as a reprisal, South Korean newsman Lee Kiyang was arrested two weeks later in Prague, Czechoslovakia, where he had flown from West Germany to cover a basketball world championship game.[8]

Economic problems of a different nature beset North Vietnam, which must walk a tightrope in order not to antagonize either the Soviet Union or Communist China. The war makes it dependent equally on both countries: Moscow supplies sophisticated weapons, and Peking delivers food as well as other military assistance. It is assumed that factions exist within the Hanoi leadership, but their composition and respective influence remain unknown. North Vietnam and China collaborate also in supporting the so-called "Thai Patriotic Front," which has been operating since 1965. Increased activity of bands in northeastern Thailand, along the border with Laos, and terrorism farther south are conducted by members of the "People's Armed Forces," trained at Hoa Binh in North Vietnam.

Regarding the war in Vietnam itself, the U.S.S.R. has been accusing China of sabotaging its deliveries to Hanoi. During 1967 these charges

8. This man disappeared in mid-April 1967, but repeated inquiries by Western governments have elicited no response from the communist regime of Czechoslovakia. *New York Times*, May 27, 1967.

specifically stated that the Chinese had "lost" some Soviet war matériel in railroad transit, replaced other equipment, and even painted their own markings on certain items. Peking did refuse to provide Moscow with an air corridor and has obstructed Russian personnel traveling to North Vietnam. A radio broadcast[9] alleged that Mao Tse-tung was attempting to "build a Chinese Wall to block the flow of Soviet supplies and to cut the lines of communication between the Soviet Union and Vietnam." It would seem that Peking is attempting to force Moscow to make its deliveries by sea and thus to precipitate a confrontation with the United States.

North Vietnam is dependent upon Chinese rice, because it had a short-fall of almost one million tons during the last harvest. Two delegations traveled secretly to Peking in 1967, probably for the purpose of allaying China's feelings of hostility toward any communist party which has remained neutral in the Sino-Soviet dispute. (During that year, about 500,000 tons of food came from the U.S.S.R. and China). Statements by the (North) Vietnam News Agency describe reports about Chinese obstructionist tactics concerning the transit of Russian aid as "sheer fabrications." It would appear that as long as ties with China are maintained, the North Vietnamese attitude in negotiations with the United States which started in May 1968 at Paris to end the war will remain unchanged. The principal Vietcong representative in Peking claimed that his organization would fight until it had won its political objectives, and Ho Chi Minh postponed accepting the U.S.S.R.'s Order of Lenin until all of Vietnam is "liberated."[10]

Complicating this matter is Hanoi's dedication to help other communist "liberation wars," especially in such adjacent states as Laos and Cambodia. North Vietnamese leaders see military operations in South Vietnam as an experience that will be useful to the revolutionary struggle of all people throughout the world. This, of course, coincides exactly with the view of the Chinese. The latter have stated that the conflict in Vietnam contributes to Mao Tse-tung's writings on people's war because Hanoi has worked out "operational lines and methods in accordance with its own conditions."[11] Although the North Vietnamese population undoubtedly suffers from problems involving morale, there are indications that the leadership will hold out until after the November 1968 presidential election in the United States.

The combination of nationalism and international communism is the reason why North Vietnam perceives its "liberation war" in a world-wide context. The present commitment represents a final test of guerrilla tactics.

9. Radio Moscow, February 12, 1967.
10. Radio Hanoi, November 14, 1967.
11. Article entitled "The Magic Weapon for Victory is the People's Revolutionary War," *People's Daily* [Jen Min Jih Pao], December 24, 1966.

In an interview carried by the (North) Vietnam News Agency in early 1967, foreign minister Nguyen Duy Trinh made the claim that "all Vietnamese people are resolutely fighting against U.S. aggressors to defend their sacred national rights and *fulfill their duty to the peoples* of the friendly countries *now struggling for their independence and freedom*" (my italics).

This avowed role as center of the national liberation struggle on a world basis was endorsed at the communist-dominated Three Continents' Conference held in 1966 at Havana. The meeting established a committee to aid liberation movements, which coordinates guerrilla and subversive activities in Asia, Africa, and Latin America. Assistance now includes training and weapons. North Vietnam is a contributor and itself a recipient of moral, political, and material help from parts of these three continents through a subcommittee in Cuba.

Apart from this "guerrilla international," relations between Havana and Hanoi involve Cuban economic aid and even military personnel for technical assistance. However, Fidel Castro has strained his relations with both China and the U.S.S.R. because he demands assistance regardless of cost. The quarrel with the Chinese came into the open during 1966, when the latter refused to supply rice or purchase Cuban sugar in the quantities suggested by Havana. Disagreement with the Soviet Union centers on tactics in Latin America.

In the summer of 1966 Castro repeatedly criticized in his speeches "pseudo revolutionaries" who talked but would not fight. *Pravda,* on the other hand, printed articles by Latin American communists on the hazards connected with premature revolutions. Finally, in a speech during mid-March 1967, Castro publicly attacked the U.S.S.R. for maintaining relations and signing trade agreements with regimes like those in Brazil, Chile, and Colombia, which are arresting communist leaders and fighting against guerrillas.

The following month Havana published an alleged message "to the peoples of the world" from Ernesto Guevara, who had disappeared early in 1965, predicting an upsurge in violence throughout all of Latin America.[12] Castro emphasized the "vital importance" of the Guevara statement and boasted of intensified guerrilla activity. The Cuban communist party's Political Bureau announced that a congress would be convened to solve "theoretical, strategic, and tactical problems of the world revolutionary movement." Havana apparently will not subordinate its militant attitude to Cuba's economic dependence upon the U.S.S.R. The chasm between such a revolutionary policy and that of most other Latin Ameri-

12. Official daily newspaper of the Cuban communist party, *Granma,* April 17, 1967. A recorded speech by Guevara was played at the May Day parade in Havana. Neither the printed message nor the speech has been authenticated.

can communist parties probably will grow, despite the death of Guevara in Bolivia, according to an interview with Castro which appeared in the December 1967 issue of *War/Peace Report*.

This may have been one of the reasons for Premier Kosygin's trip to Havana from New York back in mid-1967. Talks with Castro lasted most of the week. It is certain that the Soviet Union will continue its support of the island, both economically and militarily. There exists no alternative because Cuba remains isolated as the only communist-ruled state in the Western Hemisphere. It is interesting to note, however, that Castro has not broken off relations with Israel as did the U.S.S.R., Yugoslavia, and five other East European countries (Romania is the other exception) after the defeat of the Arab states. His independence also could be seen in the first Latin American Solidarity Conference, which was held during the first ten days of August 1967 in Havana. By a vote of fifteen to three, with nine abstentions, this conference resolved to condemn the U.S.S.R. for giving help to governments in Latin America which remained hostile toward Cuba.

From the foregoing survey it appears obvious that the Communist Party of the Soviet Union is meeting with considerable difficulty in bringing about a semblance of unity among the fourteen movements that rule their own countries. Efforts to impose a "general line" have failed. Even meetings on a regional basis for limited purposes do not seem capable of erecting the façade of a united front. In late 1965 the consensus among pro-Soviet parties appeared to favor a conference on Vietnam. The lack of support by Romania, North Korea, and North Vietnam (not to mention China or Albania) prevented implementation of this idea. Obviously there could be no meeting without the North Vietnamese themselves, who apparently feared antagonizing the Chinese.

Early in the following year the Polish United Workers' (Communist) Party sent confidential invitations for the "socialist countries" to attend a conference on Vietnam. The Albanians released this letter, together with their rejection. It was not until late fall that a little-publicized meeting of Soviet leaders and, reportedly, eight of their allies convened at Moscow. It agreed to send North Vietnam assistance in matériel and money totaling one billion dollars.[13] However, the Soviet Union has not abandoned its efforts to mount a truly international conference of communist parties that would be the third in sequence after those of 1957 with sixty-four delegations and 1960 with eighty-one delegations.

A suggestion for such a meeting was made by Todor Zhivkov, Bulgarian first secretary, at the mid-November 1966 (Communist) Party con-

---

13. Reported in *The New York Times,* October 28, 1966, from sources in Warsaw, Poland. The countries participating were not named.

gress in Sofia. Leonid I. Brezhnev, general-secretary of the Soviet party, proposed that the world conference "map out collectively our general line for the future" and use the 1960 pattern. Only thirty-eight delegations at Sofia reportedly favored the proposal, but twenty-four others remained silent. During the following month, at the party congress in Hungary, the total number of supporters rose to forty-seven after a statement that China would not be expelled from the world communist movement. Brezhnev referred again to this matter at the East German congress, when he said that communist parties should "think and consult about the concrete questions connected with the preparation of this [world] meeting."[14]

Despite the opposition of the Romanian, Yugoslav, British, Italian, Norwegian, and Dutch parties to such a conference, it appeared that the Soviet Union would continue its efforts to organize a gathering of this type. The twenty-two Theses released prior to the fiftieth anniversary of the Bolshevik Revolution, celebrated in November 1967, included the following reference: "International conferences of communist and workers' parties are a tested form of collective discussion of the most urgent problems and for working out a common program of action. . . ."[15] That same month, eighteen communist parties invited representatives from the other seventy movements to a conference on February 26–March 5, 1968, at Budapest, which would prepare the agenda for a world congress. Seven of the fourteen ruling parties did not attend this preliminary meeting, and the Romanian delegation walked out on the fourth day. It was decided, however, to convene the world congress on November 25, 1968, at Moscow.

In conclusion it should be remembered that, although differences do indeed exist among the ruling communist parties in the fourteen states of the world where they hold power, all of them still have many characteristics in common. Ideologies may appear to vary, especially in the way they are applied to justify specific policies. But all of the power elites subscribe to the view that a proletarian revolution eventually will replace capitalism with a people's or national democracy, followed by "socialism" and ultimately communism. In the words of Thesis 16, cited above: "The historic experience of fifty years, which have passed since the October [November] Revolution, convincingly supports the conclusion of revolutionary theory about the doom of capitalism." Other characteristics shared in common include the organization of governments and the leading role of the party, even though the Yugoslavs and the Chinese appear to be modifying this last element.

China also differs from other communist-ruled states by demanding

14. *Pravda,* April 19, 1967.
15. The 25,000-word Theses run four and a half pages and are entitled, "Fifty Years of the Great October [November] Socialist Revolution: Theses of the CPSU Central Committee," *Krasnaya zvezda,* June 25, 1967, pp. 1–5.

that the ideology of Mao Tse-tung be accepted as binding by all parties throughout the world. Very few have done so, because the revised Marxism-Leninism of the U.S.S.R. appears to be more attractive. The profit motive as a means of attaining the material advancement promised in the 1961 Program of the Soviet Communist Party, although adopted by the U.S.S.R. and most other East European states, still is considered a deviation by many orthodox communists even in those countries. The announcement of economic reforms does not signify, therefore, that these can be implemented painlessly or quickly, because the old apparatus workers continue to obstruct them.

Attempts by the party in the Soviet Union to restore unity within what used to be called a "bloc" is being resisted by the ruling elites of Albania, China, Cuba, North Korea, North Vietnam, Romania, and Yugoslavia, i.e., seven of the fourteen states under communist rule. Of these countries none has held a free election. It is doubtful whether any population would vote to retain communism, even that of the U.S.S.R., if given a choice.

Washington, D.C.   RICHARD F. STAAR
                                                                        July 1968

contents

list of tables and charts

Part I
Aspects of Modern Communism

1

the
communist-ruled states

JERZY HAUPTMANN

The political systems of the countries ruled by communist parties all fall under the single category of autocratic states. The same general phenomena and characteristics of autocracy are observable in these fourteen cases despite their diversity, and one could easily construct an autocracy scale in which the People's Republic of China and Yugoslavia would occupy opposite extremes.

The all-pervasive feature of these autocratic systems can be seen in the existence of very easily identifiable small ruling elites. These elites are by no means monolithic, as a superficial observation of autocracy might suggest. Within the elite of each country power struggles occur and influence future political direction. These conflicts represent a method of circulating and transforming the ruling elites. They take place with an increasing degree of sophistication. The case studies of the Soviet Union, North Korea, Cuba, the Eastern European countries, and, most recently and most dramatically, of China point to the extent to which such power struggles may develop.

These conflicts are no longer internal elite confrontations. A significant new dimension has appeared in the search for support, which leads the contesting factions within each elite to appeal to its Party organization. What form this can take has been shown well in Khrushchev's relations with his own Central Committee. Contact between the relatively small Politburo and the larger Central Committee attracts more and more attention, since those members of the former who express differing views attempt to find support for their position among the larger membership of the latter body.

This tendency sometimes is referred to as "democratization" of elite rule but remains counterbalanced by the tendency toward elevation of one person. This phenomenon is clearly visible in all fourteen communist-ruled states. Some of its recent dramatic manifestations are found in Chairman Mao's ideological glorification but also in the honors bestowed upon Brezhnev in the Soviet Union.

This elevation of a single person carries with it the dimension of charismatic leadership. It is rather difficult to find charismatic qualities in certain of the present communist leaders. But all of them definitely attempt to maintain it (Tito) or to create it despite the disadvantage of a rather bureaucratic background (Brezhnev). The person of Fidel Castro looms large in this respect, since he can look back to a relatively recent charismatic past. With the foreseeable death of the first generation of leaders (Tito, Mao, Gomulka) it will be more and more difficult to prevent a routinization of charisma. This does not mean, however, that the tendency toward one-man rule will cease and that so-called "democratization" will have to occur.

What all this amounts to is the fact that the ruling elites are undergoing spectacular change. In the Soviet Union the postrevolutionary intelligentsia comes to the fore; in Eastern Europe nonpolitical cadres are gaining preponderance over veteran Party members. This tendency, however, does not appear in the new revolutionary ideas of China, and it may be argued that even in North Korea the move is rather toward specialists in coercion and away from specialists in persuasion. These two developments seem to be contradictory, and they depend to a large extent upon the role of the military within the elites, which will be treated below.

The elites, as changing and as different as they may be, all face challenges. These challenges may be related to a weakening of legitimacy which resulted from the various de-Stalinization campaigns. The awareness of this trend most certainly has been the reason for the definite limits imposed on de-Stalinization in the several East European countries and most recently also in the Soviet Union.

Legitimacy, however, becomes crucial in view of the fact that disillusionment seems to generate among different segments of the population. This general disillusionment finds perhaps its clearest expression in the case of Cuban emigration. The fact that it is being allowed, even to a limited degree, shows on the one hand that people are dissatisfied and on the other that the regime prefers to rid itself of the disillusioned. The degree of dissatisfaction in the other thirteen states certainly demands more attention than is being devoted to it, although it would not be easy to ascertain.

More clearly visible are two other aspects of the challenge to the elite. In the first place, one must deal with the growing restlessness of the intellectuals. The trial of Sinyavsky and Daniel in the Soviet Union, the Mihajlov case in Yugoslavia, the purge of Kolakowski in Poland, and the plight of the Peking intellectuals are all examples of a restlessness which occurs everywhere. It confronts every one of the governments with the necessity to re-examine the possibility of re-establishing stricter controls over the intellectual community.

In the second place the disillusionment among the Party cadres merits attention. It has been shown most dramatically in China, but there is also evidence elsewhere, e.g., the Kuron and Modzelewski case in Poland and the 1968 changes in Czechoslovakia. Since this kind of challenge emanates, not from the broad masses nor from the always suspect intellectuals, but from within the elite of the "faithful," it demands special attention.

The Party governments of the fourteen states have attempted a variety of responses to meet these challenges. The most commonly noticed is the appeal for popular support. One observes interesting forms of it in the Soviet Union: mobilization of the primary Party organizations, attempts to involve citizens in low-level decision-making processes, the search for ways to respond to popular demands, plans to provide the individual with more legal security. Similar methods are also found in other countries, and they go hand in hand with a growing concern for some kind of improved living standard.

Another response takes the form of glorifying the revolutionary past as an attempt to regain some of the disappearing or already forgotten legitimacy. North Korea shows interesting aspects of this; in China the "Long March" recollections serve a similar role; while in Poland the appeal by a General Moczar to the "Fighters for Freedom and Democracy" is ultimately nothing else but an attempt to re-establish legitimacy.

The most dramatic method for responding to these challenges exists clearly in China, where the "great proletarian cultural revolution" confronts the leaders squarely with attempts to eradicate them. Between appealing to the people and forcing them to conform, one finds a spectrum of responses quite different from one another but still basically related to the same problem: questioning the legitimacy of the ruling elite.

Another grave crisis faces the elites in addition to internal factionalism and external challenges. It involves the matter of political change. The leading elite members are of advanced age (perhaps North Korea represents an interesting exception); some of the original revolutionary leaders have died. How can the problem of succession be solved? There is still no definite answer to this question. It occurs, as in the Soviet Union, with a certain degree of sophistication (e.g., the case of Khrushchev's removal); but it also may involve bloody civil war, as it apparently has in China recently. The institutionalization of political change remains one of the crucial difficulties facing any autocratic system, especially if charisma has disappeared.

This difficulty is compounded by the changing role of ideology. It is possible at the present time to discuss developments in the communist-ruled states without placing ideological considerations in a focal position. Yet the role played by the "Thought of Mao Tse-tung" in China's cultural revolution shows that ideology may be resurrected to influence the changes described above. What has been happening in China certainly may also transpire in other areas of the communist world. With the passage of time ideology has acquired a substantial degree of flexibility, but it still serves as a method to express the political situation at any given time. It still may be used as a kind of code or cipher which can be broken by the astute observer.

Does this all mean that even the communist world is facing a process similar to the one known in the West as the "end of ideology"? Does it really signify that ideology has been relegated to the role of a tool, used only by opportunists who themselves do not believe in it at all? This may represent too simplistic a view, since ideology (however degraded, flexible, or obscure) still remains an element of rule. Most certainly it is being criticized. Reference already has been made to the intellectual challenge vis-à-vis Party rule. It frequently assumes the form of critiques concerning ideology, referred to in Poland, for instance, as "dead speech" (*dretwa mowa*).

One may doubt, though, whether ideology can be completely de-emphasized. As the case of China shows, a reversal to complete identification with the ideology is possible. After all, ideology remains one of the major ways by which the ruling elite may legitimize its rule. Since this legitimacy is being challenged, why should one of the few remaining methods for proving it be abandoned? A growing bureaucratization and rationalization (in the Weberian sense) of the communist-ruled states certainly will require a reassessment of the role played by ideology, since ideology and bureaucracy do not go well together unless they are welded into a unified whole. When looking into the future, one cannot be certain, however, in which direction ideological development will proceed. At the present time ideology still seems to be maintaining itself.

The economic situation can hardly be discussed without reference to ideological problems. In all of the fourteen countries basic economic changes have occurred. These have found expression in industrialization and modernization, which were accompanied by a breakdown of traditional social structures. One may wonder whether the real goal in the processes of economic change was economic (industrialization) or political (social change). The processes which have occurred in these states seem to constitute, at least to a large extent, a contradiction of Marxian economic determinism. Economic change has been undertaken on the basis of political considerations and not vice-versa. The economic policies of the regimes have by no means been of the rational variety.

And so major problems arose in the economic systems of these countries. Agriculture certainly is the most important one. With the exception of Poland and Yugoslavia, not one of these countries has been able to face the dilemma between demand for increased agricultural production and the socialist dogma of collectivization. Recent developments concerning private plots are some kind of an in-between solution which requires, however, special attention. A similar dilemma has occurred in connection with industrialization. Goals were set without regard to available resources and pursued by methods which frequently endangered the attainment of objectives. Industrialization certainly has been achieved. Only one may wonder whether it really gained its economic goals. If to these two major problems others facing the communist regimes are added, such as the pressures of technology, the population increase, the growing demands of the people (after all, the revolution of rising expectations is not limited to Africa, Asia, and Latin America), the economic situation appears to be a rather difficult one.

Results are by no means uniform. One may point to relatively successful cases of solving problems, notably in East Germany and Czechoslovakia as well as in the Soviet Union and North Korea. At the same time the periodic crises engendered by the economic policies of the communist elites must be mentioned. The Chinese "great leap forward" is definitely the best example of rashness in the field of economic policy. Similar cases, however, may also be found in North Vietnam and in the recurring difficulties among the East European countries.

These difficulties, combined with a more realistic assessment of how the economic system works, bring with them a demand that priority be given to economic considerations and that politics should be placed in the background. These demands are known under the all-inclusive name "economic reform." One has to emphasize here that all of these reforms (the Liberman ideas, Yugoslav changes, the various "reforms" in Eastern Europe) occur within the state system of economic planning. They attempt to find a place for rational pricing within central planning operations, a place demanded ten years ago by Oskar Lange in Poland. It is hoped that such pricing will bring with it more rational allocation of resources and in this way eliminate previous unsuitable criteria. Yugoslav planning changes lead the way here. The ideas of the Czech economist Professor Ota Sik seem to point in the same direction.

What is not mentioned, however, although it is crucial for any kind of "economic reform," is the necessity of reasonable and rational politics as the basis for a changed and improved economic system. One has to raise the question whether this is at all possible? Can the ruling elite accept a limitation on the scope of its power by allowing an autonomous operation of the economy? Would such an autonomy not tend to spill over into other areas of life, ultimately also into politics? This represents, therefore, the major roadblock in the path of "economic reform." It explains, for instance, why previous attempts to reform the economic system of Poland after 1956 died out over the years and why current attempts should be viewed with a great deal of caution.

Regardless of the difficulties created by the operation of the economic system, another set of difficulties arises from the importance assigned to military production. The balance between production for military and civilian use tends to be a rather tenuous one. China with its nuclear program amidst an underdeveloped economy is a rather accentuated case, but all the other countries have similar problems. Even in the Soviet Union budget considerations seem to force a continuous re-examination of this balance. Most dramatic, obviously, is the case of North Vietnam, particularly in view of the damages imposed by American bombings.

Within this picture of difficulties and problems one has to point, however, to three cases which merit special consideration, since they constitute models which show some potential attractiveness for countries outside the Bloc. The first of these is Mongolia. The large amount of Soviet economic assistance granted here suggests that this country may be used as a showcase in terms of a development program. It is a rather expensive showcase, judging by the per-capita amount of Soviet aid; but still it proves to countries in Africa and Asia that definite results are possible with concentrated effort. The second model is Cuba. Here again Soviet aid is being used to create an example, especially designed for Latin America. Whether and how much it will be attractive, is still a matter for time to evaluate. The third and final model is Yugoslavia. Here, in a quite different vein, an attempt is made to show that economic problems can be solved by imaginative methods for improving the performance of planning. Due to the special position of "independence" enjoyed by Yugoslavia vis-à-vis the Bloc, the Yugoslav model for development may have a special influence on many underdeveloped countries interested in progress but unwilling to commit themselves to either of the two Blocs, even in view of their growing internal heterogeneity.

With the definite emphasis on the elite, ideology (albeit in a negative sense), and the economy, legal and political institutions seem to be pushed into the background. This does not mean that they lack importance but simply that in the present stage of development they do not attract attention. One wonders, however, if the sophisticated use of certain legal provisions, e.g., in economic relations among these countries, does not merit more attention than it receives. Legal and political institutions are still being manipulated by elites, perhaps not in such a clearly visible way as in Mongolia (with its obvious parallelism of political and constitutional development); and such manipulation, if properly understood, could provide insights regarding the relationship between law and politics in a state ruled by a communist party.

The importance of institutional arrangements is quite well ascertainable in the area of Bloc relations. The word "Bloc" must be used with a great degree of caution, since a homogeneous relationship no longer exists. At the present time the only common element among the fourteen states may be found perhaps in the fact that they are ruled by elites (not even the term Party seems to be satisfactory, in view of Yugoslav terminology) which call themselves communist and which share a common ideological past.

Two institutional relationships demand special study. The first one involves COMECON, also known as CMEA. An analysis of the development and achievements of this institution shows that it has been able to establish close economic contacts among member states and that it also has redirected traditional trade patterns, perhaps even permanently. One must admit that nationalism creates some difficulties in this respect and that from the purely economic standpoint the limited extent of capital mobility together with the nonconvertibility of currencies into gold constitute major roadblocks to closer integration. Yet at the same time a great improvement has been made from the earlier forced and imposed forms of cooperation, rarely advantageous to all parties concerned, toward a greater sophistication in a number of areas selected for integration.

While COMECON moves in the direction of some form of partnership and recognition of certain national aspirations, the Warsaw Treaty Organization (WTO) shows quite a different picture. It has a much greater degree of unity, which is maintained, however, by clear Soviet preponderance, especially in the form of nuclear monopoly. In view of this disparity in power it may be that WTO has become the most important political instrument used by the Soviet Union to achieve some form of Bloc control and unity.

To these multilateral institutions there should be added a substantial and growing number of bilateral treaties for economic, cultural, political, and other relations which have created within the Soviet Bloc a network of close contacts that does not easily fit a pattern but allows for a great degree of harmonizing efforts in the various areas covered.

When discussing Bloc affairs, one is forced at least to mention the term "polycentrism" and to examine to what extent the relations among the fourteen states have been changed since this idea received widespread publicity. The best proof of its existence can be seen in the fact that some of the Bloc countries show a degree of independence in their attitudes toward the Soviet Union. Romania is obviously the primary example here. China also definitely fits into the same pattern, especially in view of more recent developments. One could discover similar stirrings in other countries as well, but it would be advisable to add immediately that there is a limit to such centrifugal tendencies. The institutions potentially exploitable for the purpose of such limitation have been mentioned already. COMECON can definitely play this role, but in particular it is WTO which imposes severe restrictions. The presence of Soviet armed forces and the nuclear monopoly of the U.S.S.R. would make any separation from the Bloc rather difficult, if not impossible.

Certainly the growth of polycentrist tendencies has created a necessity to replace crude forms of control (as they existed, for instance, in the Cominform) with more sophisticated relations. Two aspects of this new control system require special mention. Soviet supervision is assured through close cooperation among the secret services of the various countries, sometimes combined with the delegation of Soviet personnel, especially military, to the other countries. Replacing the Cominform are also close relations among the several Parties. They exist on various levels and show a substantial degree of coordination in Party activities.

Within the Bloc, Cuba occupies a special position. Because of its remote geographical location and its special pattern of communization, Cuba is an exception to nearly every generalization made above. Still, it remains a very important member of the system just because of its unique location. This does not mean, however, that a special position brings with it also a general acceptance of Cuba as a member of the system. It is quite possible to discuss Cuba as either an asset or a liability to the Bloc, and one can ascertain variations within the Cuban policies of the Soviet Union and of other Party-states which reflect vacillations in their assessment of the role played by Cuba.

Any discussion of the Bloc would be severely limited without an analysis of the Soviet-Chinese schism. All discussions of contemporary China remain under the impact of this rift, which in the opinion of many has perhaps already acquired strains of irreversibility. One should not overlook, however, that possibilities of rapprochement are still in existence. The present cultural revolution carries within itself the seeds for development either in the direction of a deepening rift or of an approaching reversal of hostile attitudes.

While an assessment of future developments in China internally and in Sino-Soviet relations would be a matter for conjecture and speculation, one can see quite clearly their impact on the other Asian states in the system. Each of them has related itself to the China problem in a different manner. In Mongolia clear support for the U.S.S.R. is visible. Since it depends so much on economic assistance from the Soviet Union and since this aid could not be replaced by Chinese efforts, the reasons for the Mongolian choice are quite clear. If one adds to this the potential of Chinese population pressure, it is easy to understand Mongolian policy. In North Korea the situation is not that clear. Rival factions have developed within the apparatus, and although the pro-Soviet groups have emerged victorious, this may not be a final solution, especially if one takes into account the history of factional struggle in Korea. The position of North Vietnam is still more complex. It depends for military supplies as well as other kinds of support on both China and the U.S.S.R. The problem facing the North Vietnamese elite is, therefore, how to remain ideologically neutral in this rift and at the same time be assured of assistance from both of the feuding countries.

One would expect that this rift could exercise much more of an impact on the East European countries than it appears to have done. The events of 1956 had a close connection with the happenings in China at the same time. One also recalls that Bucharest has attempted variously to play the role of a "mediator" in this Sino-Soviet conflict of interests. These two facts should lead to the expectation that the rift would have major repercussions on Eastern Europe, but this is hardly the case. The elites sided clearly with the U.S.S.R. and, only some minor dissenting groups (e.g., Mijal's "Polish Communist Party"), established headquarters in Albania from which they direct small-scale propaganda warfare against the pro-Soviet establishments.

On various occasions an attempt has been made to assess the Soviet-Chinese split as essentially a national conflict. The border issue raised by the Chinese certainly emphasizes the national dimension of this schism (although the ideological dimension should not be overlooked), and it points to the problem of nationalism as also existing in other areas of the Bloc. Evidence of nationalistic expressions abounds in this area. They come not only from China and the tradition-conscious Mongols (in their Genghis Khan emphasis). They come also in Europe, other than from the Romanians. In every single country of the system the elites have found it advisable (as mentioned earlier) to manifest their own nationalism. This nationalism acts as a brake upon integrative efforts (e.g., in the case of COMECON), but one may doubt whether (at least for the present time) it plays a role more important than that of a brake. It may slow down certain developments, but one can hardly discover that it introduces as yet any sign of a major redirection. Even Romania's growing contacts with the West will not be able for quite some time to change her close relationship to the Soviet Union. The 1968 changes in Czechoslovakia also fit into the pattern of nationalistic development, but it is too early for an assessment of their meaning.

In the discussion of nationality problems in the Bloc, frequently over-looked are the nationality problems within the Soviet Union, which in herself is a multinational state. As nationalism creates problems within the system, forcing the Soviet Union toward less crude and more sophisticated forms of control, so nationalism also necessitates a revision of the U.S.S.R. approach to the "Soviet nationalities." We have recently had evidence of restlessness among Ukrainian writers; Moldavia has shown substantial tensions; and in the Central Asian republics nationality problems have again acquired major proportions. Yugoslavia, which originally attempted to duplicate Soviet nationality policies, is also gradually being forced into permitting extended autonomy for her nationalities.

If one adds to these internal phenomena certain additional aspects, the situation really becomes complex. Within some of these countries there exists a definite clash between the more and the less advanced nationalities. The more advanced ones (the Ukrainians in the U.S.S.R., the Slovenes in Yugoslavia, the Czechs in Czechoslovakia) look somewhat down at the other nationalities and resent that their capital resources are being used for the development of the remaining ethnic groups. Then minority problems also exist which have by no means been solved. If one mentions only the Hungarians in Transylvania and the Albanians in Kosmet, who are certainly affected by the nationalism of the ruling elites, one must come to the conclusion that Soviet ideology and Soviet-type governments have not been able to solve the nationality problem.

One could draw a still more involved picture by pointing to the case of the three divided countries (Germany, Korea, and Vietnam) and perhaps also to Mongolia, although it fits into a slightly different pattern because of its intra-Bloc position and the almost fifty-year-old history of its division. Nationalism cannot stop at the borders of the Bloc, and it crosses the artificial boundaries dividing these countries. Simple expansionism (as shown in Korea and Vietnam) is clearly not the solution for the division problem, but no other is yet in sight.

Cuba again requires special consideration at this place. For centuries the island has been an integral part of Latin American culture. One may even sometimes wonder whether the Castro phenomenon cannot best be explained by reference to the traditional Latin American *caudillismo* pattern. As a Latin American country Cuba is bound to have some impact upon the other countries in the area, as already was indicated before. To what extent parallels exist between Korea and Vietnam on the one hand and Cuba on the other is definitely a problem for discussion.

The issue of military doctrine and capability within the Bloc countries has remained for years one of the central concerns of the Western world. The relationship between politics and military capabilities becomes, then, a major issue. Assuming it is true, as many observers seem to believe, that the Soviet Union at the present time actually subscribes to and practices a defensive military strategy, one must still ask whether such a defensive strategy is determined by traditional defensive policies or whether by any chance the defensive strategy pushes in the direction of defensive international policies. If one takes into account the current *status quo* foreign policies of the Soviet Union and its aging military leadership, one may indeed think that the U.S.S.R. is defensive (with either politics or the military being the determinant). If, however, one observes such phenomena as the substantial WTO cohesion, which is probably greater than the cohesion of NATO, and also WTO strategy shown in recent maneuvers, then one may start to question whether the outlook is essentially defensive.

A special case in point is the antiballistic missile controversy. The Soviet Union admittedly has developed an ABM system, and now the problem facing the United States is to what extent and in what way to respond to this system. One may assume that the ABM is a real technological breakthrough and that the United States has no other choice but to develop its own system. On the other hand, one may wonder whether this is a real breakthrough and question whether the United States should respond to such a "nonexisting" threat. One may even interpret certain developments in the military past as evidence of Western gullibility in responding to nonexisting threats. Regardless, however, of whether the threat is real or not, the Soviet Union may use it as blackmail while the United States is committed in Vietnam and while the development of its own ABM system would certainly take time.

The evidence, therefore, is rather divided as to whether the Soviet Union, and with it the Bloc, show a preference for an offensive or a defensive stance in military policy. China's case seems to be much clearer. The offensive ideas, combined with a development of some nuclear potential, are certainly there. The military effectiveness of the armed forces, however, has to be described as rather negative, especially in view of the present "cultural revolution." It also is dubious whether the "Thought of Mao Tse-tung" can be an effective substitute for sophisticated equipment in a modern war.

Among all the members of the Bloc, North Korea seems to have the greatest offensive capacities, and it has expressed offensive aims many a time. One also cannot forget the role of North Vietnam. Here is a good example of the utilization of offensive capacities, even though the equipment base is not necessarily adequate.

In such situations as the last three mentioned the problem of the role of the military in politics acquires special importance. It seems that in the European states of the system, including the Soviet Union, the civilian (i.e., Party) control over the military has been clearly established. The military, with the exception of minor cases and special situations like the Zhukov episode, plays only a subordinate role within the ruling elite. (However, they may be used for decorative purposes in certain problem cases. Note, e.g., the recent 1968 elevation to state leadership posts of Marshal Spychalski in Poland and General Svoboda in Czechoslovakia.) This is not so in the Asian countries. In China, and also in North Korea, North Vietnam, and even in Mongolia, there exists a close intermeshing between the Party and the military, with the military leadership also assuming central Party positions. One should mention specifically the internal role of the People's Liberation Army in China, which may be used as an alternative to the alienated Party bureaucracy.

What do these military considerations mean in terms of foreign policy? One can clearly observe cases of the search for a *modus vivendi* by both the Soviet Union and the East European countries. Perhaps one can even notice attempts at a *détente*. In this situation of seeking a relaxation of tensions Vietnam, and possibly also Cuba, create difficulties. Even the Western countries want to build bridges to the communist-ruled countries (the United States attitude toward Cuba being a clear exception) and hope to start through trade expansion. One will have to wait before stating with certainty whether the desire for a *détente* coming from the East, coupled with the attempted bridge-building from the West, will indeed solve some of the underlying difficulties of an ideological and a political nature which have been in existence since the early postwar years.

Such a desire for *détente* obviously presupposes that the elites of the communist states will develop their foreign policies in a rational manner. One has to question whether such a trend toward rationality can be necessarily assumed. Cases are known where foreign policy has been the result of internal power struggles (e.g., in China, North Korea, and even North Vietnam), and one cannot rule out the possibility that internal developments may bring about a deviation from the apparent pattern of increased rationality in foreign policy today.

This issue of increased rationality leads to a brief exploration of the theory of evolutionism. This theory suggests that within the Soviet Bloc, as seen in the case for a rationalized foreign policy, certain forces are at work which induce the system to a gradual change toward something more closely approaching the politics of the West: less militant and less dangerous in terms of international politics. One cannot deny that certain developments of the above-indicated nature are really happening. What has to be questioned, however, is the assumption of inevitability, continuity, and irreversibility in this tendency. A change is indeed in the making, but this change may only indicate developments away from the known totalitarianism toward some form of autocracy not known before. Why should the change necessarily mean a bridging of the gap toward Western systems? When liberalization and relaxation occur (whatever these terms mean, especially if one recalls the Gomulka liberalization of 1956), does this mean that these will increase by necessity in scope and intensity? Or does it perhaps also imply that definite limits are set for these developments, as is clearly visible in the cases of the challenges by the intelligentsia related before?

It should not be forgotten that the ruling elite wants to remain in power and that this desire becomes a definite limitation on all evolutionary happenings. In this case ideology still has to be used as a straightjacket to support the determination to stay in power. One should also not generalize from isolated examples. After all, could it not be possible that Romania's deviation is deliberately accepted by the Soviet Union as an image-building proposition? History abounds in cases of deceit, and this could well be one. The current "liberalization" in Czechoslovakia also may be interpreted in many ways.

An analysis of the communist-ruled states raises two major questions. Once developments in this area are discussed as development within a system, the danger arises of utilizing generalizations from analyzing one country to help in understanding developments in another. Such a cross-country analysis is not dangerous per se, but it has two implied danger points which may lead to errors in understanding the changing scene within the Bloc. One of these danger points lies in the assumption of determinism. It is at the core of the evolutionism discussion. The fact that some form of evolution toward a more "liberal" situation occurred in one country, does not mean that such a development necessarily will take place in any kind of a situation, nor does it signify that such a development is inevitable. The social sciences have to guard against a mechanistic assumption of determinism, as in the case of evolutionism, since it makes impossible a discovery of varieties in development which the unpredictable human being can bring about. The second of these danger points is parallelism. Cases of deliberately created parallel developments are certainly known, e.g., the Chinese copying the Soviet economic developmental pattern, Yugoslavia patterning itself after the Soviet federal structure, or the quite common emulation of organizational arrangements. However, the assumption of a necessary parallelism clearly remains a limiting factor in the analysis of these countries. It would suggest that the elites have no innovating concepts of their own whatsoever and that they are completely bound to a repetition of patterns developed somewhere else. Evolutionary determinism implies the existence of an inescapable force in history; parallelism implies the existence of an inescapable human pattern. Both of these analytic tools may be used only with the greatest reservation when applied to an analysis of the communist-ruled countries.

Two other concepts, however, merit some attention when one studies current developmental patterns within the communist-ruled states. They are rationality and sophistication. It is being noted generally by observers that some development toward more rationality in public policy seems to be noticeable in these countries. Rationality is used here in the Weberian sense of "goal-rationality," that is, of actions carefully calculated to bring about the accomplishment of the established goal. The assumption of increased rationality does not mean, though, that it implies out of necessity some form of a more friendly attitude toward the West or some kind of internal "democratization." The pattern of rationality may be quite consistent with strict autocratic government. In view of the previously mentioned warning one should be cautious not to assume that a movement toward increased rationality is by nature irreversible. The case of recent developments in China shows that at least part of the leadership there seems to be inclined to reverse the trend toward rationality.

The trend toward sophistication, also noticeable in the communist-ruled countries, suggests that the methods used for the accomplishment of goals have changed their form. It is no longer necessary to proceed in a crude fashion. The same objectives may be reached in a more sophisticated manner without creating resentment and problems resulting from the utilization of unsophisticated and simplistic methods. The previously mentioned change in COMECON policies are probably the best evidence of the move toward an increased degree of sophistication. This does not mean, however, that conversation with the sophisticated communists *ipso facto* has become simpler, easier, or more fruitful. It may become such, but it also may become more complex, difficult, and devoid of accomplishment.

The utilization of such concepts as rationality and sophistication suggests the possibility of establishing a typology for communist-ruled states, depending on the degree of rationality and sophistication. These two measurements are certainly subjective in nature, but they provide a definite clue to an understanding of the fourteen states. In this typology, as seen on Chart I below, the upper right-hand quadrant includes the rational and sophisticated states, with Yugoslavia and Czechoslovakia as the best examples. On the borderline of reaching this stage are the Soviet Union and Romania. In the upper left-hand quadrant of rational but unsophisticated states are especially East Germany, Hungary, and Poland, but also Bulgaria. The lower left-hand quadrant represents the nonrational and unsophisticated states. Here are those rather close to rationality, North Korea and Mongolia; somewhere lower on the scale are Albania, Cuba, and North Vietnam. Finally, the lower right-hand quadrant consists of nonrational but sophisticated states. The only example at the present time is China, in the throes of its "great proletarian cultural revolution."

Within this chart it would be possible to have movements toward increased rationality (from the bottom toward the top) and toward increased sophistication (from the left to the right). Obviously reverse movements are also feasible. This typology does not imply any form of necessary or evolutionary movement from one quadrant to another, since this would be inconsistent with the foregoing warnings against evolutionary determinism. It does not imply, either, that one of the four types is preferable or "better" than the others. It only suggests that an understanding of the phenomena concerning communist-ruled states would be facilitated if one recognizes their differences and variations by utilizing the tools of rationality and sophistication.

The study of the communist-ruled countries suggests that the so-called "Soviet Bloc" shows signs of both unity and diversity. This analysis has clearly pointed to the still existing elements of unity and coordination, while at the same time emphasizing points of difference, which may lead even to questioning the continued existence of a Bloc.

CHART I

Typology of Communist-Ruled States

RATIONAL UNSOPHISTICATED

RATIONAL SOPHISTICATED

Rational

Soviet Union

Romania

East Germany

Hungary

Poland

Czechoslovakia   Yugoslavia

Bulgaria

Unsophisticated —————————————————— *Sophisticated*

North Korea

Mongolia   China

Albania

Cuba

North Vietnam

Nonrational

NONRATIONAL UNSOPHISTICATED

NONRATIONAL SOPHISTICATED

TABLE 1

A Statistical Profile of the Communist-Ruled States

	AREA[a] (sq. mi.)	Population (millions)	Density (per sq. mi.)	Population Growth Rate	Urbanization (% in cities of 100,000)	GNP[b] Est. U.S. $ (Billions U.S. $)	GNP[b] Per capita (U.S. $)	Number in[b] Regular Armed Forces	Estimated[b] Defense Budget (millions of U.S. $)
Albania	11,101	1.6	24.0	3	7%		—	39,000	28
Bulgaria	42,823	8.2	28.5	.9	14%	6	742	156,000	119
Cuba	44,206	7.2	24.5	2.1	26%	2–3	350–400	127,000	213
Czechoslovakia	49,362	14.1	45.0	.7	14%	21	1,489	220,000	754
East Germany	41,802	17.0	60.0	–.2	20%	28	1,631	122,000	785
Hungary	35,912	10.2	41.9	.4	24%	11	1,054	109,000	223
Mongolia	604,095	1.1	1.0	2.9	16%		—	—	—
Poland	120,359	31.5	40.0	1.3	21%	27	870	260,000	1,052
Romania	113,918	19.1	32.0	.8	17%	14	734	201,000	266
Soviet Union	8,650,000	232.0	3.7	1.6	24%	312	1,346	3,165,000	35,000
Communist China	3,768,000	700–750	27.9	1.5	8%	50–70	70–100	2,486,000	6,000
North Korea	46,814	11.0	37.7	3.0			—	368,000	—
North Vietnam	63,344	17.0	44.6	3.4			—	256,250	—

[a]Unless otherwise indicated, the source is the United Nations' Monthly Bulletin of Statistics: XX:10 (Oct. 1966).
[b]The Institute for Strategic Studies, The Military Balance 1966–67.

Differentiations within the Bloc certainly have implications for Western policy. It is not the purpose of these studies to point out the variety of challenges which exist for the West as a result of changes in the communist-ruled states. Neither is it an objective to pinpoint the danger points involved in these changes. Both opportunities and risks will be clearly visible, however, for the political decision-maker who may want to utilize the knowledge and understanding of the academic community. At the same time, those academicians may also want to express the wish and hope that increased rationality and sophistication in the communist world will find a reflection in a similar increase of rationality and sophistication on the part of Western decision-makers.

Part II
The Soviet Union

2

post-stalinist developments in soviet politics

W. W. KULSKI

The fifteen years which have elapsed since Stalin's death impress the observer with the importance of the changes in Soviet patterns of life and at the same time with the transitional nature of this period. The U.S.S.R. has become a developed, even though unevenly developed, and literate country possessing a numerous, well-trained, and bright intelligentsia. Internal political relations have undergone adjustments necessitated by the emergence from the Stalinist chrysalid of a more sophisticated society. Neither have foreign affairs remained stagnant. Moscow has ceased to be the uncontested center for the international communist movement, as it had been during the preceding twenty-nine years under Stalin's rule. World communism is now polycentric. This has compelled Stalin's successors to modify their external policies to take into account the rise of mainland China and the much lesser willingness among the other communist-controlled regimes to follow Soviet advice, the stubborn survival of Western capitalist powers, and the important international role played by the noncommunist and uncommitted governments in underdeveloped countries. The world, which had existed either in reality or else in Stalin's imagination, has changed beyond recognition. He should have detected these new trends at home and abroad, but apparently was too dogmatic to do so. The sepulchral silence of his subjects, cowed into obedience by terror as a technique of control, proved to be misleading once he had died. The population henceforth could express its grievances and aspirations half openly or by innuendo.

It no longer became possible to deny the genuine nature of the independence achieved by the former colonial territories. On the contrary, Stalin's successors discovered that the "bourgeois-nationalists" in the formerly dependent countries might become useful, though unreliable and temporary, allies in the struggle with the West for world influence.[1] The communist Chinese revolt against Soviet leadership would have come, even if Stalin had been unlucky enough to witness it himself. The same is true concerning the self-assertion by other communist parties. Finally, it should have been impossible to ignore the growing prosperity of the United States and Western Europe, which was being attained without any symptoms of a forthcoming revolution. The nuclear stalemate had frozen the status quo in Europe not only for the West but also for the Soviet Union.

All these facts on the domestic and international scenes had to be taken into account by Stalin's successors. However, adjustments to these new conditions are far from completed. Soviet rulers, like all national leaders, have been facing various policy options and have had to weigh respective advantages and disadvantages. The decision-making process has not been easier for them than for any other government. Internal and, even more so, foreign relations are in flux. Hence it is too early to say what the ultimate outcome of past and future adjustment may be. One may try to analyze, however, the scope and nature of the transformations already achieved. A good measure is to look at the Stalinist regime and its policies as of March 1953 and then to discover what has been changed since then.[2]

A cruel tyrant—but also a political genius—suddenly passed from the scene in March 1953. He left a void difficult to fill. His record of achievements and failures could not be examined dispassionately by his contemporaries, but one may try to do so after the lapse of fifteen years. In any case, an outsider may proceed with greater detachment than Khrushchev did in his impassioned indictment of his former idol at the 20th and 22nd Congresses of the C.P.S.U.

Stalin inherited from Lenin the ambition to transform the Soviet Union into a modern and fully industrialized country. It was Lenin who had coined the slogan according to which socialism was equated with electrification plus the soviets, the latter of course controlled by the Party. Stalin undertook this gigantic task, applying a different slogan of building socialism in one country. He decided to act swiftly, whatever the price in human suffering and privation. Stalin had his own reasons for accelerating the pace. The U.S.S.R. was the only socialist country in existence, surrounded by capitalist states, some frankly hostile and others suspicious of a government which controlled a vast subversive movement. The Soviet Union, in Stalin's opinion, had to acquire heavy industries quickly in order to regain its former status as a great power and the means for effective defense. As a communist, he did not forget that the U.S.S.R. also represented the only bastion in his ideological camp, and that bastion had to be strong to help in extending the revolution throughout the world. Perhaps Stalin also intended to provide an answer to orthodox Marxists who had accused Lenin of heresy in carrying the socialist revolution to an underdeveloped country. By 1939 one could say that Lenin had built the socialist vehicle and that Stalin produced the industries and a large proletariat for moving this vehicle forward. Stalin could have said on his deathbed that he was leaving a world profoundly changed by his policies. The Soviet Union by 1953 had become one of the two superpowers, and other socialist countries had taken their places beside it.

History served Stalin well. World War II weakened the great European powers and Japan; the two largest Soviet neighbors, Germany and Japan, were lying prostrate after crushing defeats; and only the United States was stronger than the U.S.S.R. Soviet territory was greatly enlarged by annexations in Europe and the Far East, and the new socialist regimes in Eastern Europe were reduced to the status of docile satellites. The U.S.S.R. zone of influence now stretched westward to the Elbe River and southward to the Turkish frontier.[3] None of the tsars had even had such ambitious dreams. Not only Russian but also foreign communists could acclaim Stalin as a great architect of socialist revolution. The communist victory in China did not owe him a significant debt, but he gained in China an ally, which fact seemed to guarantee the security of the Soviet frontier in the Far East.

Stalin gave to his country another gift—nuclear weapons. It is now known that for many years he had sponsored nuclear research and allowed his physicists to work on the basis of Einstein's theories, although they contradicted Marxist assumptions about the nature of the universe. He ordered only philosophers to attack and denounce Einstein. A few dates indicate that Soviet nuclear and space exploits were the result of long research which would have been unthinkable without Stalin's blessing. In 1949 came the first U.S.S.R. atomic explosion; in 1953, shortly after Stalin's death, the thermonuclear test took place; finally, 1957 marked the appearance of *sputnik,* proof of a highly developed rocket technology.

From both Soviet and communist points of view, Stalin's achievements were indeed impressive. His errors were impressive too. Forced collectivization of agriculture, undertaken in order to squeeze the peasants and divert a large part of the national income from agriculture to heavy industry, occurred ahead of U.S.S.R. capacity to supply machinery and chemicals required for large-scale modern agriculture. This major tragedy for the peasant has afflicted the Soviet Union with the perennial problem of inadequate food production.

Stalin's great purges cannot be rationally explained, because they extended to millions of people, including loyal Soviet and foreign communists who had posed no threat to his personal power. He dangerously weakened the Red Army by the purge of officers, including talented higher commanders. This and the blind mass terror could have caused the defeat of the U.S.S.R. in World War II. Fortunately for Stalin, he found the best ally in the Nazis, who did not encourage the mass desertion of Soviet troops, which was taking place in the first months of the German offensive. The indiscriminate treatment of Red Army soldiers and civilians as subhuman beings and their senseless slaughter effectively stopped the high rate of defection. It was the Nazis rather than Stalin who restored Russian national unity. Germany paid a heavy price for this: not only was she defeated, but the Nazis had planted, for the first time in Russian history, the seeds of a deep hatred for Germany among the Russians. The absolute veto against German unification is based partly on this emotional factor.

Stalin has never been criticized, not even by Khrushchev, for his adroit diplomacy in the years 1939–45. Exploiting Hitler's need to secure his eastern flank through Soviet neutrality, he annexed a large part of Eastern Europe to his country. Profiting from the need by the United States and Britain for Soviet military cooperation, Stalin obtained acquiescence to retention of these spoils in Eastern Europe which Hitler had first conceded, to extension of a Soviet zone of influence deep into Central Europe, and to new territorial and other acquisitions in the Far East. He has been criticized for unwillingness to believe in the warnings, coming from Britain and his intelligence service, of an imminent Nazi attack. Probably Stalin could not believe that Hitler would be so rash as to attack a rather friendly neutral power while his war in the West was far from finished. His "rational" explanation considered the warnings to be provocations, inspired by Britain in order to destroy good Soviet relations with Germany. As a result the Red Army, taken by surprise, reeled back to the very gates of Moscow.

Khrushchev's accusation that Stalin was a military ignoramus who directed operations using a schoolboy's globe was obviously farfetched.[4] Even in 1956 one needed only to read the memoirs of Sir Winston Churchill and of Americans in war time Moscow to realize that Stalin was knowledgeable in military affairs. The recent testimony in his memoirs of Marshal Georgi K. Zhukov, who has no reason for liking the generalissimo, indicates that Stalin overcame his first paralyzing fear quickly and organized national resistance. Stalin made strategic mistakes, but Sir Winston, too, is blamed for mistakes by his former generals.

Stalin maladroitly handled the dispute with Tito, unable to realize that a communist party which had come to power in its own country stood firmly anchored on national ground and no longer needed to obey Russian instructions. He delayed a self-assertion by other East European communist parties by a purge of so-called "Titoists." Stalin probably would have been too old by 1956 for an adjustment to the trend toward greater national autonomy in Eastern Europe.

The Berlin blockade also was, or rather could have represented, a dangerous miscalculation. The United States might have responded, not by an airlift, but by sending an armed convoy across East Germany. Stalin would have had either to back down or provoke a major war, which Russia, bled white during 1941-45, could not possibly have won. The initial Soviet acquiescence to the invasion of South Korea involved no miscalculation, because Stalin had the right to feel reassured by official American statements to the effect that this peninsula was not a part of the United States defense perimeter in the western Pacific. His aggressive policy in Europe and the Near East, on the other hand, overlooked the lack of adequate capabilities.

Had he lived until today, Stalin's portrait would not have been displayed in mainland China, as it is now being done to annoy the Soviet communist party. He did his best to spoil the future of Russian-Chinese friendship. In 1945 and again in 1950 he treated first the Nationalists and then the Chinese communists as a semicolonial people. With Anglo-American support given at Yalta, Stalin reimposed on China the former tsarist acquisitions in her territory, although Russia had lost them in the meantime as a consequence either of the 1905 Japanese victory or Japan's expansion into Manchuria during the thirties. Both Nationalist and communist China had to assent to the joint administration of Manchurian railroads, the acquisition of a Soviet naval base in Port Arthur and a commercial harbor at Dairen, the final recognition of "independence" for Soviet-protected Outer Mongolia; and the Chinese communists were compelled to add joint exploitation of natural resources in Sinkiang. All of this was a heavy price to pay for the Soviet alliance. Incidentally, Stalin did not help the Chinese in nuclear research; it was in 1957 that his successors promised to help China in the production of nuclear weapons; they quickly reneged on this agreement two years later.[5]

Stalin left a large vacuum to his successors. There was no one person in 1953 who could fill the vacant position. The only solution involved collective leadership. This is the form of government prevailing in the Soviet Union to the present day, despite the changing relations among the leaders. One of the many reasons for denunciation of the "personality cult" was to prevent the rise of a new dictator in the future.

Individuals who have made up the composition of collective government in the U.S.S.R. have been successively his older and then later his junior collaborators, men trained in Stalin's harsh school. This should be remembered, because mentalities stiffened by such experience might not always respond with enough flexibility to the challenges of a new domestic and international environment.

The collective leadership has been shaken by several palace *coups.* Its history began by divesting probably the most intelligent member in the Central Committee's Presidium, Georgi Malenkov, from one of the two posts he had inherited from Stalin. He remained for a time as prime minister, but soon after his protector's death he lost the more important position of C.P.S.U. First Secretary. It was surprising that some Western commentators could detect in those first months after Stalin's death the existence of a ruling triumvirate (Malenkov, Lavrenty P. Beria, and Vyacheslav M. Molotov) and at the same time overlook Khrushchev, although he held the key post of First Secretary. Perhaps his own colleagues themselves miscalculated in thinking that they had selected the most inconspicuous, hence the safest, man among them to occupy that office.

A unanimous Presidium removed Beria in the summer of 1953 by ordering his assassination, and later defamed him as a foreign intelligence agent by staging in the press his posthumous trial and—no less—posthumous execution in December of that year. He might have been a threat to them, since he controlled the security apparatus and its then numerous internal troops.

The third palace *coup* took place in the summer of 1957. The struggle for personal power marshaled almost all members of the Presidium against the ambitious Khrushchev. He won owing to support by the Central Committee hastily convoked, allegedly with the assistance of military air transportation provided by Marshal Zhukov. This outcome of the first serious crisis among Stalin's heirs, which ended in the elimination of well-known Party leaders, perhaps has created a precedent. The Central Committee, treated by Stalin very disrespectfully and rarely convoked, had emerged after his death as the most important, or rather the only truly deliberative, assembly on the national level. It meets regularly and has acquired the status of the main advisory body. It includes in its ranks the political elite of the Soviet Union, not only the highest officials within the Party hierarchy but also the highest-ranking flag officers, the leaders of professional and other organizations, as well as trusted scientists and other intellectuals. Frequently it meets in the presence of invited guests who are experts in matters on the agenda. Above all, it includes the respective political supporters of various members on the Political Bureau (called the Presidium between 1952 and 1966). One may assume that if top leaders disagree and the Political Bureau is sharply divided, this major issue will again be decided in the Central Committee.

The fourth palace *coup* occurred in October 1964. An apparently unanimous Presidium ousted Khrushchev. There was no need to have recourse to arbitration by the Central Committee, because Khrushchev's followers, with whom he had packed the Central Committee, simply deserted him.

Khrushchev's record was checkered, since his rather primitive mind inclined to make decisions on the spur of the moment, to inaugurate a policy and then contradict it by other moves, and finally to reverse himself and follow an entirely different policy. He understood the changes which were taking place throughout Soviet society and in Eastern Europe, but he handled frequently sound policies in an awkward and uneven manner. His decisions concerning agriculture, the constant reorganization of the Party and the state apparatus, his views on a new management of the nationalized economy, to cite a few examples, were chaotic and eventually produced rather dismal results. Perhaps the main foreign policy objective involved finding a workable *modus vivendi* with the United States on the basis of an implicit acceptance of the European status quo, but Khrushchev failed to elicit any significant response. In the meantime the Soviet party was losing its influence in the communist and radically nationalistic non-European world. Trading insults with the Chinese did not represent the most effective manner of gaining admirers among foreign communists. Khrushchev's highly emotional way of handling the delicate problem of de-Stalinization subverted U.S.S.R. prestige. Last but not least, he twice grossly miscalculated in international affairs. The missile crisis ended in a Soviet diplomatic defeat, as did the famous "ultimatum" on West Berlin. In 1963 Khrushchev gave Cuba a unilateral military guarantee against the United States without providing serious thought to the question of how this guarantee could be implemented: through amphibious operations in the face of American naval superiority or by a nuclear duel with the United States?

His colleagues had very good reasons for ousting this *primus inter pares* who was building his own personality cult and allegedly refusing to listen to their advice. The real enigma is why they tolerated him for so many years. The only possible explanation includes the probable feeling of uncertainty about their own futures after Khrushchev. They knew that he was not a deadly man like Stalin; but without him, could they fully trust one another?

It is impossible honestly to say how power is distributed within the current top leadership. Soviet materials provide no reliable clues. Perhaps there is one method more reliable than others, but even this may be misleading if one leaps to conclusions. Published changes within the higher Party apparatus are worth watching. When former or present close associates of one top leader are demoted and those of another promoted, this usually reflects the actual distribution of power. In the case of Aleksander N. Shelepin, a member of the Political Bureau and for a time also one of the secretaries of the Central Committee, these fluctuations and other factors seemed to have indicated his decline during a certain period of time. After the last Party Congress (March–April 1966), he seemed again firmly established. Then, in 1967 he lost his post as Secretary of the Central Committee, although he was retained on the Politburo. Some commentators in the West predicted a short career for Leonid Brezhnev and his replacement by Nikolai V. Podgorny. The C.P.S.U. Congress in 1966 gave Brezhnev the more prestigious title of Secretary General, thus placing him well above his colleagues on the Secretariat. General de Gaulle remarked that his main interlocutor in Moscow had been Brezhnev and not A. N. Kosygin or Podgorny.[6]

Another method of scrutinizing the mysteries of the Kremlin is to derive the power of each top leader from a particular interest group. However, there is no information except about the façade activities of those groups, all of them directed from above by high-ranking Party members. Malenkov was proclaimed by some Western analysts to be the leader of the state bureaucracy, probably because he was prime minister for a few years. Forgotten was that he had made his career as a Party *apparatchik* and as the principal collaborator of Stalin, although his elimination from the position of First Secretary effectively cut off all support from the apparatus. Party dignitaries frequently change their affiliations with various interest groups. Shelepin is a good example. What did his particular source of power include: the Komsomol, the Committee on State Security, the Party-State Control Commission, or now the trade unions? He has served successively at the helm of each of these rather dissimilar organizations.

If a ranking Party member has a long-term assignment to one specific interest group, he might succumb to the temptation of honestly espousing its aspirations. Even so, he could not forget that the Party apparatus remains the ultimate source of power for all leaders, including himself. What may be more probable is that the temporary leaders of interest groups would possess a sort of limited vested interest in keeping their organization satisfied. They might be and perhaps even are inclined to argue for their group in the top-level discussions concerning the allocation of national resources. Eventually they must accept a compromise solution, imposed by the over-all national priorities adopted at the Party summit. But it is naïve to suppose that any member of the Politburo or Secretariat would expect to be backed in his struggle for power by a general strike of labor unions or street demonstrations by the Komsomol or even by pressure from the security apparatus, which is now firmly in Party hands. If

Khrushchev had wanted to imitate Stalin and forge for himself a tool of power in part independent of regular Party organizations, namely, the Party-State Control apparatus with its multitude of supervisory groups on all territorial levels, then he failed. This aspect of Khrushchev's reforms has not been studied carefully as yet. An interesting factor involved the right of the Party-State Control Commission to supervise all state, *Party,* and other organizations with the exception of the highest Party and state institutions. It is true that Party secretaries headed the various territorial units of the Control apparatus, but Khrushchev might have thought that he could rely on their loyalty to him as the First Secretary. Whatever his intentions, one of the first changes after his downfall was to remove Party organizations from the jurisdiction of that control apparatus, which became downgraded generally in status and prestige.

There is one interest group which has a permanent and a professional leadership, namely, the armed forces. This explains the hopes which are sometimes voiced of a military *coup.* Nothing should be precluded regarding future human behavior. But a few caveats should be mentioned. Obviously the military leaders represent the professional interests of other career officers. It is no less apparent that they probably press for a greater allocation of resources for national defense. Their professional advice may not be lightly dismissed by political leaders, as is true in other countries. While the Party heads of other interest groups exert their pressures on their own organizations in order to make them follow Party directives, rather than on the top Party leadership to persuade it of the legitimate aspirations and needs of their groups, the marshals and admirals probably represent the only true pressure group. However, military officers suffer from the failings of all human beings. They think about their own security, promotions, the welfare of their families, and are not immune to professional envy or competition. It is impossible to forget the behavior of these military officers in the face of the terror used by the Soviet one-party system. Stalin was never endangered by his bloody purge of commanders throughout the armed forces. The remaining Soviet officers discovered that the prospect of rapid promotion had suddenly opened up for them. Marshal Zhukov perhaps would not have become a Soviet national hero if his talented superiors had survived and commanded Red armies in World War II. Hitler ordered humiliating trials for his military officers, including a field marshal who had been implicated in the July 1944 plot. They were all executed with the additional refinement of having been hanged from butcher's hooks. This was well known to German officers; yet there was no military mutiny. The partial demotion of Marshal Zhukov soon after the Allied victory did not cause any great discontent among his peers and other officers. His forced retirement in October 1957 by Khrushchev, a politican who was not feared as Stalin and Hitler had been, from the positions of defense minister and member of the Presidium did not cause any protest.

Second, both Stalin and his successors were generous with the career officers, re-establishing titles and insignia of rank, showering on them various decorations, preserving their authority regarding N.C.O.'s and soldiers, and giving them good pay as well as high retirement pensions. It is not without reason that a Russian translated the French saying *Le bien-être général* with the following: "It is good to be a general!" There is no immediate reason for a military mutiny.

Third, marshals and other flag officers are also senior Party members, a few of them even on the Central Committee. They have a vested interest in the Party's rule and perhaps a genuine attachment to it.

Fourth, they are certainly Russian patriots. The Party government is the only Russian government and the one which constantly has proved that it places the national interests above everything else, in particular by giving a high share of allocations to defense.

Fifth, a totalitarian regime is not the best place for hatching a political conspiracy. Soviet officers, whose loyalty is supervised by the Political Administration of Armed Forces, by the parallel Party organizations, and by security apparatus informers, would not have a task as easy as their professional colleagues in Latin America.

The collective leadership has functioned smoothly thus far, at least to the outside observer. Whatever fluctuations in the distribution of power actually take place, or occur only in the imagination of Western observers, the fact remains that the Soviet Union has been ruled since 1953 by a numerically small oligarchy which comprises the ultimate center in formulating all policies. This oligarchy now numbers twenty-six persons who are either members and alternates on the Politburo or secretaries of the Central Committee or both. The Politburo and Secretariat wield the greatest power, but the C.P.S.U. Rules are not completely clear on the division of jurisdiction between them. Article 39, as amended by the 23rd Congress in April 1966, states that "The Central Committee of the C.P.S.U. elects a Political Bureau to direct the work of the Central Committee between plenary sessions, and a Secretariat to direct current work, chiefly the selection of personnel and the verification of the fulfillment of Party decisions." This text assigns to the Politburo formulation of policies and to the Secretariat control over their implementation and the selection of Party cadres. The Secretariat decides such matters as the nomination, promotion, and demotion of the *apparatchiki* who in essence represent the power backbone of Soviet society. Moreover, it has at its disposal a vast number of specialists grouped in the various departments of its central office. Finally, the control over the implementation of Party decisions gives it the power of supreme watchdog over all state and other organizational activities.

This vast jurisdiction of the Secretariat explains the crucial nature of the Secretary General and his colleagues. One may perhaps guess that those members of the Politburo who are not secretaries probably require the assent of the whole Politburo to changes in the upper ranks of the Party apparatus. Otherwise they could be outmaneuvered easily by their colleagues who occupy dual positions and finally ousted from the Politburo. Promotions and demotions of higher-ranking Party officials eventually predetermine the composition of the Central Committee. One should not overlook another advantage of the Secretariat: a specialized staff allows it to act as the principal adviser for the policy-making of the Politburo, which has other advisers, for instance, among high state administrators.

Whatever the actual distribution of power between the two supreme bodies of the Party and whatever the fluctuations in this distribution, the eleven members and eight alternates on the Politburo and the eleven secretaries (these figures are not fixed in any document and actually vary from time to time) form the ruling oligarchy. Four secretaries also being members of the Politburo, the total is twenty-six persons. The stark reality of power consists in the fact that twenty-six persons rule over the population of 235 million, made up of the 5 per cent of Party members and 95 per cent of nonparty citizens. This remains true even if one takes into account the diffusion of power, unavoidable in any society. Soviet society also knows the delegation of powers and the importance of advisers who influence the formulation of policies.

Almost four years have elapsed since Khrushchev's ouster. One may now examine the kind of oligarchy that rules at the present time in Russia. It is composed of people who came from the ranks of the postrevolutionary intelligentsia. They have had a formal education. Hence their style is entirely different from Khrushchev's. Their approach to problems is businesslike and sober. Boasting, wild promises, a vulgar vocabulary, coarse humor, a constant reversal of policies, improvisation, and disrespectful treatment of members from the lower Party hierarchy have disappeared with the fallen leader. The formerly picturesque but also sometimes amusing spectacles have been replaced by serious action. This marks the advent of a new era. Stalin was a political genius, but his morbid suspiciousness, his blind terror, and sometimes his whims distorted the policies which had been rationally conceived from the Soviet point of view. Once oligarchic rule replaced the absolute dictatorship, such a system of government had all the advantages of teamwork. The personal characteristics of members of the oligarchy can be mutually balanced. This should help in devising cautious and sober policies which can be adjusted to surrounding reality.

Only a prophet could say whether the oligarchic system will last or whether a single man will again emerge as absolute ruler. On the one hand, Khrushchev was growing impatient with the restraints imposed on him by the collective leadership. On the other hand, Venice, a great power in her time, was very successfully governed by an oligarchy.

Looking summarily at the Party, one could say that it can be roughly divided into these four segments: the top leadership, the Central Committee, the whole structure of paid Party officials, and the rank-and-file members. It is appropriate to ask what the feelings of the rank-and-file members and of the general Soviet population might be. Of course, one cannot have an exact assessment of those feelings in the country where the electoral results might be predicted years ahead with mathematical precision and where the mass media serve as spokesmen for the ruling Party. But one must pay attention also to the muffled voices of dissidents and to the complaints of people who do not feel that Soviet society is better than any other.

The post-Stalinist era has brought about a notable change. Stalin reigned over a silent and terrorized population, including his closest collaborators who did not know what their own life expectancy would be. This was a conformist cemetery. Now this former cemetery is alive. A regime of reluctant half-tolerance has been observed by the top leadership.

There are various channels which transmit the voices of the population or of its important segments to the top leadership. This leadership apparently listens and adjusts to some extent its policies to appease the population. The primary Party organizations now show some signs of real discussion, whereas their meetings formerly were staged entirely by the secretary who did not admit any dissenting voice. The same phenomenon is developing within local labor union committees and their numerous commissions. This cannot be silenced by management. Individual complaints reach the newspapers through letters to the editor and not infrequently result in publicizing the abuses of local dignitaries. Grumbling in the queues and in private conversations is probably noted by security police informers and reported to the top leaders as one aspect of public opinion. The Party leadership has inaugurated fairly free and open discussions on those issues regarding which no decision has been made. These debates either extend to practically the whole population or may be restricted to specialists, depending on the nature of the issue. Such questions as the reform of criminal law and procedure, marriage and divorce, the new system of management in the national economy, or matters relating to agriculture have been the subjects for those public debates. Stalinist public campaigns survive, however. They comprise the "popular support" for Party policies, initiated and directed by the Party. This support is expressed in open meetings and in the letters to the editor.

The never-ending debate between conservative and progressive literary writers has been going on for years, with the obvious Party permission. The numerous standing committees of the Supreme Soviet deliberate and debate with cabinet ministers on the drafts of new laws to be passed later by the Soviet legislature. These discussions sometimes probably result in a modification of original drafts.

All this does not mean that the U.S.S.R. is evolving toward political democracy, but it signifies that the ruling politicians are now inclined to inquire about the aspirations and views of their subjects and to some extent to respond to them. They firmly maintain in their hands the final power on formulation of policies.

Everything indicates that one aspiration generally shared by the Soviet population is the wish steadily to improve living standards. Ideological problems do not elicit any notable interest. This indifference, particularly present among the young, worries the Party, as evidenced by the debates at the 23rd Congress and subsequent public campaigns. People seem to be tired of daily indoctrination, but they sense that the time may have come for a developed Russia to enjoy at last the fruits of previous privations.

Khrushchev and his successors have done much to improve living conditions of the urban population. Wages, especially for the lowest-paid workers, have been increased; the old bonus system continues but is now linked to labor productivity measured by performance both of the individual and of the whole plant; social security and welfare benefits have been raised or improved; medical personnel, lower grade teachers, individuals working in the tertiary sector of the economy—all receive higher salaries; the work day has been cut to seven hours, and the work week gradually is becoming one of five days with a total of forty-one hours; problems of labor safety have been given greater attention. These and similar steps will improve the well-being of the industrial working class and the lowest-paid stratum of the intelligentsia.

The upper and middle strata of the intelligentsia fare proportionately as well as they did under Stalin, the architect of present social stratification, which he devised for the sake of efficiency, the hallmark of developed societies. These socialist upper and middle strata can hardly complain. They are privileged in various respects.

This "new class" receives a disproportionately large share of that part of national income which is distributed among the population as compensation for work. Salaries, bonuses, fees, and other rewards allow its members to own a fairly spacious dwelling house which the children inherit, to accumulate bank savings for an emergency, for old age, or simply for the benefit of heirs, to buy more expensive consumers' goods, and hence to enjoy a comfortable existence. If they want to respond to the appeals of the Party for cooperative housing, they can afford more easily to buy shares in such cooperatives and own a modern apartment. One can be sure that the first buyers of new cars, to be produced in increased quantity owing to contracts with Italy's Fiat and France's Renault, will be those from the better-paid upper and middle strata.

Living standards distinguish this "new class" even externally from the workers and peasants. A greater difference is involved by the very criterion of membership in the intelligentsia, to which admission is gained by diploma from an institution of higher learning. In spite of extensive Soviet social mobility and a fairly equal opportunity for access to education, the intellectual atmosphere of the home offers the initial stimulus to children who begin the course toward well-paid careers with this advantage. Khrushchev mentioned another advantage illegally enjoyed by children of influential parents—the pressure exerted on high school teachers for padding grades and even on admissions' committees at the school of higher learning for upgrading the results of competitive entrance tests.

The higher-education diploma conditions access to better careers and thus places the intelligentsia in a commanding or supervisory position with regard to other social classes. In fact, people who count, be they rulers, advisors, or principal implementing agents, are recruited from among the intelligentsia. From this social point of view, one can say that they comprise the ruling class. They form the membership of the Politburo, Secretariat, and Central Committee; they are the speakers at national Party congresses; they are the ministers and first secretaries of Party republic and province organizations as well as the managerial-engineering personnel in industry; and if Party wishes could be fulfilled, they would be the only chairmen of collective farms. In this sense they have a share in power.

Education distinguishes them from other classes, for in the U.S.S.R., as in any other society, personal friendships are formed among people with comparable educational standards. Social stratification can best be discovered in any society by asking what kind of people are invited into the home.

Under Stalin as well as now the base of power is created by a tacit yet real covenant between the ruling politicians and the intelligentsia as a class. The rulers expect political loyalty and reward the intelligentsia with social prestige, a share in power, and higher income. The intelligentsia, taken as a whole, has a much larger vested interest in the regime than workers or peasants.

However, the intelligentsia is also the breeding ground for nonconformists. These nonconformists were suppressed and effectively silenced by Stalin. Now their voices are being heard again. Their aspiration includes two aspects: the claim to be honest with themselves and say what they deem to represent the truth, and the questioning of certain basic assumptions held by the Party. These two factors are related and involve a striving toward greater freedom of expression. The net result amounts to an undermining of Marxism-Leninism as an accepted dogma for all times,[7] a claim made by all communist parties in their statements adopted in 1957 and 1960 at the two Moscow conferences. Doubt cast on Marxism-Leninism erodes the legitimacy of rule by the Party, whose leaders have always justified their power in terms of the infallibility of Marxism and its laws of historical development as well as the Leninist concept of the elite. If Marx had been right regarding the immutable laws governing human societies, and if Lenin were not mistaken in thinking that only the most enlightened Marxists, guided by this infallible doctrine, should be the rulers, then legitimacy could be firmly rooted in the minds of all believers. If not, this legitimacy could be derived only from the longevity of the Party regime, which in 1967 was half a century old.

Soviet physicists have been the first openly to cast doubt on Marxism by publicly paying their debt to Einstein. This implied that Karl Marx's concept of the universe was as obsolete as the scientific understanding of the nature of matter and of natural laws by his contemporaries. Under Stalin scientists had acted on this assumption but could not say so; now they no longer avoid relating nuclear exploits to Einstein's theories.

More important, U.S.S.R. physicists examine the problem of the relationship between quantum mechanics and dialectical materialism with an open mind to such an extent that an eminent Soviet scientist, V. A. Fock, can now write as follows: "The discussion of physical ideas connected with broader philosophical problems is to be considered as a world-wide discussion between all scientists interested in these problems and not as a confrontation of the views of the 'Slavic' (or 'Soviet,' or 'Eastern') scientists with those of the 'Western' scientists."[8] This is a far cry from the former concept of *partiinost* expected of all Soviet scientists.

If Marxism, in its explanation of nature, had been conditioned by the knowledge available in the nineteenth century, a similar question could be raised about the social elements of Marxism, which include its laws governing human development. This is a more delicate question but has already appeared implicitly in statements by a few Soviet historians who acknowledge the contingency of past situations and the possibility of developments other than those which actually have taken place. One implication is clear: the future cannot be predicated on the basis of the simple instrument of Marxist historical determinism.

Literary writers have in a sense made a claim similar to that by other intellectuals, a claim to state the truth as they understand it. In their case, the truth means depicting Soviet reality in its fullness, including its obvious shortcomings.

Whenever a social scientist or a literary writer grows bolder in demanding the right to enunciate his truth, he challenges the Party line either in its Marxist foundations or at least in its Stalinist superstructure (such as the idea of socialist realism). This involves a kind of *lèse majesté* because it undermines the legitimacy and authority of Party rulers who cannot repudiate the title to their own ideological infallibility.

This problem became aggravated by Khrushchev's impetuous manner in dismantling Stalin's legend. No doubt de-Stalinization had to take place, because the Soviet population probably expected that the mass amnesties of concentration camp inmates would be explained by a criticism of mass terror, because Army officers probably demanded rehabilitation of their purged commanders of the interwar period, and simply because the collective leadership required a condemnation of absolute dictatorship by one man. Some criticism of the former era also could be seen in the pledge given to citizens that they would now live in peace if they only remained loyal. Khrushchev went to an extreme by ridiculing the former idol of the Party and of foreign communists, depicting him as an incapable but cruel tyrant. The image was distorted, although Khrushchev's record of Stalin's crimes was revealing yet incomplete. For instance, the Stalinist denial of any merit to Lenin's closest collaborators (Trotsky, Bukharin, Zinoviev, Kamenev, and others) remained undisturbed. These men continue to be denounced as traitors. Stalin's achievements, undeniable from the communist point of view, were not mentioned. As a matter of fact, the Chinese offered soon after the 20th Soviet Congress a more balanced picture of Stalin's record. The most serious error committed by Khrushchev was to make his speech at a secret Congress session to which foreign communist delegates were not invited. The publication of that speech by the United States took those foreign leaders entirely by surprise. They were told by Moscow in effect that for almost three decades they had worshiped an unworthy man. Their irritation, expressed immediately by Palmiro Togliatti, was understandable, because they should have been consulted. Stalin had been not only a Soviet but also an international communist leader.

The question then arose concerning the responsibility of Stalin's collaborators who, except for Beria, at that time headed the Soviet party. Were they accomplices to his crimes, or cowards who had not dared to protest or shelter their innocent Soviet and foreign comrades who fell victim to Stalin's wrath? If Stalin was a monster, what guarantee could they and their successors give that they deserved to lead the international movement? The claim that the achievements during the repressive period were due to the Central Committee but that the crimes were Stalin's own responsibility remained too ludicrous to be accepted, especially since Khrushchev insisted that the dictator's top collaborators had lived in terror with little to say about his decisions.

The polycentrism of the international Communist movement would have come about in any event for other reasons, but Khrushchev accelerated this trend with his secret speech. Moscow lost the moral right to uncontested leadership. Doubts about the infallibility of Soviet leaders spread throughout Eastern Europe and ended in the Polish and Hungarian revolts. The Romanian challenge to Moscow and the Czechoslovak unrest also have as one of their reasons the abrupt process of de-Stalinization in Russia.

Khrushchev himself was hailed by the Soviet press as a great leader. After his ouster in 1964, however, he was accused of harebrained decisions, subjectivist improvisations, not listening to his colleagues' advice, and a disrespectful attitude toward Party and state officials. The indictment was less severe than had been that of Stalin, but it again proved the fallibility of a top leader.

Stalin and Khrushchev together ruled no less than a total of almost forty out of fifty years in Soviet history. As a repercussion, the stature of Party leadership was reduced to very human dimensions. But if they were human beings with all the human defects, what right did they have to an absolute government?

These two reasons for the weakening of legitimacy regarding their absolute power cannot be overlooked by the Party leaders themselves. They must defend it. While it is extremely difficult to repair the damage within the communist movement, they still have the instruments of coercion at home. On the other hand, the repudiation of mass terror has blunted the most effective instrument. Hence both Khrushchev and the present leaders have followed a vacillating line. At one time they strongly reassert Party supremacy by deciding what is politically wise and what criteria should be respected in literature, fine arts, music, and the social sciences. At other times they seem to hesitate and allow for a regime of half-tolerance. This is best observed in the fate of the Party line regarding literature and other creative arts. It seems that composers finally are being left in peace. Modernistic music has been performed. The tribute paid by *Pravda* to Shostakovich[9] on the occasion of his sixtieth birthday anniversary in the fall of 1966 not only implicitly repudiated the criticism contained in the famous resolution on music adopted by the Central Committee in 1948 but also admitted that there existed more than one public. The former dogma that musical compositions must be easily accessible to the masses was refuted by the admission that Shostakovich might be fully appreciated only by a select audience.

It would not be surprising if the Party line on fine arts were in time also changed. After all, neither atonal music nor abstract art would endanger the regime. Probably the Party line was originally due to personal phobias on the part of Stalin, Zhdanov, and Khrushchev more than to any other considerations.

Literature presents a different problem, because any cultivated man knows that writing played a "subversive" role in prerevolutionary France and Russia. A frank criticism of Soviet reality, a true socialist realism and not the one the Party wants, could have incalculable results. The compromise policy adopted after the death of Stalin consisted until very recently of a fluctuating line. Party leaders relaxed and allowed progressive writers to publish works which were far from an apotheosis of the regime, but then the leaders vituperated and denounced those works. This uneven policy could only embolden the writers. After Khrushchev's violent and vulgar speeches in the spring of 1963 one was surprised by the reappearance of works exactly similar to those which he had denigrated. After the 23rd Congress[10] in the spring of 1966 one could have expected a more stringent Party line. Several delegates to the Congress were outspoken on this subject. *Novy Mir,* among other journals, was singled out for criticism. Yet Aleksander Tvardovsky, a respected poet, remains its editor and has not altered his attitude—something unthinkable under Stalin. However, the Party finally adopted a harsh official policy in 1968, demanding that Soviet writers toe the line. Trials of dissident writers and confinement of some others to mental hospitals during 1966–67 presaged the new attitude. One can speculate whether this harsh policy will be successful in the long run, without a return to mass terror. Is this latter phenomenon still conceivable in present-day Russia?

One can guess rather that this struggle between the progressive writers and the Party will continue, with its reciprocal successes and reverses. The most interesting aspect of this controversy is the complicity of censors. There is a dual preventive leadership exercised by the State censors and the editorial boards at all publishing houses and periodicals. If a work disliked by the Party nevertheless appears, this proves that the censors themselves are accomplices.

The Party uses other means. It may for a time refuse to print objectionable material submitted by denounced writers and thus deprive them of prospective fees. The conservative writers also never tire in their counteroffensive. Moreover, the problem is of interest only to a portion of the intelligentsia (the true intellectuals and a minority of students). Those sections of the intelligentsia that think above all about their vested interests in the regime, such as Party and state officials, the managerial and technological personnel primarily interested in their careers, the scientists or military officers absorbed in their professions, and many others, probably do not pay much attention to the aspirations of progressive writers.

The problem exists but does not seem to threaten the survival of the regime. This is the place for recalling Lenin's brilliant analysis[11] of the prerevolutionary situation. Using historical materials, he said that a revolution might succeed only if four factors coexisted. One involved a calamity overtaking a country. Another was popular discontent intensified by a disaster, whatever the nature of this disaster. The third factor was a realization by the ruling elite of its own inability to cope with the problem. The fourth included the existence of a group of prospective revolutionary leaders, capable of channeling popular discontent toward the violent overthrow of the rulers. This psychological analysis, confirmed by the history of past revolutions (French, Russian, and Chinese), remained divorced from Marxism; and perhaps because of this it is correct. It implies another truth, namely that revolutions are made by the dissident section of the educated people, while the masses are merely a tool. Only the leaders know the true objectives of the revolution, while the masses want relief and improvement in their immediate situation. Therein lies the difference between a revolution and workers' riots or peasant uprisings.

None of the conditions mentioned by Lenin exists today in the Soviet Union. No recent disaster has afflicted the country. Party policies have been on the whole successful, and prosperity is growing. The loyalty of citizens is probably infinitely greater than under Stalin for several reasons: improving living standards, greater legal security, and opportunities now offered to citizens to display initiative in the local implementation of Party policies. Party leaders show no signs of doubting their own capacity to rule the country. Finally, any conspiracy, to put it mildly, is a difficult and risky venture under a totalitarian regime.

Taken as a whole, the Soviet population is much more fascinated with the prospect of better living conditions than with freedom of expression. Party leaders are responsive. They proved this in 1965 by inaugurating a new agricultural policy which reflected the first really businesslike approach to the problem of collective farming. Contrary to the romantic view that the peasant will never work efficiently unless he owns his plot of land, and in spite of his alleged mystical attachment to the soil, the peasant is not a species different from other human beings. The vast majority of citizens in capitalist states works efficiently without owning any means of production, but rather in the hope of a fair material reward. The low productivity of the Soviet peasant is due to his desire, not for a redistribution of collective land, but for fair labor compensation. He was discriminated against by Stalin and also by Khrushchev, never having a fair share in the growing prosperity. This explains his reluctance to work efficiently and his propensity to concentrate all his hope on the so-called "garden plot," with its cow, poultry, and piece of land for the cultivation of potatoes, vegetables, and fruit.

Soviet agriculture has been afflicted by three problems: nature (droughts in the south and poor soil in the north), lack of sufficient investment in machinery and chemicals, and the denial to peasants of any real incentive. Khrushchev submitted in September 1953 a gloomy report to the Central Committee on the depressed condition of agriculture. His remedies were correct and consisted in offering a greater incentive to collective farmers and larger state investment. For reasons unknown he reversed his policies in the early sixties and began a struggle against the garden plots without giving the peasants any compensation in the form of higher income from participation in collective farming. On his orders the Union Republics passed laws cutting down the size of garden plots, while local Party and state officials put pressure on collective farmers for them to sell their private cows. The result was what could have been expected. For lack of sufficient investment and because of reduction in the relative importance of production on the adjoining plots, agricultural output began to decline. The government was compelled to raise prices for certain commodities, such as meat and dairy products, to limit the sales of others, like flour, and to buy abroad huge quantities of wheat, which depleted its fund of hard currency. After Khrushchev's fall, the Central Committee had to listen to a report on agriculture no less gloomy than the one he had submitted eleven years earlier.

The present leaders finally understand that agriculture can no longer be treated as a Cinderella, because this kind of policy retarded growth of the whole national economy. They have adopted a new course[12] which simply decided to upgrade agriculture in the national hierarchy of priorities. Vast investments are to be made in irrigation and drainage as well as in industries producing agricultural machinery and chemicals; collective farmers are to be given a tangible incentive.

For the first time in Soviet history the peasant is promised treatment as a citizen for whom the Party cares. The benefits of state social security, first granted by Khrushchev, have been extended. Collective farmers now possess the right to old-age, professional disablement, and other pensions. The drastic difference between the urban and rural areas in prices for electricity and consumers' goods has been eliminated. The pre-Khrushchev size of garden plots was restored, and cows were given back to the peasant families. Finally, a new system of payment for collective labor is being introduced. In the past collective farmers had been remunerated in compensation units of unknown value which depended each year on the size of the annual net income on each collective farm. The payments in cash and kind to each collective farmer depended upon the total results of the full agricultural year. These varied from farm to farm and from year to year. Hence the individual compensation of the collective farmer fluctuated depending on such factors as quality of soil, proximity to urban centers, weather, and variations in climate. All of these factors escaped the control of even the most laborious and conscientious peasants. There was no incentive. Now the Soviet government is introducing fixed minimum wages in cash and kind for each category of work. These payments have the highest priority on the farm's gross income. Formerly all obligations to the state and to the farm had to be met prior to the distribution of net income among the peasants according to computed units. At last the collective farmer is being placed in a position somewhat similar to that of the industrial worker, and he may hope that in the future his income will not always be less than half that of the industrial worker and even less than that of another peasant employed by a state farm.

This new policy and better weather already produced in 1966 a record harvest after several lean years. If the Party is able to maintain this policy of high priority granted to agriculture, the collective farmer certainly should respond with greater labor productivity. Other investments may also improve the situation. Eventually the Achilles' heel of the Soviet economy might become less vulnerable. The yearning of peasants for participation in the growing national prosperity then will be satisfied. This may ensure their loyalty to the regime.

The aspiration to prosperity might have been one of the reasons for Khrushchev's revivalist image of the future communist society[13] in which every citizen would receive consumer goods according to his needs and not, as is claimed now, according to his work. If Khrushchev had confined himself at the 21st and 22nd Congresses to painting an alluring image of future communist society, the heaven promised by the Marxist-Leninist "founding fathers," he would have stayed on safe ground. He was cautious enough about the gradual withering away of the Soviet state as a tool of coercion, and his successors may quote him and say that the survival of capitalist states explains the survival of the socialist state. But he was rash in promising the realization in substance by 1980 of distribution of consumers' goods according to need. It is true, he was clever enough to add that this distribution would be limited to essential needs without defining which needs were essential and which were luxuries. No less rashly, he promised to eliminate by 1980 the differences between manual and mental work and between rural and urban living. It was his secret as to how the Party would eliminate the difference between mental and manual labor. Granted that automation might help some, but differentiation of social functions would remain in the U.S.S.R. just as in any other developed society. A scientist, composer, poet, university professor, manager, or any higher administrator will never be an equal of people with lower levels of education and lesser shares in social power. Even if Soviet villages were to become *agrogorods* with many urban amenities, they will never have the cultural attraction of large cities: they cannot become a Leningrad or a Moscow, with splendid museums and theaters. Above all, would human nature change sufficiently by 1980 to dispense with material incentive, which plays such an important role in the Soviet economy? The daily Soviet press is bringing evidence of criminality as wide-spread as in any capitalist society, including juvenile delinquency, laxity toward work, and the misbehavior, semicriminal or noncriminal in nature by American standards, called hooliganism. U.S.S.R. criminal laws have been stiffened constantly during the sixties, in particular regarding economic offenses and hooliganism. The courts are busy and not lenient. The promised new Soviet man, a psychological condition for the future communist society, is nowhere to be seen. The real new man asks for greater material incentive.

Khrushchev committed the Party to the deadline of 1980, which remains an integral part of the new 1961 Party Program. This deadline will prove embarrassing to Soviet leaders. On the other hand, the U.S.S.R. citizen probably did not read into Khrushchev's bombastic speech more than the promise of higher living standards. This was enough for him.

He has received something else—greater legal security. In spite of the trial of Sinyavsky and Daniel, criminal responsibility of social parasites before popular assemblies of laymen, and a few retroactive applications of criminal laws, progress has been undeniable if one again uses the yardstick of Stalinist reality. In 1953 the state security apparatus was deprived of its former power to intern in a concentration camp or to exile any citizen accused, not of having committed a crime, but only of having been a threat to society. This was the pretext for shipping off millions, mostly innocent even by Soviet standards, to forced labor camps. It was a wasteful use of manpower for work in the far North and on big projects such as canals. Stalin's heirs realized that a free worker with family responsibility and with adequate pay would be more productive than the inmate of a camp. They released great numbers, following amnesties enacted soon after Stalin's death. Now the citizen may be called to criminal responsibility only before a regular court, except for the social parasites. The other exception involves trials of dissident literary writers which are conducted in mockery of justice, even by Soviet legal standards. The great feeling of legal security is an immense relief for millions who had lived in the fear of a knock on the door in the middle of the night and an administrative decision to deport them for no apparent reason.

Criminal legislation and procedure was revised[14] in the great reform of 1958. Responsibility by analogy for acts not forbidden under any specific article of the Criminal Codes, collective family responsibility for the desertion abroad from the armed forces, the vague general definition of a counterrevolutionary crime which made conviction by analogy easy, the decisiveness of evidence based on forced confession, the specific and general responsibility of minors in the twelve to fourteen age group (now it is fourteen to sixteen)—all were eliminated. Criminal procedure also has been improved. This is still far removed from Western standards, but it does mean progress. However, since the early sixties additional criminal offenses have been specified in legislation and penalties made more rigorous, including crimes for which capital punishment can be invoked. Courts and procurators are not indulgent: defense lawyers still play a limited role. Negligence in denouncing to public authorities about the preparation or commission of a serious crime continues to be a criminal offense without exemption for members of a family. Yet current public debates within the Soviet legal profession might promise further improvement by somewhat enlarging the role of defense lawyers and accepting the presumption of innocence as a judicial principle. Another progressive act made divorce easier and less expensive by giving the people's courts the right, not only to act as conciliators between the spouses, but to grant divorce. The legal position of citizens is far from perfect, but it has definitely improved.

Another liberal trend involves the serious effort by the Party to enlist the mass of citizens in cooperating on a voluntary basis to help devise the best means of implementing Party directives locally. This might seem like a minor change in Western eyes, but is important for Soviet people who under Stalin were used to being treated like digits, who were expected to obey local officials and to work. Now they have many opportunities to engage in local civic activities and to display their initiative under the condition that they do not question Party policies. They may actively participate in the work of various committees of local soviets, labor unions, housing committees, etc. This is not democracy, but it does give to citizens a new feeling of being important. This was probably one of the two reasons for the Party's new policy, since the citizen now feels that he bears some responsibility for local affairs which concern his immediate interest. The other reason was to elicit initiative, a difficult task under a one-party system. Yet a developed society requires such initiative. This has been understood by Khrushchev as well as by the present leaders.

Something else has changed. The intellectual level of the Soviet press has improved, especially since Khrushchev's ouster. Newspapers and magazines have become interesting, although they still remain biased. In particular, shortcomings are no longer hidden but openly criticized if they pertain to the lower echelons of Party or state administration. The image of the capitalist world is less slanted than under Stalin, probably because too many Soviet citizens have seen the West with their own eyes.

The most difficult problem facing the present leaders relates to foreign policy. *Pravda* in September 1966 carried an article written by a member of the Hungarian Politburo.[15] He frankly acknowledged the intensification of nationalism throughout the world, including the socialist countries, and warned that it would be harmful to ignore this phenomenon. He suggested a conciliation of the national interests among the various socialist countries. There were several reasons for a gradual erosion of cohesion within the world communist movement. First, there was the brutal de-Staliniza-tion which had lowered the prestige of Moscow, formerly uncontested leader. Second, there was involved the survival of communist parties in

Yugoslavia, Poland, Albania, Romania, and China, despite temporary or permanent revolts against Soviet tutelage. Now all parties feel that they may adopt a more independent line and not collapse for lack of U.S.S.R. support. They have their own states to support them and cannot but follow national interests, however these may be interpreted. Third, the open breach between the two most important parties (the Soviet and the Chinese) provided the other parties, whether ruling in their respective countries or not, with a choice: alignment on the side of Moscow or Peking, or adopting an independent attitude.

The communist movement has been unfortunate in experiencing at the same time two eras like those also known to Christianity: the great schism between Rome and Constantinople, and the Reformation with its national churches. This might become a stimulant for communist parties in the underdeveloped countries, which may now disregard Soviet or Chinese advice and determine independently their strategy in full cognizance of local conditions. As a matter of fact, if communists from one of the quarreling sects might hope for a successful seizure of power, these hopes could be confined to the underdeveloped countries where the modernization process brings in its wake political and social instability. The West is too prosperous, and its working class is acquiring the "petty-bourgeois" mentality which precludes revolutionary success even by the only large communist parties in France and Italy. These two parties face a very unpleasant choice: either they admit eventually that there is no prospect for a revolution and become in fact simply reformist parties working within the existing political framework, or they will persist in revolutionary hopes and gradually lose electoral support and party members.

Looking from the Soviet point of view, it is far from easy to cultivate the same sympathies in both European and non-European parties. The former parties either cannot become active revolutionaries, or if they are East European parties, they desire peace in order to govern their countries. An adventurous policy would not attract them, while it remains the only policy of interest for communists in Asia, Africa, and Latin America. The continuous effort by the Soviet government since 1953 to expand U.S.S.R. influence in these three continents has achieved success although not because of communist revolutions (except for Cuba) but rather because of cooperation by noncommunist governments. The same governments are frequently hostile to their native communists and even persecute them. This is one of the examples of Soviet priority to Russian national interests rather than to the much-publicized socialist internationalism. For instance, the diplomatic support as well as massive military, economic, and technical aid offered to President Gamal Abdel Nasser bought re-entry into the Near East for the U.S.S.R. but hardly helped the Egyptian communists.

It seems that Soviet leaders have become reconciled with national self-assertion by communist parties in Eastern Europe and their promotion from the Stalinist rank of satellites to that of autonomous allies. They accepted the consequences of the Polish and Hungarian revolts on the condition that the Eastern European parties maintain their rule and not disassociate themselves from Soviet foreign policy. In the case of Romania, Moscow adopted an attitude of infinite patience, strange in the capital of any great power regarding the behavior of smaller countries within its orbit of influence. The Romanians asserted their economic independence and the desire to have closer ties with Western countries (including the German Federal Republic); they have maintained their neutrality in the Soviet-Chinese split, and have raised by clear implication the problem of Moldavia, which was annexed by the U.S.S.R. Yet it would be easy to move across the border and repeat Hungarian-type military intervention.

Nationalism also undermines the cohesion of East European parties in their mutual relations. The problem of Transylvania divides Romania from Hungary, Slovaks fret under the centralizing administration of the Czechs, Yugoslav nationalities visibly do not form a fraternal family, and there is no excessive love between the Polish and East German communist parties. The old problem of nationality reminds one of the interwar period, even though the regimes have changed.

Above everything, the Chinese party decided to proceed to an open breach with Moscow. The erstwhile alliance between these two now frankly hostile powers looks like a dead letter. Unless there is an unexpected and drastic change in the Chinese leadership, there will be no chance for reconciliation between the Chinese "Trotskyite splitters" and the Soviet "accomplices of American imperialists," to apply mutual epithets. Khrushchev did not cause the split, but handled the problem in his own coarse way by responding with insults to Chinese insults. This did not win any admiration among the other parties. Since his downfall, the Soviet party has followed a wise policy of extending its hand to Peking (probably certain that it would be repulsed), refraining from vulgar criticism, and appealing for a united front in defense of Vietnam against the American "imperialists." The U.S. bombing of North Vietnam provided the Soviet leaders with the opportunity to prove to all communists that they have continued to be revolutionary Leninists.[16] Thus Vietnam has become the stake in a triangular struggle among the United States, the Soviet Union, and China. It is not the most desirable situation from the point of view of the two nuclear superpowers, because their competition might by fatal miscalculation result in direct confrontation. This confrontation is the cherished dream of the communist Chinese. They allegedly say that the best future spectacle would be to watch smilingly from the top of a mountain the two tigers devouring each other in the valley below. Thus far neither tiger is willing to provide this kind of enjoyment. If difficulties in allowing Soviet supplies for Vietnam to cross their territory continue, the Chinese probably hope that the United States will eventually respond with a naval blockade. Direct confrontation would become a fact.

Chinese competition places the Soviet party in a highly embarrassing position. Moscow fears a nuclear catastrophe as much as does Washington. Yet it must help Vietnam in order to regain positions within the communist movement lost by Khrushchev, who was only mildly interested in wars of national liberation. New Soviet tactics have brought about the isolation of Peking, which was not helped by its erroneous policies regarding the noncommunist underdeveloped countries, by the excesses of the "cultural revolution," and by its unwise advice given the Indonesian party, crushed by the army after the unsuccessful uprising. The communist parties, except for the Albanian one and the minuscule one in New Zealand as well as splinter groups in other countries, have abandoned Peking. This is true of the Japanese, North Vietnamese, and North Korean parties, which had formerly sided with China. The North Vietnamese party, forced by the reliance on Soviet aid, has gone far in reorientation. Its chief delegate at the 23rd Congress publicly proclaimed that each Vietnamese has two fatherlands: Vietnam and the Soviet Union.[17] This was the hour of greatest Soviet triumph. It may possibly be a temporary success, because the non-European parties will insist on Soviet support for revolutionary movements in the underdeveloped continents, even after solution of the Vietnam problem.[18] This is not only hazardous to Soviet security, but it would prevent the U.S.S.R. from reaching a *modus vivendi* with Western Europe and the United States.

If one may conjecture, this has been the goal in the post-Stalinist period since 1953, in spite of the current revolutionary policy regarding Vietnam. The U.S.S.R. and Eastern Europe need peace as much as does the West, and for similar reasons. Moreover, the most important Soviet problem certainly involves Germany. The Russians want to freeze the European *status quo* with its permanent division of Germany into two states. This remains the best *status quo* they could imagine. Even a Germany unified under a communist government represents a worse proposition, because it would be the strongest West European power with an independent policy probably aimed at a revision of Eastern frontiers. Such a Germany might find a friend in the other large communist neighbor (China), and the Soviet Union would be encircled, not by capitalist, but by unfriendly communist, powers.

If the present *status quo* is desirable from the U.S.S.R.'s point of view, an understanding with the United States remains vital. There is no lack of response in Washington, as evidenced by President Lyndon B. Johnson's speech of October 7, 1966. What does Moscow want? Probably it does not even expect formal recognition of the German "Democratic" Republic or the Oder-Neisse line, so far recognized only by France. The Soviet Union knows that this part of the *status quo* cannot be changed by either side because of the nuclear stalemate. But the U.S.S.R. seems sincerely to be alarmed by any prospect of West German access to nuclear weapons, because the Federal Republic of Germany is the only major European country highly dissatisfied with the present *status quo* for an entirely legitimate reason, namely, the division of the nation. What Moscow thinks is that the West German government might be pushed toward the unwise decision of unleashing a general nuclear war, acting as a trigger. The United States considers these fears to be unfounded, but nevertheless they may be genuine fears. Hence, a treaty on the nonproliferation of nuclear arms is vital to the Soviet Union, if it leaves no gaps for an M.L.F. or an Atlantic force with West German participation.[19] The competition with the communist Chinese in the revolutionary zeal over Vietnam delayed for a time the Soviet decision regarding this vital treaty. In 1968 the U.S.S.R. finally agreed with the United States not only on a draft treaty but also on parallel guarantees for non-nuclear signatory states against an attack or threat of a nuclear attack. These guarantees seem to be aimed principally at protecting Asian countries from Chinese nuclear blackmail.

For the time being, a rather unsatisfactory substitute for the United States has been found in France, but this new friendship does not solve the main European problem.

It can be assumed for the sake of argument that Khrushchev's and perhaps the current Soviet government's desire (which also has been the wish of the Eisenhower, Kennedy, and Johnson administrations) is to find a workable *modus vivendi* in Europe and the Far East (regarding China) and acknowledge the end of the cold war. Will this mean that competition in the non-European areas would be terminated? It would be naïve to expect any such development. The U.S.S.R., even if guided by its national interests, cannot be more virtuous than the Western powers which compete with one another in those areas. Each great power tries hard to maintain its influence or to increase it. The Soviet Union will remain yet another contender, fighting by nonmilitary means against each Western power and China for influence among the noncommunist countries. Improved relations with Turkey, Iran, and Pakistan might serve as a current illustration of U.S.S.R. efforts to improve its position even among nations committed to the West which become by repercussion less committed than before. One should not be surprised if the Soviet government were to use anti-Western slogans in an effort to widen its influence among the underdeveloped countries. Each government applies such slogans and means which its own ideological and social system provides. However, the U.S.S.R.

approach to those countries is less optimistic and more sober than it was in the fifties. The experience gained since the inauguration of the post-Stalinist policy during 1953–4 has not been lost on the Soviet government. If it expected that the cultivation of friendships would yield an uncompromising anti-Westernism or would facilitate the work of local communists, it must have been bitterly disappointed. It learned the same lesson as did the Western countries. Noncommunist governments in underdeveloped countries do not intend to become satellites of either the West or the Soviet Union. They welcome the coexistence of aid coming from both sources and try to counterbalance competing influences. One-party governments are no more lenient toward communists than to other political nonconformists. A friendly regime today might suddenly be replaced tomorrow by another government less friendly. The inherent instability of underdeveloped countries does not guarantee that any amount of aid would buy permanent friendship. The former revolutionary Soviet phraseology, with its advice to nationalize all Western assets and to rely only upon the aid of and trade with "socialist" countries, helped the Chinese communist rivals, who always are able to outbid the Russians in high-sounding phrases. U.S.S.R. advice has become more moderate, namely, not to hasten with wholesale expropriations and rupture of trade relations with the West, because the "socialist" countries are unable to fill the gap in the economy of underdeveloped countries. Moscow now says that the time for nationalization comes only when a given country has the qualified personnel to run the government-operated enterprises. This same more sober approach is visible regarding Soviet aid itself, which comes at the expense of the U.S.S.R. economy, including private consumption. The former readiness to finance any spectacular project wanted by a recipient government, whether economically useful or not, proved to be not only too costly but also disappointing. It eventually produced, not gratitude, but bitter disillusionment with the nature of Soviet assistance. Now Moscow wants to know whether a project is economically feasible, for instance, whether a plant can use local raw materials and also whether the repayment of Soviet credits would be in goods which the U.S.S.R. economy really needs. In other words, Moscow is more mature in its efforts to captivate the sympathies of underdeveloped countries and extend its own influence.

There will always be many occasions for disputes with the United States, but the main question is something else, namely, whether the Soviet leaders would be ready to become less zealous regarding wars of national liberation, even at the price of again losing several communist positions to China? If not, new Vietnams would preclude a true *modus vivendi* with the United States.

Soviet leaders, like all leaders, cannot eat their cake and have it, too. This is why they are now at the crossroads, or rather will be, after solution of the Vietnamese problem, in one way or another. The choice they face is between socialist internationalism and Russian national interests which are served to perfection by the present European and Far Eastern (Soviet-Chinese frontiers) *status quo.*

The unwise Chinese hostility toward two great neighbors, the United States and the Soviet Union, if persisted in, might bring about another argument in favor of Russian-American understanding. Both might be interested in containing China. They are both powers in the Far East. Then the present, unfounded Chinese accusations of Soviet complicity with the United States might become an unpleasant reality for Peking.

There is yet another reason for Soviet and East European interest in a better relationship with the West. They need Western cooperation in their economic development. U.S.S.R. contracts with Fiat and Renault and the East European desire to find the means for greater trade with the West and contacts with Western corporations, are straws in the wind. The improvement in Soviet-Japanese relations is more evidence.

In conclusion one can say that the post-Stalinist era has involved adjustment to new domestic and external conditions. Since Khrushchev's fall, a period of businesslike leadership has been inaugurated which attempts soberly to calculate its chances prior to making decisions. Depending on the national point of view, this is a leadership with which it might be easier or more difficult to find a limited common platform. The Chinese have discovered in the present leaders much cleverer, and hence tougher, opponents than Khrushchev. The United States might perhaps eventually find that it will meet in Soviet leaders rational interlocutors, despite their ideological blind spots.

Notes to Chapter 2

1. Concepts of the new Soviet policy toward the underdeveloped countries as they were defined in the fifties appear in W. W. Kulski, *Peaceful Co-Existence* (Chicago: Henry Regnery Co., 1959), pp. 203–300.

2. For a description of the Stalinist regime, see Merle Fainsod, *How Russia is Ruled* (Cambridge, Mass.: Harvard Univ. Press, 1953) and W. W. Kulski, *The Soviet Regime* (Syracuse, N. Y.: Syracuse Univ. Press, 1954; 4th edn., 1963).

3. A discussion of U.S.S.R. territorial annexations and expansion of Soviet influence in the years 1939–53 is in W. W. Kulski, *Peaceful Co-Existence,* pp. 301–88 and 448–91.

4. Khrushchev's secret speech at the 20th Congress of the C.P.S.U. in *The Anti-Stalin Campaign and International Communism* (New York: Columbia Univ. Press, 1956), pp. 1–89.

5. For Stalin's wartime and postwar foreign policy, see David J. Dallin, *Soviet Foreign Policy After Stalin* (Philadelphia: J. B. Lippincott Co., 1961), pp. 3–113, and W. W. Kulski, *Peaceful Co-Existence,* pp. 303–88.

6. *Le Monde,* No. 922, June 16–22, 1966.

7. Arthur P. Mendel, "The Rise and Fall of 'Scientific Socialism,'" *Foreign Affairs,* XLV:1 (Oct. 1966), 98–111.

8. V. A. Fock, "Comments," *Slavic Review,* XXV:3 (Sep. 1966), 413.

9. Rodion Shchedrin, "Bolshaia zhizn' muzykanta," *Pravda,* Sep. 24, 1966.

10. For debates at the 23rd Congress of the C.P.S.U., see *Pravda,* March 30–Apr. 5, 1966.

11. V. I. Lenin, *Selected Works* (New York: International Publishers, 1943), Vol. V, p. 174.

12. Guide lines for the new agricultural policy were formulated in the report submitted by L. I. Brezhnev to the Central Committee on March 24, 1965; *Pravda,* March 27, 1965.

13. For debates on the future Communist society at the 22nd Congress of the C.P.S.U., see *Pravda,* Oct. 18–30, 1961.

14. On the criminal legislation reform, see W. W. Kulski, *The Soviet Regime,* 4th edn., pp. 157–79.

15. Zoltan Komocsin, "Natsional'nye interesy i proletarskii internatsionalizm," *Pravda,* Sep. 18, 1966.

16. The Soviet stand in the conflict with China was formulated in an editorial, "Po povodu sobytii v Kitae," *Pravda,* Nov. 27, 1966.

17. Statement of Le Zuan, First Secretary of the Central Committee, Vietnamese Workers' Party, at the 23rd Congress of the C.P.S.U., as reported in *Pravda,* March 31, 1966.

18. For polycentrism within the world communist movement, see *Diversity in International Communism,* ed. Alexander Dallin (1963); Richard Lowenthal, *World Communism* (1964); and *International Communism After Khrushchev,* ed. Leopold Labedz (1965).

19. For Soviet views on Germany, see W. W. Kulski, *De Gaulle and the World: The Foreign Policy of the Fifth French Republic* (Syracuse, N. Y.: Syracuse Univ. Press, 1966), pp. 291–314; and idem, "The U.S.S.R.—France—Germany," *The Russian Review,* XXV:4 (Oct. 1966), 343–56.

Discussion

YAROSLAV BILINSKY

Professor Kulski's main conclusion appears to be that in a much more developed Soviet society the basic method of rule must undergo adaptation. Stalin killed millions of people to achieve his goals, which were mostly sound in nature. Khrushchev was more perceptive and restrained but also more chaotic in implementing his policies. The new Soviet leaders are becoming more rational, more mindful of the costs to be paid for the attainment of their objectives both in domestic and foreign policy. This involves, of course, a greater rationality of means, a greater efficiency, which they are striving to achieve. As Professor Kulski cautions, no amount of reasoning will persuade them to help democratize the country by relinquishing their power over ultimate decision-making. Under a Khrushchev or a Brezhnev the people, experts, or both may be consulted on new policies. This was done before adoption of the 1961 C.P.S.U. Program and the industrial reforms, but the final decision is always made by the top Party leaders in the Politburo or Central Committee.

There do exist areas, however, where the old Stalinist assertion of will rears its ugly head, areas that constitute aberrations from the general pattern of cost-minded rationality. If enough of these aberrations may be found, the very image of more rational collective rule may have to be revised. At the very least, one would have to conclude that the leaders would like to have the best of two worlds: the relative efficiency of a free society and the nearly unlimited effectiveness of totalitarian dictatorship. It is necessary to analyze the institutions of the regime, then its domestic and foreign policies.

Professor Kulski suggests as the watershed between Stalinist and post-Stalinist rule the abolition of wholesale terror. Party members are still being liquidated politically but not physically (L. P. Beria and associates excepted). The absence of that supreme sanction of the irreversible purge, together with some erosion of the ideology and continued lack of Party democracy, would make it most difficult to maintain legitimacy—historically an effective basis for governing. It would seem that the top Party leaders should strive to achieve among the medium and lower echelons at least a consensus on procedure to be followed in replacing the General Secretary. Such consensus is in its most rudimentary stage only. In both 1957 and 1964 (confirmation by *Le Monde*'s Moscow correspondent Tatu appeared in the issue of March 12–15, 1965, p. 2), the Party's Central Committee was involved. But in contrast to 1957, its role in 1964 appears to have been that of an auxiliary. It is reported to have heard only one denunciation of Khrushchev, made by Mikhail A. Suslov. Supreme power in the U.S.S.R. is still won by a series of quick and fundamentally unedifying, though admittedly bloodless, palace *coups*. The outside world, communists, noncommunists, and even ordinary Soviet citizens, in 1957 at least was given an official list of semiplausible charges against the "Anti-Party Group." In 1964 the new regime limited itself to a few comments about Khrushchev's harebrained schemes and withheld a forty-page indictment from all but a small circle of leaders. No amount of discussion in the Party about minor matters can compensate for the fact that the rank and file are not openly informed about changes in the top leadership.

Nor are some events at the last 1966 Party Congress designed to inspire confidence in the new ruling collective. This collectivity appears to be of a most reluctant nature indeed. If one can believe some circumstantial accounts, in 1964 at the meeting of the Presidium the main reports against Khrushchev were given by senior member Suslov and junior member (agricultural expert) Dmitri S. Polyansky. The *coup* itself was probably engineered by Aleksander N. Shelepin, who was given a full seat on the Presidium a month later. One of the main beneficiaries of the *coup* appears to have been Byelorussian Party leader K. T. Mazurov, a full Presidium member and First Deputy Premier of the U.S.S.R. since March 1965. But none of them was allowed to speak at the Congress, not even Suslov, who appears to have lent his moral authority to the *coup*. Then there is Brezhnev's immodest choice of the Secretary-General title (April 1966), which was followed eight months later by self-bestowal of the highest U.S.S.R. decoration, Hero of the Soviet Union. At the Congress, Brezhnev's final speech ranked his colleagues in terms of seniority, placing himself first, A. N. Kosygin second, N. V. Podgorny third, M. A. Suslov fourth, and A. N. Shelepin only seventh (on a Politburo of eleven). Within hours official Soviet media amended Brezhnev's ranking, rearranging it in accordance with the Russian alphabet (Christian Duevel, in Radio Liberty's *Daily Information Bulletin,* Apr. 14, 1966, Russian ed.).

One of the most fascinating and important sections of Professor Kulski's paper deals with Khrushchev's attempts to emulate Stalin in circumventing regular Party channels by establishing a system of Party-State Control bodies under Shelepin. Unlike Stalin, Khrushchev carried the attack on the regular Party apparatus to the dangerously absurd by splitting the Party into industrial and agricultural administrative branches. This bifurcation was reunited in November 1964. Dr. Duevel, of Radio Liberty's Research Department, however, has pointed out rather plausibly that until August 1965 Shelepin had tried to maintain the network of Party-State Control Committees, together with the auxiliary work of societies for the advancement of the Party-State Control Committees, somewhat independently of regular Party channels. On December 6, 1965, after several months of counterattacks in the press, the network of Control Committees almost dissolved: it could no longer control Party organs. That relatively young Shelepin (born in 1918) did not lose his Presidium status and position as Secretary upon destruction of his visible power base is in itself a tribute to his political strength and acumen. Still, it is difficult to say much about his specific responsibilities within the top leadership. There were reports as of June 1966, on the basis of his speeches, linking him to supervision over the economy (notably trade and light industry), something that before Khrushchev's fall had been handled by N. V. Podgorny. If correct, this would make Shelepin only a junior Politburo member and Secretary, not only in age but also in rank: he definitely does not seem to be the Second Secretary, a post probably held for the time being by ailing M. A. Suslov. There appears to be so much arbitrary willfulness in the Party that had the regime pursued the most rational policies, there would still be doubts about its legitimacy: in 1964, for example, several foreign communist parties challenged C.P.S.U. leaders to explain their action. The quarrel with China has, of course, not increased the stature of current Soviet leaders, even though they have been more astute in letting the Chinese damn themselves.

It can, however, be shown that the policies of the regime are not consistently rational. Professor Kulski indicated that Brezhnev has made a good start on paying the Soviet peasants a fair return for their labor. I agree that this measure was long overdue. Actually, as Jerzy Karcz points out in *New Directions in the Soviet Economy* (1966), Khrushchev also from 1953 to 1957 substantially aided agriculture. In 1958 he decided that agriculture would "take off" by itself without heavy investment and without higher prices. Brezhnev can better Khrushchev's record only if he stays with his announced plan to bolster agriculture at least through 1970. The touchstone for rationality in economic polity, however, would be the attempted reconstruction of industrial administration. Although the basic decisions were already announced in September 1965, the reforms have not yet been fully implemented; according to Gregory Grossman, completion of the reforms in both formal and real terms awaits reform of the price system scheduled for 1967–8. (For this reason, perhaps, Professor Kulski omitted the industrial sector from his discussion). It is known that the change-over from the pseudo-autonomous regional economic councils to centralized functional ministries in Moscow was conducted in some haste, immediately after the September 1965 plenum, without even waiting for the end of the planning year. The projected changes of indices emphasizing, for example, volume of goods sold rather than volume produced and reinvestment of some profits by the managers themselves, can make the economy genuinely efficient only if the prices are set in such a way that they can regulate supply and demand without a plethora of central controls. Some American economists are pessimistic about the new prices and about the willingness of the regime in Moscow to dispense with most of its supervision. It will be most interesting to see, after the price reform, whether industrial managers genuinely become autonomous or whether their authority will be whittled away immediately, as happened in Khrushchev's regional economic councils. In the industrial field the new leaders seem to have promised a large order of rationality but to have delivered only the first installment.

While these new leaders have been willing to make modest experiments in agriculture and industry and to act out the role of conservative reformers in economics, it is still true that in the realm of public law and order and in the struggle against deviationists (especially in literature), they have skirted reactionary positions. Perhaps a sort of Machiavellian rationality is involved: allow conservative Stalinists to attack ideological deviants so that they will not interfere with economic progress. To let Moscow (city) Party First Secretary N. G. Yegorychev denounce from the tribune of the 1966 Party Congress individuals who were using Stalinism as a bogey appears to be more than an attempt at setting history straight. It seems almost like a calculated de-Stalinization campaign in reverse. During 1966 the regime formally centralized its control over primary and secondary education, which heretofore had been a prerogative of individual republics.

In recent Soviet policy on nationality a distinctly pro-Russian Stalinist wind is apparent. At the 23rd Party Congress, P. M. Masherov (soon elected a candidate member of the Politburo and who is, incidentally, a Byelorussian) received delegates' applause when he referred to "the peoples of Great Mother Russia," not the R.S.F.S.R. or the Soviet Union, according to *Pravda,* March 31, 1966. Before 1917 the phrase "Great Mother Russia" used to be coupled with "Little Father" *(batyushka)* Tsar and became associated with a particularly unenlightened policy vis-à-vis the non-Russians. The regime's policy toward Jews has not basically changed, either. Ukrainian writer Yury Smolych demanded in vain the resumption of book publication in Yiddish at the fifth congress of the Writers' Union of the Ukraine in mid-November 1966 (*Literaturna Ukrayina,* Nov. 20, 1966, p. 4; *The New York Times,* Jan. 29, 1967, p. 13). Union chairman Oles Honchar publicly complained that teaching of Ukrainian in secondary and higher schools "due to certain circumstances" at times fared worse than instruction of such foreign languages as English, French, or German (*Literaturna Ukrayina,* Nov. 17, 1966, p. 5). Statements like those by Masherov and the policy which they connote are not only obnoxious to many Soviet citizens but indicate limits to Soviet political rationality.

Of even greater significance was the establishment on July 26, 1966, of a centralized Ministry for the Protection of Public Order. Dr. Andreas Bilinsky, of Munich, a German-trained jurist who was a prisoner in a Stalinist concentration camp and now specializes in Soviet law, noted with alarm certain parallels between the creation of that agency in 1966 and the All-Union People's Commissariat for Internal Affairs (NKVD) in 1934. Perhaps this is an exaggeration. Hooliganism by itself, however, is not a justification for what appears to be a new and broader campaign against crime in all of its manifestations, both civil and political. For instance, there is now information, in part confirmed by authoritative sources, that Sinyavsky and Daniel are only the most publicized victims among Soviet intellectuals. Furthermore, the names are known of twenty-two persons who between the middle of 1965 and April 1966 were arrested in the Ukraine for reading unauthorized books, distributing information hostile to the regime, and similar political crimes. A few of them were released; the large majority, however, was sentenced to as much as twelve years of jail or forced labor, one of them having already served in a labor camp from 1955 to 1957. A Ukrainian poet who recently toured the United States publicly condemned those arrests and sentences as unnecessarily harsh, at least in the case of three personal friends who had been arrested during that wave of repression. The situation has improved; sentences imposed in these twenty or more cases were less severe than they would have been in 1953. However, in 1965 a trial at Lvov before a regular court is said to have taken place behind closed doors. The system of Soviet justice, especially in the political realm, is imperfect indeed. Not only Westerners, but even Soviet citizens abroad, complain of it as being unnecessarily harsh. It may have exceeded the measure of political rationality and be reverting (though so far to a limited extent only) to the arbitrary willfulness of the Stalinist regime.

On the increased rationality in Soviet foreign policy Professor Kulski was too harsh regarding Khrushchev's unsuccessful gamble in Cuba. It appeared that during 1961–2 American policy in Berlin was so conciliatory toward the U.S.S.R. that Khrushchev might have thought more concessions might be forthcoming from the United States under pressure. In the end it turned out to be a miscalculation, but a rational miscalculation. Professor Kulski gave an excellent analysis of the Soviet predicament in Vietnam. However, as long as American planes bomb trucks, staging areas, and oil depots instead of airfields, port facilities, and ships, and as long as the U.S. commits a half million men to inconclusive jungle warfare, the Soviets may feel at ease: they can tie down major American forces and affect the American economy at rather small cost to themselves.

On the other hand, Professor Kulski may be too optimistic about indefinitely maintaining a *status quo* in Central Europe. The Soviets could have second thoughts about a strong united Germany, neutral or even procommunist. (Khrushchev is reported to have said to a leader of the French Socialist party: "You keep your Germans, and we will keep ours"). There are some pro-Chinese German nationalists. But the prize is so great that no Soviet government would miss the opportunity to assert its influence in that country: compared not only with the United States but also with united Germany, France remains a poor substitute. It would seem that the new West German government, somewhat disenchanted by the results of its close collaboration with the United States and bolstered by the Social Democrats, whose political base traditionally had been in East Germany, will increasingly turn to the Soviet Union for unification on more or less acceptable terms. If the Soviets are astute enough and West Germany edges more closely toward Moscow, this will mean the end, not only of NATO, but of the West European economic and quasi-political community, an erosion of the *status quo* in the heart of Europe of which the Soviet Union cannot but help take advantage. Rational Soviet policies can lead to serious consequences if joined by an irrational West German drive for reunification.

In connection with United States–Soviet relations, Professor Kulski alluded to President Johnson's speech of October 7, 1966. The improvement in relations between the two countries has involved atmospheric changes (exchange of cloud photographs, the consular agreement) or limited economic aid (credits for the Fiat automobile factory). What was not mentioned in that speech by President Johnson concerns the very serious increment to the U.S.S.R. arsenal, provided by the deployment of Soviet antiballistic missile systems at a time when American ABM's (thanks to the McNamara doctrine) are still in the research stage. This deployment of truly defensive weapons may represent simply a rational move to eliminate the American predominance in the balance of terror that is so well analyzed in Professor Kulski's outstanding textbook on international relations. It may, however, involve a technological breakthrough. Even if this does not provide overwhelming strength for the U.S.S.R. in an all-out nuclear war, at the very least it will increase bargaining power in future conflicts like the one in Berlin during 1958–62 and Cuba in 1962. There have also been reports of sharply stepped up ICBM production. This could be a perfectly rational policy on the part of the Soviet Union when done gradually. If armaments are rapidly accelerated, however, this could have unwanted and irrational consequences.

These comments have concentrated on disagreements and not on agreement. There are some features of Soviet institutions and U.S.S.R. domestic and foreign policies since 1953 that are still irrational; they cannot be explained other than as remnants of the Stalinist approach. They exist, like the proverbial albatross, hanging on the neck of a regime that would like to proceed to more efficient autocratic—but not democratic—rule.

3

developments in soviet foreign trade

CARL B. TURNER

The subject of Soviet foreign trade has aroused particular interest of late. After initiation of the period called peaceful coexistence by Khrushchev and, more recently, with the development of the Sino-Soviet ideological rift, there has been increasing pressure on the U.S.S.R. system to maintain less aggressive relations vis-à-vis the West and to move toward more intensive cultural, political, and economic contacts. This discussion has as its purpose a general review of the theoretical basis which the Soviets have given for the development of their foreign trade from the early days of the U.S.S.R. state to the present. An attempt then will be made to analyze recent trends, which indicate an interesting shift in Soviet thinking on international trade, and the results of actual dealings with the West in foreign trade.

The pattern of international trade is based theoretically on the principle of comparative advantage. This was enunciated clearly by the famous English economist David Ricardo, with his frequently quoted example of the trade in port and cloth between England and Portugal. His argument demonstrated that both countries would be better off economically if they were to concentrate on the product in which they had a comparative advantage. By trading, each country would obtain a larger total of goods than if it were to follow a policy of national self-sufficiency and economic isolation.

This principle is the basis for domestic trade within a nation as well as foreign trade among nations. In fact, the latter overcomes the difficulties concerning immobility of certain resources as a result of various restrictions on their movement. Hence these resources are transformed into products as they move more freely among nations. However, there are still many restrictions on trade, and the study of foreign trade concentrates largely on these barriers in order to expose them and thereby strengthen the economic argument for free trade.

In general most trading nations subscribe to the principles of free trade even though their own trading policies may run somewhat counter. In this respect the experience of the Soviet Union is at variance with Western trading nations. The U.S.S.R. has largely followed a course of autarchy, or national economic self-sufficiency, throughout the greater part of its history. However, during the post-Stalin era the Soviet Union has again made its appearance on world markets and has expressed the desire to become a member of the world trading community on the basis of an international division of labor. An official booklet on U.S.S.R. trade published in 1958 put this matter very clearly: "The Soviet Government looks upon foreign trade as an opportunity to make use of the international division of labor for the all-around satisfaction of the requirements of its people."[1] This seemingly indisputable statement represents, however, a departure from previous thinking on the part of the U.S.S.R. The Soviet Union has in fact considerably increased its trade with the world outside of its Bloc. This change-over must be seen in relation to historical developments in the U.S.S.R. itself.

The Bolsheviks came to power in a Russia which had become disorganized. Prior to World War I, Russia was primarily an agricultural country, though increasing industrial developments were having a noticeable effect. Foreign trade in the prewar period resembled this structure of the economy. In 1913 among total exports 92.2 per cent included nonindustrial items (foodstuffs, raw materials, and semimanufactured goods) and only 5.6 per cent comprised manufactured goods.[2] Russia's trade was mainly with Europe, in which Germany and England were her chief trading partners. Foreign trade was essentially of a private nature with the role of the state limited to the conventional one of customs and signing commercial treaties. Trade at this time was largely a complementary affair among participants.

When the Bolsheviks seized control of Russia in 1917, the role of the state became dominant. At first, in December 1917, the Council of People's Commissars passed a decree which introduced a permit system. All items in foreign trade had to be licensed by the authorities and were designated as contraband if not cleared in this manner. In April 1918 the Soviets decreed that foreign trade would become a state monopoly, and the People's Commissariat for Trade and Industry (later renamed the Commissariat of Foreign Trade) was given control over this nationalized sector of the economy. Since this date foreign trade has been in the hands of the state.

The early years of the U.S.S.R. were not marked by normal economic conditions. This was the period of War Communism, the civil war, and finally of the New Economy Policy. The Soviets had difficulty in establishing normal relations with other nations, which were apprehensive about the new communist regime. The U.S.S.R. protested discrimination in foreign trade relations. An early Bolshevik who was chairman of Arcos, the Soviet trading corporation in England, and later became director of the Foreign Trade Research Insititute in Moscow, has recorded some of the complaints from the U.S.S.R. point of view: "The enemies of the Soviet monopoly of foreign trade are the enemies of the whole Soviet system; they organized a gold and credit blockade; they attacked Soviet exports; raided the Soviet trade organizations abroad; organized attacks on the Soviet trade representatives; organized and paid for a campaign of slander and lies, accusing the U.S.S.R. of dumping and of the use of so-called 'forced labour'; and inspired boycotts against Soviet products, aiming at imposing an embargo on Soviet exports."[3]

To a large degree the above complaint arose from the question of settling the tsarist Russian debt, which the Soviets had repudiated, as well as claims against the Soviet government for seizing investments and property belonging to foreign citizens and companies. Despite these difficulties the U.S.S.R. managed to increase foreign trade during this period. The nature of foreign trade, however, had changed. Russia imported more raw materials and capital goods during the 1920's than she did before World War I, and during 1928–9 she exported no grains, whereas tsarist Russia had been one of the world's largest grain exporters.

During the period of the five-year plans this composition of U.S.S.R. trade was even more distinct. The Soviet Union had committed itself to a policy of industrialization as a result of Stalin's dictum on building socialism in one country. The first five-year plan called for massive imports of machinery and advanced equipment. Exports of raw materials were to provide the necessary foreign exchange to pay for imports. However, at this time the world economic crisis depressed world trade, especially for the products which the U.S.S.R. could offer for export. The Soviets continued to import industrial goods and ran into trade imbalances, as they could not sell enough abroad to pay for these goods. The U.S.S.R. was forced to accept lower world prices and drastically restrict nonessential imports. Even these severe measures failed to restore a balance in Soviet foreign trade, and credits plus gold sales made up the difference.

It was during this critical period that the U.S.S.R. was accused of dumping goods on world markets. True, the Soviets did accept low prices, but there is a distinct feature in this instance. Ordinarily "dumping" means that a nation sells surplus products for which there is no market at home. In the case of the U.S.S.R. there was indeed a market for these products at home, as foodstuffs were in very short supply. Soviet producers could easily have sold their output on the home market; but the government's policy of industrialization demanded that exports pay for imports, and so the consumer had to make this sacrifice.

After the completion of the first five-year plan, the U.S.S.R. reduced its imports and, as a consequence, was able to reduce exports. The favorable balances accumulated during these five-year plans before World War II enabled the Soviets to pay for their exports and repay the debts incurred during the first plan. Essentially trade declined as industrialization increased. Usually the reverse is the case, that is, as a nation develops industrially, its exports and volume of trade increase. Such was not the case with the Soviet Union, whose foreign trade policy was determined primarily by political considerations.

The U.S.S.R. claimed success for its trade policy during this period. Monopoly over foreign trade was defended theoretically as the only way available to control the course of economic development. It was maintained that if normal free trade were allowed, then foreign influences would have disturbed and even destroyed the young Soviet state. The U.S.S.R. was essentially correct on this point, as it would have been exceedingly difficult to control the basic sectors of a planned economy if foreign trade were to a large extent free. Other advantages appear to accrue to the state monopoly over trade in that nonessential imports can be restricted; exports may be sold at a loss to obtain necessary imports; concessions can be forced from other nations which are in need of markets; and the traditional "infant industry" argument can be applied here.

The Soviet state monopoly of foreign trade is not without disadvantages. These are readily apparent in any organization which assumes the size of this monopoly in that it tends to become bureaucratic and inefficient. The personnel are far-removed from producers and the ultimate user, which makes the communication problem a serious one. Since trade representatives are not buying or selling for their own account, they may not be concerned in obtaining the best possible prices. Lastly, the monopoly in foreign trade may prevent healthy competition for Soviet industry, thereby increasing inefficiency and distortion in the use of resources.

The foregoing represents a brief account of the Soviet foreign trade monopoly prior to World War II. The structure and the purpose of trade had changed radically from that of tsarist Russia. Economic self-sufficiency, or autarchy was the goal of the U.S.S.R., and foreign trade served this end. Soviet exports in reality were state exports and were not influenced by the conditions which affect private capitalist trade. Exports did not result from unsold goods in the home market, and they were not traded on the basis of comparative advantage or the international division of labor. Exports had to be sold to obtain imports, and whatever product was available was exported, regardless of price considerations. When industrialization had been achieved, foreign trade was reduced because vast imports were no longer necessary. A prominent Soviet economist, T. S. Ginzburg, stated in 1937: "As the volume of our imports began to decline, the necessity of forcing our exports disappeared."[4]

The U.S.S.R. economy suffered a severe shock from the invading German army in 1941. Economic life became disrupted, and serious shortages occurred in both the industrial and agricultural sectors of the economy. The Soviet Union needed material and equipment of all kinds to carry on the war. The United States came to the assistance by offering huge amounts of aid via lend-lease arrangements. The total value of this aid amounted to $9,128,875,000, according to L. T. Crowley, the U. S. Foreign Economic Administrator. Of the total American exports Soviet Russia received 17.6 per cent in 1942, then 23.1 per cent in 1943, and 24.3 per cent in 1944.[5] Other countries, mainly England and Canada, also contributed significantly to help the U.S.S.R. during the war. There was a tremendous amount of sympathy and admiration for the Soviets in their struggle against Germany. This feeling plus the enormous quantity of aid sent to the U.S.S.R. by her allies gave rise in the West to hopes of increased foreign trade with the Soviet Union in the postwar period. The U.S.S.R. economy had suffered severe disruptions and would need a large amount of reconstruction after the war. Although the foreign trade organization remained intact throughout this period and despite the fact that there was no change in the status of the U.S.S.R. foreign trade monopoly, somehow it was hoped that trade would increase between the Soviet Union and her wartime allies. This was quite understandable under the circumstances.

Soon after the war a considerable amount of literature was published on this subject which chiefly reviewed the history of Soviet trade and offered conclusions about the future of this trade with the West. There was general agreement that the Soviet Union would be welcomed back into the world trading community. Some writers appeared more optimistic than others. Eric Johnston, then president of the United States Chamber of Commerce, wrote the following in a foreword to one of the books on the subject of foreign trade:

> We can do business with Russia. Every day that I was in the Soviet Union I had evidence from top Soviet officials with whom I discussed the problem that they are very glad to do business with American businessmen. . . .
>
> Though our economic and political systems are completely opposite, Russia being the most collectivized state and we the most individualistic nation in the world, we do not want to interfere with our respective systems. Marshal Stalin and I took it for granted that capitalism could do business with communism. In fact, I see no reason why we cannot cooper-

ate. We have no conflict of interests. Neither one of us, I am sure, wishes territorial aggrandizement at the expense of the other, neither of us is a competitor with the other in the markets of the world, and I see no reason why we cannot form bridges between our respective nations for greater trade after the war.[6]

There seemed to be a common ground in all of these works on the assumption that the Soviet Union would need trade to restore her economy. Only the West could provide the necessary exports. The U.S.S.R. would have difficulty in paying for the imports, since she had little to export, and even if there were surpluses in the Soviet Union, the West might be reluctant to accept them, as sales could not be guaranteed. Hence the problem centered on credits and especially the need for long-term credits. These studies also mentioned other problems, such as the Soviet desire for bilateral trade agreements, but they all hoped that the U.S.S.R. would abandon her autarchic policies and join the world trade community.

These hopes were soon dashed, as the Soviet Union refused to participate in the reconstruction of Europe. The U.S.S.R. charged that the proposed aid from the United States represented an imperialist device to subvert the national economies of the participating countries. Moscow countered this with the formation of the Council for Mutual Economic Assistance (CMEA) among the satellites in Eastern Europe. According to the Soviet version, CMEA arose for the following reasons: "Above all, this unification was a natural result and the consequence of the appearance and development of the world socialist system." The author went on to say that Lenin had foreseen this development. He also noted another important reason for the formation of CMEA: "The foreign factor—the policy of the imperialist states—hastened the process of the economic rapprochement of the U.S.S.R. and the people's democracies. The major capitalist powers, not wishing to accept the loss of their ruling position in Central and Southeastern Europe, organized in reality an economic-trade blockade of the Socialist States. The main weapon of this policy was the so-called 'Marshall Plan.'"[7] This was in line with an earlier statement that the U.S.S.R. and the people's democracies had refused to participate in the Marshall Plan because they did not wish to compromise their sovereignty and the interests of their national economies.

Basically the people's democracies followed the Soviet pattern of development through emphasis on heavy industry. Trade arrangements were made on a bilateral basis, with the Soviet Union enjoying very favorable terms of trade. This area together with Communist China became the major trading bloc for the U.S.S.R. in the postwar period. Two writers noted this development in the following words: "Before the war those countries accounted for very little of the U.S.S.R.'s foreign trade, but when they had switched over to socialism the road to international economic cooperation was opened to them."[8]

Prior to World War II, as already noted, the Soviets followed a trade policy of self-sufficiency, or autarchy. As a result of the ideological realignment among states following that war, the U.S.S.R. expanded its trade with the newly-formed socialist countries. In Soviet terminology this area has become known variously as the socialist system of world economy, the democratic camp, or the socialist world. This division of the globe into two camps resulted in the formation of parallel world markets: one socialist and hence "democratic," the other capitalist. This trend can be observed by the following figures: the U.S.S.R. exported 57.7 per cent of its total exports to the socialist countries in 1946; then 83.3 per cent in 1950; later 79.8 per cent in 1955; an even 75.0 per cent in 1956; and 75.4 per cent in 1957. This increase in trade with the "democratic camp" was also reflected in Soviet imports: 51.6 per cent came from socialist countries in 1946; next 77.6 per cent in 1950; then 78.7 per cent in 1955; a drop to 76.2 per cent in 1956; a decline to 71.5 per cent in 1957. The remaining percentages in the above figures indicated the amount of trade with the so-called "capitalist" countries.

The value of Soviet foreign trade increased considerably during these years over the prewar period. For instance, trade turnover[9] amounted to 1.1 billion rubles in 1938; but 7.4 in 1946; an even 13.0 billion in 1950; and 25.9 billion in 1955. This increase in the volume and extent of trade was based on the theory of an "international socialist division of labor." This term meant that the principle of comparative advantage, based on this division of labor, supposedly operated throughout the socialist Bloc. In reality a system of arbitrary prices precluded any resemblance to the principle of comparative advantage as it functions in the West. Despite these differences the Soviets have moved toward enlarging their markets in comparison to prewar performance but, until recently, only within their own sphere of political influence. The term "international socialist division of labor" is still current in Soviet economic literature, and there is much discussion concerning it.

Following the death of Stalin, Khrushchev initiated the era of peaceful coexistence at the famous 20th Party Congress in 1956. This policy called for economic competition as well as peaceful coexistence. The program was to be implemented on all fronts, and foreign trade was designated an area for expansion. Khrushchev himself campaigned very strenuously on behalf of this policy during his many visits to foreign countries. He continually called for more trade wherever he went. The following utterance is typical of his views: "Foreign trade provides a sound and stable basis on which to construct peaceful coexistence among states with different social and economic systems. Further, economic ties offer a good foundation for improving political relations among nations. The extensive development of trade plays an important role in strengthening mutual trust among peoples and in reducing international tension."[10]

This policy had some success, as foreign trade continued to grow, and more significantly, the amount of commercial exchange with the industrialized West increased. Soviet foreign trade turnover (value of exports and imports) totaled the equivalent of $8.647 billion (U.S. dollars) in 1958; then $11.826 billion in 1960; later $13.486 billion in 1962; and $15.420 billion in 1964. See table 2. This amounted to an annual rate of increase of 10.7 per cent, which compares favorably with previous periods. Using 1953 as a base year, the dollar value of U.S.S.R. trade by 1963 grew 2.7 times. Furthermore, Soviet trade turnover for 1963 in dollar value amounted to approximately 35 per cent of the total trade turnover of the United States. The bulk of U.S.S.R. trade (some 70 per cent) was still with communist-ruled countries. Soviet trade with China has been reduced considerably, while Cuba's share has risen substantially. Approximately 19 per cent of all U.S.S.R. trade was with advanced nations and only 11 per cent with underdeveloped countries.[11] As to commodities, the Soviets exported mainly machinery, equipment, fuel and petroleum, and raw ma-

TABLE 2

Soviet Foreign Trade in 1965–7

(millions of rubles at current prices)

Category	1965	1966	1967
Total trade turnover	14,610	15,076	16,400
of which Soviet exports	7,357	7,957	8,700
of which Soviet imports	7,253	7,119	7,700
Hence, Soviet balance	+104	+838	+1,000
Trade with socialist countries	10,050	10,023	11,100
of which Soviet exports	5,001	5,286	5,700
of which Soviet imports	5,049	4,737	5,400
Hence, Soviet balance	—48	+549	+300
Trade with non-Socialist countries	4,560	5,053	5,300
of which Soviet exports	2,356	2,671	3,000
of which Soviet imports	2,204	2,382	2,300
Hence, Soviet balance	+152	+289	+700

NOTE: The official rate of exchange is one ruble for $1.11 in Moscow.

SOURCE: U.S.S.R., *SSSR v tsifrakh v 1967 godu* (Moscow: Tsentralnoe Statisticheskoe Upravlenie pri Sovete Ministrov SSSR, 1968), p. 30.

terials; whereas imports included machinery, equipment, consumers' goods, and chemicals. It must be noted that the Soviet Union is a net importer of machinery and equipment.

The increased trade with the industrialized countries of Western Europe together with Japan has caused much comment in Soviet economic literature. Heretofore the emphasis has been on the international socialist division of labor, which represented the basis for trade within the communist Bloc. Naturally the U.S.S.R. could not apply this theoretical framework for trade with the noncommunist West. Hence the Soviet Union produced a "new" term, long familiar to Western economists: the international division of labor. This idea has been explained as follows:

> Despite the availability of sufficient natural riches and stable economic conditions for the unlimited development of production, the Soviet Union and other countries of the world socialist system do not strive towards autarchy. In the first place, autarchic tendencies contradict the policy of peaceful coexistence, the economic base of which is the broad development of trade and other economic relations among the countries of the two systems. In the second place, from an economic point of view autarchy is disadvantageous as it brakes the development of productive forces, slows down the growth of labor productivity. In fact, the tendency to produce everything yourself, including those products which are more costly to produce in the home market than to buy in the world market, does not signify a saving but a squandering of social labor. But the participation of that country in the international division of labor allows that country to economize on the expenditures of social labor and raise its productivity. The Soviet Union and other socialist countries have not locked themselves within the framework of national markets or the world socialist market but are striving to exploit the advantages of the international division of labor on a worldwide scale.[12]

The above statement reveals a complete *volte-face* on the part of Soviet theoreticians and could be placed in a textbook on international trade in the capitalist West with few economists taking exception to it. References to the international division of labor have become more frequent in Soviet economic literature, but comments about the international "socialist" division of labor still persist. It is maintained that the latter represents a new type of economic cooperation among socialist states and that this relationship needs further development.

These two principles of a "socialist" division of labor and an international division of labor continued to coexist peacefully. They were brought together in the directives of the 23rd Party Congress for the development of the new five-year plan during 1966–70 as follows:

> *In the field of foreign economic relations the most important tasks of the five-year plan are:*
>   —to develop further the economic ties of the Soviet Union and the socialist countries and to use the advantages of the international division of

labor on the basis of Leninist principles of proletarian internationalism and fraternal mutual assistance in the interests of strengthening the world socialist system;
—to increase economic cooperation with the developing nations by means of strengthening trade relations and giving them economic and technical assistance to strengthen the independence of their national economies;
—to develop trade with other foreign countries.[13]

Henceforth foreign trade is to be divided into three geographic parts: the socialist area, the underdeveloped lands, and the other foreign countries (i.e., capitalist states). In connection with the last category the directives were expanded as follows: *"To develop further foreign trade with industrially developed capitalist countries"* which show a readiness to develop trade with the Soviet Union."

In order "to utilize fully the advantages of the international division of labor, to increase the economic effectiveness of foreign trade, and to better satisfy the needs of the Soviet people"[14] the directives called for an increase in exports of manufactured goods and a thorough study of foreign markets. Comment by way of journal articles soon appeared with the pledge to fulfill this program and to master the new tasks.

The next issue of *Vneshnyaya torgovlya* carried a lead editorial about "The 23rd Congress of the C.P.S.U. on the Foreign Economic Ties of the U.S.S.R." in which a program for the international socialist division of labor was discussed. Then the article went on to analyze the international division of labor and called for a broadening of trade and foreign credits to facilitate this trade. In a subsequent issue of *Vneshnyaya torgovlya* the U.S.S.R. Minister of Foreign Trade further explained the new program.[15] He followed the classification laid down by the 23rd Party Congress directives in dealing separately with each world trading area.

However, articles still appeared which continued to refer only to the area of the socialist countries, as, for example, the following paragraph: "This program [23rd Party Congress directives] which includes the tasks of increasing the effective and national forms of mutual economic ties envisages a fuller utilization of the advantages of the international socialist division of labor in the interests of further strengthening the world system of socialism."[16]

The foregoing has included a review of the theory and the ideological basis for U.S.S.R. participation in foreign trade. It is well to recapitulate briefly the change that has taken place. The Soviet foreign trade monopoly was introduced very early in the history of the regime and has remained in force to date. In the theory of trade the U.S.S.R. has held a variety of positions. At the beginning of the five-year plans the theory of autarchy was stressed. Exports were justifiable only to offset necessary imports which helped build socialism in the one country "imprisoned" by capitalist encirclement. With the territorial gains following World War II the Soviet Union imposed on the newly-formed socialist countries the theory of the international "socialist" division of labor for the world socialist market. This remained in force during the Stalinist period. With the era of peaceful coexistence following Stalin's death the U.S.S.R. has insisted on the international division of labor in a world-wide context and even repudiated autarchy. At present the Soviets adhere to both theories of the division of labor, the socialist and the international. It appears that this represents a convenient device, similar to peaceful coexistence and world revolution: both theories allow maximum flexibility for whatever policy the circumstances might require.

With the above brief outline on the course of Soviet foreign trade theory in mind, it might be possible to gain a better understanding of recent developments in U.S.S.R. commercial transactions, particularly with the countries of Western Europe and the United States. The Soviets have stepped up their trade activities in their attempts to increase the volume of trade, especially with the United States. Since the U.S.S.R. has reversed itself in the field of theory, it is interesting to see if this change has produced any effect on the actual volume of trade with the West.

Prior to the current period of peaceful coexistence, trade between the Soviet Union and the United States suffered from the effects of the cold-war period under Stalin, especially with regard to American exports to the U.S.S.R. As a result of the cold war and the concomitant restrictions, U.S. exports to the Soviet Union dwindled from $149 million in 1947 to $27.8 million in 1948, then $6.6 million in 1949, down to $55,000 in 1951, and finally as low as $19,000 in 1953. Since that time American exports have increased, but they did not go over the million mark until 1956, when they were valued at $3.8 million. Soviet exports to the United States were more stable by contrast: from $77.1 million in 1947 to a low of $10.7 million in 1953 and then up to $24.5 million in 1956.

It is apparent from the above trade figures[17] that Khrushchev faced some difficulty when he attempted to increase trade. However, such was his aim, and he even visited the United States in 1959 to further this purpose. His desire was understandable, for the United States is the leading industrial power in the world and produces the most advanced technical goods. The sheer efficiency and productive ability of the United States have always been admired and envied by the Soviet Union. With due respect to Khrushchev's efforts, he was unable to lower American trade barriers. Even Anastas I. Mikoyan, the successful and most prominent of U.S.S.R. commercial negotiators, visited the United States and failed to obtain a general agreement on trade.

In the United States support for more trade with the Soviet Union has increased slowly. There are a variety of reasons for this changing attitude. In particular the general lowering of international tension seems to call for a decrease in restrictions. Furthermore, the United States is experiencing a balance of payments problem and has even been running a deficit in its account with the Soviet Union. Then there are the usual free trade arguments, and some firms are anxious to seize an opportunity for more sales in the Soviet market.

This problem was recognized officially in the 1966 Annual Report by the Council of Economic Advisors:

> The United States is also giving increased attention to the lowering of barriers to trade with the countries of the Soviet bloc. For both political and economic reasons, this country has not fully participated in the steady expansion of East–West trade during the past decade. U.S. trade with the Soviet bloc amounted to barely 1 per cent of total U.S. foreign commerce in 1964. Last year, the President's Special Committee on U.S. Trade Relations with East European Countries and the Soviet Union recommended an expansion of peaceful trade with the European Communist countries and urged that the President be given discretionary authority to remove trade restrictions against those countries.[18]

A number of high-ranking U.S. government officials responded by giving this position their support. Secretary of Commerce John T. Connor called for the separation of trade from politics. Deputy Under-Secretary of State Foy D. Kohler spoke in favor of greater flexibility in East–West trade. He expanded on this subject to an interested party, a meeting of the American Legion in Orlando, Florida. In addition to increased trade President Johnson called for an exchange in skills and ideas with the Soviet Union and other advanced societies.[19] The President appointed McGeorge Bundy, of the Ford Foundation, to explore this area.

Despite this official support there has been little gain in the actual volume of trade. It appears that the public is not in sympathy with the administration on this matter, partly because of existing cold-war attitudes and the current Southeast Asian conflict in which the Soviet Union is openly supplying North Vietnam. Various groups have strongly negative feelings about U.S.S.R. trade and are quick to act on their convictions. The International Longshoreman's Union, for example, refused to load wheat for shipment to the Soviet Union unless 50 per cent of the cargo were carried in American ships. East–West trade presents economic hazards to private firms as well. There was the case of the Firestone contract with Romania which suffered adverse publicity, as stores were picketed by organizations protesting this agreement, and finally Firestone was forced to cancel it.

There are also political repercussions in advocating greater trade. In the 1966 American elections a candidate would hardly have improved his chance for office in most regions if he had called for increased trade with the U.S.S.R. The public does not readily differentiate among the various brands or types of communist states. Communism is treated much like a commodity in economics. A commodity includes all items or articles of a similar kind which are perfect substitutes for one another. Hence it is difficult to identify the specific producer. A product, on the other hand, after processing carries a brand name and can be associated with its firm, producer, or manufacturer. That there exist various brands of communism, some of which are at great odds with one another, is a factor which the America public has been slow to grasp.

National security is the basic reason why the United States has restrictions on trade with the Soviet Union. The aim is to prevent strategic goods from reaching the U.S.S.R., thereby affecting her military capability. There is a difference of opinion as to what constitutes strategic materials. Economists maintain that in the long run resources can be transferred from one kind of production to another, subject to varying costs, and are hesitant to call one material more strategic than another. In the short run, however, definitions can be adopted for strategic goods. In any case the list of strategic items does not appear to have hampered the Soviet military effort. Further, alternative sources of supply have been available to the U.S.S.R. if necessary. Soviet trade specialists[20] contend that the U.S.S.R. has even exported goods which are on the restricted list in the United States.

One can understand why there is reluctance on the part of American business firms to seek trade with the Soviet Union. There are difficulties in the way of restrictions at home, which are involved with bureaucratic procedures. Furthermore, difficulties exist on the U.S.S.R. side if trade does develop, since it involves a private firm negotiating with a state trading organization. Other doubts are always present. Will Moscow buy only capital goods? Will the purchase be a one-shot affair, such as a complete industrial plant, with no prospect of continuing trade? These questions together with the inconveniences of travel, currency, negotiations, service, and lack of promotional arrangements in the U.S.S.R. may well deter even the most aggressive business firm from trading, although such a firm might participate in this trade through part-ownership in a West European firm which is exporting to the Soviet Union.

Nevertheless if restrictions in the United States were lifted, this would in all likelihood increase exports to the U.S.S.R. However, Moscow would want to sell more of its goods in return. This would be difficult because Soviet products would face strong competition on the American market. Soviet manufacturers have had little experience in producing for sale in any competitive market. They have had even less exposure to or contact with the consumer, since they are represented by state trading agencies.

U.S.S.R. economists have written a great deal negatively about capitalism and its shortcomings. They have neglected to study demand analysis, price theory, business administration, and other related disciplines which are essential for success in the American market. This has been noticed by certain Soviet writers, who have mentioned it in their discussion of these problems. Five years ago a Soviet academician lamented the fact that no business schools existed in the U.S.S.R. and mentioned the Harvard Business School favorably as an example of such an institution in the West.[21]

The Soviets have tried to sell certain of their internationally recognized products such as vodka to the West. American newspaper readers may have noticed a recent advertising campaign for *Stolichnaya Vodka* which carried the caption "from Russia with ice." If the U.S.S.R. has any success here, it is to be feared that they will try further toxic subversion with that old favorite *kvass*. In addition to the need for greater advertising the Soviets have also recognized the long-standing problem of quality in their exports. The Minister of Foreign Trade during a Moscow television symposium on foreign trade stressed this point in his closing statement: "I would like to take this opportunity to express my wishes to the collectives of the enterprises whose production is for export to strive for excellence in the quality of everything that carries the mark *Sdelano v SSSR* [Made in the U.S.S.R.] as called for by our Party and Government."[22]

The Soviets seem to realize that for the time being they have little opportunity to gain a foothold in American foreign trade. Their products have the additional disadvantage of being denied "most favored nation" treatment, which makes them prohibitively expensive. Hence the plea for credits to expand trade. Every Soviet writer dealing with foreign trade and the West mentions the need for long-term credits to finance U.S.S.R. purchases. These credits have not been forthcoming from the United States, and this has further discouraged Soviet purchases, aside from the huge 1964 grain deal.

If the U.S.S.R. has not had much success in the American market, it has fared better in trade with Western Europe. The Soviet campaign began in the usual manner, with high-ranking personalities visiting various countries. After Stalin's death Malenkov visited England. He was followed by Khrushchev, who toured most of Europe before his retirement. Recently the U.S.S.R. president Nikolai Podgorny, traveled to Austria and Italy; Premier Kosygin visited France. During these trips discussions were initiated by the Soviets which invariably brought up increased trade. It is interesting to note that even the Ministry of Foreign Trade is bypassed at this level. After the political leaders secure a commercial agreement, the Ministry then follows up with detailed arrangements. As a result of this campaign the value of Soviet trade with Western Europe is much greater than with the United States. In 1963 total U.S.S.R. foreign trade amounted to $344.9 million with England, $284.2 million with West Germany, $174.4 million with France, $272.8 million with Italy, $133.8 million with Sweden, $133.8 million with Belgium, $77.8 million with the Netherlands, but only $52.7 million with the United States.[23]

Several reasons can be offered to explain Soviet success in this area. The chief one appears to be that the U.S.S.R. has been able to obtain long-term credits from these countries, as the Foreign Trade Minister has stated: "The growth of the exchange of goods is not the only index of the interest of the Western powers in the development of trade with the U.S.S.R. but the fact that in recent years England, France and Italy granted financial credits for the placing of huge Soviet purchases."[24] The largest of these purchases arranged on long-term credit was the agreement the U.S.S.R signed with the Fiat company of Italy to build an auto plant near Moscow. The plant will have the capacity of producing 600,000 cars a year. Fiat granted a ten-year credit of $300 million to the Soviets for their purchase. This agreement has many interesting aspects. There are political considerations, such as the size of the communist party in Italy and the fact that the plant will be built in the town of Togliatti, U.S.S.R. Of particular interest is the fact that the Soviets have purchased an entire factory rather than build one themselves. This may represent a gain from trade on the basis of the international division of labor. However, if Italy is more efficient in producing cars, it should be more feasible to continue production of these cars in Italy in exchange for oil, timber, and other products from the Soviet Union. Greater gains for both sides might have resulted from such an arrangement.

The recent Gallic flirtation with the Soviet Union and their trade and cultural agreements, signed during October 1966, are further proof of increased U.S.S.R. trading stakes in this area. When General de Gaulle visited the Soviet Union in June 1966, Moscow spared no effort in making him feel that he was indeed the world's most distinguished statesman. Following this trip discussions on trade between France and the U.S.S.R. resulted in protocols on bilateral cooperation which call for the adoption of the joint Soviet-French SECAM-III color television system, combined research efforts at the atomic research center of Serpukhovo, substantial purchases from as well as technical cooperation with the Renault and the Peugeot automobile firms, and a substantial order for housing construction equipment with the firm of Camus and Company. During Premier Kosygin's visit to France in December 1966 he spoke on French television about peace, friendship, and cooperation.[25] Expanded trade relations, he maintained, would further these goals.

It appears that the U.S.S.R. will continue its efforts to increase trade with Western Europe. The Soviet economy is growing more complex and requires advanced techniques and products from the West. Since these items are difficult to obtain in the United States, the U.S.S.R. has turned to Western Europe. The reception of the Soviets in Western Europe has been favorable, and trade in all probability will increase. Furthermore, the U.S.S.R. is in some ways more acceptable politically in Western Europe, and this facilitates trade. Western Europe does not depend heavily on Soviet trade, so there is no question of any dominance or economic penetration involved. Western Europe realizes the importance of the Soviet market and will exchange its products for traditional Russian exports which were acceptable in West European markets during past history.

There is not much immediate prospect for greatly expanded trade between the Soviet Union and the United States. For reasons outlined above the U.S.S.R. still has achieved no trade agreement and has not received "most favored nation" treatment. Progress is slow but not without hope. The recent signing of a civil air agreement is a step in this direction. Above all, an objective appraisal concerning the merits of trade is long overdue. In the last analysis much depends on the political climate, which for the present has not been propitious.

In the meantime the Soviets have improved their trade outlook. Theoretically they participate in the socialist market and in the world market on the basis of the convenient twin doctrines of the international "socialist" division of labor and the international division of labor. They have given up autarchy and have opted for greater material benefits to be gained from an increase in foreign trade. They have become more sophisticated in their methods and more successful in their endeavors. On the surface, it would certainly appear that substantial and significant changes have taken place. Basically, however, the U.S.S.R.'s trading structure and objectives have not varied. There still remains the state monopoly over foreign trade, which initiates and controls trade according to planned goals. And the primary goal is to strengthen the world socialist system, and this, strangely enough, is being accomplished by the Soviets with the benefits obtained from trade according to the principle of the international division of labor.

Notes to Chapter 3

1. V. Alkhimov and V. Mordvinov, *Foreign Trade of the U.S.S.R.*, Soviet Booklet No. 37 (London, 1958), p. 19.

2. H. G. Moulton and L. Pasvolsky, *Russian Debts and Russian Reconstruction* (New York, 1924), p. 73.

3. J. D. Yanson, *Foreign Trade in the U.S.S.R.* (London, 1934), p. 29.

4. T. S. Ginzburg, *Vneshnyaya torgovlya S.S.S.R.* (Moscow, 1937), p. 11;

quoted in M. V. Condoide, *Russian-American Trade* (Columbus, Ohio, 1947), p. 68.

5. A. Baykov, *Soviet Foreign Trade* (Princeton, 1946), pp. 76–7, 89.

6. Hans Heymann, *We Can Do Business with Russia* (Chicago-New York, 1946), pp. vii, ix.

7. V. I. Morozov, *Sovet ekonomicheskoi vzaimopomoshchi: soyuz ravnykh* (Moscow, 1964), pp. 6–7.

8. Alkhimov and Mordvinov, *Foreign Trade of the U.S.S.R.,* p. 12.

9. L. I. Frei, "Foreign Trade," ed. Robert Maxwell, in *Information U.S.S.R.* (Oxford–New York, 1962), pp. 360–1, is the source for the preceding and the following statistics.

10. *Pravda,* March 7, 1959.

11. These figures are taken from U.S. Congress, Joint Economic Committee, *Current Economic Indications for the U.S.S.R.* (Washington, D.C., 1965), pp. 151–3.

12. B. Vagonov, "Leninskie printsipy vneshneekonomicheskoi politiki," *Vneshnyaya torgovlya,* No. 2 (1965), p. 5.

13. *Pravda,* Feb. 20, 1966. The foreign economic relations directives were reprinted in *Vneshnyaya torgovlya,* No. 4 (1966), pp. 3–4.

14. *Vneshnyaya torgovlya,* No. 4 (1966), p. 4.

15. *Ibid.,* No. 5 (1966), pp. 3–5; N. Patolichev, "Vneshnyaya torgovlya SSSR v novoi pyatiletke," *Vneshnyaya torgovlya,* No. 7 (1966), pp. 3–7.

16. B. Ladygin and Y. Shiryaev, "Voprosy sovershenstvovaniya ekonomicheskogo sotrudnichestva stran SEV," *Voprosy ekonomiki,* No. 5 (1966), p. 81.

17. L. M. Herman, "Soviet Foreign Trade and the United States Market," in U.S. Congress, Joint Economic Committee, *New Directions in the Soviet Economy* (Washington, D.C., 1966), Part IV, p. 943.

18. *Economic Report of the President* (Jan. 1966), p. 146; transmitted to Congress.

19. *The New York Times,* Nov. 12, 1966; Dec. 12, 1966; and Dec. 16, 1966.

20. Alkhimov and Mordinov, *Foreign Trade of the U.S.S.R.,* pp. 26–7.

21. K. Plotnikov, "V chem prav i neprav E. G. Liberman," *Voprosy ekonomiki,* No. 11 (1962), p. 114.

22. N. S. Patolichev, "Dlya razvitiya ekonomiki, dlya blaga naroda," *Vneshnyaya torgovlya,* No. 3 (1965), p. 3 (supplement).

23. H. W. Heiss, "The Soviet Union in the World Market," in *New Directions in the Soviet Economy,* Part IV, p. 925.

24. N. S. Patolichev, "Vneshnyaya torgovlya SSSR v novoi pyatiletki," *Vneshnyaya torgovlya,* No. 7 (1966), p. 6.

25. *Pravda,* Dec. 9, 1966.

Discussion

Mose L. Harvey

Current trends in Soviet foreign trade present the same basic question as does U.S.S.R. policy in general: Is the Kremlin changing course, or is it merely tacking in the face of strong winds? To note this puzzle is to strike a familiar chord. For near fifty years outside observers have recurrently wondered whether shifts by Moscow came for opportunistic reasons or signified a real change in attitude.

Thus it was with Lenin's New Economic Policy (NEP); with the triumph of "conservative-nationalist minded" Stalin over "world revolutionary" Trotsky; the turn to the West for machinery and technical know-how during the industrialization of the first five-year plan, with its subtheme of Soviet good faith in paying off debts and fulfilling commitments; the "United Front for Collective Security" line of the thirties; the sweeping wartime adjustments at home and in international stance, including dissolution of the Third International; the early postwar discussion of massive trade with the West, and especially the United States; Stalin's lifting of the Berlin blockade, which many hailed as inaugurating the end of the cold war; the "Malenkov reforms" and the peace offensive following the death of Stalin; the 20th Party Congress with its repudiation of Stalinism and its dual emphasis on "peaceful coexistence" and the "peaceful road to socialism;" and the retreat during the Cuban missile crisis.

What has made the Soviet puzzle such a continuing enigma is that much of the outside world has been convinced from the very seizure of power by the Bolsheviks in 1917 that virulent communism could not possibly endure in Russia:

(1). For some it has been a matter of faith in the basic humanity of man, belief that any group of men ruling a great state in the modern era would over time necessarily come to put the well-being and progress of their own people above the dangerous and costly pursuit of world revolutionary objectives. This faith first manifested itself in the widespread belief that Lenin would be "sobered" by responsibility and power, subsequently in the thought that Lenin's successors would necessarily be "more rational," and then that the "next generation" would assuredly take a different course, and so on.

(2). Others have believed that the U.S.S.R. system could not work over the long term, that it was only a matter of time before it would become too bogged down in problems and difficulties of its own making. Soviet leaders would have no choice then but to turn to the capitalist way of operating and to a new relationship with the noncommunist world itself.

(3). A third group has felt that U.S.S.R. hostility and aggressiveness derive more from deep-rooted suspicion of the capitalist West, reinforced by Western policies and actions, than from positive purposes of the Soviet leaders themselves. If reasonably reassured and enticed by the Western side, these leaders would steadily, albeit cautiously, move toward an accommodation with the West and even to a modification of their totalitarian practices at home. According to this line of reasoning these last aspects have largely resulted from the state of siege in which the regime has always felt itself to be.

Each time that the Soviets have fallen on troubled days, and each time that they tempered their conduct or even their tone, flurries of excited expectations have swept the West: "Is not the great metamorphosis at last underway?" And then a beguiling game has invariably begun, a contest in searching for (and happily finding) clues and signals of the basic change in attitudes and policies so long wished for and anticipated. That the U.S.S.R. has consistently ended this game by abruptly reverting to type has not dampened the enthusiasm with which it has been started again whenever a new opportunity offered.

For several years now excitement has been building to a high pitch. This has been due in part to acknowledged difficulties the Soviet Union is having with its economy, i.e., making the system work. It has also been caused by other reasons: the change in style of the post-Khrushchev leadership, both in its relations with other countries and in its method of rule at home (that the Khrushchev period had itself brought a change in style would seem beside the point); the absence over a prolonged period of any Soviet-generated major crisis, with the last and doubtless the most dangerous having occurred all of five and a half years ago; the re-establishment of United States technological superiority, i.e., "assured" American leadership in the space race; renewed Western confidence regarding its irreversible strategic superiority, i.e., the bolstering influence of the McNamara assurance; and the turn of the world-wide tide against U.S.S.R. policies and enterprises, about which there can be no doubt at least for the time being.

The prime factor, however, has been the Soviet break with China. The reasoning here is quite simple, although whether it is equally sound remains highly questionable: Moscow has become the enemy of Washington's enemy. Ergo it must be or become our friend. The Chinese bait and insult the Soviets, even as they attack and denigrate the United States. The Chinese threaten to bring ruin down upon the Soviet world, just as they threaten to destroy the capitalist world. Thus however much the U.S.S.R. may still profess to be engaged in a struggle with the United States, it must necessarily view China as the real enemy and, beneath the façade of continuing hostility, is moving closer to the Western way. Or put in other terms, the Chinese have carried communism and communist zeal for world revolution to a logical conclusion and, in doing so, have reduced both to an absurdity from the standpoint of a country like the Soviet Union.

Once again the feverish search for signs and signals has commenced, and it will bear the usual predictable results. Speeches are read and assurances drawn from the fact that Russian adjectives to decry the "bestiality" of American policy in Southeast Asia are fewer or less vivid than they might have been. A step-up in Soviet arms shipments for use by the North Vietnamese against United States forces is examined in terms of the increased friction likely to be produced between Moscow and Peking. A change in economic practices that looks toward greater efficiency in the centralized management of the economy is interpreted as a step toward the adoption of capitalism. A fairly meaningless consular agreement with America, and one sought principally by the administration in Washington, is taken as an augur of far-reaching political understandings and agreements.

It is against this background that the chapter analyzing recent developments in Soviet foreign trade must be read. Professor Turner is obviously well trained in the art of trying to explain U.S.S.R. intentions. On the one side, he is fully aware of the *possible* significance of departures from traditional practices and of the need to give these the most careful attention and weight. On the other, he is alert to a basic characteristic of the Soviet leadership, and that is the deftness with which it follows the adage that there is more than one way in which to skin a cat.

Professor Turner should be commended on spotting and analyzing shifts and turns in Soviet foreign trade practices and in Soviet theoretical thinking about the role of foreign trade in a socialist order over the past ten years. His account entirely justifies the summary conclusion that "on the surface it would certainly appear that substantial and significant changes have taken place."

The disquieting aspect about the innovations is their inconclusiveness. They are intriguing and suggestive, as indeed are any changes in the U.S.S.R. way of doing things. But are they of a nature and do they go far enough to qualify as basic? Professor Turner answers this question in the negative: "Basically . . . the trading structure and objectives have not varied. There still remains the state monopoly over foreign trade, which initiates and controls trade according to planned goals. And the primary goal is to strengthen the world socialist system, and this, strangely enough, is being accomplished by the Soviets with the benefits obtained from trade according to the principle of the international division of labor."

The only quarrel with this judgment is the implication that it is novel for the Soviet Union to take advantage of "the principle of the international division of labor" in an effort to strengthen itself. The use of trade with the outside world for this purpose has been, as a matter of fact, standard operational procedure for the U.S.S.R. government since its establishment. There have been long periods, of course, when for one reason or another Moscow severely limited its exchanges with capitalist countries. But given a special need, Soviet authorities have repeatedly and as a matter of course turned to capitalist sources of supply.

The real issue is, not whether the U.S.S.R. for the moment is trading more with the West, but whether it has abandoned the old objective of carrying on foreign trade in order, as it has said, to end the need for foreign trade. In Professor Turner's view, such is indeed the case: "They have given up autarchy and have hoped for greater material benefits to be gained from an increase in foreign trade."

Unfortunately such a basic change in Soviet purposes, one that would be truly revolutionary in its implications and consequences for the U.S.S.R. system as we have known it, can hardly be substantiated. A few Soviet voices have been heard on the advantage of a true international division of labor, but these have been feeble in the extreme and for the most part spoken within the context of special efforts to stir up Western interest in the U.S.S.R. market. (Even Stalin was willing to dangle "billions in trade" before the eyes of an Eric Johnston.) Meanwhile, and as Professor Turner stresses in his paper, the pattern of Soviet trade with the capitalist countries remains singularly as it has been over the past five decades: export of raw materials and semimanufactured goods in order to buy machinery and equipment, including complete plants, needed to build up the U.S.S.R.'s capacity to satisfy its own requirements.

Exception might also be taken to Professor Turner's generalization that the Soviets "have become more sophisticated in their methods and more successful in their endeavors." The U.S.S.R. always has shown sophistication when it wanted something badly enough. But in routine trade relations it has been, and evidently remains, heavy-handed. Instructive in this connection is a lament of *The Economist,* one of the strongest advocates of maximum British trade with the Soviet Union, in its issue of February 11, 1967: "Behind Mr. Kosygin's fine words about trade with Britain lies a sad story for this country and a lesson for Russia. What is wrong with the two countries' trade is not any unwillingness in Britain to buy Russian goods: the charts show this clearly. . . . Part of the answer lies in inefficient communist state trading, i.e., horse trading, with its double-think and even treble-think, until the experts can hardly work out whether they are going to make a profit or a loss. . . . Export promotion, communist style, consists of carrot-and-stick bilateralism. The trouble is that the west is well used to the carrot vanishing."

The *Economist* makes another point of key importance: if it is to enter the mainstream of international trade, i.e., truly adapt to an international division of labor, "Russia must get into a growth sector in exports, and that means manufactures."

But this is precisely what the U.S.S.R. is not doing, which is exactly why the strongest reservations must be taken regarding the significance of the "new" Soviet position on foreign trade. The regime is attempting to use increased foreign trade to escape from a serious economic bind, to start the country moving again. At the same time, however, it refuses to make domestic adjustment, i.e., to change long-established priorities in resource allocation that aim at expanding and strengthening the economic power base of the country, which are essential if the U.S.S.R. is to become a genuine participant in an international division of labor.

Should the Soviet Union bring itself to make, or be forced into, such adjustments, the consequences would be so far-reaching as to leave no doubt that a true change in course were under way. But as long as this does not happen, one can only conclude that the purpose of the U.S.S.R. remains to exploit in support of its system the resources and energies of the rival system, which it still would bury.

4

ideology and soviet military strategy

JAMES M. MCCONNELL

The thrust of Soviet military strategy since 1917 has not always been in the same direction. In part, change has been dictated by new weapons and scientific-technical developments. In large part, however, the impetus can be traced to transformations in Soviet intentions and objectives. As is known, in the U.S.S.R. a special emphasis is placed on the intimate connection between political and military affairs; to the Soviets (following Clausewitz), war is only a continuation of politics by other means. U.S.S.R. military strategy, therefore, cannot be understood apart from U.S.S.R. political strategy; and behind political strategy, which concerns the exercise of power, lies ideology, the fountainhead of political purpose.[1]

There can be no question but that over the years alterations have occurred in communist ideology and in the political policies derived from it. In discussing these changes two questions remain in the forefront: (1) the basic nature of change in the U.S.S.R. and (2) the significance of these transformations.

As to the basic nature of change in the U.S.S.R., Soviet politics betray an unstable dualism, often referred to as the "consciousness" and the "spontaneity" syndromes. When the "consciousness" syndrome is in the ascendancy, the ideologues emphasize more strongly the obligation to transform the world through the action of the state and in the interest of the movement-regime. Initiative comes from above, from the Party and the state; the people are objects, not subjects, of the political process. When the shift of the Party line is in the direction of "spontaneity," on the other hand, the pressure from the regime against Soviet society and the external world tends to subside. It is important to emphasize that when change does occur, it tends to take place on a broad front, on an across-the-board basis; the new line is almost always revealed, more or less simultaneously, both in foreign policy and in domestic policy (economics, military affairs, the arts, etc.)

In assessing the significance of changes in the U.S.S.R., Brzezinski makes a distinction between that portion of ideology which can be called doctrine and that portion which can be called the action program. Although a clear dichotomy cannot always be made between the two levels, doctrine seems to comprise "the philosophical assumptions, the broad historical laws, the ultimate ends—in brief, the *a priori* assertions which form the foundation stone of ideology." It includes such conceptions as: the general crisis of capitalism; the objective necessity of the transition from capitalism to socialism on a world scale; dictatorship of the proletariat; the leading role of the Communist Party, etc. The ideological action program, on the other hand, reflects "contemporary problems of applying the unchanging doctrine to the changing realities of the time. . . ." It has to identify the basic features of the immediate phase within the epoch of the transition from capitalism to communism and to lay down the broad guidelines for action during this phase.[2]

These levels of ideology, i.e., the doctrine and the action programs, have corresponding levels in Soviet political art—primarily in the levels of grand strategy and strategy. The highest level of Soviet political art can be called grand strategy; it pursues the fundamental and ultimate objectives of the communist movement, objectives which persist throughout all changes of strategy. Grand strategy flows from ideological doctrine. However remote some of these doctrinal tenets appear from the everyday world, the consistent aggressiveness which doctrine imparts to Soviet grand strategy accounts for much of the difficulty which the peoples of the U.S.S.R. and of the rest of the world experience in dealing with the Soviet regime. When the general thrust of Soviet strategy coincides with that of grand strategy, as it did under Stalin, the result is totalitarianism. On the other hand, even when U.S.S.R. strategy is more accommodating, as in the post-Stalinist period, the hostile and offensive grand strategy in the background surrounds even the *détente* achieved with an unwholesome air of mutual suspicion and tension, tension which has been channeled into large-scale military preparations by both protagonists.

Strategy is the next highest level in Soviet political art. It emerges from the most fundamental portion of the ideological action program. If grand strategy can be said to measure the future by epochs, strategy measures it by decades. The latter takes the long view but not as long a view as that of grand strategy. There is another difference between grand strategy and strategy which is worth noting. Grand strategy (and the doctrine from which it stems) is the product of a long historical evolution. Its acceptance in Soviet society is based upon an ultrasecular trend in the conditions, psychological and other, of that society and in its interaction with the world. Once adopted, it undergoes only slow alterations over time. Strategy, on the other hand, is more subject to change; its acceptance in Soviet society seems to be based, not upon ultrasecular trends, but upon secular trends.

Thus the Soviet Union can be said to have had three strategies since its inception. The first strategy was based on the Lenin-Trotsky action program of "permanent revolution," which largely determined the character of the Leninist era. The second strategy depended upon the Stalinist action program of "socialism in one country." The third is based upon a post-Stalinist action program that can be described by the term "peaceful coexistence," provided one understands this slogan as the crown, or one of the crowns, of a whole series of ideological constructs that are similar in nature.

If one compares and contrasts these three strategies in terms of the already-mentioned dualistic character of the Soviet social process, one finds that Leninism, relatively speaking, tended toward the "spontaneous" pole, that Stalinism represented a marked shift in the direction of "consciousness," whereas post-Stalinism as a trend seems to revert once more to spontaneity. It can be seen from this tendency for strategy to shift alternately from relative hostility to relative accommodation that strategy might often find itself in basic conflict with a grand strategy that has been consistently aggressive. Although a formal attempt is always made by the Soviets to prove the compatibility of the action program with doctrine and of strategy with grand strategy, the demonstration is not always convincing. For example, today doctrine and grand strategy dictate the road to full communism for the U.S.S.R., which implies the disappearance of a money economy. The thrust of action program and strategy, on the other hand, is today in an opposite direction, toward an expansion of the role of money in the Soviet economy.

From the standpoint of understanding the significant changes in Soviet military policy, attention should be focused on the strategic level of the political art, since grand strategy is assumed to be relatively constant, while Soviet tactics and grand tactics (which are based on short- and mid-term trends and fluctuations around the secular trend line) are not adhered to long enough to permit a fundamental alteration in military development programs.

Leninist Political Strategy

The Bolshevik strategy of permanent revolution, in the last analysis the joint work of Lenin and Trotsky, took its point of departure from the traditional social democratic two-stage theory of the anticipated revolution. Russia, it was conceded, appeared ripe in the initial stage only for a revolution aimed at securing radical bourgeois reforms; "objective" conditions (the low level of economic development and the lack of a proletarian majority among the population) would not permit any decisive steps toward socialism immediately following the revolution. The essence of the dispute among Russian Marxists in this period can be reduced, not to the question of whether social democracy could build socialism in Russia unaided—this did not become a subject of controversy until 1924 with the promulgation by Stalin of the alternative strategy of "socialism in one country"—but to the question whether a revolution led by the middle class and capable of solving urgent bourgeois tasks was any longer possible. Bolshevism contended that the Russian *bourgeoisie* could not assume a revolutionary role because it was weak and because it feared its own workers, whose cause in the long run would be enormously strengthened by a thoroughgoing middle-class revolution. Only the proletariat could be consistently revolutionary. The task of social democracy in the first stage, therefore, was to seize power and complete the bourgeois revolution.

But the revolution could not stop here; the revolution was supposedly "permanent." Left on their own, the workers of Russia could not hope to take more than tentative steps toward socialism. But the Russian workers would not remain alone. Since Europe had become objectively ripe for socialism, the Bolshevik seizure of power and the subsequent implementation of its bourgeois-radical "minimum" program would break the conservative crust of Europe's society and stimulate a successful socialist revolution on that continent. This second victory would then radically transform the perspective for permanence of the revolution in Russia. The balance of forces would no longer be calculated on a national scale (here admittedly the working class was weak) but on an international scale, where the working class was strong. Backed by the resources and the class-conscious enthusiasm of a socialist Europe, the Russians could then win the third victory—a decisive transition to socialism.

An analysis of the strategy for permanent revolution reveals a strain of passivity not often given the attention it deserves. To be sure, with respect to the bourgeois revolution, the Bolsheviks did not have this fatal passivity; they did not rely upon an external force compelled by history to do their bidding; their strategy stressed leadership rather than "tailism." A tendency toward a deterministic passivity, however, revealed itself in the course of action to be followed in the aftermath of the bourgeois revolution, when the problem of the transition to socialism was on the agenda; here the key role in the "telescoping" of the two revolutions was to be played by European workers. To be sure, the victory of the proletarian party in Russia would provide a powerful stimulant to revolution in Europe; and once the red flag had been raised there, with the issue still in doubt, there could be no principled reason why insurgent Russia would not render assistance even to the extent of a revolutionary war. Nevertheless, despite the important role cast for Russian Bolshevism, this role was subsidiary; the moving forces of the European socialist revolution were located in the indigenous workers' movement of the West. Just as in the Menshevik scheme the Russian proletariat had to adapt its activities passively to the initiative of the *bourgeoisie* in the struggle for the bourgeois revolution, so in the Bolshevik scheme the Russian proletariat had to tailor its activities to the success or failure of the European proletariat in its struggle for socialism. If the latter failed in its task, the will to socialism in Russia would be paralyzed by objective circumstances.

Leninist Military Strategy

The rejection of "voluntarism" in political strategy (tactics and grand tactics are another matter) was paralleled by a similar rejection of voluntarism in military strategy during the Leninist era. Instead of a strategy based upon the offensive and designed for export of world revolution, spokesmen of the majority insisted that strategy should aim at the defense of the Soviet state. As War Commissar Lev Trotsky put it, "Foreign military powers fulfill in a revolutionary process, not a fundamental, but an auxiliary role." At the same time he and others, including Lenin, pointed to the lack of material and cultural prerequisites in Russia for an offensive strategy even if it were to be judged politically feasible.[3]

In line with this "objectivist" and deterministic approach, the theorists of permanent revolution advocated a mixed, cadre-territorial militia system instead of a uniformly regular standing army as the foundation for a defensive military strategy. Although the Red Army during the civil war comprised a regular army, strategically it had been regarded as an improvisation, not a model to be followed once victory came. Consequently even in the midst of the war resolutions on the transition to a militia system had been adopted. After experimentation in 1921 the definite transformation began early in 1923. In the long run, according to Trotsky, all divisions of the army would correspond territorially to factories, mines, villages, and other organic groupings, with a local commanding staff and local stores for arms and supplies. In the short run, however, since the backwardness of Russian communications would constrain rapid deployment in the initial weeks of a war, a small regular army for the border districts was required along with the territorial militia to cover mobilization.

In its inexpensiveness as well as local and defensive nature, the territorial militia represented yet another reflection, according to Carr, of the compromise with the peasant which marked the whole post-civil war system, a system with a spirit "unpropitious to any form of military enthusiasm." By the end of 1923 the regular forces consisted of 560,000 men, compared with the 1.2 to 1.5 million constantly maintained by the tsar in the years before World War I. In 1913 the military establishment had taken 30.5 per cent of the state budget; whereas such expenditures in 1925–6 accounted for only 15.8 per cent of a budget 40 per cent smaller in real and comparable terms. By 1924–5 the defense share of GNP amounted to a mere 1.8 per cent.[4]

There is no reason to question the sincerity of the theorists of permanent revolution in attributing their defensive strategy to "objective" circumstances. The strategic primacy of base over superstructure, of "objective" over "subjective," was fundamental to every sphere of Russian thought in the post-October 1917 period down to the very end of the Leninist era. Soviet leadership might abstractly prefer socialism, yet the economy after the end of the civil war remained oriented toward the market. The creation of a proletarian art and literature (the germ of "socialist realism" was advocated by a minority), but this approach was rejected, *inter alia,* because the economic base was thought to be too weak to support such an ambitious superstructure.

It is interesting to note also how the actual methodology of Soviet philosophy reflected this impasse (reflected it "spontaneously," since the Party had not as yet interpreted *partiinost'* to mean that the highest level of the superstructure, politics, dictates to the lower level, philosophy). A mechanistic materialism in various forms was the dominant philosophy in the Soviet Union until it was challenged in 1925 by the Deborin dialectical school, which constituted the philosophical counterpart to socialism in one country. In its treatment of the ontological hierarchy, mechanistic materialism tended to de-emphasize the qualitative distinctions between the various levels of being, to regard the ladder of being as a discrete continuum, and to dissolve the "higher forms of matter" in the forms beneath. The movement within each system in the existential hierarchy was more derivative than autogenetic, and the impetus for movement was envisaged as coming "from below," i.e., the more highly organized system adapted its movement to the less highly organized; the aim of this adjustment was the maintenance of equilibrium. The mechanist theory of movement also proved interesting from another standpoint. Continuity was stressed rather than discontinuity, quantitative changes rather than abrupt qualitative transformations; the dialectic was blunted so that change came smoothly, even mechanically. It is difficult not to see in this philosophic postulation of mechanical rather than dialectical materialism a reflection, whether conscious or unconscious, of the view that the era of revolution following October 1917 had ended and the period of evolution had just begun. It is also difficult to avoid interpreting the tendency to "democratize" the hierarchy of being as a philosophical counterpart of subjecting the superstructure to the base in the social sphere.

This epiphenomenalism, so to speak, of the higher forms of being (at times it almost amounted to a "withering away" of the higher forms of being) was reflected in the attitude of the philosophers toward scientific disciplines in the substratum. Philosophy might be the "queen of the sciences," but in the view of the mechanists it reigned at best, as a constitutional monarch," but did not rule. "For the Marxist," said one of the leading mechanists, "materialist philosophy consists in the latest and most general findings of modern science." The self-depreciation of the superstructure as against the base was as much reflected in the individual sciences as in philosophy. "In theory and in fact," observed one authority, "social phenomena may equally well be subjected either to qualitative sociological investigation, or to quantitative analyses on chemical, physical and biological lines."[5] Psychology revealed the same reductionist tendencies as sociology. For a time after the 1917 Revolution the discipline per se was virtually annihilated and replaced on the one hand by the "base" sciences of physiology and biology and on the other hand by sociology, an extreme example of the "withering away" of the superstructure. Even where psychology was accepted, there appeared a tendency to view the internal superstructure of the psyche, consciousness, as determined by the unconscious base, the seat of psychic spontaneity. Under the circumstances it is not surprising that Freudian depth psychology was popular; Trotsky, for example, favored a fusion of Freudian theory and Pavlovian method for a correct materialistic model of human behavior, and he used the concept of the unconscious as an argument against the theory of an officially sponsored "proletarian culture." Art, in his view, had to be spontaneous rather than consciously tendentious, the exact opposite of the later premise for socialist realism.

There is, then, no real reason to question the sincerity of the explanations given for Leninist defensive strategy; the basic thrust of Soviet thought proceeded in the direction of objectivism and spontaneity. One should not single out some isolated factor, such as the failure of the counteroffensive on Warsaw in 1920 or the temporary poverty of Russian industry and agriculture after the civil war, as the "pragmatic" explanation for a defensive strategy and for the fact that "the Red Army had been almost strangled with purse-strings"[6] under the New Economic Policy (1921–8). Strategy is built of more substantial stuff than tactical defeats and temporary economic distresses; it takes the long view: defeated and poor today, it prepares for a victory tomorrow. Not so much the lack of an objective "economic margin" restricted Soviet military ambitions as did the lack of a "psychological margin"—the relative absence of enthusiasm in

Soviet society for expenditures on arms and for probing the West with bayonets. The deterministic inhibitions in the strategy of permanent revolution had been rooted in that general sentiment. It required a basic devitalization and demoralization of Russian society and a revolution from above by the apparatus to reverse this political strategy and to reshape the military strategy which flowed from it.

Stalinist Political Strategy

Stalin's action program for socialism in one country involved a critical turning point in the development of Soviet ideology. The theory of permanent revolution had insisted that the Russian base was inadequate for a decisive advance toward socialism, that the base for socialism in Russia lay in Europe, and that Russia would have to adapt its progress toward socialism to the pace of the European socialist revolution. Such passivity was not to Stalin's taste. Straining every possible text to find support in Lenin, he asserted his conviction that the socialist revolution in Russia would only draw its forces from within Russia itself. Since a socialist strategy could not be justified by prevailing "objectivist" criteria, Stalin had no choice but to reverse the flow of cause and effect in Marxist determinism. Instead of the base determing the superstructure, the superstructure had to be understood as autonomous, even determing the base; or as Stalin himself less heretically put it, the superstructure had a "reactive" effect upon the base.

Stalinist philosophy fully reflected the new conception. The mechanistic materialism dominant before 1925 had envisaged the motion of higher-order systems in the scale of being as derivative from the motion of lower-order systems; and this motion was conceived of as relatively smooth, mechanical, continuous. Against this the Stalinist philosophers postulated the theory of autogenetic movement; each system in the hierarchy of being had its own lawful development which could not be explained by the laws of motion for the system below. The mode of movement was not envisaged as continuous, mechanical. Just as the mode of movement in the past had been dialectical, by way of the transformation of cumulative quantitative changes into a new qualitative synthesis (resulting in the present hierarchical structure of being), so the mode of movement in the future would be equally discontinuous, depositing qualitatively new systems as it progressed through a struggle of opposites.

It was hardly the intention of the dialecticians simply to assert the autonomy of higher-order systems, their mere negative freedom from lower-order leveling. Could one system move at one, a second system at another, and a third at still a different pace? The mechanists had envisaged coordinated movement, with initiative below and adaptation, the maintenance of equilibrium, above. Coordination was also implicit in the Stalinist scheme, with the exception that the laws of the higher system took precedence over and legitimately suspended those of the lower. The mechanists, standing at the bottom of the ladder of being, saw only responsiveness and pale imitation above, a withering away of the superstructure. The dialecticians, glancing downward from the vantage point of the ladder's apex, saw an equal amorphousness below, the absence of a legitimate claim to autonomous movement, the withering away of the base. Totalitarianism had been projected upon the cosmos.

At the apex of the totalitarian system was the "leader" (*vozhd'*, the equivalent of the German *Führer*), the incarnation of the organized consciousness and rationality of society. The secular growth in what the post-Stalinist era was to call "the cult of personality" resulted in a *de facto* suspension of the normal collective decision-making processes of the Party in favor of the leader and his so-called "private secretariat," the Special Sector of the Central Committee. The will of the leader was supreme; his laws, arising from an autogenetic movement, superseded the laws of lower systems in the Party and state, even if this conflicted with rational administrative practice and with the interests of the state as such. This was always the point to the permanent purge, to make way for the displacement of the laws of higher-order systems onto lower-order systems, producing that phenomenon of "organized amorphousness" characteristic of totalitarian movement regimes. The aim of the purge was to shatter the structure and atomize the components of the lower-order systems, suspending their autogenetic movement and creating an unimpeded channel for the flow of movement, based on different principles, from above.

The logic of displacement downward was carried out by the Stalinists to the grim end. Instead of economics strategically determining politics, as in the Leninist era, the political superstructure (armed with higher laws) hurled itself with dialectical abruptness on the economic base, collectivizing agriculture and imposing a central plan that dispensed with spontaneity in both production and distribution. In the process the "law of value," which guides the invisible hand of the market, was modified to accord with planner's preferences; and the planner, it was made clear, preferred to distribute the social product so that it nourished the superstructural "metal eaters" and not the masses. The result was a drastic decline in returns to labor. Over the period 1900–28 the real take-home pay of workers had increased by at least one quarter, with a work week shorter by 12 to 18 hours. During the period 1928–50, on the other hand, while the work week increased from 37.3 to 42 hours, the real wage fell more than 40 per cent;[7] and the peasants suffered just as severely.

In view of the logic of displacement downward, it was only natural that the laws of politics should also be forced on other systems of the superstructure as well as on the base of society. The Leninist era had held that the artistic process was determined spontaneously by the artist's sub-conscious and his general social environment and that as a part of the superstructure the artist was responsible to the "public"; at the same time he was free from artistic dictation by higher systems of the superstructure. Stalinism reversed the flow of cause-and-effect. In the first place the artistic process was now determined by the conscious side of mental life. Art became tendentious, and it had to reflect reality dialectically, not naturally, i.e., it revealed a transformed reality. However, it was not the artist's own conception of this transformed reality which was to be reflected. By virtue of the law of displacement downward, the point of view of the Party must define the purpose of literature and direct all Soviet art. The artist was no longer responsible to his public; he was only responsible to the Party for reshaping the consciousness of this public in the Party spirit.

Philosophy, too, had to be dominated by *partiinost'*, since practice (politics) always has been superior to mere theory; and the Bolshevization of philosophy by the Party was paralleled by a similar assertion by philosophy of its authority over the sciences. The grim hunting down of spontaneity went forward in psychology, too. The "superstructure" of mental life, consciousness, now carried out a revolution from above against its "base," the subconscious. Conscious, purposive action became the central focus of Stalinist psychology. Along with the depreciation of the subconscious within the psyche went a depreciation of spontaneous environmental conditioning as a basic determinant of individual psychology. At the same time the Stalinists also denied that psychic processes were simply the obverse, seen from the subjective side, of physiological processes. In their view the psyche represented instead a qualitatively new synthesis of matter, an autonomous superstructure of the body with its own autogenetic movement, the laws of which were not reducible to those of the physiological base. The character of these psychic laws is such that the individual can carry out "self-training"; he can "react" upon the physiological base by transforming conscious behavior into reflexive automatic behavior. The depreciation of the general environment as a formative factor and the elevation of consciousness to a "leading role," as against spontaneous processes, was not intended to promote individual freedom and self-determination. The displacement of consciousness onto the unconscious and the physiological base was only a necessary prelude to the introjection of the "social command" into the psychic vacuum left by the displaced consciousness. The values, goals, and morality of the individual were not his own; they represented the internalized values, goals, and morality of the regime.

The ultimate in the logic of displacement was reached in 1948, when Lysenko was installed as dictator over biology. Here the aim was to remove the very base of mechanistic continuity and spontaneity in living phenomena, the gene; the revolution from above was to be made permanent by displacing and fixing onto the genetic structure itself the physiological results of extensive training and self-training in Bolshevik virtue. Further than this, it would seem, the revolution in biology could not go. Actually it went further, blurring the boundaries between the animal and vegetable kingdoms: a rudimentary form of consciousness, the gift of foresight and the ability to adapt to foreseen circumstances, was actually displaced by Lysenko from the animal kingdom onto the plant world. Lysenko was not led to this and similar standpoints "by the weight of carefully sifted scientific evidence, but by the imperatives of transformist ideology,"[8] by the logic of displacement, whereby the laws of higher systems supplant the laws of lower systems.

Stalinist Military Strategy

The emphasis on developing "socialism in one country" did not lead the Stalinists to an abandonment of world revolution as a goal; they simply recast their strategic conception of this task from a "revolution from below" to a "revolution from above," emanating within the Soviet power complex. The movement of the international system was envisaged as being determined by the contradiction between the principle of consciousness (socialism) and the principle of spontaneity (capitalism). War between the champions of these two principles had a strategic inescapability; it might be avoided tactically, but in the long run it was "inevitable," i.e., desirable. Stalin was motivated mainly, not by defensive considerations nor by a fear of freedom in the outside world, but by offensive considerations, by an aggressive hatred of freedom, since he felt that the tide was moving his way strategically, that the capitalist system was disintegrating while the socialist system was gaining in strength; his strategy was optimistic and offensive.

Violence being "the midwife of every old society pregnant with a new one" (Marx), it followed that the Soviet Union needed a superior military establishment and an offensive military strategy to terminate the gestation period of an emerging all-socialist world. By 1929 a strong bias for the offensive was already firmly grounded in Soviet military doctrine. "Wars of a proletarian army," it was said, "must be distinguished by consciousness, activity, initiative. . . ."[9] As Garthoff notes, behind this heavy Soviet emphasis on seizing and maintaining the initiative lay an ideological impulse displaced on the military impulse, supplementing and intensifying the latter. Indeed, so strong was this stress that defensive doctrine (which probably would have been generated rationally in the absence of ideological displacement) appeared to be instilled inadequately throughout the army. It was necessary to teach and partially recreate defensive doctrine in the course of the costly retreat during the early phase of World War II. At the time of the German attack in 1941, by Soviet admission there existed no plan for strategic withdrawal. Not until 1942 was defense explicitly admitted to be "a normal form of combat"; but even after the experience of that conflict, Soviet military doctrine in the pastwar period continued to stress the role of the offensive.

The stress on the offensive required the Soviets to aim at a general superiority in men and matériel; as Stalin sloganized in 1934, the Red Army had to be stronger than any possible armed combination against the U.S.S.R. At least from a quantitative standpoint the achievement was remarkable, the value of armament output in real terms increasing more than 7,000 per cent over the period 1928–50. To be sure, the economic base was also expanding rapidly, but not at the same rate. Consequently the real burden of defense is said to have increased from 1.3 per cent of GNP in 1928 to 13.1 per cent in 1955; in addition there was a tenfold increase in military manpower.[10]

Not only did the Stalinists aim at a general superiority; they had as their objective also a balanced predominance, applicable to each major armed force component. They did not single out any particular branch as the main one; there was to occur all-around development and all-around superiority. The U.S.S.R. seemed especially critical of what it called "the pseudo-scientific theories of bourgeois military men" that strategy should be based on a small, elite army relying either upon mobility of tank formations or air power. Rather than the primacy of one massive arm, Soviet doctrine accented the mass employment of all arms: infantry, artillery, tanks, and aviation. In addition, paratroops (which the U.S.S.R. invented) were to be dropped on a large scale to destroy the enemy in depth. Strong strategic reserves would be maintained. The Soviets almost had an obsession with numbers. Already by 1933 they were reputed to have had 2,000 tanks, but this was only the beginning. "By 1941, the total strength of the Soviet tank forces was in the region of 21,000–24,000 tanks, more than four times as many as the Germans had, and more than all the other tank forces of the world put together." As for the Soviet air force, its combat strength had quadrupled between 1932 and 1936, making the U.S.S.R. the largest air power in the world; the Soviets seemed to be aiming "at nothing less than the air hegemony of all Europe."[11] On the eve of the German invasion the U.S.S.R. had 10,000 combat aircraft, while the Luftwaffe, according to Garthoff, used but 1,300 to 3,000 planes in its Eastern campaign. As for artillery, more emphasis was probably placed here than on other types of weaponry; to Stalin artillery was the "god of war." In 1941 the Soviets also had more airborne troops than any other power, not excluding Germany.

Prodded by the ideological militancy of the period, it was perhaps inevitable that a more active strategy should be worked out for the Soviet navy also. The Leninist era had neglected the navy even more than the army, the fleet tonnage falling from 548,000 in 1917 to 82,000 in 1928. The five-year plans saw a reverse trend, with a build-up to 600,000 tons already attained by 1940. So persistently was submarine construction fostered that as early as 1937 the U.S.S.R. had the world's largest underwater fleet. In the postwar era the submarine was still emphasized. The total inventory at its peak in the mid-fifties reached 450 to 500 units, about 280 of which were long-range by the standards of that time. The primary mission apparently comprised interdiction of sea and ocean lines of communication during a protracted war. This was more than twice the 220 submarines of Germany at the height of the battle for the Atlantic.

The world's largest submarine fleet was not enough, however, to slake the ambitions of the Stalinist era, despite the "straitjacket of geography" which has always placed formidable obstacles in the way of a Russian high-seas effort. Because of its inherent limitations the torpedo attack submarine is strategically almost by definition a defensive weapon. Tactically, of course, it is an offensive weapon. At best, it can harass the enemy's navy and disrupt his lines of communication. It cannot secure the belligerent's own lines of communication; it cannot assume command of the seas, as an offensive surface fleet can. These are the classic rules which Stalin apparently understood very well. By 1934 the Soviet leadership had apparently decided upon a shift from the naval strategic defensive to a more offensive stance, a decision which "marked the start of an all-out warship construction effort seriously intended to make the U.S.S.R. if not the greatest naval power in the world, at least a major naval power."[12]

Although the Nazi invasion had brought all warship construction to a halt, U.S.S.R. statements in the immediate postwar period suggested that the development strategy of the thirties had not been abandoned, despite pressing reconstruction priorities which inhibited immediate implementation. In 1946 Admiral Alafuzov reiterated the line of the prewar period that "the surface forces have always been, and still are, the basic and most universally useful element of the Navy." The necessity for including aircraft carriers in the composition of contemporary postwar navies (by then the battleship was regarded everywhere as outmoded) also became affirmed explicitly in the general staff journal at this time. In view of the fact that, for reasons of morale, the Soviets since the Stalin era have been reluctant to recognize the usefulness of weapons which they do not intend to acquire, the affirmation of the value of carriers read like a powerful plea for a militant presence on the high seas. The impression derived from this was supported by the re-establishment in 1950, when reconstruction needs were satisfied, of a separate Navy Ministry, which signified a higher priority for naval requirements. The generally aggressive thrust of ideology during this period suggests that the testimony of a former Soviet naval officer concerning a ten-year capital shipbuilding program should be taken at or near face value. Under this reported program the U.S.S.R. would begin with the construction of *Sverdlov*-class cruisers, progress to the construction of several *Stalingrad*-class battle cruisers, and, on the basis of the experience gained, build four aircraft carriers.[13] If true, this represented an ambitious step for a power which only two decades previously had possessed a pygmy fleet and was now challenging a single overwhelmingly superior power that has all the advantages of geography, advanced bases, wealth, and experience.

Post-Stalinist Political Strategy

Beginning in 1949–50, but especially after the death of Stalin in 1953, the secular social trend again seems to have shifted direction. The subjective to a certain extent retreated from the objective, and the superstructure from the base; the suspended laws of lower systems in the Soviet hierarchy began to function again; determination no longer came overwhelmingly from the top downward. The transformation occurred on an across-the-board basis, affecting every sphere of life in the U.S.S.R.—ideology, politics, economics, philosophy, the arts and sciences, foreign affairs, and military strategy.

The overthrow of the Leader principle appeared to be most important of all. A relatively gentle downgrading of Stalin during the period 1953–5, stripping him of the superhuman attributes and retroactively converting him into a humble instrument of the Central Committee, was succeeded by the ruthless denigration in Khrushchev's secret speech at the 20th Party Congress and by press statements which condemned Stalin for the "terrible muddle" made of the "Marxist conception of the interrelations of base and superstructure of society."[14] The decision to destroy the Leader principle was manifestly strategic. As the 1959 history of the Party put it, "The campaign against the cult of personality was primarily needed to create firm guarantees that similar phenomena would never arise again in the Party and in the country, and that the Party leadership would be carried out on the basis of the collective principle."[15] At the same time, under the slogan that socialist legality must be fortified, the state security service was stripped of much of its power, shrinking and subduing the indispensable instrument for displacement downward of the Leader's self-generated laws. This development has been accompanied by elevating the "base" of the Soviet legal system, namely, the procuracy.

In the heyday of the Leader principle the Party had constituted only one of the many levers of Stalin's power, the others being the secret police, the army, and the administrative as well as economic-bureaucratic organs of the state. Since 1953 the Party has resumed its place at the apex of

Soviet society. However, the Party has not simply assumed the Leader's functions and plenary power. Without mass terror the ideologues can no longer remold society at will; indeed, the secular trend seems to be in the direction of a partial remolding of the Party by society. The most recent 23rd Party Congress's decisions and plans bear, in Soviet terms, "a deterministic character"; the leaders are confronted "not by theoretical, invented laws but by real laws of economics, politics, psychology and logic. . . . In the face of these laws, the communist leaders find themselves not on the offensive but rather on the defensive, in a position in which they have to adapt themselves to their environment." From Stalin to Malenkov to Khrushchev to Brezhnev the erosion of ideology has been steady, if gradual. This has resulted not so much in the outright repudiation of ideological tenets as in pushing items of the action program back into doctrine, negating Stalinist strategy by transforming it into grand strategy, eliminating inconvenient, strategically forfeited goals by projecting their realization forward into the period of the "second advent."

On the domestic scene the evolution seems to be away from the totalitarian rigidities of the Stalin era and toward a more relaxed form of dictatorship and one-party rule with increasing consultation of upper- and middle-echelon elite groups in framing policy and with more autonomy granted to the creative intelligentsia and its special disciplines. Philosophy, for example, seems to have returned *de facto* to the more complaisant position of constitutional monarch over the natural sciences, while *partiinost'* no longer quite dominates the humanities and social sciences. Within philosophy, while the word "dialectical logic" has been retained for the sake of appearance, formal logic is emphasized in fact. Literature, too, has seen the emergence of an approach to life which stretches the framework of socialist realism to the limits of elasticity. In this respect Khrushchev's speech to the 1959 Writers' Congress seems remarkable by contrast with the Stalinist era; not only did he eschew categorical Party controls (the comrades were asked not to "burden" the authorities with the resolution of their own quarrels), but he also suggested that the reading public should judge the value of a work of art and hinted at a far-reaching change in the conception of psychology and its relation to the artistic process, including the tolerant recognition of unconscious determination of psychic phenomena.

In the economic sphere there also has been a roll-back of ideology and an evolution away from the older "command economy" in the direction of a semi market-collectivized economy operating within a central planning framework. The campaign against the "cult of personality" in economics has been sharp, leading to a real improvement of the consumer's position. For the period 1950–8 alone the net average annual real wage in industry seems to have increased more than 60 per cent, with a decrease in the average work week from 42 to 39 hours; and there has clearly been improvement since that time, though not at the same dramatic pace.

In Eastern Europe the outcome of de-Stalinization has been far-reaching. The policy which Stalin had carried out in this area from 1939 on had involved a repetition of the earlier U.S.S.R. experience: revolution from above carried out at the point of a gun, installation of the totalitarian Leader principle, the permanent purge, central planning, and ruthless economic exploitation. To prevent cohesion these countries had to live in enforced political and economic isolation from one another as well as from the outside world; what one found at the base of the Bloc was an undifferentiated congeries of compartmented "socialism in one country," revealing how little real internationalism appeared in the Stalinist action program.[16]

The situation has, of course, changed substantially since 1953, in spite of the grand-tactical return to repression in the aftermath (1957–61) of the Hungarian rebellion. The overthrow of the Leader principle in the U.S.S.R. has led to a situation in which the Soviets cannot enforce unity of organization, doctrine, or foreign policy. This is far removed from the monolithic unity of a decade or so ago. Within its sphere the C.P.S.U. no longer enjoys the "leading role," an ideological euphemism for unconditional authority over other communist parties; the leading role has been renounced for the more modest role of "vanguard," a glorified first among equals, entitled to respect but not to unquestioning loyalty and subordination. The East European leaders have regained their morale and capacity for resistance; partly because of this and also because of a general softening of communist ideology the Soviet grip has relaxed. The Yugoslav concept of different roads to socialism has been recognized ideologically; economic exploitation by the U.S.S.R. has ceased; multilateral political and economic ties have emerged within the Bloc; increasingly the principals have felt free to develop extra-Bloc relations; some liberalization of domestic political and economic systems have taken place; and more emphasis is given to consumer welfare and freedom of expression. The autonomy of the East European countries now seems so extensive and firmly planted that it is probably an abuse of the term to call them satellites.

Of more direct interest is the perceptible retreat of ideology as a determinant in extra-Bloc affairs. As has been noted, by the time of the 20th Party Congress the Soviet "compulsion to dichotomize the image of the world was no longer operative. The two-world conception faded out, giving way to the picture of one world in which two rival systems of states, the Socialist and the Capitalist, compete for a preponderance of world influence. . . ."[17] Subsequent events (disintegration of the Sino-Soviet alliance and the simultaneous loosening of NATO) have modified even this limited dualistic concept, leading to a far more pluralistic Soviet view of the world than was possible in Stalin's day. One of the preconditions for the Stalinist strategic political offensive abroad, in addition to its own inner drive in that direction, had been a parallel world trend toward weakening of spontaneous forces, a conspicuous shift in the world mood favoring the imposition of authority, whether of the native or imported variety. From the standpoint of attaining greater weight in world affairs, this gave a certain advantage to regimes that were ready to exploit the authoritarian drift. Since the Korean War, however, the secular trend in world psychology seems more encouraging. Just as the Soviets have had to deal with a new mood at home and within the Bloc, which places limits on their freedom of action, they also have had to deal with a greater capacity for resistance in the world at large; strategically, the tide is no longer running in their direction.

In general the 1950's and 1960's have witnessed a dramatic recovery of confidence and strength in the noncommunist world. The countries of Western Europe, politically vulnerable and economically prostrate during the first Soviet postwar offensive, have reacquired their old vigor and stability. The upsurge of the so-called "third world" represents another sign of the general turn for the better that has been visible in both the committed East and the committed West. Since real independence is not born in a day, the instability of the emerging nations, the delicate and fluctuating balance that often exists there between the forces making for viability and those contributing to political despair as well as economic decay, have created tactical and grand-tactical opportunities for Soviet diplomacy and subversion. However, the essential long-run healthiness of this upsurge, and its development on a basis at variance with the traditional Stalinist scheme, has forced the U.S.S.R. to make a sweeping revision of its inherited ideological action program and the strategy that flows from it.

The cornerstone of the new post-Stalinist strategy was the abandonment of the two-camp theory of the late forties, which left no legitimate place for a "third world" of countries uncommitted either to the socialist or capitalist bloc. Today the Soviet Union implicitly recognizes that "bourgeois nationalism" is a formidable force, requiring a more positive response internationally by Soviet diplomacy and domestically by native communist parties of the respective countries.[18] Domestic cooperation with bourgeois nationalism, of course, has assumed many grand-tactical forms, depending upon the mid-term trend. In 1955–6, for example, at the height of a mid-term drift toward *détente,* the U.S.S.R. advocated the formation of people's fronts led by the nationalists, with the native "proletarian vanguard" in a subordinate role; at the same time it was understood that "national liberation" from imperialist domination could take place by peaceful means. In 1960–1, on the other hand, at the high point of a mid-term drift toward international intransigence, the ideologues formulated the grand-tactical conception of "national democracy" for the underdeveloped world. In the people's front envisaged by this program the "leading role" seems to have been reserved ambitiously for the native communist party, though still in cooperation with a national *bourgeoisie* now described as vacillating and unstable. At the same time the Soviet Union declared wars of national liberation to be inevitable, i.e., desirable. With the failure of this approach the U.S.S.R. decided, in its grand-tactical program of "revolutionary democracy" (from the summer of 1963 to date), to proceed consistently with bourgeois nationalism, even to the extent of permitting the dissolution of native communist parties and absorption of their individual members into one-party, nationalist-dominated movements. When it was further accepted ideologically that many of these countries might even be able to take the road to socialism (without a communist party in the leading role, the party which was formerly held to possess alone the key to scientific socialism), it is small wonder that the C.P.S.U. has aroused the contempt of the Chinese for its "ideological disarmament of the proletariat," especially when the new program of revolutionary democracy was followed shortly after (1964) by the quiet announcement concerning the noninevitability of war in the struggle for national liberation.[19] Depending upon tactical and grand-tactical opportunities, the Soviets now strive for and welcome either the maintenance of true neutralism or, if possible, the conversion of Western-aligned nations into true neutralists and true neutralists into "positive neutralists," with the hope that all will be led by stages (grand strategy) along the road to "scientific socialism" and integration with the socialist Bloc. Strategically U.S.S.R. ambitions are today less grandiose; to this extent there has been some normalization of the international political process.

The crown of the new post-Stalinist foreign policy, however, is the strategy of peaceful coexistence adopted with regard to the capitalist "second world." The theoretical underpinning involves the thesis that while the danger of war will continue as long as imperialism exists, neither socialist-capitalist nor interimperialist wars are any longer "fatalistically inevitable"; wars can be banished from the life of society even before the triumph of socialism on a world scale. Skeptics who know Soviet history have not been unreasonable in questioning the depth of the U.S.S.R. commitment to peaceful coexistence; after all, it had been proclaimed on several occasions in the past both as a tactical and grand-tactical expedient to cope with a "temporary stabilization of capitalism" and then abandoned as soon as a "revolutionary situation" appeared. It should be noted, however, that since the newest restatement of peaceful coexistence in 1956, Soviet leaders have consistently denied its tactical character and proclaim it without the standard qualification, namely, that the stabilization phase would last at the most only a "prolonged" period of time. The approach used in presenting the formula openly as a departure from traditional Marxism-Leninism would favor a straightforward interpretation. It is true also that the U.S.S.R. has adhered to the formula longer than in the past, even throughout the Soviet grand-tactical offensive of 1957–62. Certainly this offensive subjected the idea of peaceful coexistence to severe strain; one need only recall in this connection the Cuban confrontation, the attempt at military-political blackmail during the Berlin crisis, and the temporary exclusion by Khrushchev of "national liberation" wars from the peaceful coexistence formula.

Because of these grand-tactical lapses and above all because of the continuing harshness of grand strategy in the background, one should not overemphasize the contrast between the Stalin and the post-Stalin eras. Alongside welcome change there has been drab and depressing continuity, and it might prove a difficult task indeed to determine which aspect should be the more heavily stressed. Despite all qualifications, however, there does seem to be a distinct difference between the strategic concepts of the two eras. Today the regime may see the peasant and the intellectual at home, the capitalist abroad, even the foreign comrade, as enemies to be curbed; but it must pay greater deference to each. In the strategic sense the regime is on the defensive. It periodically goes over to the offensive, but only on a tactical scale (e.g., the 1964–5 trend toward re-engagement in Southeast Asia) or on a grand-tactical scale (as during the second postwar offensive of 1957–62).

Post-Stalinist Military Strategy

If one is correct in assessing post-Stalinist political strategy as essentially defensive, then it would be reasonable to anticipate a reorientation of military strategy in a less militant direction. Although the problem of establishing the degree of continuity or discontinuity between the military strategies of the Stalinist and post-Stalinist eras is complicated by the emergence of nuclear technology during the transition period, the expectation of a contrasting strategy which leans to the defensive seems to be born out by doctrinal discussions as well as by an examination of the direction of development given the Soviet armed forces over the last dozen years.

In the first place the real burden of defense on the Soviet economy seems to show a secular declining trend from 13 per cent in 1955 to 10.2 per cent in 1960, roughly the same as in the United States at that time. Judging purely on the basis of overt budgetary allocations, the weight of defense on the Soviet economy probably has declined further since then. The military manpower drain also underwent a reduction of about 45 per cent since 1952.[20] The trend in both the real burden and manpower indices suggest a secular diminution in the "quantity of aggression" in Soviet society.

The second point to be noted is the post-Stalinist tendency to show less concern about quantitative superiority in major offensive forces, a Stalinist prerequisite for an offensive strategy. Under the current military scheme, provision for general nuclear war assumes top priorty. Despite the emphasis on preparing for this type of war, the U.S.S.R. leadership can hardly be under the illusion that its capabilities for general war have given the Soviets superiority over the United States. They have the means to devastate North America in a countervalue strike, but their inadequate counterforce capability and lack of an effective antiballistic missile system certainly should be enough to dissuade U.S.S.R. leaders from initiating a nuclear exchange. Subsequent damage from a retaliatory blow by the United States could not be held down to acceptable levels. In short the Soviets have a general war capability that is sufficient only for deterrence. Unlike the Stalinist era, they no longer base their developmental strategy upon superiority in the offensive. They did not attempt to compete strenuously with American heavy bomber deployment in the late fifties or to forge ahead in ICBM deployment in the sixties. There exists enough economic margin for more competition; lacking is the psychological stimulus.

The third point to be noted involves the unusual Soviet practical stress on strategic defensive weapons in preparing for a general war. Today U.S.S.R. strategic personnel, offensive and defensive, number about 525,000, or more than the United States total of 330,000. However, when one examines the ratio of offensive to defensive personnel, it can be seen that the Soviets allot more than 60 per cent of their strategic personnel to air defense, while fewer than 40 per cent of the comparable U.S. force performs this function. The comparison becomes even more one-sided when one notes that the entire United States strategic offensive force is assigned to or serves weapons which can hit the U.S.S.R. The Soviet strategic arsenal, on the other hand, includes large numbers of continental range ballistic missiles (750 MRBM's and IRBM's) and bombers of continental range. The problem can also be approached from the standpoint of aircraft allocation, the U.S.S.R. assigning more than 4,500 fighters to its strategic Home Air Defense *(PVO strany),* although there are only 1,350 fighters, including Canadian, attached to the North American Air Defense Command. The Soviets have a penchant for deploying defensive systems, often at the expense of long-range offensive weapons, exhibited in the current and perhaps technically premature deployment of the antiballistic missile. Since investment in offensive missile systems is said to be only a fifth to a quarter as expensive as defensive antimissile systems from a cost-effectiveness standpoint (the best defense being the best offense), it is difficult to justify the U.S.S.R. decision on rational military grounds. It is tempting to attribute it, if only in part, to a deep-seated, doctrinally grounded predilection for the defensive as such.

The fourth point to be noted is the contrast between the strong Stalinist emphasis on all-around development of the armed forces and the post-Stalinist establishment of the Strategic Missile Troops as the "main" branch of the Soviet armed forces. Stress on the Missile Troops, of course, is not absolute but relative. As one Soviet military commentator expressed it, "While assigning a decisive role to the Strategic Missile Troops, the Party at the same time bears in mind that the safety of the Motherland and, in case of war, victory will be insured by the efforts of all branches of the armed forces. Therefore it displays a constant concern for the harmonious development and perfection, based on the newest weapons and equipment, of the Troops of Air Defense of the Homeland, the Ground Troops, the Air Forces, and the Navy."[21] Thus from a primary accent in Stalin's day, the principle of "harmonious development" of all arms now receives a secondary emphasis.

The singling out of Missile Troops for special doctrinal attention apparently does not so much reflect a Soviet devotion to this branch as it does an intention to stress preparations for general nuclear war rather than other types of war. According to figures from the Institute of Strategic Studies, for example, the Soviets allot 33 per cent of their military personnel to specialized general war missions as against 17 per cent by the United States, i.e., relatively speaking, the U.S.S.R. assigns almost twice as many men.

At one time the preponderance of emphasis on general war capabilities could be justified doctrinally by the "inevitable escalation" formula which refused to recognize the possibility of limited wars between the two alliance systems. As the Soviet authors of the authoritative work on military strategy wrote, "One of the important tenets of Soviet military doctrine is that a world war, if unleashed by the imperialists, will inevitably assume the character of a missile-nuclear war. . . ."[22] This categorical way of resolving the question had become almost obligatory in Soviet doctrinal discussion until a few years ago. The formula has now been modified to admit the possibility of conducting conventional wars and even limited nuclear wars without such conflicts necessarily being solved at the apex of the escalation ladder. However, the Soviets still speak uncertainly and ambiguously to the question of whether limited war can be carried on in the heart of Europe as opposed to other areas where the interests of the great powers are less deeply involved. In 1965 an article bearing some of the marks of a consensus on this point did not exclude the possibility of nonescalation, nor did it really affirm it. It stressed in general that if the nuclear powers become involved in local wars, the "probability of escalation into a nuclear world war is always great and in some circumstances inevitable." As a consequence the relatively new Soviet willingness to consider a broader spectrum of conflict situations should not prompt the assumption that priority attention is no longer being given to developing capabilities for general nuclear war. As the U.S.S.R. chief of the general staff wrote, "The Strategic Missile Troops—the main means for containment and complete destruction of an aggressor—remain in the center of attention, as in the past. . . ." At the same time Marshal V. D. Sokolovskii and his collaborator, Major General Cherednichenko, insisted that *"the most pressing problem of strategy under existing conditions is the development of means for conducting a nuclear-missile war. . . ."*[23]

While it would seem likely that the relative de-emphasis regarding a flexible response posture in Soviet doctrine has had some retarding effect on U.S.S.R. capabilities to wage limited war, it is difficult to determine the magnitude. Current estimates give a slight advantage to the active duty strength of NATO over the Warsaw Pact, i.e., 3.2 million men as against 2.9 million, but manpower is only the beginning. The mix of weapons and specialities as well as logistic support is more crucial. One might expect, for example, that since general nuclear war is emphasized by the U.S.S.R., there might be a greater tendency to substitute tactical missiles for tactical aircraft. Perhaps the fact that the density of tactical aircraft is almost three times greater in American than in Soviet ground forces reflects this tendency. With respect to artillery the Institute of Strategic Studies reports that conventional firing power of a Soviet division remains as great as, but presumably no greater than, that of most divisions in NATO.

As for ground-force logistics this might be expected to have suffered, too, by a doctrinal preference for general war, since general nuclear war presumably would not bear the protracted character of conventional war. Sometimes U.S.S.R. writers emphasize that under conditions of mass nuclear missile employment "the initial period of the war can be the decisive and essentially the only period." Others, however, give a strong secondary stress to the possibility of a protracted, "broken-back" nuclear war. Last year a writer noted the "widespread opinion" that in a nuclear war the outcome would be decided in "the relatively short initial period" and stressed that the Soviets must prepare for this type of war. He also felt that "forecasts on the brevity of the war may not be warranted and, consequently, the economy has to be prepared for a protracted war."[24] Ground-force training, it might be noted, continues to concentrate on the movement of tank and missile-artillery formations across ground contaminated by radiation. The stress appears to be still on large-scale advances at high speeds (100 kilometers a day) in the initial period of a war to take advantage of mass nuclear strikes. If the major accent in logistic planning is actually on this announced goal of rapid advance, such a rate would permit Soviet spearheads to reach the English Channel in perhaps ten days and Gibraltar in three weeks. However, logistic capabilities in a conventional conflict might not come up to standard under such circumstances.

The flexible-response deficiencies of the U.S.S.R. armed forces can be seen more by contrast with the guidelines of the Stalinist era than with current Western forces. It should be noted, too, that in many cases effort devoted over the last decade to improving Soviet general war capabilities has probably been of equal advantage from the standpoint of less destructive forms of combat. Certainly the Soviet ground forces still possess a formidable capability to wage limited war. One cannot ignore almost seventy U.S.S.R divisions at or near full strength and another seventy at less than full strength in any kind of war. But this capability is probably not what it would have been, had the Stalinist principle of "harmonious" development continued to receive major stress. The main ground-force doctrinal emphasis for many years has been geared to preparation for general nuclear war, and this emphasis probably has not provided the type of support needed for a truly vigorous diplomacy to achieve limited or practical ends. Such a diplomacy requires conventional troops to make credible the background threat and to ensure preparedness for less lethal forms of combat than general war, should a more aggressive policy unintentionally lead to a solution "by other means."

The relative Soviet restraint in developing general purpose forces for limited war might represent a better index to Soviet intentions than the failure to strive for superiority in the deployment of ICBM's. Nuclear war is of problematic feasibility even for the markedly superior power, and given greater American resources and a determination to match Soviet ICBM deployments, it seems highly unlikely that the U.S.S.R. could hope to achieve strategic superiority, barring an asymmetrical weapons breakthrough. Even if the Soviets aimed at an offensive strategy, therefore, it is questionable whether this purpose would be reflected in their strategic general war capabilities. They might prefer to settle for strategic deterrence rather than superiority and concentrate their main effort on troops for fighting conventional wars. If the potential gains are more limited and the struggle more protracted, the hazards are less awesome and the possibilities of success more promising. Deterrence of general war requires relatively small expenditures, but between deterrence and a war-winning capability there is a great gap. Enormous expenditures and a striking offensive-defensive superiority are required to overawe a nuclear opponent or to defeat him in a general war without incurring unacceptable losses. Conventional war does not demand the same degree of superiority. As a matter of fact, over-all conventional superiority is not even a prerequisite, provided that a greater force can be applied locally as a result of favorable geopolitical conditions and a superior military and political strategy. The limited-war approach should have been especially appealing to a power whose productive capacity is relatively small compared with that of the United States.

Mainland China, it seems, understands the argument very well, and in its general struggle against revisionism of Marxism-Leninism it has found room for the logically related special struggle against "revisionists in the military domain." As one writer in the Chinese communist camp stated, the Soviet preoccupation with nuclear weapons reflects a failure to understand that "armed class struggle has many forms and sizes" and that the revolutionary armies of many countries may have "to engage in minor wars before engaging in major wars, and use conventional weapons before using nuclear weapons." This writer continued: "He who does not study all categories of wars, and make full preparation for them . . . detaches himself from the political tasks of the world revolutionary movement. . . . He who fails to counterattack the imperialists . . . and sees only the necessity to prepare for world war has fallen into a state of negative defense and deprived himself of an opportunity to take the initiative. . . . The modern revisionists' errors have had disastrous effects on the military activities of the socialist countries. . . ."[25] In the view of Mainland China the imperialists intend to prepare, not only for a general war with nuclear weapons, but also for regional wars with conventional weapons and for antiguerrilla wars against national liberation movements. The socialist countries, therefore, should be prepared equally at every level of escalation so as to counter all imperialist moves; in short the socialist Bloc should have a capability for "flexible response."

If the "dogmatists" do not see a flexible response capability in the Soviet ground forces, they are even less likely to find it today in the Soviet navy. Western writers "completely fail to appreciate how . . . completely the Soviet navy is committed to a largely deterrent and defensive posture and how very limited are its actual offensive capabilities. . . ."[26]

In the first and, perhaps least important, place the Soviet navy appears to have suffered a personnel reduction of almost 25 per cent since 1955, i.e., from 600,000 down to 465,000 men. This has been accompanied by an overt repudiation of the Stalinist emphasis on quantitative superiority. As the commander-in-chief of the U.S.S.R. navy put it some years ago, "The might of a navy is now determined. . . . not by the number of pennants, but by the quality of the warships and by their modern military equipment and weapons. . . ." This point was recently reiterated by another admiral as follows: "Formerly it was considered that numerical superiority over an enemy was the primary factor, whereas at the present time such superiority is not given decisive significance. . . ."[27] Despite statements to the contrary the Soviet naval establishment cannot make up in quality what has been forfeited in quantity.

In the second place, as in the case of other general-war strategic offensive systems (ICBM's and heavy bombers), the U.S.S.R. has not attempted to achieve superiority over the United States in the number of fleet ballistic missiles; today the Soviet Union is reported to have 150 FBM's compared with 624 in the West. This does not entirely exhaust the unfavorable comparison.

> The lack of nuclear propulsion in four-fifths of Soviet ballistic missile submarines and the non-availability of any forward bases like the U.S. possesses at Holy Loch, Scotland, at Rota, Spain, and at Apra Harbor on Guam, means a long, slow, time-consuming, and hazardous journey from Soviet Northern Fleet and Pacific bases through the Greenland-Iceland-UK line and that of the Sea of Japan and Kuriles, to reach stations within range of the continental United States. Of equal seriousness, by the time that the diesel-powered units have finally arrived on station, it can only be a relatively short time before they have to quit station in time to begin the long trek back. The inescapable consequence of this, of course, is that the number of submarines that can be maintained on station is very greatly reduced. . . .[28]

Since the death of Stalin the U.S.S.R. has not shown any interest at all in building up what might be referred to as a general-purpose strategic offensive capability. The United States has sixteen attack carriers. If the Soviet leaders in Stalin's day ever had invidious ambitions in this regard (and there is some evidence that they did), the goal has been abandoned. Nor does the U.S.S.R. attempt to compete in strategic amphibious capabilities: American amphibious personnel number 165,000, whereas the Soviets allegedly can claim only a few thousand naval infantrymen, to be used for tactical amphibious landings in support of the ground forces, such as seizing straits leading out of the Baltic and Black Seas. Without a blue-water offensive capability to pave the way and protect lines of communications, the U.S.S.R. could not begin to plan for strategic amphibious landings.

For some time now in the post-Stalinist era the primary mission of the Soviet navy has been defense against Western seaborne strategic nuclear attack: Polaris submarines and carrier strike forces. Because of the emphasis on these missions the main forces used to combat them (submarines assisted by naval aviation) have been declared to be the basic elements of the fleet. No longer does one hear, as in Stalin's day, of surface forces assuming the elevated role of basic elements. Against the Polaris the U.S.S.R. stresses the use of nuclear antisubmarine warfare (ASW) attack submarines and specially equipped land-based ASW aircraft. Without mobile air cover, surface ships would be highly vulnerable. However, the problems of combatting Polaris are so difficult, considering the expanses the Soviets have to cover and their geographical as well as other disadvantages, they may well be "quasi-insoluble."

The U.S.S.R. would have a much better chance of dealing with American carrier task forces. Over the last decade Soviet naval aviation has been reorganized to participate more fully in such missions. Older accounts suggest that naval aviation of the fleets formerly had played the role of tactical air forces in naval theaters. During 1958, for example, naval aviation was said to have 4,000 aircraft, including fighters. Almost a decade later it apparently has only 850 aircraft, some 500 of which are medium reconnaissance and missile-carrying bombers and apparently no fighters. Naval aviation obviously has been streamlined largely as a strategic defensive element against approaching carrier task forces. About forty cruise missile-launching submarines are also deployed almost entirely in the open-ocean fleets. Their primary mission probably involves carrier task forces, although they could be used against land targets. Aside from cruise missile submarines and naval aviation, it is said that bombers of the long-range aviation command and nuclear as well as conventionally powered torpedo attack submarines of the navy have been assigned anticarrier roles.

The allocation of torpedo attack submarines to primary anti-Polaris and anticarrier missions raises the question of whether the Soviet Union still envisages an anti–merchant shipping mission for its submarine force. Under Stalin this was a major consideration. The massive investment program begun under his aegis gave the U.S.S.R. from 450 to 500 torpedo attack submarines in the mid-fifties. With the shift to a general nuclear war strategy in 1955, however, attention was concentrated on ballistic and cruise missile submarine production, and torpedo attack submarines were cut back so sharply that output in the long run has not equalled retirements. Instead of 450 to 500, the Soviets in 1967 were said to have only about 315 attack subs. Of these the 100 or so in the Baltic and Black Sea fleets would not be able to participate in a *guerre de course* until the Skagerrak and Dardanelles exits had been secured, unless the U.S.S.R. were willing to give strategic warning of an impending attack by mass predeployment to the open ocean. In the abstract this would leave about 200 torpedo attack submarines in the northern and Pacific (open ocean) fleets available from the outset of a war for division among the various strategic defensive missions, i.e., ASW, anticarrier, and anti–merchant shipping.

In spite of this seeming potential for a *guerre de course* one has the impression that in the Soviet view very few submarines can be spared for this mission because of the stress on general war and the consequent emphasis on the primary anti-Polaris and anticarrier missions. At the same time the concentration on general war necessarily carries with it a corollary regarding the decisive nature of the initial period of war and the possibility of a shorter war, reducing the value of an assault on lines of communication. An article in the U.S.S.R. navy journal about three years ago addressed itself to this very point:

> If there should blaze up a new war of the capitalist countries against the countries of the socialist camp, it would, in the opinion of many military specialists, certainly be a missile-nuclear war. The mass employment of powerful weaponry makes it highly probable that such a war would be short, and its outcome on the whole would be decided in the initial period by the operations of those forces and means available at the outset of the war.

For this reason, the author concludes

> that ocean communications will be of no vital significance in the initial period of a general thermonuclear war under existing conditions, and consequently combat operations either to disrupt or to secure intercontinental transport can play only an auxiliary role within the framework of other missions to be executed by naval forces.[29]

A somewhat similar stand was stated more recently by a Soviet admiral who agreed that in the past

> armed combat at sea was never limited only to the destruction of the basic forces of the enemy fleet. It always included operations for the disruption of enemy communications and for the defense of one's own. . . .
>
> This was the case, but it is impossible to maintain that it will occur again in the event of a missile-nuclear war.
>
> Certain foreign military figures consider that the rapid pace of events and the power of the blows will not permit large-scale ocean transport in the initial period of a war; nor apparently will there be any requirement for them, since combat operations will be conducted with the forces and means accumulated in the theaters of military operations in peacetime. . . . Shipments in support of the economy can play only a secondary role at the beginning of a war and will not exert a direct, decisive influence on the course of the armed struggle during the indicated period.
>
> All this, they consider, permits the supposition that in the initial period of the war the requirements for sea and ocean transport under existing conditions will be significantly less than in the second world war and that the role of transport can increase only if the war is protracted.[30]

The U.S.S.R. stress on the danger of escalation would appear to place the navy in a relatively poor position for conducting a limited war in the course of which the struggle against lines of communication would have a bigger payoff. It would seem necessary for the Soviets to reserve their fleet for its primary missions, releasing it only after the latter task had been accomplished. Could the U.S.S.R. afford to expend substantially its general-war strategic defense capabilities in a *guerre de course* under the constant threat of escalation? The Soviets have a large number of torpedo attack submarines, but they also have formidable priority missions which will tax their capabilities to the full.

It would appear on balance, then, that the essentially defensive political strategy of the Soviet Union is reflected in its naval strategy, i.e., in the rejection of a "command of the seas" concept; a minor stress on the general war strategic offense; a major stress on the general war strategic defense; and a doctrinal downgrading of cutting lines of communication as a mission.

The present relative Soviet de-emphasis on flexible response, if one can call it that, would appear to be at variance with the Stalinist military tradition. One cannot, of course, be certain of this in the absence of equivalent conditions in weapons technology. It would have been morale-shattering only if Stalin had coupled an offensive political strategy with a recognition of the primacy of strategic weapons and the decisive character of the initial period in a war as long as he had insufficient nuclear weapons in his arsenal. But if Stalin overtly ignored or deprecated nuclear weapons, this does not mean that he really did so in the quiet of the Kremlin. His research and development efforts were focused precisely on acquiring a nuclear capability to neutralize the American strategic advantage. At the same time he maintained large conventional ground forces which could overrun Europe; he apparently prepared to build the foundations for a more aggressive surface navy. It does not seem likely that Stalin would have followed up the successful atomic test of 1949 with ambitious long-term plans for expanding his navy if he had thought it compatible with his political strategy to plan mainly for a single contingency (general war) rather than for a flexible capability to respond to a range of situations. It is tempting to see in this possible contrast between the military development strategies of the two eras confirmation of the relative decline of political militancy in the post-Stalinist period and the shift in military strategy from offensive to defensive considerations.

Notes to Chapter 4

1. Zbigniew K. Brzezinski, *The Soviet Bloc: Unity and Conflict,* rev. edn. (New York: 1961), p. 383.

2. *Ibid.,* pp. 387, 392–3; David D. Comey, "Marxist-Leninist Ideology and Soviet Policy," *Studies in Soviet Thought,* II: 4 (1962), 304.

3. Trotsky, *The Revolution Betrayed* (New York, 1945), pp. 211–14.

4. E. H. Carr, *Socialism in One Country* (London, 1958–64), Vol. II, pp. 392, 399, 393, 247, 259; A. Yugoff, *Economic Trends in Soviet Russia* (London, 1930), p. 246. Yugoff made deductions from the 1913 budget for the areas later lost after the Revolution and not included in the U.S.S.R.

5. Gustav A. Wetter, *Dialectical Materialism* (London, 1958), p. 141.

6. John Ericson, *The Soviet High Command* (London, 1962), p. 366.

7. Solomon M. Schwartz, *Labor in the Soviet Union* (New York, 1951), pp. 130f.; Manya Gordon, *Workers Before and After Lenin* (New York, 1941), p. 69. Janet G. Chapman, "Consumption," in *Economic Trends in the Soviet Union,* ed. Abram Bergson and Simon Kuznet (Cambridge, Mass., 1963), p. 238.

8. Robert C. Tucker, *The Soviet Political Mind* (New York and London, 1963), pp. 92–4.

9. Quoted by Raymond L. Garthoff, *Soviet Military Doctrine* (Glencoe, Ill., 1953), p. 91.

10. P. Wiks, "Western Research into the Soviet Economy," *Survey,* No. 50 (Jan. 1964), p. 76; Abram Bergson, *The Economics of Soviet Planning* (New Haven, 1964), p. 309; Jerry Godaire, "The Claim of the Soviet Military Establishment," in U.S. Congress, Joint Economic Committee, *Dimensions of Soviet Economic Power* (Washington, 1962), p. 43.

11. R. M. Ogorkiewicz, "Soviet Tanks," in *The Soviet Army,* ed. B. H. Liddell Hart (London, 1956), p. 300; Ericson, *op. cit.,* pp. 365, 408f., 445.

12. Robert W. Herrick, "Soviet Naval Strategy—Theory and Practice, 1921–1965" (diss. Columbia Univ., 1965), ch. IV.

13. *Ibid.,* ch. VI; N. G. Kuznetsov, *Nakanune* (Moscow, 1966), pp. 258 f.

14. Cited by T. B., "Ideology and Philosophy," *Studies in Soviet Thought,* II (Sep. 1962), 222.

15. N. Nikolai Galay, "The Twenty-Third Party Congress: Its General Significance," Institute for Study of the U.S.S.R. (Munich) *Bulletin,* XIII (May 1966), 11.

16. Brzezinski, *op. cit.,* pp. 84, 122–4, 458.

17. Tucker, *op. cit.,* p. 177.

18. T. P. Thornton, "Communist Attitudes Toward Asia, Africa and Latin America," in *Communism and Revolution,* ed. C. E. Black and T. P. Thornton (Princeton, 1964), pp. 247, 251.

19. V. K. Sobakin and R. A. Tuzmukhamedov, article on "The International Legal Basis for the Armed Battle of Nations for their Freedom and Independence," in *Mezhdunarodnoe pravo,* ed. F. I. Kozhevnikov (Moscow, 1964), p. 143.

20. Institute for Strategic Studies, *The Military Balance, 1966-1967* (London, 1966), p. 48.

21. Col. I. Prusanov, article on "Activity of the Party in Strengthening the Armed Forces When Military Art Is Undergoing a Revolution," *Kommunist vooruzhënnykh sil,* No. 3 (March 1966), p. 12.

22. V. D. Sokolovskii, ed., *Voennaya strategiya,* 2nd edn. (Moscow, 1963), p. 242.

23. Marshal of the Soviet Union Matvei Zakharov, article on "A Mighty Step," *Tekhnika i vooruzhenie,* No. 4 (Apr. 1966), p. 6; Sokolovskii and Cherednichenko, article on "Contemporary Military Strategy," *Kommunist vooruzhënnykh sil,* No. 7 (Apr. 1966), p. 64.

24. Col. P. Trifonenkov, article on "The Objective Laws of War and the Principles of Military Art," *Kommunist vooruzhënnykh sil,* No. 1 (Jan.

1966), p. 11; Maj. Gen. Kh. M. Dzhelaukov, article on "Economic Potential in Modern War," *Morskoi sbornik*, No. 3 (1966), p. 17.

25. Hoang Van Thai, "It is Necessary to Hold Fast to the Party Military Line and Check the Revisionist Influence in the Military Sphere," *Hoc Tap* (Hanoi), No. 4 (Apr. 1964), quoted in T. W. Wolfe, *Trends in Soviet Thinking on Theater Warfare, Conventional Operations, and Limited War*, RAND Memorandum RM-4305-PR (Dec. 1964), pp. 73f.

26. Herrick, *op. cit.*, Introduction.

27. Admiral N. M. Kharlamov, article on "Trends in the Development of Navies," *Morskoi sbornik*, No. 1 (Jan. 1966), p. 34.

28. Herrick, *op. cit.*, ch. IX.

29. Captain 1st Rank S. I. Filonov, article on "Armed Conflict and Ocean Communications," *Morskoi sbornik*, No. 3 (March 1965), pp. 39–41.

30. Kharlamov, *op. cit.*, pp. 35f.

Discussion

KENNETH R. WHITING

Mr. McConnell has covered a large subject in a brief space which prevented him from developing his thesis adequately. He apparently is arguing that Soviet grand strategy has passed through three radical changes in the last half century. The first strategy (in the sense that Mr. McConnell uses the word), because of Lenin's adherence to the "permanent revolution" program, was defensive in nature. Then, as a result of Stalin's action program of "socialism in one country," the strategy became offensive. Finally, in the post-Stalinist period, there has been a return to the defensive strategy. In his argumentation Mr. McConnell is consistent. Even changes in the force structure of the Soviet military are attributed by him to over-all shifts in ideology.

Before discussing a few particulars in Mr. McConnell's paper, perhaps a much less sophisticated theory could be advanced concerning the successive Soviet shifts in strategies. First of all, it seems much simpler to assume that when the international situation is such that an offensive strategy appears feasible, then the Soviet leadership attempts to exploit this. When such a strategy is judged dangerous to the safety of the U.S.S.R., then the leadership moves toward the defensive. Secondly, the various Soviet military doctrines, which reflect the changes in strategy that have come and gone over the last half century, seem to have been based on such factors as combat experience (e.g., the civil war and World War II), the state of the art in weaponry, economics, and the external threat. Ideology has been just one more factor among the foregoing.

Now to be more specific. Mr. McConnell states that the Leninist defensive strategy was derived from the "permanent revolution" thesis, i.e., the assumption that revolutions in the more economically advanced nations were necessary if the revolution in Russia were ever to attain socialism. This would seem to imply an offensive strategy. This was the period (1918–24) in which the new regime reconquered all the former tsarist holdings that it possibly could: the Transcaucasus, the Ukraine, Central Asia, and Siberia. It also achieved hegemony over Outer Mongolia. It even envisaged the expansion of communism into Western Europe by means of Red Army bayonets in 1920, when General M. N. Tukhachevsky advanced upon Warsaw.

In his description of the military organization that emerged in the 1920's, the relatively small cadre army supported by a large territorial militia, Mr. McConnell asserts that it was the "lack of psychological margin" and not the absence of an "economic margin" that induced the regime to cut back its military commitment so severely. Although seemingly plausible, it would appear a little too ingenuous as an explanation for a very simple fact. Lenin came up with the New Economic Policy for good economic reasons, and the decision to opt for an inexpensive Red Army during that same period was motivated by the same dearth of economic resources.

Stalin's offensive strategy, according to Mr. McConnell, derives from the "socialism in one country" thesis. It is just as reasonable to describe Stalin's strategy as a defensive one. He needed a *détente* in order to devote all Soviet energies to the forced industrialization program and the collectivization of agriculture. Furthermore, the fiasco in China during 1927, the increasing Japanese threat, and the rearmament of Germany made Stalin fully cognizant of the necessity for modernizing the Red Army and of building the required industrial base for its accomplishment. Stalin's foreign policy, the rapid shifts from isolationism to united fronts to collaboration with Hitler, indicates a devotion to the defense of the Soviet Union rather than an offensive strategy.

Even the military doctrine that prevailed from 1925 to late 1941 largely came from the Red Army's experiences in the civil war, tempered by its technological level. It was really M. V. Frunze's doctrine, and he had worked it out in its main outlines before Lenin's death. As for Stalin's "obsession" with numbers, with masses of men and tanks, even the tsarist generals had the same obsession. Given Russia's enormous population and its relatively low technological level, this would seem less of an obsession than a logical development. In addition, such an "obsession" is just as easily explained as the result of a defensive syndrome as it could be on the basis of an offensive strategy. Mr. McConnell himself points this out when he discusses the enormous manpower allotted to *PVO-strany* in the current Soviet military structure.

Stalin's great offensive period came between 1944 and 1950. The collapse of the German and Japanese empires resulted in the creation of power vacuums at both the western and eastern borders of the U.S.S.R. Thus the international situation invited a shift to an offensive strategy. Communist ideology undoubtedly helped influence Stalin, but given the opportunities, it is doubtful that even a tsarist regime could have withstood the temptation to occupy some of the territory so temptingly available.

Mr. McConnell states that in the post-Stalinist period, the Soviet leadership reverted to a defensive strategy for ideological reasons. It is difficult to describe the invasion of Hungary in 1956, the Berlin offensive in 1961, or the Cuban missile end-run in 1962 as obsessively defensive. Mr. Mc-Connell himself admits that there was a Soviet "grand-tactical offensive" in the 1957–62 period. Would it not be just as simple to say that Khrushchev misjudged the situation and, in typical Soviet fashion, attempted to exploit it? And like Stalin after 1950, he found the situation much tougher than anticipated and reverted to the defensive.

Mr. McConnell suggests that the movement away from mass armies to sophisticated weapons systems, the present emphasis on defensive systems, raising Strategic Missile Troops above other services, and the lack of a "flexible response" capability in the Soviet armed forces are all part and parcel of a shift in ideology. It seems more reasonable to explain these phenomena as Soviet reactions to both technological developments in military hardware and the desperate need for investment funds to stimulate a lagging economy.

Between 1945 and the mid-1950's the U.S.S.R. lacked both nuclear weapons and strategic delivery vehicles. Stalin could do little else but come up with a military doctrine that exaggerated the efficacy of masses of men, tanks, fighter aircraft, and artillery while at the same time denigrating surprise, strategic aircraft, and nuclear weapons as ephemeral factors which could not determine the course or outcome of war. By 1955 the Soviet Union had enough nuclear weapons and strategic aircraft at least to bluff a deterrent capability. At this point it changed its military doctrine to take into account these new tools of warfare. Experimentation with nuclear weapons, however, also led Soviet leaders to appreciate the enormously destructive nature of their new acquisitions. At this time, probably, the "peaceful coexistence" thesis was literally forced upon the Kremlin leadership. If an all-out clash between competing ideological systems were inevitable, as ideology had always held, it was obvious that even a Soviet victory would be a Pyrrhic one. The men in the Kremlin had no ambition to further the world revolution at the cost of their homeland being reduced to a heap of atomic ash, even if Mao Tse-tung could contemplate such an event with equanimity. The awesome power of the nuclear weapon itself made a change in ideology and strategy a necessity.

Once the Soviets had acquired nuclear weapons and long-range delivery vehicles, the need for mass armies backed by enormous numbers of tanks and guns could be debated. One does not have to be ideologically motivated to see the uselessness of expending vast sums on infantry and artillery when in all probability a general war will be a spasmodic exchange of nuclear strikes. It is harder to explain the tenacity with which the Soviets have held on to the concept of mass armies than to explain why they are now stressing the pre-eminence of their Strategic Missile Troops. Furthermore, the suspicion arises that geography, the lack of sea and air lift capabilities, and inadequate experience have had more to do with the Soviet lack of a "flexible response" than ideological considerations.

Finally—without my wishing to be more of an economic determinist than the Marxists—it seems to me that Mr. McConnell has advanced ideological reasons for much in Soviet military doctrine that is the result of economic scarcities. The U.S.S.R. decision not to build Bisons in large numbers, not to go all out in the manufacture of ICBM's, is explainable in terms of a defensive strategy derived from an ideological *volte-face,* but it is much easier to interpret this in other terms: the fact that these are extremely expensive gadgets. As long as Soviet leaders could bluff the United States successfully first with the "bomber gap" from 1955 to 1957 and then with the "missile gap" between 1958 and 1961, why expend scarce resources on bombers destined to become obsolete and on first-generation, liquid-fuelled ICBM's? Khrushchev's almost hysterical reaction to the American re-evaluation of the "missile gap" in late 1961 and his attempt to overcome the "reversed gap" by placing Soviet missiles on Cuban soil would seem to provide some corroboration for the simpler explanation.

In brief, the main reasons for Soviet defensive strategy include the U.S.S.R. conviction that the United States will not launch a first strike, the enormous cost of building a superior long-range missile force, and the fact that the Kremlin still holds half of Europe as a hostage. The case may be somewhat overstated, but the relationship of the Soviet leaders to their ideology is somewhat analogous to the relationship of Mr. Gladstone to his conscience, as Disraeli commented: it is not so much a guide as an accomplice.

Part III

Eastern Europe

5

polycentrism in eastern europe

RICHARD F. STAAR

Preliminaries

The experiment of maintaining a single organization, the Communist In-formation Bureau, or Cominform, to control Eastern Europe politically from Moscow existed less than nine years. It is doubtful that this instru-ment could have been used at all following the death of Stalin. Only one eyewitness account of the Cominform's establishment exists in print.[1]

This organizational meeting took place during September 22–7, 1947, at Szklarska Poreba (the former Bad Schreiberhau) in the Giant Moun-tains of Silesia, which Poland had taken from Germany at the end of World War II. Representing the host country's communist party was Wladyslaw Gomulka, who signed the original Cominform manifesto de-nouncing the Marshall Plan and condemning the United States as "an arsenal of counterrevolutionary tactical weapons." The other delegates came from the remaining East European parties, in addition to those from Italy and France, where, it was assumed, the communists would shortly be in power.

The second meeting came at the beginning of 1948 in Belgrade, where Cominform headquarters functioned for a brief period of time. The next session at the new center in Bucharest issued the communiqué excluding the Yugoslav communist party from the organization. A fourth meeting at Budapest toward the end of 1949 devoted its time to planning the world drive for signatures to a so-called "peace manifesto." After that, little was accomplished and the Cominform was all but forgotten until April 1956 and its dissolution, apparently as part of the price for reconciliation between Belgrade and Moscow.

Abolition of the Cominform, the existence of which had manifested itself during the last few years only by publication of the weekly newspaper entitled "For a Lasting Peace, For a People's Democracy," left a vacuum in the Soviet Bloc. This coincided with what has become known as de-Stalinization, and was apparently aimed at transforming the image of East European leaders from Moscow agents to respectable "national communists" *à la* Tito. Nikita S. Khrushchev had launched the process with his secret speech in February 1956 to the 20th Party Congress. Apart from denigration of Stalin, this elite gathering also heard enunciated the formula of different roads to socialism.

Whatever may have motivated Khrushchev to repeat his denunciation of Stalin publicly at the 22d Congress in October 1961, sweeping changes in Eastern Europe had to be avoided at all costs. The simple fact of the matter remains that many regimes would have fallen if de-Stalinization had been implemented. Most leaders in power today had at one time or another been ardent supporters of Stalinist techniques, and some might even like to revert to them at present. Hence de-Stalinization was restricted to changing the names of streets and cities as well as taking down statues of Stalin, including the one in Prague made from a solid piece of marble and weighing five tons, and removing mummified bodies of "little Stalins" from mausoleums. However, nothing ever came of Khrushchev's 1961 proposal to "erect a monument in Moscow to perpetuate the memory of comrades who fell victims to arbitrary rule," either in the U.S.S.R. or elsewhere.

Eastern Europe's Leaders

The men controlling communist regimes within the Soviet Bloc, even those in Albania and Yugoslavia, share many characteristics. They are all hard-core apparatus workers, i.e., professional revolutionaries who reached the top post after having served in less responsible work, also when their parties were banned by the prewar governments. They had all proved themselves to be dedicated communists, some of them in "capitalist" and even in their own postwar communist prisons (see Table 3).

Enver Hoxha is the best educated among these eight communist leaders in Eastern Europe. Definitely of "bourgeois" origin, he was graduated from the French secondary school at Koritsa and then studied one year at the University of Montpellier, in France. Back in Albania after having worked in Paris and Brussels over a period of five years, he taught the French language at a secondary school prior to the Italian occupation. Hoxha became secretary-general of the Albanian communist party when it

TABLE 3

Eastern Europe's Communist Leaders, 1968

Country	Leader's Name and Party Position	Year of Birth	Father's Occupation	Joined Communist Party	Profession	Years in Prison	Spent World War II in	Years in U.S.S.R.	Government Position	Year Joined the Party Politburo
Albania	Hoxha, Enver First Secretary, 1941–	1908	Small land-holder	1941	Teacher	1939 (briefly)	Albania	None	None	1941
Bulgaria	Zhivkov, Todor First Secretary, 1954–	1911	Peasant	1932	Printer	None	Bulgaria	1936–41(?)	Prime Minister	1951
Czechoslovakia	Dubček, Alexander First Secretary, 1968–	1922	Auto-worker	1939	Engine-fitter	None	Czecho-slovakia	1925–38; 1955–8	None	1963
East Germany	Ulbricht, Walter First Secretary, 1950–	1893	Tailor	1919	Carpenter	1918; 1930–2	U.S.S.R.	1933–45	Chairman, Council of State	1934
Hungary	Kádar, János First Secretary, 1956–	1914	Peasant	1932	None	1933–5; 1951–4	Hungary	None	Member, Presidential Council	1956
Poland	Gomulka, Wladyslaw Secretary-General, 1943–8; First Secretary, 1956–	1905	Oil-field worker	1926	Black-smith	1932–4; 1936–9; 1951–4	Poland	1934–6	Member, Council of State	1943
Romania	Ceausescu, Nicolae Secretary-General, 1965–	1918	Poor Peasant	1936	None	1936–9; 1940–4	Romania	None	Chairman, Council of State	1954
Yugoslavia	Tito, Josip Broz Secretary-General, 1937–66; President, 1966–	1892	Peasant	1920	Metal-worker	1915–17; 1928–34	Yugo-slavia	1915–20; 1934–36	President (for life)	1934

SOURCES: Radio Free Europe, *Eastern Europe's Communist Leaders*, 5 vols. (Munich, 1966); for Dubček's biography, *Krasnaya zvezda* (Moscow), January 7, 1968; and current identifications from the East European press.

was founded in 1941, and he has directed the movement ever since. After his Yugoslav mentors had been expelled from the Cominform in 1948, he took advantage of this development to become the protegé of the U.S.S.R. A second opportunity came at the 22d Party Congress in Moscow when the Albanian communists were read out of the world movement loyal to the Soviet Union. Hoxha had already shifted his allegiance to Peking, much farther away geographically.

Bulgaria's leader, Todor Zhivkov,[2] also spent the war years in his own country as one of the anti-German partisans. However, here the resemblance to Hoxha ends. Born into a peasant family, Zhivkov only completed a few years of elementary school. Between 1936 and 1941 he may have been in Moscow undergoing communist political training, since there is a gap in his biography to cover these years. Zhivkov succeeded the notorious "little Stalin" Vulko Chervenkov as a member of the new collective leadership. He has never deviated from the Moscow line and rivals his communist East German colleague in this respect.

The leader in Czechoslovakia is Alexander Dubček, who joined the underground communist movement in his country at the age of eighteen during the Nazi occupation. He had spent thirteen years (1925–38) in the Soviet Union with his parents and worked at the Skoda plant during most of World War II. Dubček fought in the Slovak Uprising, where his brother was killed. After four years as a factory worker at Trencin, he became a full-time Party aparatchik. During 1955–8, Dubček attended the higher school attached to the Central Committee of the Soviet communist party at Moscow. Four years later, he became a member of the Czechoslovak party's Presidium and in 1963 First Secretary of the Slovak communist party. Prague is headquarters for the monthly *World Marxist Review,* successor to the long-defunct Cominform weekly newspaper, certainly an indication of confidence by the Kremlin.

Perhaps among all East European leaders Walter Ulbricht,[3] in the so-called "German Democratic Republic," remains the most submissive in his relations with the Soviet Union. A member of the *Spartakus Bund,* he joined the communist party when it was founded and even represented it in the Reichstag. Ulbricht served as an international Comintern agent as far back as 1924 and worked briefly for the Soviet secret police (NKVD) during the Spanish Civil War. He has been Moscow's viceroy in East Germany since the time he returned to East Berlin in the uniform of a Red Army colonel at the end of the war. In 1963 Ulbricht became a "Hero of the Soviet Union," apparently for services rendered.

Another man who has also spent his entire adult life in the service of communism is János Kádár, in Hungary. Although he lived inside his native country during the war, by 1948 he had become deputy secretary-general of the Party. The following year Kádár betrayed his best friend, the Interior Minister Laszlo Rajk, who was executed. Despite this action he was swept up in the anti-Titoist purge and spent thirty-two months in prison. Kádár next turned traitor to the Imre Nagy government, of which he was a member, by clandestinely establishing a counterregime at Uzhgorod in the Soviet Ukraine and calling on the U.S.S.R. at the end of October 1956 to suppress the freedom fighters in Hungary. Two years later Nagy was executed. Since the Hungarian revolt Kádár has always done Moscow's bidding.

Like his counterpart at Budapest, Wladyslaw Gomulka spent World War II in his native country and also became a victim of the anti-Titoist purge. As secretary-general of the Party in the early postwar period he had been just as adept at employing Stalinist techniques against the opponents of communism as any other East European leader. Although not apprised that Gomulka would become the first secretary in October 1956, the U.S.S.R. accepted this decision after an all-night confrontation. Since that time, and perhaps because Gomulka had been trained in Moscow at the International Lenin School for Political Warfare during the mid-1930's, relations between the two communist parties have been excellent.

Another leader in the Bloc is Nicolae Ceauşescu. He, too, like Go-mulka, had been imprisoned by the precommunist government of his country. Always advancing to more important positions, Ceauşescu spent the war in Romania, most of the time in jail. His contacts with the Soviet Union have included repeated visits ever since 1957, when he represented the Romanian communist party at the 40th Anniversary Celebration of the Bolshevik Revolution. However, no delegation from Bucharest went to the March 1–5, 1965, preliminary (to a world conference) meeting of communist parties in Moscow. The Albanians and the Chinese also refused to attend. On the other hand, Ceauşescu did host the Warsaw Pact and Council for Mutual Economic Aid (CMEA) sessions during July 1966 in Romania. His party also sent delegates to the 66-party preliminary consultative conference at Budapest, but they walked out on February 29, 1968, the fourth day of this meeting which was called to prepare the agenda for a world congress to be held the end of the year at Moscow.

Finally, a man unique in Eastern Europe is Josip Broz Tito,[4] whose relationship with the Soviet Union goes back to 1917 and membership in a Red Guards unit at Omsk, Siberia. He returned to Yugoslavia but left again for Moscow, where he taught in the mid-1930's at the International Lenin School for Political Warfare, while Gomulka was one of its students. Moscow appointed Tito in 1937 general-secretary of his Party and sent him back to Yugoslavia for clandestine work. Here he spent the war and emerged as leader of that country, only to have his Party expelled from the Cominform by Stalin. The rapprochement which started with Khrushchev has continued under the new Soviet leadership.

Unity in Diversity

As can be seen from the foregoing, the backgrounds of these eight communist leaders would indicate that they might be difficult to manipulate. Oddly enough, it was a communist from outside the Bloc who contributed more to the development of polycentrism than anybody else. Palmiro Togliatti, the late secretary-general of the Italian communist party, is credited with already having used this term in 1956. While Stalin was still alive, this man had been among the most subservient of foreign communist leaders. However, in 1964 he wrote a memorandum during a vacation at Yalta in the U.S.S.R. intended to represent the basis for discussions with Khrushchev. These never took place because Togliatti died. His body and the memorandum were removed to Italy.

Leonid I. Brezhnev, today general-secretary of the Soviet communist party, represented Moscow at the funeral in Rome. He first learned of the memorandum there and attempted to have it suppressed. Although it never would have appeared if Togliatti had lived, the new Italian communist leaders under Luigi Longo decided to publish it.[5] *Pravda* then carried a translation five days later but without any comment. Subsequently the press of most other East European communist parties also printed the memorandum. Many of these ideas, of course, had already appeared in one way or another.

Togliatti emphasized that the Soviet Bloc had been developing a "centrifugal tendency," i.e., individual parties were moving away from centralized control exercised by Moscow. He also spoke out against any proposal to create once again an organization like the Comintern (1919–43) or Cominform (1947–56). Togliatti rebuked the U.S.S.R. and other communist-ruled states in Eastern Europe for their slowness and resistance in "overcoming the regime of restrictions and suppression of democratic and personal freedom introduced by Stalin." Finally, to quote the memorandum, "one must consider that the unity one ought to establish and maintain lies in the diversity and full autonomy of the individual countries." Togliatti proposed in brief an Eastern Europe based on polycentrism.

If translation and publication of the Togliatti memorandum were allowed by Khrushchev, it is only because the latter's attitude toward Eastern Europe had been based on an effort to eliminate the master-servant relationship existing under Stalin. The goal appeared to be introduction of more flexible contacts with the various communist parties, whereby common policies might be reached by means of discussion, although the U.S.S.R. would still maintain a decisive voice because of its power position. This grand design failed for various reasons, including the half-measures which Khrushchev allowed, the unexpected strength of nationalism, the effects of incomplete de-Stalinization, and the impact of the Soviet dispute with China.

It should be noted that ever since the dissolution of the Cominform the day-to-day business of handling relations among the various Bloc communist parties is being conducted through special departments within the Central Committee apparatus of each organization. Mikhail Suslov, chief ideologist for the C.P.S.U., indicated that international discipline no longer involves orders "from above" but is voluntary.[6] Apparently the most that he and Khrushchev regarded as obtainable could have involved an international system of "democratic centralism," i.e., minority accepts majority decision in foreign policy (see Table 4).

TABLE 4

Bloc Party Foreign Departments, 1966–8

No.	Country	Director	Unit Designation
1.	Albania	Bita, Piro	Dept. of International Relations
2.	Bulgaria	Tellakov, Konstantin*	Foreign Policy & International Relations Dept.
3.	Czechoslovakia	Kaderka, Oldrich**	International Dept.
4.	East Germany	Markowski, Paul**	International Relations Dept.
5.	Hungary	Puja, Frigyes*	Dept. of Foreign Affairs
6.	Poland	Czesak, Jozef*	Commission on Foreign Affairs
7.	Romania	Vlad, Vasile**	Foreign Relations Section
8.	Soviet Union	Rusakov, Konstantin V.***	Section for Liaison with Communist & Workers' Parties of Socialist Countries
9.	Yugoslavia	Popović, Vladimir*	Commission for International Relations

NOTES:
*Member of Central Committee
**Candidate Member of Central Committee
***Member of Central Audit Commission
SOURCES: (1) Department of State, *Directory of Albanian Officials* (Washington, D.C.: Nov. 1966), p. 24; (2) Bulgarian Telegraphic Agency, May 30, 1967; (3) Department of State, *Directory of Czechoslovak Officials* (Washington, D.C.: Nov. 1967), p. 58; (4) Bonner Fachberichte aus der Sowjetzone, *Die SED* (Bonn: Bundesministerium für gesamtdeutsche Fragen, 1967), p. 76; (5) *Krasnaya zvezda,* Feb. 18, 1968; (6) *Radio Warsaw,* Jan. 21, 1968; (7) *Radio Bucharest,* Jan. 29, 1968; (8) *Krasnaya zvezda,* Feb. 25, 1968; (9) *Wissenschaftlicher Dienst Südosteuropas,* XV:10 (Oct., 1966), 156, based on official Yugoslav source materials.

Fall of Khrushchev and After

Togliatti had dealt with the lack of freedom in communist-ruled states, and the manner in which Khrushchev was dismissed enhanced the impact of his memorandum. The slogan "unity in diversity" can best be observed in the various reactions to the editorial in *Pravda* on October 17, 1964, explaining the change in leadership at Moscow. Even the most obedient among the East European regimes finally had come to the realization that it did have some bargaining power vis-à-vis the Kremlin. Nowhere was this truer than in Romania.

Bucharest published the following day a summary of the Soviet editorial but gave a full translation of the paragraph describing Khrushchev's deficiencies. This probably was meant to indicate dissatisfaction with the deposed leader, who had attempted to pressure the Romanians into giving up certain of their more independent policies. In the cases of Hungary, Czechoslovakia, and Poland, irritation could be discerned, since Khrushchev had only recently visited these countries. Here communist spokesmen all praised him.

Kádár, who had been placed in power by Khrushchev, returned from a visit to Warsaw and admitted that the change in Moscow had caught him by surprise. In this same speech he declared the following: "I am of the opinion that Comrade Khrushchev has very great merits in the struggle against the Stalin personality cult. . . . The hundreds of thousands of Hungarians who not long ago this year, here in our country, were able to greet Comrade Khrushchev and did so whole-heartedly as representative of the great C.P.S.U. [Communist Party of the Soviet Union], State and people . . . did well to do so and have nothing to reflect on subsequently."[7]

The following day the principal Czechoslovak communist newspaper reprinted the *Pravda* editorial. Three days later the party's Presidium issued a statement which remarked that "the news of the decision by the C.P.S.U. Central Committee on relieving Comrade Khrushchev was received by our whole Party and the public with surprise and emotion" and then went on to repeat Kádár's praise of the man. This marked the first time that an official pronouncement in Prague deviated from the Moscow line. Khrushchev had toured Czechoslovakia in late August and early September 1964, endorsing the Novotny leadership. (Novotny himself was ousted on January 5, 1968, from First Secretary and on March 22, 1968, from President.)

Only in one case did the new Soviet duumvirate travel outside the U.S.S.R. to explain in person why they had deposed Khrushchev, and that was to Poland. Gomulka, who praised the former leader, also admitted in his speech that he had been taken by surprise. He may have been concerned about the forthcoming extension of the April 1945 twenty-year friendship treaty with the U.S.S.R. which Khrushchev had promised would include a specific guarantee of the Oder-Neisse boundary line. At any rate the meeting took place in the Bialowieza Forest, near Bialystok, with Brezhnev, Premier Aleksei Kosygin, Gomulka, and Premier Jozef Cyrankiewicz. The brief announcement on October 25, 1964, merely stated that the talks had been conducted in an atmosphere of "friendship, cordiality, and complete identity of views."

It was the East German communists, and specifically Ulbricht, who showed most apprehension over events in the Kremlin. Apart from the Politburo statement mentioning the "profound stir" that Khrushchev's departure had caused, a rally of all political parties and mass organizations "unanimously consented" to the Soviet changes. These groups pledged themselves "to activate" the U.S.S.R.–East German friendship treaty. This reference to the June 12, 1964, pact probably indicated a real fear concerning future Kremlin policy in Germany.

Bulgaria alone made no comment about Khrushchev himself. All newspapers carried photographs of the new leaders, Brezhnev and Kosygin, with factual information about the changes. Zhivkov's telegram of congratulations plus their biographic sketches appeared together with the *Pravda* editorial on front pages. The same day a Central Committee meeting pledged support for the C.P.S.U. line and promised to "march side by side in unflinching unity with the great party of Lenin." Only the Albanian communists sent no congratulatory message, in contrast even to the communist Chinese.

On the other hand, the first authoritative comment from Yugoslavia reflected the anxiety of Belgrade at what had occurred in Moscow.

> The situation in the international workers' movement today requires a thorough analysis, and the changes in Moscow can not be isolated from this situation. . . . The changes are of special importance in view of the role played by the international workers' movement and the prominent role played by Comrade Khrushchev, together with other Soviet party and government leaders, in eradicating the Stalinist heritage, not only in the Soviet Union, but also in the international worker's movement, and particularly in relations between the Soviet Union and other Socialist countries and Yugoslavia.[8]

The day before this appeared in print, Foreign Secretariat spokesman Dušan Blagojević indicated that the events in Moscow were the internal affair of the Soviet Union. He further acknowledged that the Yugoslav government had found significant the affirmation by the U.S.S.R. of its policies based on decisions of the 20th and 22nd C.P.S.U. Congresses.

Thus in general the fall of Khrushchev at first caused bewilderment throughout almost the whole of Eastern Europe. Whereas previous changes of this kind had been accepted without hesitation by all communists, this time comment involved questioning and in many cases even criticism. Demands for more detailed explanations as to why Khrushchev had been deposed continued, and the new Soviet leadership found itself compelled to state its case in Moscow to delegations from a number of communist parties. Some of this could be taken care of during the traditional anniversary celebrations of the Bolshevik Revolution in November. It is not known from the communiqués issued at various times whether these delegations were satisfied with the results of these talks.

The Post-Khrushchev Era

Khrushchev had scheduled a twenty-six party preparatory conference to be held at Moscow on December 15, 1964, which was to draw up the agenda for a world congress of representatives from the international communist movement. The high-level Chinese delegation, headed by Chou En-lai, that attended the anniversary celebrations in the U.S.S.R. during the preceding month probably influenced the new Soviet leaders to postpone the conference until the following spring. Finally, it was scheduled definitely for March 1–5, 1965.

Only eighteen of the parties invited sent delegations, plus an observer from an additional one; and the gathering became merely a "consultative meeting", which meant that it could make no decisions binding upon the absent communist parties. In addition to the Albanians, who, like the Chinese, refused to attend, the only other East European communist party that decided not to send any representatives was the Romanian. The communiqué issued five days after the end of the meeting dropped for all practical purposes the idea of holding a world congress but left open the possibility in the future, providing conditions change.

Previously the Albanians had been invited by the Polish hosts to the seventh meeting of the Warsaw Pact's political consultative committee. They refused to come, even though the reconciliation would have involved a new Soviet leadership. Perhaps there existed a suspicion that the gathering might be used as a vehicle for establishing a new political relationship and not restrict itself to purely military affairs. Albania also did not participate in the eighth meeting[9] at Bucharest, although it is now known that no invitation was extended this time.

It is interesting that the Romanian communists would have hosted this session, and this tends to undermine the hope frequently voiced concerning that country's desire to withdraw from the Warsaw Treaty Organization. Economic nationalism is another matter. Already on April 26, 1964, the Central Committee of the Romanian communist party issued a declaration which included the following:

> During the development of the relations of cooperation among the socialist countries which are CMEA members, ways and means have been sug-

gested, such as a joint plan and a single planning body for all member countries, interstate technical-productive branch unions, enterprises jointly owned by several countries and interstate economic complexes . . . these measures are not in keeping with the principles which underlie relations among sovereign states. . . . Transmitting such levers to the competence of superstate or extrastate bodies would make of sovereignty an idea without content.[10]

The U.S.S.R. under Khrushchev and his successors has been unable to supply Romania's needs in full and thus cannot respond satisfactorily with economic pressure to that country's defiance (see Table 5).

TABLE 5

Fuel and Raw Material Imports from U.S.S.R.
(percentages of consumption)

Country	Coking coal	Oil	Iron ore	Cotton
Bulgaria	82.5	87.5	45.0	65.7
Hungary	65.5	79.0	79.5	61.2
East Germany	78.0	94.0	58.7	91.2
Mongolia	——	89.0	——	——
Poland	4.1	89.5	70.0	58.6
Romania	32.1	——	54.5	43.4
Czechoslovakia	——	97.0	74.6	59.6

SOURCE: *Voprosy ekonomiki* (Moscow), No. 10 (Oct., 1967).

The struggle for economic independence is closely related to the process of removing Soviet political influence. For a brief period Bucharest even suspended publication of the "World Marxist Review" in the Romanian language. When resumed, it came out with reduced contents and specific deletion of articles that might embarrass Bucharest's neutrality in the Sino-Soviet dispute or contradict its position on other political and economic matters. At the communist-front World Federation of Trade Unions meeting in Warsaw during October 1965 Romania even went so far as to support China against the U.S.S.R.

To a certain extent many of the East European leaders are exploiting feelings of nationalism in order to obtain some identification with the people. In the case of Romania this has led to an overtly anti-Soviet attitude. On the other hand, Gomulka in Poland has had to discourage the deep feelings of hostility against Russians in general and Soviet communists in particular. His nationalism has become diluted as the years have passed. Only the Bulgarians do not even pay lip service to nationalism; and the East German regime, of course, is in no position to do so.

Many of the East European peoples (in contrast to their rulers) for good historical reasons have been traditionally antagonistic toward the colossus in the East. Germans fought against Russians in both world wars. The same is true of the Hungarians, even though many of them may have done so reluctantly. In June 1940 Romania ceded northern Bukovina and Bessarabia after a direct threat of force by the U.S.S.R. The people of Poland, steeped as they are in history, remember that Russia (tsarist and communist) participated in all six dismemberments of that country: 1772, 1793, 1795, 1939, and 1945. Neither have they forgotten the suppression of revolts in the nineteenth century, the mass deportations following the Hitler-Stalin pact, the massacre of prisoners of war at Katyn Forest, and the failure of the Red Army to assist the 1944 Warsaw uprising against the Germans.

Conflicts within Eastern Europe

Apart from this negative attitude toward the Soviet Union, there exist many traditional enmities among the East European countries themselves. The image of East Germany is affected by memories of Nazi occupation or domination. Although the communist regimes attempt to channel these feelings against the Federal Republic of (West) Germany, much of the hatred toward all Germans still remains. This is especially prevalent in both Czechoslovakia and Poland. Even between these two countries, however, the differences in temperament and attitude toward the U.S.S.R. have been complicated ever since the seizure of Cieszyn (Tesin) by the Prague government in 1920 during the Polish-Soviet war and its recovery by Poland in September 1938 with the use of an ultimatum at the time of Munich.

Minority Problems

The most important potential area of Bloc conflict involves the Hungarians in Romania. Forcible assimilation of these people was intensified after the 1956 uprising in Hungary, when the possibility of contagion seemed imminent. Budapest has made no public effort to intercede on behalf of the Magyars in Transylvania. However, even Hungarians within the communist party may feel strongly about the repression of their kinsmen across the border. There also exists the problem that parts of Hungary other than Transylvania, like the city of Oradea Mare (Nagyvarad), are currently in Romania.

Czechoslovakia, too, has its Hungarian minority, where the assimilation process has continued. For example, the Slovak communist party weekly stated that "the participation of workers and collective farmers of Hungarian nationality in the country's economic upsurge will depend on the extent to which they can master Czech and Slovak technical literature as well as on their expertise in their respective fields."[11] It is noteworthy that bus lines between Czechoslovakia and Hungary were not opened until 1964 and that the bridge over the Danube between the two countries at Esztergom had not been rebuilt by the following year.

The best illustration of minority problems is Yugoslavia, with its many nationalities. Bulgaria has alleged from time to time that the Bulgars in Macedonia are being persecuted by the Yugoslavs. These charges became particularly vociferous during the second (1958) Soviet-Yugoslav dispute. However, even six years later the main communist party newspaper in Belgrade printed editorially a listing of then current anti-Yugoslav speeches and articles still referring to Macedonia as Bulgarian.[12] Officially, however, friendship is being proclaimed between the two countries. There are also some 900,000 Albanians living in Yugoslavia, and a steady stream of denunciation comes from across that border.

Internal Nationality Problems

Two of the countries in Eastern Europe, namely Czechoslovakia and Yugoslavia, are faced with the question of how to preserve unity among their different ethnic groups and yet not erase national identities. The two states involved have not existed long enough to change the fundamental individualism of their minority components. Slovaks remember their brief separate statehood during World War II, and even the communists are proud of the 1944 uprising against the Germans in Slovakia. After that war, local autonomy was granted Slovakia, but resentment flared in 1960 when the Slovak Board of Commissioners, symbolizing that self-rule, was dissolved under the new "socialist" constitution.

The dismissal during 1963 of two notorious Stalinists of Slovak extraction, Karol Bacilek from headship of the communist party of Slovakia and Viliam Siroky from the premiership of the entire country, only contributed to further demands for restoration of autonomy. The new premier, Josef Lenart, had been president of the Slovak National Council, and his appointment could be interpreted as a concession. The powers of this latter agency were increased the following year.[13] However, the primary task of this Council remains to fulfill the state economic plan. Slovakia will continue to strive for more freedom, although it certainly has no future as an independent entity under communism, even with Dubček as First Secretary.

The problems in Yugoslavia are more complex. After the final reconciliation between Khrushchev and Tito at the end of 1962, a general domestic relaxation led to a revival of nationalism within the individual republics which must have worried the communist leaders in Belgrade. Tito complained about this, and in his 1963 address to the 7th Congress of the Yugoslav People's Youth he attacked unnamed persons who confuse the nation with the state. Economic overtones also appear to be significant, especially in connection with subsidies given by more developed Croatia and Slovenia in the north to Serbia and Montenegro in the south.

Opening the 8th Congress of the Yugoslav Communist Party, Tito warned against wanting "to create something new and artificial—one unified Yugoslav nation, which is not unlike . . . centralism" and against "chauvinism"; in Yugoslav "socialist integration" all nationalities would find their individual interest.[14] However, nationality problems most assuredly will play a part in the leadership succession. The fact that Tito is a Croatian may be insignificant, but this will not be the case with regard to his successor. Aleksandar Ranković is a Serb, and his replacement as vice president in July 1966 by Koča Popović came from that same nationality, indicating that the ethnic balance is important.

Conflicts Within Communism

The communist system was imposed upon the countries of Eastern Europe against the wishes of the overwhelming majority of the populations involved. This basic conflict between the people and their rulers exploded during 1953 into riots at Pilsen (Czechoslovakia) and East Berlin as well as demonstrations during 1956 at Poznan and Warsaw, culminating with the full-scale revolt at Budapest. Other conflicts on the interstate level have involved Yugoslavia twice and Albania once with the U.S.S.R. since 1948 and 1961 respectively. These two countries broke away completely from the Soviet Bloc, although Yugoslavia again seems to be a member in good standing. The most recent case in which independence is being asserted involves Romania and overtly dates back only to 1964, as mentioned already. Finally, differences in both politics and economics exist among the East European regimes themselves which in turn affect their relations with the U.S.S.R.

Although intervention by Soviet armed forces crushed the revolution in Hungary, apart from the initial postrevolt terror, there has been no return to the Stalinist type of government which had precipitated the uprising. János Kádár soon demonstrated firmly the impossibility of an alternative to the communist regime, and it seems that the population has indeed come to terms with reality. This situation is reinforced by the continued presence of some 50,000 Soviet troops permanently garrisoned in Hungary. Although a sensitive problem, Kadar has indicated openly that these forces will remain as long as they are needed.[15]

Although no U.S.S.R. troops have been stationed in Romania since 1958, and perhaps because of this situation, the communist leadership in Bucharest has dared to exploit nationalist sentiments domestically. This included a deliberate attempt to underemphasize the role played by the Red Army in establishing the present system throughout Romania at the end of the war. Compulsory study of the Russian language has been discontinued in secondary schools; Soviet names of streets in Bucharest have been changed; and even the anniversary of the Romanian-Soviet friendship treaty was celebrated in 1965 on a much smaller scale than ever before. This campaign culminated with the publication of previously unknown manuscripts by Karl Marx on late eighteenth- and early nineteenth-century Romanian history which indicted tsarist Russian policies. Finally, a book on the early period of the communist party in Romania discusses Comintern interference with appointments in 1920 to the leadership of the former.[16] In mid-January 1967, Bucharest exchanged ambassadors with Bonn which probably incurred the displeasure of Moscow and several other East European capitals.

As these developments have been taking place in the various East European countries, with internal relaxation and even attempts at asserting some degree of independence vis-à-vis the Soviet Union, one of the Bloc states remains locked in the vise of Stalinism. East Germany's position will continue to be unique because it is part of a divided country. Ulbricht must counter all polycentrist tendencies and prevent domestic relaxation, because this might lead to ferment and agitation for union with the much larger and wealthier Federal Republic of (West) Germany. That is also the reason behind Ulbricht's drive for recognition of the so-called (East) "German Democratic Republic" as a sovereign state in its own right.

The agreements to establish West German trade offices in Poland, Romania, Hungary, and Bulgaria have made Ulbricht uneasy. Negotiations by the Krupp combine for economic cooperation and joint enterprises in Eastern Europe have political as well as economic overtones. Obviously a growing trade with Bonn will make the Bloc partners less sensitive to the needs of Pankow. That is why East German propaganda has been stressing the danger of subversive activities by the trade missions and raising the specter of economic blackmail by the West.[17]

On the other hand, Yugoslavia has supported East Germany and extended official recognition to the Ulbricht regime despite the sanction applied by West Germany under the Hallstein Doctrine. No diplomatic relations existed between Bonn and Belgrade from October 1957 to January 1968, when they were resumed. Attitudes by the Bloc toward Yugoslavia have varied, depending upon Moscow. During two periods, 1948–55 and 1958–62, Tito found himself to be ostracized. However, by December 1962, when he visited the U.S.S.R., Khrushchev conceded that Yugoslavia was indeed a socialist country. The following month a Yugoslav communist delegation attended, for the first time since 1948, another Party congress in the Bloc namely, the one held at East Berlin.

At the interstate level also the then Yugoslav foreign minister, Koča

Popović, paid a visit to Bulgaria in January 1965, the first such trip by a cabinet member since November 1947, when Tito came to Sofia. Ulbricht and Novotny both had arrived in Belgrade during September 1964, although at different times. There existed less of a problem at reconciliation with either Poland or Hungary because Gomulka and Kádár had been imprisoned as "Titoists." Romania did not stage any trials for nationalist deviation, and even during the second Yugoslav-Soviet dispute in 1958 maintained its attacks at a low level. All but one of the East European parties and governments now accept Yugoslavia as a member of the Socialist camp. Only little Albania continues to denounce its communist neighbor.

The reasons for this continued hostility include the fear of annexation by Yugoslavia and the Albanian minority within Yugoslavia, which equals to half the total population inside Albania's own borders. Toward the end of 1960, at the conference of eighty-one communist parties in Moscow, Enver Hoxha also attacked the Soviet Union and accused it of attempting to starve Albania into submission. During the spring of 1961 the U.S.S.R. and Czechoslovakia stopped aid to Tirana, which had totalled the equivalent of $600 million over the preceding thirteen years; by the end of the summer all Bloc experts and technicians had left for home.

After the 22nd C.P.S.U. Congress, at which Khrushchev openly attacked the Albanian leadership for "resorting to force and arbitrary repression," diplomatic relations were severed between the two countries in December 1961 at the instigation of Moscow. Since that time Tirana has not attended any Warsaw Pact or CMEA meetings, although never expelled from either organization. The other Bloc countries followed the example of the U.S.S.R. and reduced their ranking diplomatic representative to the level of *chargé d'affaires*. Only the Romanians kept on friendly terms with Tirana. Bucharest even sent a delegation to the twentieth anniversary of Albania's "liberation" in November 1964, the only East European capital to do so, perhaps as an indication of its neutrality in the Sino-Soviet dispute.

Sino-Soviet Dispute

Besides the conflicts between the U.S.S.R. and individual countries within Eastern Europe, as well as among the latter states themselves, the Sino-Soviet schism has made an impact on the Bloc through the differing attitudes toward this rift. Ideologically, of course, all communist parties except the Albanian support Moscow. However, they are not unanimous in agreeing with the manner in which the dispute has been handled by the C.P.S.U. As mentioned already, Romania has proclaimed its neutrality and also attempted to mediate the quarrel in 1964 with the dispatch of a delegation to Peking. Bucharest is definitely against any excommunication of communist China and remains opposed to a world conference that might precipitate such a move. Romania even refused to attend the 1965 "consultative" conference in Moscow for this reason. It was also absent from the meeting of twenty-four European communist parties on April 25–6, 1967, at Karlovy Vary, Czechoslovakia.[18] The leaders in Bucharest, however, did send a delegation to the consultative conference for all parties in the world, held at the end of February 1968 in Budapest but then walked out.

The leaders of East Germany, Bulgaria, Czechoslovakia, and Hungary support the Soviet position both in terms of communist doctrine and of the tactics used to handle the differences. Spokesmen for the regime in Poland have indicated their hesitation at giving the C.P.S.U. full backing, and these statements make it apparent that the communist leadership at Warsaw is not very enthusiastic about the future. At any rate, certain of the other regimes in Eastern Europe may follow the Romanian example and try to exploit the Sino-Soviet dispute for their own ends. However, this had not been done at the Bulgarian communist party congress in November 1966 or at the subsequent Hungarian congress which ended early the following month or even at the East German congress in April 1967.

It would have seemed natural for the Romanians to utilize the arrival of Chou En-lai in June 1966 for another demonstration of independence. At the same time the Chinese premier undoubtedly timed his visit just three weeks prior to the Bloc summit meeting of Warsaw Pact members for the purpose of influencing this session by exploiting the strained relations between Romania and the Soviet Union. Chou praised his hosts for "fighting against all attempts at control or interference from the outside." He added that by standing up for their sovereignty, they were defending the correct basis for relations between communist parties and states.

An attack on C.P.S.U. leaders as "modern revisionists" at a banquet was deleted from reports on Chou's speech by Romanian censorship, and he apparently desisted from any further criticism of the U.S.S.R. during the one-week visit. Although nothing is known about the private talks which took place with Ceauşescu, there could not have been much agreement on substantive matters. Even the farewell rally had to be delayed some two hours, which would indicate a clash regarding Chou's address. The final statement had little to say about the exchange of views except that these had "led to increased knowledge."

If this visit diminished Chinese prestige, and it was, paradoxically, in 1960 at the Romanian communist party congress in Bucharest that China first attacked the Soviet Union openly, there still remained one country in Eastern Europe where Chou could receive full support for his views. Arriving in Tirana, he saw portraits of Stalin and Mao Tse-tung together with those of Marx and Lenin. Here the spokesman for communist China denounced the "treachery and collusion" of Soviet and United States leaders, whose alleged plans to dissolve NATO and the Warsaw Pact meant a plot to encircle China. Albanian premier Mehmet Shehu echoed the visitor at a mass rally in Durres.

The Limits of Relaxation

It would seem that the attainment of some freedom from Soviet control throughout Eastern Europe would be connected with a loosening of the totalitarian control exercised by each regime upon the population concerned. That this is not necessarily true can be seen from the example of Albania, which has been *de facto* outside the Bloc since the end of 1961, when the U.S.S.R. severed all relations with that country. The leadership in Tirana continues its harsh rule and hence will not be discussed in this section.

Regarding the other Bloc countries, three have delayed any internal *détente* longer than the others because the leaders do not seem able to overcome their Stalinist background. Thus the nationalism of the Slovaks and the general intellectual ferment forced Novotny to make some concessions before his ouster. East Germany, on the other hand, has had no relaxation to speak of and recently "celebrated" the seventh anniversary of the Berlin Wall. The domestic "thaw" in Romania has been gradual and maintained under strict control, in sharp contrast to assertions of independence within CMEA and the Warsaw Pact.

Comparing the two remaining countries, both of which played main roles in the events of 1956 major differences can be seen. Kádár, who had been put into power by the U.S.S.R. and betrayed the Hungarian government of Imre Nagy, has by and large tried to obtain the support of the population and relaxed domestic conditions. Gomulka, conversely, on whom so much hope had been placed in Poland, has pursued a constant policy of retrogression[19] so that today the country stagnates politically and economically. Restrictions on freedom of speech, a violent campaign against the Church, but only cautious economic reforms have been undertaken.

Despite some of the foregoing changes, it should be emphasized that the communist regimes in Eastern Europe remain more similar than they are different. Not one of them has indicated an abandonment of one-party rule or a centrally planned economy. Regardless of wishful thinking, even Romania will most probably not leave CMEA or the Warsaw Treaty Organization. It is true that secret police have been less in evidence throughout the Bloc, but detailed card files are being maintained.[20] Last but not least, the ouster of Khrushchev in 1964 and of Novotny in 1968 remind the average citizen that change may come suddenly in Eastern Europe.

TABLE 6

Eastern Europe, Basic Data, 1966–8

Country	Area (sq. miles)	Population (millions)	Party Members (millions)	Socialized Sector (percentage of total)		Trade		GNP
				Industry	Farm Land	Wholesale	Retail	
Albania	11,101	1.9	0.066	99.5	82.0	100.0	92.9	90.5
Bulgaria	42,823	8.3	0.611	99.5	98.1	100.0	99.9	99.5
Czechoslovakia	49,370	14.3	1.690	100.0	93.5	100.0	100.0	95.0
East Germany	41,659	17.1	1.770	89.0	94.0	100.0	77.0	83.0
Hungary	35,915	10.2	0.627	98.0	95.2	100.0	98.8	96.6
Poland	120,359	31.8	2.000	99.6	14.6	100.0	98.5	76.9
Romania	91,699	19.1	1.700	99.6	94.1	100.0	100.0	95.7
Yugoslavia	98,766	20.0	1.050	100.0	17.5	100.0	99.0	n.a.
Total	491,692	122.7	9.514					
Average				ca 98.2	ca 73.6	100.0	ca 95.1	ca 91.0

NOTE: n.a.—not available. The validity of certain data remains questionable, especially in the agricultural (farm land) column. Unfortunately, sources do not always define the terms used.

SOURCES: Compiled from *Kommunist vooruzhennykh sil* (Moscow), XLVI:3–4 (Feb. 1966); Radio Free Europe, *Situation Report* (Munich), Aug. 25, 1967, for communist party membership figures; and *Reader's Digest 1968 Almanac and Yearbook* (New York), passim, for area and population.

The concessions that have occurred do not seem to affect the membership in the various communist parties. If anything, these have increased. Czechoslovakia claims the highest proportion of Party members (11.4%) to the total population. In other Bloc countries this ranges from 5 to 10 per cent (see Table 6). Drives to increase membership alternate with purges, so that despite the apparent size of the communist movement in each country, it can no longer guarantee effective administration of the government. Thus a trend which had its beginning in Hungary has been spreading throughout Eastern Europe whereby professional qualifications rather than Party service may in the future determine who occupies certain positions in the economy and public administration. The resulting conflict between the young, by and large nonpolitical, cadres and the old Party members without any training in management is becoming acute.

The need for economic reform is closely connected with this struggle between the young managerial elite and the Party apparatus workers. Most countries in the Bloc now realize that progress cannot be achieved without a more realistic pricing system, at least some decentralization, and appropriate incentives for workers. This is not a return to capitalism: all measures are to remain within the framework of central planning. Begun in Yugoslavia during 1949–50, such measures did not appear in any other East European country until Poland made a few steps in the same direction eight years later. Here, however, opposition in 1957–8 stymied any progress for a full year.

The impetus to reform did not come until after the publication of U.S.S.R. Professor Yevsei Liberman's article in 1962. His ideas affected East Germany without too much publicity. They also led to a study in Czechoslovakia, following the negative performance of that country's economy in 1962–3, and subsequent reform. The regime in Hungary announced during November 1965 that fundamental changes were required but would be introduced gradually. After some experimentation the Politburo in Bulgaria released its "Theses" in December 1965 according to which the individual factory will be self-supporting but within the framework of the central control under the five-year plan. Yugoslavia has proceeded further than any other Bloc regime by withdrawing subsidies from enterprises that do not make a profit.

Recently there has appeared also a trend toward allowing the small remaining amount of private initiative to develop. A contribution may have come from comparing the figures which show higher production by the small garden plots in relation to the socialized sectors in agriculture. All countries except Yugoslavia and Poland have announced the victory of collectivization. However, incentives are being provided to maintain the private plots. East Germany, Hungary, and Poland even allow craftsmen to operate on their own within certain limits. Recently similar regulations in Czechoslovakia and Bulgaria permit a limited degree of private enterprise in the services area which should make life somewhat easier.

These developments have been accompanied by more contacts with the West, even in the case of regimes which have maintained the tightest control over their own populations. Although tourism is recognized as a major source of foreign exchange, Western visitors are still considered to represent a danger from the ideological point of view. In the opposite direction, only Romania and Bulgaria have an almost complete ban on foreign travel by their own citizens. East Germany, of course, is unique in that no West European country recognizes it. Currency restrictions probably are the reason why it has become more difficult for Hungarians and Czechoslovaks to obtain passports to travel in the West.

Perhaps this threat of Western ideological corruption has also caused the reimposition of stricter controls on cultural life in Eastern Europe. Throughout the Bloc it seemed that in 1962 and 1963 there was a beginning of greater freedom for writers. This could be observed especially in Czechoslovakia, Hungary, Poland, and even Yugoslavia. Since that time journals have been closed, editorial boards changed, and some individuals indicted. Especially pertinent are well-publicized cases of Polish philosophy professor Leszek Kolakowski and Yugoslav university instructor Mihajlo Mihajlov, the latter serving a prison term in 1967–8.

Although a certain degree of relaxation has taken place in Eastern Europe during the past several years, it is strictly limited and subject to sudden reversal. If developments in the Soviet Union may serve as a rough model, one should anticipate a struggle for power within the communist parties of the individual Bloc countries as soon as or even before the current leaders pass from the scene. More of these key individuals may yet be overthrown as Khrushchev and Novotny have already been.

Any thaw in Eastern Europe must be limited because of the common desire on the part of the respective regimes to remain in power and in posts they have never held by the will of the peoples concerned. This, then, is the broad framework within which the communist systems operate: they cannot permit complete freedom of expression, and their choice of policies is limited by the ideological straightjacket of Marxism-Leninism. Perhaps the only hope for Eastern Europe should be sought in the laws governing the development of human society, which in fact represent communism's invincible enemy.

Notes to Chapter 5

1. Eugenio Reale, *Nascità del Cominform* (Rome, 1958), p. 51; see also Günther Nollau, *Die Internationale: Wurzeln und Erscheinungsformen des proletarischen Internationalismus* (Cologne, 1959), pp. 193–6.

2. Radio Free Europe (RFE), *Eastern Europe's Communist Leaders*, 5 vols. (Munich, 1966), provides excellent biographical data on the Politburo members in the countries to which RFE broadcasts.

3. Untersuchungsausschuss Freiheitlicher Juristen, *SZB-Biographie* (Bonn, 1964), p. 360.

4. Biography in *Krasnaya zvezda* (Moscow), March 25, 1965.

5. *Renascità* (Rome), Sep. 5, 1964.

6. *Pravda* (Moscow), Apr. 3, 1964.

7. Radio Budapest, Oct. 18, 1964.

8. *Borba* (Belgrade), Oct. 23, 1964.

9. For names and identifications of participants see *Krasnaya zvezda*, July 5, 1966, and July 6, 1966.

10. The full declaration appeared in Agerpres, *Statement on the Stand of the Rumanian Workers' Party* (Bucharest, 1964). Excerpts have been printed in "A Rumanian Manifesto," *East Europe*, XIII: 6 (June 1964), 25–30.

11. *Predvoj*, Jan. 19, 1961.

12. *Borba*, Apr. 2, 1964.

13. "Resolution on the Slovak National Council by the Central Committee of the Czechoslovak and Slovak Communist Parties," in *Rude pravo*, May 22, 1964.

14. Speech carried live by Radio Zagreb, Dec. 7, 1964.

15. Radio Kossuth, Feb. 11, 1965.

16. Unc Gheorghe and Dan Mihaela, article on "Documents Concerning the Struggle for the Creation of the Romanian Communist Party, 1916–1921," *Lupta de clasa*, No. 6 (June 1966).

17. Note the five articles in *Neues Deutschland*, May 18, 19, and 20, 1965; see also *The New York Times*, Feb. 2, 1967, which discusses the recent agreement to exchange ambassadors between Bonn and Bucharest.

18. The parties are listed in *Krasnaya zvezda*, Apr. 28, 1967.

19. See R. F. Staar, "The Hard Line in Poland," *Current History*, LII: 308 (Apr. 1967), 208–13, 244.

20. A good example of this relationship between the KGB and East European secret police services was the arrest in Czechoslovakia of the American citizen Vladimir Kazan-Komarek, whose non stop Moscow to Paris flight on Oct. 31, 1966, was diverted to Prague for this purpose; after considerable U.S. pressure he was released. *The New York Times*, Feb. 5, 1967.

Discussion

ALEX N. DRAGNICH

Professor Staar has given us an excellent picture of Eastern Europe in transition. Not only has he brought together a great deal of useful and pertinent material but, in addition, has provided real perspective. There are places, of course, where one might wish that his treatment could have been more thorough, but it must be remembered that he has dealt with a very large and complex topic. These observations will be limited mainly to two matters that require further study and elaboration. The first deals with theory, and the second with a country (Yugoslavia) that is more familiar to this commentator than any one of the other states in Eastern Europe.

In discussing the Togliatti memorandum Professor Staar is correct in stressing diversity among the Eastern European states. But if polycentrism is to be the rule in practice, what, then, becomes of Marxian, or Marxist-Leninist, theory? For a good many years all communist leaders stressed the monolithic nature of communist parties and communist systems; this was their pride and joy. Marxist-Leninist theory in the Soviet Union was identical with Marxist-Leninist theory elsewhere. It did not allow for deviations, and so long as there was one communist center, doctrinal deviations could be dealt with successfully and expeditiously. But with many communist centers, how can theory be kept pure?

Ideologically speaking, communist polycentrism is a contradiction in terms. Marxist-Leninist doctrine has not admitted of different ways of looking at things. There was only one correct view; all else involved deviation. If individual countries which regard themselves as having communist systems go their separate ways, will this not lead to important differences in doctrine? Is Marxism to become a generic term like Christianity, with sectarian interpretations being more controlling than the basic theory?

These questions are raised because ideology has been such an important ingredient in all communist movements and parties. If polycentrism in practice brings about ideological diversity, it may be important to consider the impact of the latter upon the domestic communist systems as well as upon their relations with other states.

The second observation concerns Yugoslavia, or more concretely its nationalities problem. This is indeed a complex question, as Professor Staar points out, and he could not have been expected to deal with it within the confines of his paper. Nothing more will be attempted than to point to some aspects of its complexity.

When the Yugoslav communists achieved power, they openly attempted to copy the Soviet model, i.e., national autonomy. This was more apparent than real. Aside from the central government retaining all real power, the territorial division of Yugoslavia followed nationality lines only in part. In this division the Serbs were discriminated against the most. This was not too surprising in view of the fact that charges of hegemony had been leveled against Serbia during the interwar period, particularly by the Croatian nationalists and by communists of all stripes. The territory of Serbia was reduced in several ways: first of all, some areas of southern Serbia were either given to the newly-created republic of Macedonia or incorporated into the autonomous province of Kosovo-Metohija; secondly, the predominantly Serbian region of Vojvodina was also made an autonomous province; thirdly, Bosnia-Herzegovina was made a separate republic, where Serbs predominate but where many Croats and a smaller number of Moslems (some Serbs and some Croats) also reside; fourthly, the Serbs of Montenegro were given their own republic, in part because a large number of important communists came from that area.

Perhaps the most important ramifications of Yugoslav communist nationality policy have been economic. In the immediate postwar years the largest economic investments were made in Croatia and Slovenia. Serbia, because it was the richest in agriculture and raw materials, paid the heaviest price. In turn it received mostly monuments. Croatia, in which over 500,000 Serbs were massacred during World War II by the Croatian *Ustashi,* and Slovenia, which produced the shrewdest communist leaders, forged ahead of Serbia in terms of income per capita. In more recent years the Yugoslav communists have increased their investments in the less developed areas, notably Macedonia, Montenegro, and Bosnia-Herzegovina. The Croatians and Slovenes, in turn, now feel that they are paying a large part of the price for these newer investments.

The Serbs are still contributing substantially to the development of other republics. Serbia has received some investments in more recent years, but the latest figures show that it contributes well over one half (some figures suggest two thirds) to the total national budget while receiving less than one fourth of the national expenditures. Most symbolic of Serbian complaints is the fate of the Belgrade-Bar railroad. Begun in the early 1950's with the aid of United States funds, its construction has been interrupted and it is still not completed. In this, Croatian and Slovenian communists have been particularly influential because the port of Bar would take away much freight traffic now flowing through Croatian and Slovenian ports.

Yugoslavia's efforts to inaugurate some decentralization in the economy have also had their impact. If, for example, a washing-machine, radio, refrigerator, or other type of consumer-goods plant were located in one of the republics, then all of the other republics demanded similar plants. Often this has led to expensive duplication and waste of scarce capital and other resources.

But all of the differences have not stemmed from economic factors.

Indications of nationalism and national pride have been labeled by the controlled press as chauvinism, particularly when this occurred in Serbia. Individuals were even hailed into court for singing the old Serbian anthem, at a time when other national groups were relatively free to sing theirs. More recently some relaxation has taken place, but not without recriminations. In 1964, during the fiftieth anniversary of little Serbia's gallant struggle against the Austro-Hungarian rulers, the film enterprise in Serbia produced the motion picture "March on the Drina." This film resurrected heretofore forbidden Serbian national songs. While the Serbs were pleased, the Croatians, most of whom in 1914 were also under Austro-Hungarian rule, became displeased with this show of Serbian pride.

There are, of course, other aspects to the Yugoslav nationalities problem. The Croats and Slovenes point to Belgrade as the capital, where significant sums of money are spent on governmental and other buildings and where much expensive entertainment of foreign dignitaries takes place. They also point to Ranković, a recently ousted Serb, as the architect of the Yugoslav secret police and therefore the man most responsible for consolidating the communist regime.

These are some of the aspects of a most complex question. If they were free to do so, the noncommunists would probably be the most vociferous in voicing differences. Publicly they are forbidden from doing so. Therefore the airing of differences is done almost exclusively by the communists themselves. This explains—in part, at least—why these differences center on economic questions and rivalries and are couched in Marxian terms. The recent discussion of linguistic differences, for example, is in the nature of "window-dressing," which tends to obscure more fundamental conflicts. In conclusion, it seems obvious that there is room for considerably more research on the Yugoslav nationalities problem and its different ramifications.

6

economic integration of eastern europe

Hermann Gross

The conditions under which the first intergovernmental economic organization of the East European Bloc, the Council for Mutual Economic Assistance (COMECON or CMEA) was established in 1949 were characterized by the world political and economic situation immediately after World War II. The first attempt to rehabilitate Europe's economy came through the Marshall Plan in 1948. This comprehensive American aid project was designed to promote economic reconstruction. In that same year the Organization for European Economic Cooperation (OEEC) was founded in Paris, uniting the European countries which were to receive Marshall Plan aid. The OEEC was entrusted with carrying out the European Reconstruction Program (ERP).

The U.S.S.R. and the other East European countries within the Soviet sphere of influence were also asked to participate in the Marshall Plan but declined or, like Poland, Czechoslovakia, and Yugoslavia, were forced to withdraw their acceptance under pressure by Moscow. According to Lenin's concept, the Soviet Union and other people's democracies were to develop their own ideological and political reconstruction programs.

As a reaction to the Marshall Plan, COMECON was founded at Moscow in January 1949 by the U.S.S.R., Poland, Czechoslovakia, Hungary, Romania, and Bulgaria. The following states joined COMECON later: Albania in 1949 (but since 1961 she has not participated in any meetings and has ceased to pay her dues); the Soviet Occupation Zone, i.e., the so-called "German Democratic Republic" in 1950; and Mongolia in 1962.

Yugoslavia, owing to her conflict with the U.S.S.R. and the Cominform, did not participate in the establishment of COMECON. After her reconciliation with Moscow in 1955, Yugoslavia's cooperation with COMECON countries has varied according to her political relations with the Eastern Bloc generally and with the Soviet Union in particular. The Asian people's democratic republics, North Korea and North Vietnam, as well as Cuba participate in COMECON as observers and maintain close economic relations with its members. China made regular use of her observer status only between 1956 and 1961. Chinese attendance since then has varied but never canceled, although commercial and economic policies of Peking have become quite independent of COMECON in the last several years.

Purpose, Organization, and Development

Integration comprises any movement directed toward uniting various members to form a common superior entity, where a division of labor is practiced. If the combination is to become sound economically, this new entity must produce for all concerned a decisive increase in wealth on a higher level of economic development and show a greater economic potential. According to the statutes of COMECON (Article I), "the purpose of the Council for Mutual Economic Assistance is to promote, by uniting and coordinating the efforts of the member countries of the Council, the planned development of the national economy, the acceleration of economic and technical progress in these countries, the raising of the level of industrialization in the industrially less-developed countries, a steady increase in the productivity of labor and a constant improvement in the welfare of the peoples of the member countries of the Council."[1]

It was not until 1962 that the "Basic Principles of International Socialist Division of Labor"[2] could be adopted; they state that this concept "makes for maximum utilization of the advantages of the world socialist system, for a balanced economy in each country, rational distribution of the productive forces throughout the world socialist system, efficient employment of labor and material resources, and enhancement of the defense potential of the socialist camp."

The achievement of these goals has been hampered by considerable difficulties. Thus integration through COMECON meets with the obstacle of discrepant economic potential and the varying stages of development of the member states. "The COMECON community is characterized by great differences in the economic level of the different states, differences in social labor productivity, the structure of industrial production, and finally living standards."[3] It is worth mentioning that the COMECON secretary-general also considers differences in stages of economic development among the member countries as being mainly responsible for the present difficulties.

All of the states united in COMECON after World War II had pursued with almost equal intensity the policy of forced industrialization as understood by Marx and Lenin, the object being to stimulate the growth of capital or producer-goods industries. Every long-term plan, worked out for periods of five or six years, was cast in precisely the same manner. It attempted to impose the Soviet structure in its totality upon the new Bloc members, repressing any attempt at national adjustment and narrowing the scope for exchange.

Furthermore, an optimum integration within Eastern Europe is made difficult by the fact that each individual national central planning authority tends to favor self-sufficiency, both in the various branches of national production and in the national economy as a whole. Nevertheless integration through COMECON has achieved a relatively high degree of cooperation in certain fields for political and technical reasons. This is also due to the fact that the central planning system can allow for integration on a nonprofitable basis at the expense of national resources and the general standard of living. International economic integration, under which economic development of the underdeveloped countries has become a recognized objective "like national integration, is at bottom a much broader problem than trade or even than economics. It involves problems of social cohesion and practical international solidarity, and the building up of machinery for accomplishing intergovernmental agreements and large-scale political settlements."[4] In addition to the economic factors, political and social aspects are decisive for the success of any integration which depends in the last analysis on the insight and general willingness of the population to cooperate.

Organs of COMECON

The organization functions and powers of the principal agencies within COMECON are regulated by the charter. The Council is the supreme organ which determines basic development, since 1962 in close contact with conferences of the leaders of communist and workers' parties from governments of the member states. The Council is empowered to discuss all matters of economic as well as scientific and technical cooperation and to adopt recommendations and decisions in accordance with the present statute. The Conference of Representatives from countries in the Council has been superseded after 1962 by an Executive Committee, composed of deputy premiers from member states and endowed with decision-making powers at the highest level. As a permanent organ the Executive Committee directs, coordinates, and controls the functions of the Secretariat and of the Standing Commissions. In 1963 a bureau, i.e., a subcommittee of members on the Executive Committee, was created for integrated planning problems. Its task is "to prepare proposals for coordinating the economic development plans of member countries and to give direct assistance in promoting broad cooperation between their respective planning bodies on specific matters."⁵

The Secretariat has its seat in Moscow and is concerned with administrative tasks and preparing the work and planning of the Council. Standing Commissions were established in 1956 as permanent bodies for the purpose of promoting the further development of economic relations among member states. Each country delegates an expert as its representative on the various Standing Commissions. There are at present fifteen sector commissions for the different branches of production and seven general commissions for the coordination of economic policy, such as Economic Questions, Transportation, Foreign Trade, Currency and Finance, Standardization, Statistics, etc. The Standing Commissions were each placed in the member country most interested in the respective branch or sector: the Commission on Agriculture has headquarters in Sofia; Coal Mining in Warsaw, with an office at Katowice; Iron and Steel in Moscow; Nonferrous Metals in Budapest; Chemical Industry in East Berlin; Oil, Gas, and Transportation in Bucharets; Engineering in Prague.

Differences between COMECON and EEC

Because of the origin of COMECON and the economic system in the centrally planned states of Eastern Europe, adopted from the Soviet Union, the ways and means for integration differ from those of the Western market economies in the European Economic Community (EEC) and the European Free Trade Area (EFTA). So far there have been no plans for an Eastern "customs union" nor indeed for any agreements concerning a free commodity exchange or mobility of capital and labor. Such freedoms cannot be reconciled with the principles underlying controlled economies, which are subject to centralized administration.

According to regulations of the General Agreement on Tariffs and Trade (GATT), COMECON cannot be regarded as a customs union, a free trade area, or an internationally recognized preferential-tariff zone. For this reason it cannot act as an international entity so far as commercial policy relations with the outside world are concerned. Having been founded as a loose agreement, based on unratified international law, COMECON was given a definite organizational framework only by the 1959 Charter, which came into force the following year, over a decade after its establishment. "The Charter endowed COMECON with an international form, but the national delegations continued to play a major part in its manpower."⁶ As an institution COMECON is an intergovernmental agency. It always had a U.S.S.R. national as secretary-general and deputy secretaries from each of the East European members.

Furthermore, there is a fundamental difference between the constitutional foundations of COMECON and the EEC. All recommendations and decisions by the COMECON Council as well as by its Executive Committee and the Standing Commissions can only be adopted with the consent of all interested member countries, i.e., by unanimous vote. According to the Charter (Art. IV), decisions can be made only "on organizational and procedural matters," whereas substantive affairs such as "matters of economic, scientific and technical cooperation" are the subject of recommendations.

In contrast to this constitutional arrangement, EEC institutions (Council of Ministers and Commission) make decisions by majority vote and are invested with legislative power directly binding upon individuals and business concerns in the member states. Through a staged replacement of the unanimity principle by majority voting in the supranational bodies of EEC, the individual member veto gradually will become attenuated, and new common solutions to problems can be provided. On the other hand, COMECON member states are able to pursue aims of economic and political nationalism which do not conform with common aims. The effect of recommendations and decisions of the Council do not extend to countries which have declared their lack of interest in the question concerned.

Coordinating the International Division of Labor

Looking at aims and methods, it is possible to distinguish three phases of the interstate division of labor coordination within COMECON. During the first period, from the establishment of the organization in 1949 until 1955–56, "activity of COMECON chiefly consisted of the strengthening and extension of trade links between member states because, at that time, the predominant form of economic cooperation was trade relations."[7] A network of long-term commercial agreements was concluded which took into account the new redirection of East European commodity exchange from West to East, within the framework of the foreign trade monopolies.

The regional shift of traditional Bloc foreign trade during the initial decade after World War II was primarily brought about by so-called "reparation deliveries" to the Soviet Union, the U.S.S.R.-controlled "mixed companies," the one-sided favorable buying and selling conditions within the Bloc,[8] and Russia's position as the intermediary in trade with the most valuable East European products. The recommendations of COMECON in these years were concerned with bilateral deals and two-way balancing. "Basic Indicators for the Application of Operational Reports on Foreign Trade" and a "Uniform Foreign Trade Contract" were agreed upon. These covered conditions of delivery, quality of goods, packing, guarantees, payments, compensation, and arbitration. During this initial phase the first principles of procedure for scientific and technical cooperation were developed. This cooperation consisted primarily of delegating Soviet experts into the decision-making organizations and into the enterprises of the people's democracies and in training skilled personnel of the member countries inside the Soviet Union. This is sure to have promoted decisively the acceptance of economic planning and control by the Soviet model.

Gradually a network of bilateral agencies on a reciprocal basis could be created for the exchange of scientific as well as production experience, linking not only each member with the Soviet Union but every member with all others. During this phase relatively few conferences were convened, and those that did meet had the character of *ad hoc* gatherings. In 1954 the member countries resolved a priority scale for the coordination of individual sectors under which heavy industry received absolute first place. Compared with this, light industries, chemicals, engineering and power production were assigned secondary rankings. In this phase efforts were also made to obtain more consideration for the people's democracies within COMECON through resolutions by creating the Conference of Representatives of member countries in the Council.

During the second phase (1956 to 1962–3) integration activity by COMECON substantially intensified, following the 1956 events in Poland and Hungary and the conclusion of EEC and EFTA treaties. Eastern integration policy is marked by the slogan that the combination of Western states into common markets represents a threat which calls for rapid and far-reaching coordination of economic development within the socialist countries. The chief activity of COMECON has shifted from coordination of foreign trade to the synchronization of economic plans and a rational division of labor in key branches.

The already-mentioned Standing Commissions, created in 1956, have become the most important instruments for planning and specialization in the various sectors of the Bloc economy.[9] They begin to work on integration from the bottom, so to speak; that is, they coordinate specific production sectors on the lowest level and gradually work their way up until common, so-called "perspective plans" can be evolved. The object is to produce a more sensible adjustment and division of labor by means of greater differentiation among the various subsections of production in different branches of industry. In the meantime the chief stress, as far as cooperation is concerned, has shifted from engineering to the chemical industry and the iron, steel, and nonferrous metals industries as well as to the generation of power.

Apart from a gradual reinforcement of integration in this phase, a further institutional strengthening of COMECON was achieved through acceptance of a formal Charter in 1959 and by establishing an Executive Committee. With the exception of the Soviet Union, joint investment projects (whereby foreign capital is directed toward a specific project, and repayment and interest are financed from the eventual output) as well as mixed planning commissions for joint enterprises in which ownership itself was mixed were established within COMECON by Poland and the other members. Multilateral projects, such as the COMECON "Peace" electric power grid and the "Friendship Pipeline" to transport crude oil from the Soviet Union to East European countries, have begun operating. "General Conditions for Deliveries of Goods among Foreign Trade Corporations of the COMECON Members" replaced the separate agreements attached to annual protocols. Agreements also have been made for subassemblies, and product specialization within the framework of COMECON and sector balances for different branches of industries and agricultural products have been discussed. Foreign trade planning has been revised. Now bilateral deals for the next round of long-range economic plans are being drawn up before, instead of after, the production targets are set.

This successful activity of COMECON has been in effect since 1958 through meetings of communist party leaders and the premiers from the various COMECON states. However, further development of COMECON to a higher institutional form of integration on a multilateral basis, as intended by Poland and the U.S.S.R. under Khrushchev, could not be implemented because of the crisis in world communism which had already started during this phase as well as the Sino-Soviet dispute and its repercussions upon the attitude of Romania. This changed situation within the socialist camp already came to light at the fifteenth meeting of the Council in December 1961 as a result of the absence of an Albanian delegation and the Chinese observers. The groupings of less-developed and more-advanced member states became more and more evident as the years passed.

The third phase in the development of COMECON (since 1963) is marked by more or less differing views and expectations concerning further integration within the organization. These differences were produced because of divergent political and economic interests of members, which became more and more manifest as economic development progressed. These interests are better served through bilateral trade agreements and coordination-of-production pacts than by multilateral cooperation. This could be seen, for instance, in Romania's attitude toward the Soviet suggestion in July 1962 on establishment of a common central planning organ, empowered to compile joint plans and to decide organizational matters. The main purpose of such an organ was to involve selection from among the various sector-perspective plans (target year, 1980) of investment projects for a rational allocation of investments which would serve the area as a whole. Such long-term projects were to be jointly financed and become common property.

Khrushchev had justified the Soviet proposal as follows: "At present there exist all possibilities not only to coordinate certain key indexes on the volume of industrial production, but also to elaborate over-all economic proportions by mutually coordinated efforts, taking into account our common interests in order to create a kind of balance which would constitute a collective plan for the economic development of all the countries of COMECON. It was stated quite rightly at the [16th Conference of the Council] that we must begin with the elaboration of unified plans for the principal sectors of production. The organization of COMECON considers it to be its task to elaborate a system which guarantees the transition from bilateral to multilateral planning and regulation of trade and payments among the socialist countries."[10]

Even scholars in the West are of the opinion that integration endeavors by COMECON are doomed to failure as long as the allocation of resources is not directed by a supraregional collective plan. From the economic point of view such an argument is justified, because a rational allocation of investment through a multinational plan in large capital-investment projects would serve the area as a whole more than it would the limited market of one country. But such a procedure presupposes that the member states will transfer certain aspects of national sovereignty to the organs of COMECON, as has been done already in part by the members of the Common Market.

Romania definitely refused to agree with these proposals, both at the seventeenth meeting of the Council and at the sixth session of the Executive Committee in 1962 as well as at the conference of party and government leaders in July 1963. The Romanians "objected to the Soviet proposal according to which the state plans of CMEA [COMECON] members should be coordinated through a central organ. They rejected the establishment of bilateral Soviet-Romanian Governmental Commissions for supervising the implementation of long-term bilateral agreements. The Romanians also opposed the development of joint companies among CMEA members."[11] At the same time, Romania became seriously annoyed over a suggestion published during the spring of 1964 by Professor E. Valev at the University of Moscow concerning the future formation of an entire territorial interstate production complex within the Danubian parts of Romania, Bulgaria, and the Soviet Union. This was considered to be an infringement of Romanian national sovereignty. The Romanians interpreted the Soviet suggestion as a revival of plans for partial federation announced by Stalin in 1948 and of U.S.S.R. annexation goals inherent therein.

The Romanian communist party Central Committee issued a precise statement of that country's objections to all supranational projects in a declaration during April 1964:

Our Party has very clearly expressed its point of view, declaring that, since the essence of the suggested measures lies in shifting some functions of economic management from the competence of the respective state to the attribution of super-state bodies or organs, these measures are not in keeping with the principles which underlie the relations between socialist countries. The idea of a single planning body for CMEA has the most serious economic and political implications. . . . The planned management of the national economy is one of the fundamental, essential and inalienable attributes of the sovereignty of the socialist state—the state plan being the chief means through which the socialist state achieves its political and economic objectives. . . . Transmitting such levers to the competence of super-state or extra-state bodies would turn sovereignty into a notion without any content.[12]

The Soviet-Romanian conflict of interest mainly concerned the industrialization of the latter. "The Soviet leaders, working within the framework of CMEA, wished the Romanians to implement the principle of the socialist division of labor by concentrating on the development of petrochemicals, synthetic fertilizers, food processing, and agriculture. The Romanian leaders, on the other hand, wished to develop a 'heavy' industry, producing iron and steel, complex machinery, and the like. Their principal project was a huge iron and steel combine (ultimate capacity, 4,000,000 tons of steel per annum) to be built at Galati on the lower Danube."[13]

There are more reasons for the relentless attitude of the Romanians toward Soviet proposals. After World War II sixteen mixed companies *(Sovroms)* were operated under Soviet orders and were not dissolved until 1954–5, substantially later than the disappearance of similar organizations on other ex-enemy territories. The burden of reparations on the population and national income had been much heavier than in Hungary or Bulgaria.

Such exploitation had clearly impeded the industrialization of Romania. And at the very time the Soviet leaders were opposing the construction of Galati, they granted the Bulgarians a credit of 650 million rubles (December, 1960) for the expansion of the Kremikovtsi steel works. The Romanians must also have been well aware of the fact that Soviet aid for the years 1945-62 came in their case to $10.00 a head, whereas the corresponding figure for Poland was $33.00, for Hungary $38.00, for Bulgaria $73.00, and for the GDR $78.00. . . . The key element in this confrontation is the fact that the Romanian communist leaders were placing the national interests of Romania, as they understood them, above the interests of international communism, as interpreted by the Russians.[14]

So far the concepts of national sovereignty and patriotism have proved to be stronger than solidarity among communist parties and Marxist ideology.

The attitude of the other COMECON states varies between insistence upon multilateral supranational planning, which conforms with the Soviet view, and a refusal to accept such plans as in the Romanian example. In this respect it is interesting to note the attitude of Czechoslovakia, which recently defended Gomulka's proposal for "differentiated" integration (i.e., subregional instead of comprehensive integration) in COMECON.

It seems that conditions are not yet ripe among the COMECON states for multilateral coordination aimed at directly implementing the international division of labor, i.e., multilateral coordination of the complex national plans. . . . A more realistic approach today is to coordinate selected programs of development instead of coordinating the national economic plans. And it seems that bilateral negotiations will prevail for the time being. As far as economic cooperation goes, especially in the processing industries, the possibilities are much greater for an agreement (either on specialization or on investments) between two or three countries than in COMECON as a whole. Multilateral coordination is most important at present in solving a narrow circle of key problems related to raw material supplies, transport, tariffs, foreign currency, etc. . . . In view of the different levels of interest in the introduction of progressive forms of economic cooperation among the COMECON countries, the principle of national interest will have to be applied to a much greater extent than in the past. This means that important problems of economic cooperation should be discussed among the countries that are specifically interested. . . . This would make it possible to tackle a number of questions that have so far been "kept on ice" because of differences of opinion among the member countries.[15]

A "differentiated" integration of this kind might prove a feasible means for achieving a more far-reaching division of labor in COMECON, to the extent that the other preconditions of this division of labor are also fulfilled.

In speaking of the differences of opinion in COMECON concerning the primacy of a bilateral or a multilateral division of labor among the member states, it is worth mentioning that the Warsaw Pact, which contains at least statutory authority to pursue economic purposes, in Article VIII envisages multilateral economic clauses. One writer contends that the conflict of competencies between the Warsaw Pact and COMECON is out of keeping with the idea of an international division of labor.

Until 1962 a military-political concept of the Eastern Bloc prevailed in theory and practice. The provision in the Warsaw Pact relating to multilateral economic and cultural cooperation was looked upon as the fundamental principle of East European integration, which is concretely expressed in bilateral agreements and the Charter of COMECON. According to this opinion, COMECON comes under the reservation contained in Article VIII of the Warsaw Pact, and the legality of its Charter is merely derived. This manifest hierarchy of East European integration rights was based on the primacy of political and military elements. Since 1962, however, efforts are evidently being made to assign more independent importance to the economic factor. Reformers in the Eastern Bloc are convinced that communist integration may be encouraged by recognizing the principle of economic effectiveness and making COMECON independent in the meaning of international law. After the "Fundamental Principles of International Division of Labor" were recognized on June 17, 1962, the economic function should have been transferred entirely to COMECON. On the other hand, it must not be forgotten that this tendency to free COMECON of political implications is restricted through bilateral alliances. The Soviet-

Polish extension pact of April 8, 1965, in Article II, obliges both contracting parties to practice economic collaboration within the framework of COMECON. Article VIII of the pact between the Soviet Union and the GDR, dated June 12, 1964, envisages the same kind of cooperation.[16]

This development may assume some importance because integration policy has taken a visibly new turn since the fall of Khrushchev. While Khrushchev largely used COMECON in pursuing his integration plans, Brezhnev and Kosygin have attached greater importance to the Warsaw Treaty Organization. It is rumored that there is a more formal link between the Economic Commission of the Warsaw Pact and the Defense Industry Commission of the COMECON.

Results and Prospects of Integration

As already mentioned, the discrepancy in economic potential and stage of development among member countries is characteristic of COMECON's economic structure and configuration. The rich and enormously large economic area of the Soviet Union, which both has the position for and is desirous of aspiring to autarchy, contrasts with the small people's democracies whose resources vary considerably from one country to another. Their economic growth and national product depend precariously on extensive and profitable foreign trade and on importing foreign capital and expertise. During 1962 the Soviet share of industrial production in COMECON totaled 70 per cent; of oil, 93 per cent; of iron ore, 92 per cent; and of steel, 76 per cent. The U.S.S.R. delivers 70 to 80 per cent of COMECON raw-material requirements.

The removal of historical differences in levels of economic development among members, a declared aim of COMECON, has not been achieved. There are still substantial differences in this regard between the individual states. During the past decade all COMECON countries have made remarkable progress in developing their national economies, and some of the formerly agricultural countries were able to reach the higher agricultural-industrial stage. Intensive economic policy, directed toward a forced exploitation and development of existing resources, produced a relatively high rate of growth in industrial production and national income, particularly in the more backward countries. In the more advanced economies like those of the GDR and Czechoslovakia, however, this policy was less successful, and growth rates either became stagnant or declined. In any case, progress achieved in economic development would seem largely due to national efforts. It is very difficult, even impossible, to determine in detail how far progress may be attributable to cooperation through COMECON. The opinion prevails that economic growth was mainly induced by mutual capital aid and the free exchange of experience, patents, and licenses rather than through trade and specialization in the production sector. The less developed states were the ones to benefit most from mutual assistance in the fields of capital aid and the exchange of technical expertise. It is interesting to note the above-mentioned Czech opinion:

> The positive results achieved in COMECON are offset by the fact that coordination to date has remained focused on accounting relations and has only indirectly touched upon production (that is, production plans and investment programs) through bilateral negotiations on the drafts of the individual countries' Five-Year Plans. Essentially this means that the COMECON states still confront each other to a large degree as closed economic units. This in turn impedes implementation of one of the basic goals of the international division of labor—that is, the rational distribution of production forces and the optimum utilization of manpower and raw materials within the framework of COMECON. . . .[17]

Along with progressive economic development, foreign trade among COMECON states has expanded steadily. In countries which depend on foreign trade it has increased at a faster rate than the national income. However, the development of foreign trade by itself cannot serve as a criterion for judging the value of integration. The exchange of commodities among COMECON countries, where state trading with a self-sufficient orientation in production is the rule, is unlike foreign trade in market economies and does not by itself lead to progressive specialization in branches of production with comparative cost advantages (see Tables 7 and 8).

There is still a remarkable discrepancy between the economic potential of East European countries, on the one hand, and their share in international trade, on the other. Although COMECON countries produce about one third of the output of the total industrial world, their share in world trade only amounts to about 10 per cent.[18] These rather feeble international trade relations are primarily concentrated on intra-COMECON trade. Considering the enormous political and economic preponderance of the U.S.S.R., the network of trade in COMECON is concentrated with the Soviet Union. An average of 65 per cent (varying from 60 to 75 per cent) of foreign trade from all East European Bloc countries is with COMECON, of which about 38 per cent (between 35 and 65 per cent) is with the Soviet Union.

The share of the less developed members in COMECON trade has declined. While Czechoslovakia and Hungary increased theirs, the GDR and Poland have remained at the same level. Only 20 per cent of their foreign trade is with the advanced industrial states in the West, which formerly used to be by far the most important trade partners and creditors of all East European countries. From the standpoint of developments in world trade up until after World War II and the structure of the world economic division of labor, this close commercial interlocking relationship among states which (apart from the GDR, Czechoslovakia, and perhaps

TABLE 7

COMECON National Income (A), Industrial Output (B) and Foreign Trade (C) (1961–5)
(percentage changes from preceding year)

	1961			1962			1963			1964			1965		
	A	B	C¹	A	B	C¹	A	B	C¹	A	B	C¹	A	B	C¹
Bulgaria	2.8	11.7	10.6	6.2	11.0	17.2	7.5	10.0	13.5	9.6	11.4	14.8	7.1	13.7	20.1
Czechoslovakia	6.8	9.1	8.8	1.4	6.3	4.8	-2.2	-0.6	8.3	0.6	4.1	10.4	3.7	7.9	8.5
Eastern Germany	3.5ᵃ	5.9	2.7	2.2ᵃ	6.2	5.6	2.9ᵃ	4.3	5.4	4.5ᵃ	6.6	10.9	4.6ᵃ	6.2ᵇ	5.0
Hungary	6.1	11.0	11.4	4.7	8.4	9.4	5.7	7.1	11.7	4.7	8.8	13.3	1.1	4.8	6.7
Poland	8.2	10.4	13.1	2.1	8.6	10.6	6.9	5.5	6.3	6.8	9.3	11.5	7.0	9.0	9.6
Romania	10.0	15.3	18.4	4.0	14.8	9.4	10.0	12.5	10.3	11.4	14.1	11.8	9.6	13.1	9.0
Soviet Union	6.8	9.1	9.4	5.7	9.7	14.0	4.1	8.1	6.4	9.3	7.3	7.6	7.2	8.7	5.0

¹Medium of percentage changes of imports and exports;
ᵃAt current prices; ᵇThe figure for 1965 refers to "commodity production" which is not strictly comparable with gross production because the former excludes work in progress.
SOURCES: United Nations, *Economic Survey of Europe 1963* (Table 26, p. 56); *1964* (Table 2, p. 6); *1965* (Table 1, p. 2; Table 3, p. 6; Table 28, p. 53)

TABLE 8
COMECON Foreign Trade By Region[1] (1955–65)

	1955		1960		1964		1965	
	Billions of U.S. $	Percentage	Billions of U.S. $	Percentage	Billions of U.S. $	Percentage	Billions of U.S. $	Percentage
Imports:								
Total World	7.31	100.0	12.93	100.0	18.10	100.0	19.04	100.0
of which from:								
COMECON-states	4.75	65.0	7.72	59.7	11.96	66.0	12.52	65.8
Western industrialized countries[2]	1.18	16.2	2.52	19.5	3.93	21.7	4.08	21.4
Developing countries	0.41	5.6	1.18	9.1	1.53	8.5	1.84	9.7
Other countries[3]	0.97	13.2	1.51	11.7	0.68	3.8	0.60	3.1
Exports:								
Total World	8.03	100.0	12.98	100.0	18.38	100.0	19.63	100.0
of which to:								
COMECON-states	4.75	59.2	7.72	59.5	11.96	65.0	12.52	63.7
Western industrialized countries[2]	1.51	18.8	2.53	19.5	3.65	19.9	4.04	20.6
Developing countries	0.39	4.8	0.83	6.4	1.89	10.3	2.07	10.5
Other countries	1.38	17.2	1.90	14.6	0.88	4.8	1.0	5.2

[1]COMECON countries, excluding Mongolia
[2]Excluding trade of West Germany with East Germany
[3]Rounded off; including China, Mongolia, North Korea, and North Vietnam
SOURCE: *Neue Zürcher Zeitung*, Nov. 20, 1966; Foreign edition.

the Soviet Union) must be regarded as moderately developed countries, represents an entirely new and artificial phenomenon (see Table 9).

TABLE 9
Intra-COMECON Trade (1950–65)
(percentages of total trade)

Country	1950	1960	1963	1964	1965
Albania	100.0	88.6	35.5	—	—
Bulgaria	83.6	80.3	79.6	75.0	73.6
Czechoslovakia	53.6	64.1	69.5	68.4	68.2
East Germany	72.3	67.7	74.6	72.2	69.5
Hungary	61.4	63.3	66.3	65.7	65.4
Poland	58.4	56.8	61.1	59.6	60.5
Romania	—	66.8	64.5	64.9	60.6
Soviet Union	59.9	54.3	59.1	59.3	58.2

SOURCES: W. Gumpel, "Progress and Limits to COMECON Collaboration," paper read at conference of the Deutsche Gesellschaft für Osteuropakunde in Heidelberg on Oct. 13, 1966, Table 7 (to be published); *Statistischer Jahrbuch der Deutschen Demokratischen Republik 1966* (East Berlin, 1966), and *1967* (Table 14, p. 17*).

This is not an immediate result of COMECON but owes its origin to power and political systems rather than to economic factors. The reasons include a reorientation of foreign trade by East European countries from West to East, as enforced by the Soviet Union since the period 1945–8, the embargo policy of NATO, and differences in economic and trade systems between East and West. The structure of intra-COMECON trade is determined by the stage of development within the group of countries concerned as well as by the internal configuration of economic power. As a center of gravity the Soviet Union stands between the highly developed group which comprises the GDR plus Czechoslovakia and the group of agricultural-industrial states like Hungary, Poland, Romania, and Bulgaria. Accordingly the U.S.S.R. mainly imports capital goods, chemical products, and durable consumer goods from the East European industrial states, while at the same time supplying a decisive proportion of the raw materials, fuel, and food requirements to COMECON states. In 1964 COMECON countries procured 70 per cent of their raw material requirements from the Soviet Union, the share of which in intra-COMECON trade of raw materials and fuel increased from 41 per cent in 1955 to 56 per cent in 1964. The most important trade partner of the Soviet Union is the GDR, from which the former bought 28 per cent of its 1965 imports of investment goods. These amounted to 60 per cent of all U.S.S.R. imports from the GDR. Some 21.3 per cent of the Soviet Union's imports of industrial goods came from Czechoslovakia and 10 per cent from Poland. The West had a share of only 19 per cent in the East's imports of these products, which were, however, of decisive significance.

The GDR and Czechoslovakia are also important suppliers of valuable industrial products to other member countries. But it is remarkable that the less developed COMECON states, like Bulgaria and Romania, as industrialization progresses, are intent and dependent upon exporting industrial products (semifinished and finished goods) to partner countries, but mainly to the Soviet Union. Accordingly the share of the item "machines and equipment" in Romania's total exports to COMECON countries went up from 6.1 per cent in 1955 to 24.5 per cent in 1965, the relevant figures for Bulgaria being 2.8 per cent to 29.9 per cent. In exporting these products, East European countries depend considerably on the COMECON markets. The sale of industrial products in Western markets is seriously hampered by inferior quality and design, the lack of marketing organizations, pricing, and other obstacles arising from centrally planned systems and trade monopolies.

The one-sided development of production and trade in machinery and equipment makes it more difficult in some cases for traditional suppliers like Czechoslovakia to sell the industrial goods concerned and endangers integration with COMECON. As a Yugoslav writer points out:

> Prevailing conditions in the common markets induced every country—including the less developed ones—to increase the proportion of machinery and equipment in their exports, for these brought higher profits not only because of the differences in profitability of investments at home, but also on account of some peculiarities in the COMECON market. Contrary to the practice in world trade, suppliers of equipment and machinery in COMECON do not grant purchasers any credits, they do not offer any advantages for bulk ordering. They ask guaranteed, fixed prices without regard to the quality of the machines or supply and demand. The result of this situation was that the COMECON market was becoming more and more disadvantageous for the buying countries, and that equipment became more expensive, independent of the prices agreed upon. The tendency to restrict imports of these products from the partner countries caused difficulties with the industrially more developed COMECON states, especially as the latter installed part of their capacities exclusively for supplying the COMECON market. The unused surplus capacities in the Czechoslovak machine industry, for instance, was caused to a considerable extent by the reorientation of the Soviet Union, Romania, and Bulgaria, which import "technology" from the West; for these three countries were the main buyers of machines in COMECON.[19]

During the years 1958–65 the growth rate of intra-COMECON trade (110 per cent) only exceeded the over-all growth rate of foreign trade in the area by somewhat less than one fifth (18 per cent). During the same period, however, intra-EEC trade expanded over three times (202 per cent), while total EEC trade volume only doubled (106 per cent). The share of intra-COMECON trade in the total foreign trade of the member states rose from 58 to 65 per cent on the average, although there were considerable differences from one country to another. The U.S.S.R.'s share in intra-COMECON trade has remained relatively stable at about 38 per cent (see Table 10).

TABLE 10

Commodity Structure of Intra-COMECON Trade (1955–65)

Country	Percentage of Machines and Equipment in Total Exports to COMECON Countries		Percentage of Raw Materials and Food in Total Imports from COMECON Countries	
	1955	1965	1955	1965
Bulgaria	2.8	29.9	39.9	45.0
Czechoslovakia	51.1	56.3	75.6	59.3
East Germany	53.6	58.6	82.9	78.6
Hungary	37.6	42.8	74.6	59.2
Poland	17.4	48.7	50.8	48.0
Romania	6.1	24.5	50.5	51.5
Soviet Union	17.3	18.0	47.7	31.6

SOURCE: *Hospodarske noviny* (Prague), Jul. 22, 1966; published in *East Europe*, XV:11 (1966), 28.

In comparing the development of intra-COMECON trade with that among the member states of the EEC, the following must be taken into account: (1) the proportionate share of trade within the area, even in 1958, was twice as large in COMECON (58 per cent) as in the EEC; and (2) the volume of intra-COMECON trade increased from 12 to 25 billion dollars (equivalent) between 1958 and 1965, while the internal foreign trade volume of the EEC increased from 13.6 to 41 billion dollars over the same period.

Although the COMECON countries noticeably have not increased their share in world trade (it is still 10 per cent), these countries buy relatively more from Western countries and sell more to them. Changes in the economic policy of Eastern Europe and the new orientation given to planning objectives have eliminated certain difficulties. The Soviet Union, and particularly the East European states, are more than ever interested in a further intensification of their economic relations with the West and in particular the EEC. Since these countries are aspiring to and forging ahead in transition from an extensive to an intensive phase of economic growth, they are becoming increasingly dependent upon a division of labor even between themselves and the industrial countries of the West. Only the latter are able to supply the COMECON states with the most up-to-date capital goods and techniques and to import COMECON products as income and purchasing power rise.

Specialization and Coordination of Production

The numerous bilateral agreements in the production sector, at least on the basis of their existence, cannot teach us how far the attempts at an intensive division of labor in this field were successful. Specialization particularly has been promoted in a number of branches of the engineering sector, to which a key position is attributed in the development of the entire industry.

Until 1965 proposals for a specialized production of about 1,600 different machine and equipment items had been adopted in 1964 and 1965. A total of 525 recommendations in this area were issued. Almost half the total output of plant and equipment for the chemical industry, 50 per cent for the mineral oil industry, and 85 per cent for rolling mills are now specialized. However, these are exceptions. Up to 1965 it had been possible to specialize only in 5 per cent of the total output of machines. Besides, only 3 per cent of engines produced and 6 to 8 per cent of combine-harvesters and tractors are handled in intra-COMECON trade, although specialization in these branches has been completed already.[20]

The astonishingly small percentage of specialized machines and equipment in intra-COMECON trade shows what little progress has been made in the industrial division of labor (see Table 11). Two Soviet economists, Ladigan and Terekhov, emphasize this fact by the following statement:

> The estimates of various organizations agree that the share of production in COMECON which has undergone specialization is still very small. Besides, the recommendations accepted by the Council fix the division of labor between the countries where it is already practiced in the production of machines, equipment, and other products. In other words, these recommendations refer not so much to restricting the assortment of products in the respective countries but rather to stopping the extension of assortments.[21]

In addition to quantitative aspects, the qualitative factor also gives reason for criticism. Otakar Simunek, deputy premier of Czechoslovakia and a very prominent expert on COMECON, formulates this criticism as follows: "If the results arrived at up to the present in specializing the engineering sector are considered unsatisfactory, the reason will mainly be that specialization has contributed little toward improving the technological standard and the quality of production."[22]

Technical and Scientific Cooperation

More progress seems to have been made in the field of technical and scientific cooperation. The exchange of technical data, licenses, and inventions seems to be suitable for intensifying the division of labor and accelerating the adjustment of economic progress among the socialist countries. In 1960–2 COMECON states reciprocally exchanged 38,000 items of technical and scientific information. It is characteristic, however, that the Soviet Union has passed on more technical data to the less developed countries than it has received from them, while the exchange with Czechoslovakia and GDR nearly always balanced.

TABLE 11

Specialized Engineering Products
(machines and equipment) in Intra-COMECON Trade (1964–5)

Country	Exports (1964)	Imports (1965)
Bulgaria	6.0%	3.4%
Czechoslovakia	4.5%	12.0%
East Germany	20.7%	4.8%
Hungary	8.3%	6.9%
Poland	16.7%	7.7%
Romania	9.8%	2.1%
Soviet Union	10.0%	14.3%

SOURCE: D. Arsić, article in *Medjunarodni problemi,* Institute for International Politics and Economy, Belgrade, XVIII:1 (1966), 21 (estimates from publications in the various COMECON countries).

The regulation according to which technical data must be exchanged free of charge appears to be a retarding factor. According to the U.S.S.R. economist Bogomolov, certain states frequently preferred to wait until the procedures or technology had been developed at great cost by another country and then could be applied by them without having to spend anything on the development.[23] For this reason the industrialized countries of COMECON have suggested that in the future licenses and technical inventions should be exchanged at world-market prices. This, in the meanwhile, has been agreed upon.

Although intraproduct specialization demands common technical standards, the efforts at standardization have not been very fruitful in COMECON. Up to the present no more than about three hundred uniform and binding norms could be agreed upon; most of them involve testing and measurement standards applicable to ferrous metals, textiles, and electrical engineering industries. Standard models for shipbuilding and the production of engines, wagons, and special trucks were also developed. According to a program submitted to all Standing Commissions by the COMECON Institute for Standardization in Moscow, thousands of groups of standards are to be unified between 1966 and 1970.[24]

Cooperation in Transportation

For many years the transport sector had been badly neglected in COMECON. Nevertheless cooperation has achieved remarkable success since 1957–8 in this area where international cooperation suggests itself quite naturally. In this field activity has concentrated upon the improvement and new construction of interstate railroad and water transport, especially on port and frontier-station facilities in border regions between the Soviet Union and the East European countries along the Baltic and Black Seas. Mention should also be made in this connection of the non-COMECON agencies among socialist countries, like the Common Freight Car Pool, the Organization for International Railway Cooperation, the Organization for Cooperation of Socialist Countries in Telecommunications and Mail, and the Common Freight-Chartering Bureau.

Common Projects

A few important agreements among several states have been concluded outside the competence of COMECON. These include "Friendship" pipeline for transporting crude oil from the Soviet Union to the GDR and Poland; the electric power grid "Peace" between the East European countries, and the "Intermetal" organization which is to promote cooperation in the steel industry. "Intermetal" was established by Czechoslovakia, Poland, and Hungary in 1964. In the meantime the Soviet Union, the GDR, and Bulgaria joined the organization. Romania has kept apart. "Intermetal" deals with specialization and coordination of investment plans and the standardization of technical norms in the steel industry.

Cooperation in these fields has been quite successful. Thus the transportation of crude oil via the "Friendship" pipeline increased from 8.4 million tons in 1964 to 13.2 in 1965; the exchange of electrical power via the "Peace" grid jumped from 1.6 billion kwh. in 1960 to 5.6 billion in 1965. The establishment of joint enterprises has been difficult to implement up to the present owing to the rigidity of the state planning system, which hampers entrepreneurial coordination. The few existing enterprises of this kind are operated under the legal form of a joint stock corporation, as for instance the Hungarian-Bulgarian companies "Intransmash" (internal factory transport machinery) and "Agromash" (fruit and vegetable processing machinery) and the Hungarian-Polish company "Haldex" (processing of coal slag). Joint stock corporations may attain greater importance, provided the present reforms in the economic systems leave enterprises wider scope for independent decision-making. This kind of corporation then might also be used in multilateral agreements with Western firms.

Economic Limits on COMECON Integration

Unrelenting centralist economic planning and the foreign trade monopoly as well as authoritarian fixing of prices not only obstruct the organic development of the East European economies but also stand in the way of a rational economic division of labor among COMECON countries and prevent intensive economic relations with Western market economies. Central planning necessarily demands a rigid organization of foreign trade. Operations are entrusted to governmental foreign trade corporations which monopolize all trade involving the various economic sectors. They place an opaque screen between foreign exporters and national users, between local producers and foreign importers.[25] Thus foreign markets are unable to encourage domestic production in a manner fit to intensify an economical division of labor. Here foreign trade resembles a system of isolated barter relations. Besides, the lack of flexibility and of commercial experience on the part of foreign trade monopolies seriously hinders the development of trade.

Therefore, besides the institutional foreign trade organizations, the development of a communications system which might form a link between foreign and domestic markets is equally important in the state-trading countries. It has been pointed out that in the Western world such considerations were often ignored because here such problems lie in the realm of management by Western trading firms. Greater attention has been paid in the East European economies to problems of information-gathering since the late 1950's: "The statistical reporting system was improved: more aggregative statistics, such as trade-price and volume indices were made; and more emphasis was laid on the use of statistics in decision-making. The gathering of information on foreign markets was improved through the placing of greater emphasis on market research and intra-Bloc advertising as well as on alternative channels of communication, such as trade fairs and missions."[26] This also applies to seeking better knowledge of export and import opportunities in Western countries and adjusting the products of East European countries to the conditions of Western markets.

The changes which are taking place in the methods of managing the economy and external trade of COMECON countries and in the management of enterprises in the Eastern Bloc area might be of great importance for the development of intra-COMECON trade as well as for expanding East-West trade. The most recent attempts to reform the economic and foreign trade system tend toward relaxing the governments' foreign trade monopoly. External trade plans have become more indicative, and centralized indexes are increasingly replaced by general directives. Industrial enterprises which produce for foreign markets are to be given some influence, enabling them to acquire rights in their own name and for their own account. A certain amount of decision-making is to be conceded to them, side by side with the official foreign trade corporations and the specialized associations of the various commercial branches, while central control will continue to be exercised over foreign trade operations. In a number of countries, like Hungary, a transformation of the central foreign trade corporations toward the role of liaison organs has taken place. This may lead to closer relations between production on the one hand and foreign trade and markets on the other.

The foreign trade policy of the COMECON countries is still being decisively determined through the system of centrally planned economies. Imports and exports are subject to central controls so as to fit them into the overall macro-economic plan. Planning on the basis of material balances is and will remain for the near future the standard technique within COMECON. But these balances cannot gravitate toward an optimum solution which is attainable in a market mechanism.

The price systems, which do not correctly render cost relations in the various countries, together with the immobility of national labor and capital, prevent Eastern Bloc resources from being utilized rationally. This is so because prices are fixed and manipulated by the state planning authorities, often disregarding the actual cost of investment and production. Accordingly, high or low prices are no real measure of production costs and productivity, and it is impossible to determine which COMECON country would most economically and advantageously produce certain goods. "Decision-makers, employing no criteria independent of their own authority, lack a yardstick to measure national against extranational interest."[27] Therefore the division of labor which is developing within COMECON is technical rather than commercial and does not assure that an optimum result will be achieved. The problem of fixing prices in the foreign trade of COMECON countries has not yet been solved despite many efforts and, in recent years it has become the subject of heated discussions.

Intra-COMECON trade was and is carried on approximately at capitalistic world market prices. These "corrected world market prices" were more or less stabilized over a lengthy period, like 1953 to 1957 to 1965. In the future these prices are to represent guidelines only, whereas the actual price is to be determined through bilateral negotiations.

Since 1966 prices in intra-COMECON trade have been based on average world market levels of 1960 to 1964, which brought about a reduction in the cost of raw materials. The Soviet Union, being the largest supplier of raw materials, fuel, and semifinished goods in the Bloc (see Table 12), argues that this will cause it considerable economic damage. For this reason the U.S.S.R. demands that other COMECON states give it investment aid for opening up and utilizing Soviet raw material resources. Thus Czechoslovakia already has agreed to provide credits equivalent to 500 million dollars between 1966 and 1974 for the extraction of oil resources from minerals in western Siberia.[28]

Since the foreign trade relations of all COMECON countries still remain subordinated to strict planning, bilateral commercial treaties prescribing rigidly fixed quotas as well as barter-trade agreements are practically the only ones applicable to centralized economic plans in the various Eastern states. All digressions of foreign trade turnover from planned imports and foreign exchange-earning exports have a very disturbing effect on economic development in the countries concerned. COMECON states may, however, only negotiate binding quotas for goods to be taken or delivered among members of their own group or those developing countries having planned economies. Besides, the trade structure and coordination of production plans (imperfect though they are) necessarily give rise to a built-in preference favoring producers from COMECON countries.

TABLE 12

Intra-COMECON Trade in Raw Materials and Fuel (1955–64)

Country	1955	1964
Bulgaria	5%	2%
Hungary	4%	4%
East Germany	10%	11%
Poland	15%	9%
Romania	11%	7%
Czechoslovakia	13%	10%
Soviet Union	41%	56%

SOURCES: *Mirovaya ekonomika i mezhdunarodnye otnosheniya,* No. 5 (Moscow 1966), p. 18; quoted in *Godisnjak 1965* (Belgrade, 1966), 147. N. B.: Percentages apparently rounded off.

These are some of the main technical and economic reasons why, despite limited opportunities for mutual complementation and substitution, foreign trade relations among COMECON states are so disproportionately and unilaterally close and why trade with the developing countries is being stimulated so forcefully.

Trade among COMECON countries is seriously hampered by the non-transferability of currencies and the absence of a multilateral payments system. All foreign trade business of members is conducted strictly on a bilateral basis. Such a clearing system will naturally break down as soon as commodity movements between two states predominate in one direction. These difficulties were to have been removed at least in part by the agreements on multilateral clearing between COMECON members concluded in 1957 and, after its failure, again in 1963 with the "International Bank for Economic Cooperation" in Moscow. Each COMECON member has the right to draw from the bank. But swing credits are permissible during the calendar year only, and each party is obliged to plan for equilibrium in its balance of payments with the rest, including settlement of any debit balance at the bank. An important innovation came with meetings of parties in multilateral negotiations to implement supplementary exchanges. The new clearing system offers the possibility of trilateral deals, to be settled on the basis of transferable rubles.

Genuine transferability within the group would add to an easing of rigidity in bilateralism. But as long as the ruble is transferable among COMECON members only and not made convertible to outsiders, the new clearing system will involve rather restricted practical importance. It has been pointed out that free convertibility in COMECON cannot be attained from the payments side only. "At the same time, this will call for corresponding multilateral agreements on the interstate exchange of commodities . . . to the extent the system hitherto practiced will be retained, the economic function of multilateral clearing will be restricted to making it easier for the planning administrations of the participating countries to balance inevitable deviations between the planned payment items and the actually realized receipts."[29] Experience will show how far COMECON succeeds in utilizing the new clearing institution for integration purposes in more than a mere technical respect.

Outlook for COMECON

The many disappointments over the unsatisfactory technical rather than economic division of labor in COMECON forces all its members, particularly those East European people's democracies which depend on foreign trade, to seek immediate and close cooperation with the nonsocialist countries of the world. These include first and foremost the Western industrial states, both in the field of foreign trade as well as in research and technology. This is revealed by the above-mentioned attempts at cooperation with the West on the basis of enterprise-to-enterprise relations and by the efforts to gain admittance to the GATT and to participate in the Kennedy Round.[30] For the state-trading countries of COMECON would not automatically share in the benefits of the further reduction of tariffs and the removal of other barriers against international trade agreed upon in the Kennedy Round and thus would become even more isolated.

Therefore Poland and Czechoslovakia have made quantitative counteroffers in exchange for automatic extension of concessions negotiated within the framework of the Kennedy Round and the granting of additional concessions. This involves either an obligation to buy minimum quantities of certain products from GATT members or else an obligation to increase, by a minimum annual percentage, imports from these same countries collectively. This seems like an interesting idea, although it does not involve an adequate concession, as both countries are forced to increase their imports from the West under any circumstances.

The development of COMECON to date and dispute in recent years regarding the future and reform of the economic systems have shown with startling clarity how unsuited are the criteria now being used by the centrally planned states of Eastern Europe for rational allocation of resources as well as economic division of labor among member states and the rest of the world. Without a thorough reform of their economic systems, which would have to proceed far beyond the present experiments at reforms, COMECON states will continue to remain outside of the international economic community and GATT, the members of which account for about 85 per cent of all world trade.

The Yugoslav example shows that such an operation can be carried out by a socialist country without abandoning its fundamental economic and political structure. In the "socialist camp" Yugoslavia alone has managed to participate in international trade under conditions comparable with those governing commerce among market economies. Yugoslavia has recently (1966) become a full and active member of GATT, after having fundamentally modified its economic, financial, and commercial structure in a manner necessary for it to enter directly into the international economic community.

Since its expulsion in 1948 from the COMINFORM, the organization of communist parties, Yugoslavia has discarded the central planning system and assumed some of the aspects of a free-market economy by granting more autonomy to individual, self-managed enterprises. Foreign commerce regulations have been liberalized; and foreign trade is being gradually decentralized, not only by the establishment of autonomous commercial enterprises, but also by allowing factories to deal directly with foreign customers as well as suppliers. For the rest, Yugoslavia has developed and expanded her economy mainly in close economic, financial, technological, and scientific cooperation with the West, not least with aid from the United States (amounting to $2.5 billion). About 70 per cent of Yugoslavia's foreign trade is with the West and only about 30 per cent with COMECON countries. Yugoslavia acquired nearly all of its foreign licenses, designed to develop and improve production, from the West. In connection with the acquisition of these licenses a remarkable amount of cooperation and coproduction has developed between Yugoslavia and individual Western private firms.

In recent years, however, Yugoslavia has also tightened its relations with COMECON countries, especially the Soviet Union. After reconciliation with Moscow, Belgrade entered COMECON as an observer in 1956 and kept this status until 1958, when it ceased to receive invitations to meetings. The COMECON session of December 1961 offered Yugoslavia full membership but refused to continue its observer status. In September 1964 Yugoslavia finally became associated with COMECON by being admitted to several Standing Commissions.[31] Belgrade takes an active

part in this work. During the years 1964 and 1965, critical for the economy, Yugoslavia's trade with COMECON expanded, mainly as a result of
the special willingness of Moscow to take Yugoslav products which could
not be readily sold on the world market. The share of COMECON in
Yugoslavia's foreign trade, which used to be about 25 per cent until 1963,
increased to 31 per cent and then to 35 per cent during ensuing years.
However, as the economic situation has become consolidated following the
reforms of 1965, the share of the West (particularly in Yugoslav exports)
has again risen noticeably in 1966.

Among all countries of the socialist camp Yugoslavia is most closely
connected economically with the West. Of those states outside the Soviet
Bloc, Yugoslavia has the most intensive relations with COMECON, both
economically and politically speaking. It will be interesting to watch how
Yugoslav links with COMECON will continue to develop after the country
has approached the type of foreign trade system in Western market economies by means of her economic reforms. Yugoslavia might provide some
stimulating ideas for COMECON states in adjusting their economic systems to the requirements of an economically more efficient division of
labor, both among themselves and with the rest of the world.

Notes to Chapter 6

1. See text in Michael Kaser, *COMECON: Integration Problems of the Planned Economies* (London, 1965), pp. 181ff.

2. *Ibid.*, pp. 190ff.

3. J. Smilek, article on "Coordination of the Economic Development of COMECON Member States" in *Hospodarske noviny* (Prague), Jul. 22, 1966; tr. in *East Europe* (Aug. 1966), p. 27.

4. Gunnar Myrdal, *An International Economy* (London, 1956), pp. 339ff.

5. Kaser, *op. cit.*, p. 98.

6. *Ibid.*, p. 168.

7. *Ibid.*, p. 46.

8. It is estimated that the Soviet Union in this manner, by 1956, had been able to make a profit equivalent to at least one billion dollars per year from trade with the people's democracies; see Zbigniew K. Brzezinski, *The Soviet Bloc: Unity and Conflict* (Cambridge, Mass., 1960), p. 283. In this context it is worth mentioning the Polish agreement with the Soviet Union to cancel debts of $525 million in consideration for Polish deliveries of 65 million tons of coal from Silesia during 1946–53 at a price covering only the transport costs, a Soviet gain at world coal prices of around $14.00 per ton, or some $900 million. See Kaser, *op. cit.*, p. 70, and *Trybuna ludu* (Dec. 20–30, 1956).

9. See Hermann Gross, "The Common Market and Eastern Bloc Integration," in *Berlin and the Future of Eastern Europe,* ed. David S. Collier and Kurt Glaser (Chicago, 1963), pp. 193ff.

10. N. S. Khrushchev, "Nasushchnye voprosy razvitiya mirovoi sotsialisticheskoi sistemy," *Kommunist,* No. 12 (Moscow, 1962), pp. 3ff.

11. R. V. Burks, "The Rumanian National Deviation—an Accounting," in *Eastern Europe in Transition,* ed. Kurt London (Baltimore, 1966), p. 97.

12. Quoted from Kaser, *op. cit.,* pp. 94 and 28.

13. Burks, *op. cit.,* p. 97.

14. *Ibid.,* pp. 99–100.

15. J. Smilek, *op. cit.;* as quoted in *East Europe* (Aug. 1966), pp. 27ff.

16. Alexander Uschakow, in an article on "The Council for Mutual Economic Assistance," in *Das Parlament* (Jan. 12, 1966), pp. 41ff.

17. Smilek, *op. cit.*

18. See *Neue Zürcher Zeitung,* Nov. 20, 1966.

19. *Godisnjak 1965,* Institute of International Politics and Economy (Belgrade, 1965), pp. 147ff.

20. See V. P. Sergeyev, *Ekonomicheskie svyazi stran sotsializma* (Moscow, 1965), p. 31.

21. See *Mirovaya ekonomika i mezhdunarodnye otnosheniya* (Moscow), No. 11 (1965), p. 16.

22. T. Engel, in an article on "Specialization and Collaboration in COMECON," in *Osteuropäische Rundschau,* XII: 11 (1966), 17.

23. See *Voprosy ekonomiki,* No. 2 (1966); also *Kommunist,* No. 18 (1966).

24. See G. Elsholz's article on "Limited Integration in COMECON," *Wirtschaftsdienst,* XLV (1965), 302; and Kaser, op. cit., pp. 134ff.

25. Concerning the problems of coordinating and harmonizing decision-making between production and foreign trade enterprises, see F. L. Pryor, *The Communist Foreign Trade System* (London, 1963), esp. pp. 60–3.

26. *Ibid.,* p. 96; see also *Der Volkswirt,* No. 19 (May 13, 1966), Frankfurt/M.; Supplement.

27. Kaser, *op. cit.,* p. 26.

28. See T. Engel, *op. cit.,* p. 21.

29. E. Klinkmüller, article on "Multilateral Clearing Among COMECON States," in *Osteuropa-Wirtschaft,* XI: 3 (1966), 224 and 226.

30. See *Economic, Industrial, Scientific and Technical Cooperation Between Countries of Eastern and Western Europe,* from a round table organized by the European League for Economic Cooperation in Brussels, Feb. 24–25, 1967 (Publication No. 41, pp. 120). With the exception of Czechoslovakia, the Eastern Bloc countries are not full members of GATT. Even Czechoslovakia, though a full member since 1947, does not enjoy the liberalization measures undertaken within GATT or the benefits of the most-favored-nation clause because, as a state-trading country, it is largely unable to fulfill its obligations under these headings. Poland has been an associate member of GATT since 1960 and can participate in the work of the contracting parties by special arrangement; it became a full member of GATT in 1967. Romania and Hungary

as observers have attended meetings of the GATT Council and its Committee on Trade and Development since 1957 and 1966, respectively. Bulgaria was admitted to GATT in 1967 as an observer. None has participated in the Kennedy Round talks, in contrast with Czechoslovakia and Poland.

31. These include: Foreign Trade, Currency and Finance Questions, Ferrous Metals, Nonferrous Metals, Chemical Industry, Radio Engineering and Electronics Industry, and Coordination of Scientific and Technical Research.

Discussion
STANLEY J. ZYZNIEWSKI

Professor Gross's comprehensive treatment of COMECON (evolution, practices, failures, and obstacles) leaves this discussant in an unenviable position because of the judicious balance and highly informative analysis he has presented.

From the standpoint of perspectives or interpretation, however, two points may be worthy of consideration. Both deal with stereotypes shared by many Western observers. First of all, most accounts about the establishment and development of COMECON accept at face value the objective officially stated in January 1949: that Stalin initially held real economic integration of Eastern Europe as a primary goal. It would perhaps be more realistic to recognize that during Stalin's last years COMECON remained moribund. Originally it was just another instrument used to reinforce Soviet domination and exploitation, while priming the pump for rapid industrialization. Stalin's assertion that a "parallel world market" would arise represented merely a euphemism for Soviet hegemony. To assign economic integration as a motive for establishment of COMECON in 1949 is to perpetuate a myth.

What Stalin saw in COMECON and how his successors began to view it are quite different matters. Coincidental with Stalin's death, the primitive or "heroic" stage of rapid industrialization in Eastern Europe ended. Growing strains upon Soviet sources of raw materials for this wasteful approach toward individual East European autarchy were increasingly felt. Only then did this magnitude of waste prompt the new leadership to pay more than lip service to slogans of integration. In this respect the institutional maturity of COMECON actually began in 1959. Hence it would be misleading from a historical perspective to ascribe present ills and defects in COMECON to the supposedly conscious approach selected by Stalin. Ironically the Stalinist legacy, which in recent centrifugal tendencies has presented obstacles to integration (perpetuation of differences in economic development among Bloc members as a result of the previously under-taken drive for autarchy) really stems from the absence of any real inten-tion to integrate at the time Stalin dictated the formation of COMECON.

Another often-repeated statement about the nature of East European economic relations during the past twenty-two years holds that the sharp reversal in direction of East European trade immediately after World War II was artificially induced by political considerations. This, of course, is true; but maintaining this emphasis today is either irrelevant to contem-porary problems or misleading because of the inference that a return to prewar patterns seems highly desirable. Of relevance is that the direction of trade and economic relations forged at that time exists today, and what-ever the shortcomings from the standpoint of integration, a considerable intra-Bloc dependence has matured. It reaches such a magnitude that if a Bloc member were hypothetically capable of drastically altering its politi-cal orientation, it could not do so rapidly in economic relations without extreme trauma, if not chaos. This high degree of economic intermeshing among members of COMECON is a reality seldom voiced at length when discussions broach a pan-European *détente,* German reunification, etc. Such political considerations cannot ignore the economic challenges involved in the fact that grids and networks of energy and raw materials tie these states closely together.

Professor Gross has aptly underscored the nature of the shortcomings and obstacles which prevented real integration within COMECON. These roughly fall into categories of technical and nontechnical impediments. On the one hand, autarchic traditions, nationalism, and ideological diver-gences exist. On the other hand, the absence of methods for comparing members and the attendant obstacles to an international division of labor remain at the core of this failure. Except for some inferences, Professor Gross did not dwell on immediate and long-range prospects of COMECON. Yet one may engage in some speculation on the basis of recent developments.

Professor Gross observed a recent trend among East European com-mentators in discussing "differentiated integration," i.e., a more modest approach toward subregional integration as an alternative to the heretofore unsuccessful campaign at multilateral coordination. This phenomenon, when related to other considerations, would seem to indicate that the late 1960's and early 1970's will be a critical juncture and that the role and nature of COMECON may be radically altered at this time.

Highly significant also are the current domestic reforms within each economy, varying in scope and tempo. Common to most is the attempt to accept some elements of supply and demand as interaction upon produc-tion, in order to expedite efficiency and economy. Although these efforts have been modest, they could induce results whose ramifications would be mirrored in intra-Bloc relations from the standpoint of comparability, transferability, capital mobility, etc. While one should not assume that anachronistic practices of bilateralism, centralized planning, and material-balances in accounting would quickly disappear, it is not unreasonable to surmise that within the context of "differentiated integration" some significant transformations might arise.

The probability of such changes in the pattern of Bloc relations may be further induced by other existing pressures, especially regarding those related to the technological needs of Bloc members. The more advanced northern tier of COMECON is already experiencing difficulty in exporting machine products in the face of competition and the growing capabilities of other members and, concurrently, from the failure to keep pace with technological advances. This latter development has been partly reflected in recent United Nations data showing that Eastern Europe has reversed its previous attitude by importing more from the West than it exports.

Finally, there are those Western commentators who insist that the greater progress non-COMECON economic groupings achieve toward integration, the greater impetus will be given COMECON members to accept realistic accomodations with these groupings, willingly or unwillingly.

In the time allotted for discussion the foregoing can serve only as broad markers pointing to the critical juncture facing COMECON. These strongly indicate that major changes will be forthcoming, both in the focus and role of COMECON. Developments of late appear to have impressed upon Soviet leadership that the economic interests of socialist states are not alike and may even be contradictory, that the concept of multilateral coordination via COMECON as the supranational planning authority is highly premature. In the face of reforms now being instituted in the various economies of Bloc members, with the more sensible and less grandiose advocacy of "differentiated integration" among East European commentators, COMECON probably will function less as an active agency directing wholesale integration and more as a clearing house as well as an advisory body fostering smaller, more patient steps toward sectoral coordination among Bloc members.

the warsaw pact and western security

WILLIAM R. KINTNER

The Warsaw Treaty Organization (WTO) was created by the Soviet Union on May 14, 1955, five days after Germany had joined NATO. The charter members of the Warsaw Pact included the Soviet Union, Albania, Bulgaria, Czechoslovakia, East Germany, Hungary, Poland, and Romania. Albania, while still a *pro forma* member of the Warsaw Pact, no longer participates in its activities.[1] In 1955 the Soviet threat to Western Europe was considered acute, and the Soviet Bloc regarded as a monolith. In the thirteen years that have passed much appears to have changed.

The 1955–62 period was dotted with a series of crisis-laden events, reaching their zenith during the October 1962 Cuban crisis. Some of these were the Suez invasion of 1956, which occurred almost simultaneously with the Hungarian revolt; the launching of sputnik in 1957; the Berlin ultimatum of 1958, relieved briefly by the spirit of Camp David; the U-2 incident, and the renewed Berlin crisis during 1961–62.

The end of the Cuban missile confrontation marked the beginning of a general de-escalation in the Cold War. Despite the growing magnitude of the conflict in Vietnam, a number of major developments have contributed to an East-West *détente* atmosphere, including the Test Ban Treaty, the Hot Line agreement, the "Wheat Deal," and the anti-proliferation treaty. Most noteworthy, within the present context, has been a growing disunity and diversity within the communist world, stimulated by the Sino-Soviet dispute, which has become increasingly aggravated since 1962. Taking advantage of the feuding communist giants, the East European satellites of the Soviet Union have gained for themselves a measure of independence.

In 1961 Albania defected from the Soviet Bloc altogether and sought the protection of the communist Chinese. Romania came into the spotlight when it openly disagreed with the U.S.S.R. and other Bloc members on the question of its own national economic development. Formerly among the most subservient of Soviet satellites, Romania surprised the world by seeking better trade and cultural relations with the West, applying for membership in GATT, and apparently taking independent initiative in mediating the Sino-Soviet dispute. Cracks appeared in the monolithic Soviet Bloc.

Communism itself seems to have been adjusting to the economic realities of the sixties. "Libermanism" has gained gradually in the Soviet Union and Eastern Europe, spearheading a great debate over the advantages and disadvantages of economic centralism.

The entry of mainland China into world affairs as a competitor of, rather than a collaborator with, the Soviet Union has shifted Western attention to Peking. Relatively little has been heard during the past four years of Soviet efforts to bring communists to power in the underdeveloped countries. Such communist attempts as have occurred in Southeast Asia and Africa of late have been credited to China rather than to the U.S.S.R. The Soviet hand in the recurrent Middle East disturbances has been more conspicuous.

Many leaders in the West have come to feel that the U.S.S.R. threat to Western security has significantly diminished. The aftermath of the confrontation over Cuba led to the conclusion that reason, not missiles, was the only feasible means of settling international disputes. A "new Cold War" had developed, this one between Moscow and Peking. The view became widespread that increasing fear of the Chinese would persuade the Soviet Union to draw to the side of the West, even to the extent of becoming a part of Europe.

As this perception has gained ever increasing currency, the Western capitals have begun to re-evaluate their security requirements. Significant changes have transpired both within NATO and the military establishments of the individual Western powers. It is beyond the scope of this introductory section to dwell in detail on these changes in the West vis-à-vis the Soviet Bloc and the security of NATO. The purpose here has been to sketch in a perspective for an analysis of the Warsaw Pact which is to follow.

Potential Value of WTO for the Soviet Union

It is difficult to say with certainty what reasons were uppermost in the minds of Kremlin leaders for establishing the Warsaw Pact. The treaty was signed five days after West Germany had joined NATO, and the stated purpose was to counter the possibility of German aggression.[2] Equally significant, however, may be the fact that one day after the creation of WTO, the Austrian State Treaty was signed, requiring the U.S.S.R. to withdraw its forces from Austria and thereby depriving the Soviets of any valid legal grounds for maintaining the Red Army in Romania and Hungary. The Warsaw Pact placed on a new legal footing the continued occupation of these two countries, as well as of Poland and East Germany.[3]

Thus in 1956 the Warsaw Pact provided the legal framework for the Soviet military intervention in Hungary to suppress the revolt.[4] The U.S.S.R. troops used to crush the Hungarian revolt were moved across Romania. Although the Soviet Army has been withdrawn from Romania since that time, it continues to occupy East Germany, and U.S.S.R. forces are deployed in Poland as well as in Hungary. News reports on May 10, 1968, of Soviet troop movements in Poland, close to the border of "revisionist" Czechoslovakia indicated that the specter of Soviet military intervention still haunts dissident satellites. Soviet soldiers are seldom seen in public; they are confined to the compounds of their units, an isolation probably made necessary by the hostility prevailing in the countries in which they are stationed.

Undoubtedly, then, one of the benefits derived by the U.S.S.R. from the Warsaw Pact involves a power base in several of the Bloc countries, providing a means of direct military influence. Since the extent of control actually exercised by the Soviet Union over the Warsaw Pact countries has been a subject of increasing doubt in the West, perhaps some further elaboration would be appropriate here.

A study of changing trends in East Central Europe made at the Foreign Policy Research Institute sought to determine the influence of the Soviet Union on the transformations that have occurred throughout the Bloc (by comparing the countries of East Central Europe, according to the same indicators of change, with one another, and with the Soviet Union). Deviations from the Soviet patterns of rule and policy occurred during the 1950's as well as during the 1960's. They point to stresses within the communist system and to strains on Soviet-satellite relations. Stresses and strains are to be expected, even in command-type societies and relationships. But as of the present time, it would be premature to conclude that the Soviet Bloc has been rent asunder.

Specifically, with regard to the control exercised by the U.S.S.R. over the member states in the Warsaw Pact, a look at the structural organization of the command at the highest level may be illuminating. The commander-in-chief of the Warsaw Pact, as well as his chief of staff, has invariably been a Soviet marshal or general. The defense ministers of the member countries, except the Soviet Union, are deputy commanders-in-chief, that is, deputies to the Soviet commander. Thus into the chain of command of the Warsaw Pact the East European member nations are tied at the ministerial level. The Soviet commander-in-chief of Warsaw Pact forces, of course, is responsible first and foremost to the U.S.S.R. government. Admittedly not all of the forces of member countries (with the exception of East German troops) are integrated with the Warsaw Treaty Organization.[5] But the fact that the defense ministers are deputies of the Soviet commander-in-chief indicates that there is great flexibility of commitment, in accordance with U.S.S.R. desires.

To what extent the Soviet government has a voice in the selection and appointment of individuals to the post of defense minister in WTO countries is not known. But it is known that by and large the satellite general officers have undergone military training in the Soviet Union. It is also interesting to note that throughout the postwar period most satellite defense ministers have had careers as political commissars; their assignment to the military forces may be taken as a measure designed to assure the reliability of the armed forces to the satellites, as well as to the Soviet Union.[6]

The locus of power for each communist-controlled country in East Central Europe is the Party politburo. At this level, there are direct lines of communication between Moscow and the capitals of the WTO member countries. Face-to-face consultation between the chieftains of the Soviet Union and Bloc countries occurs on an average of three times or more a year, if not in the political consultative committee of the Warsaw Pact, then in a different context. Between 1960 and 1965 meetings among Politburo members of the Soviet and East European communist parties, with the exception of the Romanians, increased in frequency.

Another means of U.S.S.R. control over WTO member states is the network of Soviet security police, supervising and working with the secret services of the satellite countries. This, of course, is not properly a part of the Warsaw Pact, but it deserves mention here because of its known role in the suppression of the conspiracy to oust the Bulgarian communist government during April 1965, in which several high officers of the Bulgarian army were implicated.[7]

Occasionally the West benefits from the disclosures made by high-level defectors from the secret police of satellite countries. I personally had the opportunity of communicating with one such defector, who categorically asserted that the secret service represented the main control mechanism of the Soviet Union in East Central Europe.

Prior to the formation of the Warsaw Pact the Soviet Union relied primarily on other means for its control of satellite military establishments. One of these included infiltration of U.S.S.R. personnel into the satellite armed forces. Although many of these Soviet nationals have since been withdrawn, those who remain can be assumed to act still as agents of Moscow control over satellite military establishments. For example, in 1956 about thirty senior Soviet officers were sent back to the U.S.S.R. by Gomulka. As late as 1965, however, at least two hundred others, slightly less senior, held positions of importance in the Polish armed forces. Presently two U.S.S.R. officers remain in high positions: Major General Jozef Urbanowicz, the Third Deputy Minister and Chief of the Main Political Administration for the Armed Forces; and Vice Admiral Zdzislaw Studzinski, the Navy CO.[8]

The WTO and NATO: Force Levels and Strategic Doctrine

An understanding of the role which the Warsaw Pact plays in Soviet calculations may be gained by comparing force levels, resources, and military doctrine of WTO with those of NATO. The Soviet Union has some 20 divisions deployed in East Germany, in addition to 2 divisions in Poland and 4 in Hungary. Poland, East Germany, and Czechoslovakia combined muster about 34 divisions. These three countries comprise the so-called "Northern Tier" of the Warsaw Pact area, geographically located in the front line of any East-West confrontation.

These combined 60 Soviet-satellite divisions appear to be at about two thirds of the personnel strength for comparable NATO divisions.[9] Their fire power, however, is believed by some Western military commanders to be superior to their NATO counterparts. In case of hostilities Warsaw Pact forces would, of course, be reinforced by Soviet troops now deployed in the European part of the U.S.S.R. There is a wide range of estimates as to the actual number of combat-ready Soviet divisions close to its western borders, and it is difficult to predict how quickly these divisions could be deployed westward.[10] Undoubtedly one obstacle to speedy troop movements is the limited number of broad-gauge interchange points for railroad traffic between the Soviet Union and Eastern Europe.[11] The U.S.S.R. does have an airlift capacity, and judging by geographical distance alone, it seems fair to conclude that Soviet troop deployments into Eastern Europe would pose a much smaller problem than comparable American troop deployments across the Atlantic.

More important is modernization of Warsaw Pact divisions, which has occurred during the 1960's. Prior to 1960 the satellite divisions in the Warsaw Pact were equipped essentially for defensive warfare. There is evidence, however, that during the past decade the U.S.S.R. has provided the countries of East Central Europe with advanced radar systems, surface-to-air missiles, and high-speed fighter interceptors. Frontline attack aircraft have been supplied to Poland, Czechoslovakia, and East Germany. These three Northern Tier countries also received short-range tactical rockets which can be armed with nuclear warheads, high explosives, or chemical charges. Nuclear warheads apparently remain under firm Soviet control.[12]

Training of Warsaw Pact forces has been intensified during the 1960's. It is only in this decade that Warsaw Pact forces have been deployed in joint training exercises. The standardization of equipment, organization, and military techniques for WTO forces, including the Soviet Army, is now virtually complete.[13]

Long of critical importance has been the reliability and morale of the armed forces in the East Central European area as allies of the U.S.S.R., particularly in a war of an offensive nature. It is difficult to estimate the troop morale of any army in advance of combat. It should be borne in mind that most of the officers in the East German, Czechoslovak, and Polish armies are themselves members of their respective communist parties and that the troops of these nations receive constant indoctrination concerning the alleged revanchist schemes of West Germany. The personal security of the men serving in these armed forces would be endangered in the event of a Warsaw Pact defeat. It is to be expected that the Soviets, if deciding to undertake military operations of an offensive nature, would attempt to pin the label of aggressor on the NATO countries. It is also likely that the U.S.S.R. would, as it did in World War II, incorporate the troops of other WTO states into Soviet army groups in order to insure the loyalty of the former.[14] For these reasons one must rate the Polish, East German, and Czechoslovak forces as generally reliable during the initial phase of a conflict in East Central Europe. Their reliability would remain high if Soviet troops demonstrated battle superiority. Only in the event of serious military reversals is it likely that the Warsaw Pact forces, especially those of the Northern Tier, would cease to be dependable.

It is significant that the U.S.S.R. has increasingly embraced a nuclear strategy at the very period during which the United States has sought to persuade its European allies to adopt an almost completely conventional posture. Soviet divisions, trained to fight under tactical nuclear conditions, are prepared to execute a rapid thrust westward following a nuclear exchange. U.S.S.R. military writings increasingly emphasize preparation for a nuclear conflict. Typical is an article by a Soviet colonel which appeared in a monthly army magazine. Illustrative of the content are the following remarks:

> The role and significance of *surprise* has grown still more. For example, the surprise use of the nuclear weapon permits the bringing of very great losses to the enemy, it depresses his troops morally, sharply lowering their combat ability, it quickly changes the relationship of forces and upsets command, thus creating conditions for completing his defeat. An indispensable condition for achieving surprise is secrecy. However, achieving it is not easy. For this, along with arrangements for counter-measures of the

enemy's reconnaissance, it is necessary to perfect constantly the means and methods of camouflage and misinformation, to raise the tactical training of officers, their knowledge of the enemy, his tactics, and strong and weak sides. . . . The most important part of the principle is the *constant struggle with means of nuclear attack* with all available means and methods.[15]

According to a commentary which originally appeared in France, the U.S.S.R. excludes the possibility that in a war against an adversary equipped with nuclear weapons it would hold its own nuclear striking force in reserve.

The Soviet armored and mechanized divisions are not organized and equipped to fight a battle of attrition, but rather to conduct a rapid exploitation after a massive strike of nuclear and chemical weapons. Thus, more and more the Soviet Army assumes the shape of a force conceived for a single form of war, an organization that has been tailored to meet the requirements of a new doctrine.

The evidence seems to justify the belief that the development the Soviet ground forces have undergone in structure, objectives, organization, and equipment has reached a point from which reverse is difficult. A reconversion of these forces designed to adapt them to another form of war is conceivable only in the improbable event of revolutionary scientific discoveries which call for a complete revision of the fundamentals of the modern military art. In any case, it took more than a decade for the current Soviet doctrine to mature, and such a reconversion would undoubtedly be a long and difficult undertaking.[16]

Warsaw Pact field exercises have increasingly emphasized the Soviet doctrine that nuclear weapons will almost automatically be employed in the event of a conflict in Europe. This is exemplified by the scenario for "October Storm," the joint maneuver held October 16–22, 1965, in which NATO forces invade the (East) German Democratic Republic, are stopped by WTO troops in conventional combat, and decide in desperation to use atomic warheads. Inevitably, of course, NATO forces are defeated by WTO defenders with more powerful and more numerous nuclear strikes.[17]

NATO in Contrast to WTO

At the beginning of 1963 U. S. Secretary of Defense Robert S. McNamara declared the following: "In central Europe NATO has more men and more combat troops on the ground than does the Bloc. It has more men on the ground in West Germany than the Bloc does in East Germany. It has more and better tactical aircraft, and these planes carry on the average twice the payload twice as far as their Soviet counterparts. These facts are hard to reconcile with the familiar picture of the Russian army as incomparably massive."[18] Mr. McNamara's assessment of NATO superiority over the Warsaw Pact has not gained universal acceptance. It reflects the conclusions reached by some of the civilian systems analysts within the

Pentagon. I myself have had several conversations with leading American military commanders in Western Europe, none of whom subscribes to the view that NATO enjoys over-all superiority. Some of these officers, in fact, have questioned the feasibility of NATO's forward strategy; for they believe that at the line of contact WTO forces have a preponderance of manpower, tanks, and artillery and are maintained in a higher state of combat readiness.

A numerical count of divisions allegedly available to NATO may look impressive on paper. Far more important, however, is a realistic assessment of the effectiveness of Western divisions relative to those of the Warsaw Pact. NATO has been variously estimated to have anywhere from twenty to thirty divisions in Western Europe for defense against possible Soviet aggression.[19] The six American divisions stationed in Europe, together with the British Army of the Rhine, have by far the highest combat rating among all NATO forces. Of late, however, the United States has withdrawn from the Seventh Army several thousand of its most highly trained military personnel for service in Vietnam, apart from the 35,000 troops and 100 aircraft withdrawn in 1968. In all probability, therefore, the combat readiness of American forces in Europe is lower today than two years ago. How long the 50,000 British troops will remain on the Rhine is an open question, since London has declared that it cannot afford to pay for them and West Germany has been unwilling to take up this burden, although Bonn did offset some of the costs by agreeing to purchase British military equipment.

West Germany's 12 divisions comprise by far the largest ground commitment to NATO. The effectiveness of these troops, however, is highly problematical in view of the acute shortage of noncommissioned officers and officers of field and staff rank. The West German army might not be fully effective in combat against Warsaw Pact forces. The difficulties with Star fighters, West Germany's air power contribution to NATO, are well known. Primarily because of a lack of sufficiently trained technicians, required for the maintenance of such sophisticated aircraft, the mortality rate of Star fighters reached such high proportions that the Bonn government decided to keep these aircraft temporarily grounded.

France continues to maintain two divisions in West Germany. But de Gaulle's recent pronouncements regarding the French relationship to NATO make it problematical whether these forces would be available to the West in the event of an emergency. Whereas the commitment of national troops to NATO is automatic for all member countries in case of an attack, de Gaulle has recently declared that France insists on retaining the option to decide whether it wants to be engaged in a conflict.

Unlike the Warsaw Pact, NATO has achieved very little standardization of military hardware and has not yet pooled its logistical support facilities.[20] All of the nuclear weapons that could be used in tactical operations against communist forces in Europe are tightly controlled by the United States.

Control over and potential employment of nuclear warheads in NATO strategy has been a most controversial issue within the Western alliance. As long as the strategic superiority of the United States was unquestioned by both East and West, the problem could be managed. However, since the Soviet Union acquired a sizable nuclear stockpile and an array of aircraft as well as missile delivery systems, the European members of NATO have sought to play a greater role in strategic planning.

The United States seems to have placed its wish to prevent the spread of nuclear weapons above its desire to maintain the cohesion of NATO. During 1966 Washington advanced the idea of the so-called "Mc-Namara Select Committee" to develop contingency plans for the possible employment of nuclear weapons. This committee has been created; its permanent representatives include the United States, Britain, West Germany, and Italy. Whether or not such a committee will satisfy the demands of nonnuclear NATO members for a voice in the deployment of nuclear weapons—and thus contribute to the cohesion of the alliance— remains to be seen.

Ironically this question already has been superseded by a more fundamental one, namely, whether or not the allies (including the United States) perceive the need to maintain a militarily strong and cohesive alliance. To ask this question is merely to acknowledge the tremendous changes that have occurred over the years in the world outlook of Europe, changes which have affected the assumptions of Western statesmen regarding their security interests. West European NATO countries no longer appear to be very much concerned about the possibility of Soviet aggression. Rather they seem to have allowed the focus of their attention to shift toward further improvement of East-West relations, especially with the states in East Central Europe. Even West Germany, whose relations with the communist world have long been restricted by the Hallstein Doctrine, has embarked on a new policy of forming closer ties with East European countries. Speaking before the Bundestag on December 13, 1966, Chancellor Kurt Otto Kiesinger, declared: "For centuries Germany was the bridge between East and West Europe. We would like to fulfill this role in the present age and are therefore interested in improving relations in all fields of economic, cultural, and political life with our eastern neighbors who have the same desire, and even opening diplomatic relations with them whenever the circumstances allow it."[21] In January 1967 Romania and West Germany established diplomatic relations.

With this change in attitude, the need for NATO in its present form and strength has come into question. If this trend in attitudes continues, it is even doubtful that NATO will continue to exist after 1969 as a militarily effective alliance.

It might be useful at this point to bring into focus the contrast between NATO and WTO by summarizing concisely the points outlined above.

(1) Throughout the sixties the Soviet Union has continuously bolstered the effectiveness of WTO through better coordination, improved weapons systems, and joint maneuvers; concurrently, France has withdrawn its troop commitments from NATO, many NATO members have reduced their forces, and the United States has transferred many of its most highly skilled technicians from Europe to Vietnam.

(2) The Soviet Union has placed increasingly heavy emphasis on nuclear strategy and tactics in any possible engagement against NATO; the United States, preoccupied with nonproliferation, seeks to persuade its NATO allies to bolster their conventional forces.

(3) Because of the command-type relationship within the Warsaw Pact, the Soviet Union appears to have little difficulty in organizing WTO forces with a nuclear deployment potential; the United States, on the other hand, has been unwilling or unable to satisfy the demands of its allies for an effective voice in nuclear decision-making.

(4) The cohesion of the Warsaw Pact has been maintained by virtue of the control exercised by the Soviet Union over East Central Europe and is reinforced by a continuous propaganda barrage about the alleged aggressive intentions of the German Federal Republic; NATO, on the other hand, becomes progressively disunited.

Bucharest Declaration of 1966

The foregoing analysis on the effectiveness of the Warsaw Pact brings up the question of Soviet objectives in Europe. Throughout the existence of WTO, proposals have issued from behind the Iron Curtain concerning arrangements for peace and security in Europe. At its second conference in January 1956 the political consultative committee of WTO called for the establishment of a nonaggression pact with NATO and/or an all-European collective security treaty. This proposal was repeated in 1958 and 1960. During 1963 the U.S.S.R. on at least four separate occasions called for a nonaggression pact between NATO and WTO states.[22] Over the past few years the Soviet Union has repeatedly asserted in official statements that if NATO were disbanded, there would be no more need for the Warsaw Pact alliance. The most eloquent and comprehensive expression to date of this trend of thought can be found in the "Declaration on Peace and Security in Europe," issued in the summer of 1966 by the WTO political consultative committee at its meeting in Bucharest.

This declaration probably would not have attracted as much attention as it did in the West, had it not been for the dissident attitude shown by

Romania during the prelude to the WTO conference. This in turn led to the widespread belief that trouble had developed in the Warsaw Pact. Indeed, Romania during the three years prior to this event had been publicly at odds with the U.S.S.R. and other Bloc countries over questions of Soviet control in general and economic cooperation in particular. The publicity given in the West to Romania's disagreements with other Bloc governments has been responsible more than anything else for the exaggerated notion that the Soviet Union no longer controls the countries of East Central Europe.

From a detailed examination of Romania's role in the events leading up to the Bucharest Conference, it may be possible to derive some implications pertinent to the security of the West. On June 5, 1965, *The New York Times* printed a report based on "the highest authority" that more than six months earlier Romania had quietly begun limiting its role in WTO and that this move was proving to be a source of continuing friction with the Soviet Union. Thus Romania alone among WTO members in 1964 reduced compulsory military service from 24 to 16 months, and apparently had done so without prior consultation with the U.S.S.R. Furthermore, the Romanian army was cut from 240,000 to 200,000 men.

In September 1965 Soviet Party chief Leonid Brezhnev, in a speech to his Central Committee, emphasized the need to strengthen the Warsaw Pact. By the spring of 1966 some Western observers noted that the WTO political consultative committee, which according to the treaty, should meet twice a year, had not been convened since its meeting in January 1965 at Warsaw. Certain analysts saw in this a possible indication of difficulty in the Soviet bloc. As a matter of fact, there was nothing unusual in this time lapse between meetings, for the political consultative committee has never been convened twice during the same year.

Nevertheless something was brewing behind the scenes, and it erupted into public view on May 11, 1966. On that day a speech was published by Romania's Party leader, Nicolae Ceauşescu, which he had delivered on the occasion of the Romanian Communist Party's forty-fifth anniversary. This speech attacked the infallibility of Soviet leaders. Under the guise of being honest with history, Ceauşescu dwelt on the mistakes made in the formulation of Comintern policy as well as some of the errors in the development of Romania's communist party during the Stalinist period. His speech implied that what is good for the Soviet Union may not always have been appropriate for countries in East Central Europe. Ceauşescu stated explicitly that it is impossible to direct from one center the many communist parties of the world which operate under diverse national conditions.

The part of this speech which received most attention in the West concerned Ceauşescu's view of military blocs. According to some Western analysts, it equated the Warsaw Pact with other alliances. Calling for recognition of the sovereignty of nations, noninterference in internal affairs, and similar international rights of which the satellites are still deprived, Ceauşescu stated: "The military blocs and the existence of military bases and of . . . troops on the territory of other states is one of the barriers in the path of collaboration among the peoples. The existence of blocs as well as the sending of troops to other countries is an anachronism incompatible with the independence and national sovereignty of the peoples and of normal relations among states."

Two days after Ceauşescu had made this speech, Brezhnev arrived in Bucharest on a secret visit. Whether this trip occurred as a result of the speech or whether in making this speech the Romanian leader had meant to convey his views to Moscow in anticipation of Brezhnev's arrival, is not known with certainty. The intimate details on the discussion between the two party chieftains have not been revealed either. But after Brezhnev's departure, Romanian official statements set forth the dissolution of NATO as an essential precondition for abolition of the Warsaw Pact.[23]

On May 16, 1966, *The New York Times* printed information about a position paper, allegedly submitted by the Romanian government to the U.S.S.R. and other members of the Warsaw Pact, prior to Brezhnev's visit. It reportedly made the following points: (1) there was no longer any justification for stationing Soviet troops on foreign soil; (2) if a Warsaw Pact member state required Soviet troops on its soil, that country should negotiate bilaterally with Moscow and arrive at a status of forces agreement; (3) Bucharest was no longer willing to contribute to the cost of stationing U.S.S.R. troops in Eastern Europe; (4) governments allied in the Warsaw Treaty Organization should have a voice in determining the use of Soviet nuclear weapons; (5) the supreme command of WTO should be rotated.

Since this position paper reputedly circulated before Brezhnev arrived in Bucharest, it may have been one of the reasons for his visit. During the two days following the appearance in *The New York Times* of the article on this matter the Romanian Foreign Office would not commit itself to either a confirmation or a denial of the report. Then on May 18, 1966, a Romanian official who preferred to remain anonymous emphatically denied that Bucharest had voiced any opposition to the stationing of Soviet troops on East European territory. The same official asserted the belief of his government that "the Warsaw Pact is sufficiently strong to meet present needs."[24]

In June 1966 the foreign ministers of member states in the Warsaw Treaty Organization met at Moscow. Here again the Romanians distinguished themselves by allegedly opposing agreement on Bloc policy. The Warsaw Pact foreign ministers conference lasted four times longer than had been originally scheduled.[25] According to the Yugoslav press, Romanian Foreign Minister Cornel Manescu demurred at supporting any open condemnation of West Germany as the chief trouble-maker in Europe, which reportedly made up part of the proposed text for a joint WTO declaration. During the conference debate the Romanians allegedly were accused of treason to the communist cause by delegations from East Germany and Hungary. At this point Manescu is said to have threatened to walk out of the meeting. He was persuaded to stay only after a promise by the Soviet delegation that he would be granted an interview with Leonid Brezhenv.

On June 12, 1966, *Pravda* published Ceaușescu's "Speech of Independence" given the previous month. Rarely does *Pravda* publish material offensive to the U.S.S.R. The publication of this supposedly hostile speech may have involved the preparation for de Gaulle's arrival in Moscow eight days later. Aware of the difficulties confronting NATO, the Soviets apparently wanted France to take other steps which would further separate that country from its Western allies. To allow Romania, the "France of the Balkans," a forum from which to speak so freely against the Soviet Union might encourage de Gaulle to act more openly against the United States.

Thus the stage had been set for the evening of July 4, 1966, during which top-level delegations from all Warsaw Pact countries except Albania met as the WTO political consultative committee in Bucharest. After the first hour, taken up with the usual introductory amenities, five delegations reportedly departed from the conference hall. This left the Soviets and the Romanians locked in a closed session. As far as is known, such an occurrence had no precedent in the history of the Soviet Bloc. Western observers have interpreted it as another sign of friction between Romania and the U.S.S.R., something to be resolved bilaterally. But the real explanation for this event might be traced to an interview between Brezhnev and Manescu in Moscow a month before; the Romanians and the Soviets merely may have been implementing a prior agreement to consult only on a bilateral basis.

For the following morning, July 5, with almost no debate or plenary consultation, party and government leaders active in the Warsaw Pact signed a lengthy and comprehensive declaration on the peace and security of Europe. The declaration, which in all probability had been under consideration at the foreign ministers conference at Moscow in June, viciously attacked Bonn. It was so vitriolic in its denunciations of alleged West German militarism and revanchism as to lead some observers to suspect that the Romanians traded their objections on this point for a Soviet agreement to shelve existing plans for "strengthening" the Warsaw Pact.[26]

The underlying burden for the Bucharest Declaration is that the continued existence of NATO is not only unnecessary but even counterproductive to the goal that West Europeans really desire: a general settlement in Europe. NATO, according to this document, is a tool of West German militarists who, in alleged collusion with the United States, want to re-embark on the course of conquest which they followed twenty-five years previously. Hence NATO by implication is an obstacle to peace and security in Europe. The Declaration ends with a number of specific conditions prerequisite to a general European settlement. Among these are the following: (1) Germany must never have access to nuclear weapons; (2) Germany's borders, as they exist at present, must be recognized as irrevocable with all claims to territory beyond these borders emphatically rejected; (3) all foreign bases must be liquidated, which means that NATO and WTO should be simultaneously dissolved; (4) flights by foreign aircraft carrying nuclear weapons over the territory of European states must be prohibited, and bases in Europe for nuclear-armed submarines of foreign powers must be abolished; (5) economic relations among all European states should be pursued without discrimination; (6) East and West Germany should reduce the numerical strength of their armed forces by mutual agreement.

According to the tone of this Declaration, the peace and security of Europe is a matter of concern solely to European states (including the U.S.S.R.) but not to the United States. In the document it is suggested that an all-European conference be convened in order to determine the conduct of relations between European countries. While no power would be excluded if it wished to attend, the document makes clear that the proposed conference should be specifically limited to Europeans.

If the issue primarily in dispute between the Soviet Union and Romania were that of strengthening the Warsaw Pact, the latter country's view may be assumed to have prevailed at the Bucharest Conference. The final communiqué does not mention any agreement regarding this point. On the other hand, the Bucharest Declaration, which was signed by Romania (whether willingly, under duress, or in exchange for a Soviet concession to forego strengthening the Warsaw Treaty Organization is open to debate), may in the long run outweigh any benefits the Soviets had hoped to attain through a strengthening of the WTO. In the meantime, Romania maintained its formal "active status" in WTO by engaging in a seven-day joint military exercise with Soviet and Bulgarian troops in August 1967.

There is little reason to doubt the sincerity of Soviet intentions to dismantle the Warsaw Pact in exchange for the dissolution of NATO, if all other essential conditions contained in the Bucharest Declaration are met. Should the United States withdraw its divisions from Europe, the U.S.S.R. would remain the preponderant military power on the continent. Moscow would no longer need the Warsaw Pact for security or policy objectives. By virtue of its military preponderance the influence of the Soviet Union in Western Europe would increase; its control over the communist states of East Central Europe unquestionably would be assured. Therefore, by achieving a consensus within the Warsaw Pact on the Bucharest Declaration concerning peace and security in Europe, the Kremlin may have paved the way to its lasting control over East Central Europe and perhaps even laid the groundwork for an extension of its power in the future from the Urals to the Atlantic.

Summary Conclusions

The foregoing assessments can be summarized in the following points:

(1) The Soviet Union attaches far more importance to the crucial central front than to the southern approaches to the U.S.S.R. via Bulgaria, Romania, and Hungary.

(2) There has been no corroborated disagreement on essentials of either security or foreign policy matters between the Soviet Union and the Northern Tier countries of Poland, Czechoslovakia, and the GDR, Czechoslovakia's domestic liberalism notwithstanding.

(3) The paradoxical aspect of Romania's behavior appears to be that it does not conform to the historical pattern of servility toward its powerful Russian neighbor. At the same time, for reasons of geographic propinquity the Soviet capacity to exercise pressure upon Romania is extremely great. It is not inconceivable that the Soviet leaders, fully aware of the resources at their disposal, may see certain political advantages in Romania's "independent" stand.

(4) Romania's so-called "independent policy" on matters of security and foreign affairs may reflect either real divergences with Moscow or joint tactical maneuvering designed to lessen Western perceptions of the Soviet threat. In any event, Romania's support of the Bucharest Declaration has helped to foster divisive trends within NATO.

(5) It is noteworthy that the Bucharest call for a pan-European conference (without the United States) to work out European security arrangements was echoed in the joint statement issued by de Gaulle and Kosygin following the latter's visit to France in December 1966.

(6) Unless the U.S.S.R. makes some unmistakably hostile move toward Western Europe, the cohesive forces within NATO are likely to become weakened still further.

(7) Whether or not the United States continues to maintain sizable forces in Western Europe, its influence on NATO policy can be expected to decline as Western perceptions of the Soviet military threat to Europe diminish.

(8) In the meantime the Soviet Union can exploit the real or latent fear of West Germany to preserve the operational cohesion of the Northern Tier group within the Warsaw Pact.

(9) A weaker NATO is likely to confront an increasingly powerful

Soviet Union, whose decisions will continue to dominate the Warsaw Pact states, particularly those of the Northern Tier.

(10) If, through a combination of antiballistic missile defense and increased production of ICBM's the U.S.S.R. should achieve strategic parity vis-à-vis the United States, the greater cohesion of the core area in the Eastern Bloc would become a significant Soviet advantage in any future East-West confrontation. Soviet determination to achieve strategic parity, if not superiority, has become increasingly evident, and since 1967 the U. S. Defense Department has admitted that the production and deployment of offensive missiles in the U.S.S.R. has been underestimated. It appears likely that the Soviet Union will be able to match the strategic power of the United States by 1970.

(11) In summation, the rate of diminution of cohesion within the NATO alliance is considerably greater than the decentralization trends thus far observable within the Warsaw Pact. To what extent the Soviet Union will want, and be able, to capitalize on these divergent patterns in order to launch a new diplomatic-military offensive against the West cannot be predicted at this time.

Notes to Chapter 7

1. U. S. Congress, Senate Committee on Government Operations, 89th Cong., 2d Sess., *The Warsaw Pact: Its Role in Soviet Bloc Affairs* (Washington, D.C.: 1966), p. 2.

2. *Ibid.,* p. 24.

3. Hanson W. Baldwin, "Communists 'NATO' Tightens Soviet Grip," *The New York Times,* May 5, 1955, p. 5.

4. For a report on the U. S. Department of State's view on this matter, see "West Seeks Way," *The New York Times,* October 27, 1956.

5. Richard F. Staar, "Military Threat to NATO: The Warsaw Pact," appearing in U. S. Congress, House of Representatives, Committee on Foreign Affairs, 89th Cong., 2d Sess., *The Crisis in NATO* (Washington, D.C.: 1966), pp. 287–90.

6. *Ibid.*

7. *Ibid.,* pp. 296–7.

8. *Ibid.;* Major Edgar O'Ballance, "Poland: Keystone or Weakest Link?" *Military Review* (April 1963), p. 58.

9. The Institute for Strategic Studies, *The Military Balance 1966–1967* (London, 1966), pp. 4, 21; "The East German Army," *Military Review* (August 1962); Dan Partner, "Bulgaria Called NATO Thorn," *Denver Post,* October 7, 1965; R. T. Rockingham Gill, "The New East-West Military Balance," *East Europe* (April 1964) pp. 3–6; "The East-West Military Balance," *East Europe* (July 1964), pp. 22–4.

10. *Ibid.*

11. Staar, *op. cit.,* p. 290.

12. Raymond L. Garthoff, "The Military Establishment," *East Europe* XV:9 (Sep. 1965), 2–16.

13. *Ibid.*

14. *Ibid.,* pp. 15–16.

15. Colonel N. Miroshmichenko, article on "Changes in the Content and Nature of Modern Combat," *Voennyi vestnik* (October 1966); tr. Harriet Scott (italics added).

16. "L'Adaptation des forces terestres Sovietiques á une guerre nucléaire," *Revue de Défense Nationale,* XXX (Feb. 1966), 223.

17. Staar, *op. cit.,* pp. 288–9.

18. Quoted by Rockingham Gill, *op. cit.,* p. 4.

19. The Institute for Strategic Studies, *op. cit.,* pp. 13–14; Rockingham Gill, *op. cit.*

20. Maj. Gen. A. L. Ratcliffe, "The Strategic Balance," *Military Review* (Apr. 1963), p. 38.

21. Quoted in *The New York Times,* Dec. 14, 1966, p. 18.

22. Sydney Gruson, "Action in Prague," *The New York Times,* Jan. 29, 1956, p. 1; William J. Jorden, "Soviet Army Plans to Quit Rumania in Near Future," *The New York Times,* May 27, 1958, p. 1; "Text of Statement of the Warsaw Pact Members Issued After Moscow Meeting," *The New York Times,* Feb. 5, 1960, p. 4; "Soviet Proffers a Pact With NATO at Geneva Talks," *The New York Times,* Apr. 10, 1963, p. 1; "Reds Renew Bid at Geneva for Nonaggression Accord," *The New York Times,* May 18, 1963, p. 2; Seymour Topping, "Kennedy and Khrushchev Call Pact a Step to Peace But Not a War Preventive," *The New York Times,* Jul. 27, 1963, p. 1.

23. Max Frankel, "Hint of Warsaw Pact Split Is Seen in Rumanian Stand," *The New York Times,* May 14, 1966; Henry Kamm, "Rumanians Avoid Denial of Hint of Rift with Soviet on Arms Pact," *The New York Times,* May 15, 1966; "Bucharest Denies It Seeks Pact's End," *The New York Times,* May 19, 1966.

24. Henry Kamm, "Rumanian Rebuff to Soviet on Cost of Pact Reported," *The New York Times,* May 17, 1966.

25. Raymond H. Anderson, "Warsaw Pact Sets Bucharest Meeting for Early in July," *The New York Times,* June 17, 1966.

26. Joseph Lelyveld, "Red Bloc Assails U. S. Over Vietnam," *The New York Times,* Jul. 7, 1966; Joseph Lelyveld, "Red Bloc Invites West Europeans to Security Talk," *The New York Times,* Jul. 9, 1966.

Discussion

RICHARD F. STAAR

This commentary on Dr. Kintner's outstanding analysis will involve several points which he did not explore fully, in view of the limited scope of his presentation. First of all, it is certainly unwarranted at this time to say that the Warsaw Treaty Organization (WTO) has become weakened due to the alleged behavior of Romania. Much of the information reported by *The New York Times* may conceivably have been inspired in anticipation of President de Gaulle's visit to Moscow during December 1966 for purposes of weakening NATO even further. On the other hand, WTO has been strengthened in the meantime through the series of twenty-year bilateral friendship and mutual (military) assistance treaties signed during the first two weeks of March 1967 by Czechoslovakia and Poland, East Germany and Poland, and Czechoslovakia and East Germany in that order. These are the first pacts of a military nature concluded by the Pankow regime outside of the multilateral WTO framework. (Note the East German commentary by the communist party secretary for security and armed forces, Erich Honecker, as cited in *Krasnaya zvezda,* March 21, 1967.) They all state that West Berlin represents an "autonomous political unit," confirm *de facto* borders, and declare that reunification of Germany must proceed through negotiations between the two "sovereign" German states.

The three countries involved with this new sub-bloc are called the "Northern Tier" by Dr. Kintner and indeed may comprise the most effective and perhaps even the most reliable allies of the Soviet Union in any possible conflict with the West in Central Europe. Poland, Czechoslovakia, and East Germany also have been identified in Soviet military publications as the "first strategic echelon" of WTO. The most recent Institute for Strategic Studies issue of *Military Balance 1967–68* (London) confirms Dr. Kintner's figures from this same source during the previous year of approximately 60 divisions in these three countries, including 35 that are indigenous and another 26 from the U.S.S.R. These latter units are stationed in the Soviet Zone of Occupation in East Germany (20), Hungary (4), and Poland (2). Optimistic reports concerning a transfer of between 3 and 5 U.S.S.R. divisions from Central Europe to the Far East, allegedly to the Sino-Soviet border, have not been substantiated to date. Dr. Kintner's point about the capability for rapid deployment of more troops from European Russia to the Northern Tier area via transport aircraft has been demonstrated repeatedly in annual maneuvers, most recently during September 1966 under the code name "Operation Vltava." These field exercises involved troops from the U.S.S.R., East Germany, Czechoslovakia, and—for the first time in a quadripartite situation—from Hungary. Large-scale airborne landings of Soviet units from European Russia, as reserves, took place simultaneously with attacks upon the "aggressor" by WTO armored and motorized rifle divisions. The scenario began with an attempt by NATO to force the Vltava River in Czechoslovakia. Tactical nuclear weapons came into play very quickly. That current military doctrine of the U.S.S.R. and its allies has shifted radically from a defensive to an offensive nature can be seen from a statement by Admiral Waldemar Werner, first deputy defense minister of East Germany, published in Russian for Soviet military readers in *Kommunist vooruzhënnykh sil,* No. 4 (1966), p. 78, as follows: "The mission of the [East German] National People's Army is to be prepared for and capable of . . . *destroying the aggressor on his own territory by decisive, offensive action* together with the brotherly socialist armies and to assist progressive [i.e., communist] forces in West Germany to liquidate its imperialist system." In case of hot war the matter of reliability arises. Dr. Kintner points out the difficulty of assessing this factor prior to actual combat.

The relatively high percentage of officers who are members of the local communist parties, ranging between 70 per cent in Poland and 96 per cent in East Germany, may or may not represent a criterion for measuring such reliability. However, Dr. Kintner's point about the constant political indoctrination and the fostering of hatred toward West Germany as the alleged heir to the Nazis is significant. It remains especially important in Poland, where over six million citizens, or one fifth of the total population, lost their lives during World War II as a result of Nazi extermination policies. If this assessment holds true for the Poles and perhaps also for the Czechs, it is not necessarily applicable to other WTO members where the hostility toward Germans is absent. The one country on which Dr. Kintner spends most of his analysis in this connection is Romania. It is obvious that Bucharest cannot possibly go beyond certain limits in its "maverick" behavior. Although the agreement on January 31, 1967, to establish diplomatic relations with West Germany appears contrary to Bloc policy, and despite the fact that only a deputy foreign minister represented Romania at the WTO conference the following month in Warsaw, the highest ranking delegation from Bucharest visited Moscow during March 17–18, 1967 (communist party general-secretary Nicolae Ceauşescu; Premier Ion Georghe Maurer; and communist party secretary and deputy leader Paul Niculescu-Mizil). They discussed "Soviet-Romanian relations and the problem of European security," according to the communiqué, with their U.S.S.R. counterparts. As far as is known, Romania contributed its share of the war material and other supplies totaling the equivalent of one billion U.S. dollars during 1967 for North Vietnam, as agreed upon by the U.S.S.R. and its allies during a conference in late October 1966 at Moscow. The meeting of European communist leaders during April 24–6, 1967, at

Karlovy Vary in Czechoslovakia might have provided some clues to the attitude of Bucharest. It did not send any representatives. However, during 1966 trade between Romania and West Germany trailed that between Bonn and Warsaw, Prague, and even Belgrade (with which diplomatic relations had been severed during 1957–68 because of the Hallstein Doctrine). Bucharest only led Sofia and Budapest, both much smaller in area and population on a country-wide basis, in commercial exchange with Bonn (*Das Parlament,* Feb. 8, 1967).

Part IV

Mainland China

8

the elusive élan: problems of political control in communist china

RICHARD L. WALKER

When on October 1, 1966, the aging Chinese communist leader Mao Tse-tung and his "close comrade in arms, Comrade Lin Piao" mounted the Gate of Heavenly Peace in Peking, they reviewed a parade of more than 1.5 million people. This vast organizational display by the "revolutionary masses" was hailed in the mainland Chinese press and radio as "the biggest parade since the founding of new China" seventeen years before.[1] On the surface, at least, it would seem that the Chinese communist leaders, who gazed down on the masses they had helped to organize, masses raising red-covered copies of *Quotations from Chairman Mao's Works* and shouting and singing, had succeeded in keeping alive the revolutionary enthusiasm which had greeted them on the first day of October 1949, when Mao had proclaimed the founding of the Chinese People's Republic (CPR).

On that first day of communist rule in mainland China there had been a general atmosphere of optimism and hope. Mao and his comrades had waged a successful military and political campaign, and millions of Chinese, including those who were not necessarily sympathetic toward the communists, looked with favor and indeed enthusiasm on a rule which promised peace and stability. China had been through too many heartrending and economy-wrecking years of war. The communists spoke of a new era, a new China, and offered to the Chinese (students and intellectuals particularly) an opportunity for a kind of unity which might restore China's position in the world after what they regarded as more than a century of national humiliation. As a historian has noted, when Mao Tse-tung declared that China had stood up, "he was echoing the wishes of millions of Chinese, including the 'reactionaries' whom he had vowed to liquidate."[2]

There can be no gainsaying the initial élan within the People's Republic of China. The Chinese communist leadership was closely united. It seemed to represent the wave of the future. Though Mao Tse-tung warned that the communists would have to learn many new skills, particularly in the field of economics, his unified communist party exuded self-confidence. It had come to power against great odds, and members had faith in their ideology, their leaders, and their formulas for the application of Marxism-Leninism to China. The noncommunists who joined with Mao Tse-tung in the People's Political Consultative Conference, the initial ruling united front, felt that some of the communist dogmatism would be modified by the realities of the Chinese scene and that they in turn could accommodate themselves and China as a whole would adjust to the new era of Mao Tse-tung.

Seventeen years later observers of the anniversary parade, noting the mass discipline and the seeming enthusiasm of the marchers, would have been justified in concluding that the communists had succeeded in maintaining those initial qualities of verve and support which had offered so much hope for "new China" in 1949. Certainly the outward forms were there, and many of these had come to characterize the Chinese style of communist rule: massive displays of organizational power, boasts of China's vast population, claims of identity with and support by the "people" of the world, and assertions of infallibility for China's omniscient leadership.

Beneath the surface, however, the quality of rule in mainland China had by 1967 changed dramatically. The initial climate which brought broad-based enthusiasm and support had all but evaporated. The years 1966 through 1968 witnessed frenzied and frenetic developments which bespoke an almost desperate effort to recapture the former élan. There was a major and continuing purge affecting even the topmost leadership of the Chinese Communist Party (CCP). The activities of the Red Guards, composed for the most part of adolescents aged fourteen to eighteen, had disrupted the economy and stability and had even brought attacks on the bureaucratic structures of the CCP and its Communist Youth League in many of the provinces. The young zealots issued denunciations of top CCP leaders in the capital city of communist China itself. The "great proletarian cultural revolution" of 1966–8 brought cries of bewilderment and dismay from fellow communists around the world who had once been so enthusiastic about Mao's China. The entire outside world wondered about the long-range impact of such activities as a New China News Agency dispatch (August 25, 1966) reported:

> In the afternoon of 24 August a revolutionary fire was ignited in the Central Institute of Arts to destroy the sculptures of emperors, kings, generals, ministers, scholars, and beauties, images of Buddha, and niches for the Buddha sculptures. The revolutionary students and teachers of the institute said: "What we have destroyed and crushed are not only a few sculptures, but the whole old world."
>
> The masses of revolutionary students and teachers of the Central Institute of Arts, together with the revolutionary students and teachers of other fraternal schools and institutes of higher learning such as the Peking Normal College and others who came to support them and join their rebellion, were in high spirits. They cast out from their classrooms, studios, and storerooms the sculptures of the goddess of mercy, princes, the fierce-looking gods of Shu Yu and Yu Lu which they had collected from various temples in China, the stone horses and stone tigers which they had collected from paths in front of imperial tombs, and the sculptures of King David of Israel, of the "hero" David in the Bible, of the "goddess of love and beauty" Venus of Greek legends, of Apollo, and so forth which were purchased abroad, and they completely destroyed these by burning and crushing.

The official position of Peking toward those who questioned the rationality of the "great proletarian cultural revolution" and toward the activities of the Red Guards was stated forcefully in a *People's Daily* editorial (October 1, 1966) which greeted the seventeenth anniversary celebrations:

> Today the imperialists headed by the United States, the modern revisionists with the Soviet Communist Party leadership as the core, and reactionaries of all countries are having fits of hysteria. They are doing their very utmost against the great proletarian cultural revolution in China, slandering it, distorting it, inciting against it, and defaming it. They are screaming themselves hoarse and competing to see who in the anti-China chorus can shout the loudest. In fact, the desperate howling of these overlords cannot hide the fear in their hearts.
>
> Gentlemen, haven't you placed your hopes of "peaceful revolution" on our younger generation? Too bad, you miscalculated! It is precisely this great cultural revolution that is tempering and forging tens of millions of our younger generation into the staunchest fighters against imperialism and revisionism. And you—the garbage of history—will inevitably be swept right off the face of the earth by the revolutionary people of the whole world.

In former years the major displays of organizational power had been limited to parades and demonstrations on International Communist Workers' Day (May 1), Chinese Red Army Day (August 1), and the anniversary of the CPR (October 1), and to mass displays in connection with foreign policy issues such as those frequently staged against "American imperialism." But between August 18 and November 26, 1966, there occurred eight mammoth gatherings of Red Guard stalwarts from all over China reviewed by Mao Tse-tung in Peking. According to the *People's Daily,* more than eleven million Red Guards were involved: "This is a great creation without parallel in the history of China's proletarian revolution and in the international Communist movement."[3] Observers outside and inside China, noting the activities of the Red Guards and more particularly the length of time required to have them return to their home districts from Peking, wondered with good reason whether matters had developed beyond control, whether the extremes of irrationality might lead to a major internal conflagration in China.

The derangement and extremism and the purge at the top levels in Peking assumed an even more serious significance, given the fact that by mid-1968, communist China had detonated seven atomic devices, one a bomb delivered on target by a missile. Following its fifth nuclear test in late 1966 Peking had begun a nation-wide showing of a color documentary film dealing with the first three Chinese communist atomic tests, a movie entitled "The Great Victory of Mao Tse-tung's Thought." The *People's Daily* (October 9, 1966) reported that after seeing the film at the time of the anniversary celebrations in Peking, "representatives of the workers, peasants, and soldiers" stated: ". . . We realize that Chairman Mao's thesis that the atomic bomb is also a paper tiger is entirely correct. To heroic people, the atomic bomb is nothing to be afraid of. The senseless statement of the revisionists [the Soviet leaders] that atomic bombs 'will wipe out mankind, wipe out everything' is a downright lie to deceive people." It has been argued that if the mainland regime has spent so much of its scarce capital to create its own "paper tiger," then it is guilty of "magnificent conspicuous consumption."

Given the new status as one of the world's five nuclear powers and the many developments for which the Chinese communists can claim credit (industrialization, public health, education, to name three outstanding achievements), why, then, was it necessary to mobilize the teen-agers to sustain revolutionary fervor? What happened to the spirit of "new China?" Was the "great proletarian cultural revolution" something new on the Chinese scene, like the "people's communes" of 1958, or could it merely represent an intensification of already existent patterns?

To answer such questions it is necessary to examine the major features of almost twenty years of communist rule in China. In that period the Chinese communists developed a number of formulas and institutions which, taken together, constitute a uniquely Chinese version of Marxism-Leninism and method for operation in a communist state. They have relied on these formulas and institutions with a stubbornness bordering on fanaticism; and while any one of them might be viewed as an essential characteristic of any communist or totalitarian state, it is the intensity and manner of their combination which have made the communist political process in China *sui generis.*

The Consolidation of Inflexibility

In many respects the pattern of rule in communist China has involved the application of those formulas which the Chinese communist leaders, particularly Mao Tse-tung, found successful in their surge to power. They drew on experiences in administering guerrilla areas and in creating cadres during the Kiangsi Soviet period, the Long March, and especially World War Two; and at that time the great teacher and model for their work was Stalin.[4] Stalinism left its indelible mark on the approach of Mao to rule in China.[5] But there are other factors which have helped to shape the politics of the CPR. These would include, for example, the great problems of the Chinese scene: a massive population problem, given the ratio of people to scarce resources, national minority antagonisms, and difficulties in communication and transportation exacerbated by low-level income and inadequate economic bases. Perhaps even more decisive is the Chinese tendency (one with great historical resonance) to look inward and use their own experience almost exclusively as the basis for judgment in the selection of policy alternatives.

Although during the initial years of the CPR there was a conscious borrowing from the Soviet Union, particularly while Stalin was alive, more and more it became Chinese formulas which determined politics and policies in Peking. It is necessary to note that in China, as in other communist states, life remains dominated and its style dictated by the all-powerful Party apparatus; perhaps more meaningful would be to examine the politics of communist China by concentrating attention on those formulas which the leaders in Peking have indicated by word and action are the most important. These characteristics became intensified—in fact, exaggerated —as the Chinese communists progressively turned away from the Soviet Union and turned toward their own experience and understanding of Chinese reality as the touchstone of validity. These Chinese communist prescriptions for "true Marxist-Leninist" rule have also interacted with one another to intensify the totalitarian qualities of the regime as it has moved further and further from the possibility of relating judgments to the real world outside of China.

An analysis of the history of the CPR suggests that the communist revolutionary process has become frozen and Peking's phantasy world extended as attention has been concentrated on general formulas to which have been ascribed almost magical qualities by the communist leaders, especially since 1958, the year of the "great leap." In the totalitarian pattern of stressing their infallibility, the leaders in Peking have insisted that theirs are the only correct formulas. Six deserve some elaboration:

(1) The Doctrine or Mao's Version of Marxism-Leninism

Mao Tse-tung is a great sloganizer and simplifier; and though he has added some Chinese decorations to his interpretations of Marxist-Leninist lore, it is rather his emphases—his concentration on a few key ideas— which provide the major justification for Peking's assertion that "Comrade Mao Tse-tung is the greatest Marxist-Leninist of our era. Comrade Mao Tse-tung has inherited, defended and developed Marxism-Leninism with genius, creativity and in an all-round way, and has raised Marxism-Leninism to a new stage."[6] Apotheosizing the "Thought of Mao Tse-tung" (TMTT) has become associated with quasi-religious fanaticism and puritanical exhortations unequalled in previous communist experience A first area of the Marxist-Leninist tradition emphasized in the laudatory references to TMTT in communist China are Mao's theories of contradictions and class struggle within all societies. Within Mao's overly simplified view of a world in its final life-death struggle between imperialism and socialism, there can be no middle ground. He has insisted that the contradictions between two forces, capitalism and socialism, persist even within socialist states and will continue as long as imperialism exists. The Chinese communists have therefore rejected—in fact, denounced—the U.S.S.R. view that such contradictions no longer are applicable within Soviet society. For them, therefore, a dual world of antagonistic forces exists everywhere, and particularly on the Chinese scene, where the class conflict continues. Since the CCP and particularly its Chairman Mao are viewed as the mystical embodiment of the purest forces of socialism, any questioning of their decisions or their interpretations can only be regarded as proof of the contradiction between them and the forces of the enemy. Mao's double vision of the world has allowed little latitude for diversity or tolerance, particularly when handling intellectuals in China who can sometimes be capable of intricate and devious subtleties, as the experience with Wu Han and other Party intellectuals must have reminded the Chinese leader after 1961.

A second major area of doctrine which TMTT tends to emphasize more than other communists do is attention to the masses. Mao has attributed phenomenal capabilities to them in an almost sublime belief that "if the masses are organized, anything can be accomplished." The attempts at modernization through mass mobilization, as, for example, at the time of the "great leap forward" with its backyard iron furnaces and "people's communes" in 1958 and 1959, attest the seriousness with which the Chinese communists accept Mao's thesis that the masses are the infallible vehicle of progressive socialist development if properly guided by the CCP. The attention to the masses as represented by "workers, peasants, and soldiers" in China has provided background for Peking's emphasis on austerity, simplicity, and egalitarianism. It probably reflects Mao's distrust of China's intellectuals whose influence he would like to offset by the counterforce of great numbers. Thus one finds, for example, the final 1965 number of *Philosophical Studies,* the leading philosophy journal in mainland China, devoting itself to special articles by workers, peasants, and soldiers. In hailing this special issue, the *People's Daily* (January 10, 1966) asserted: "They are fine articles of rich content, written in an animated style and abounding with fresh ideas. Analyzing their own practical experience from the philosophical plane, their varied experiences and analytical findings are thus totally beyond the knowledge of those theoretical workers who year after year have confined themselves to their studies, pouring over books and learning by rote. . . . In comparison to those articles on concepts and generalities written by writers who lack purpose and bemoan themselves for some inexplicable reasons, they offer a distinctly fresh approach to views and problems."[7]

There is a seeming contradiction between reliance on the masses and the third general area of Mao's emphasis in his commitment to Marxism-Leninism: the belief expressed in communist China that "the individual is everything." This belief has been stretched to such extremes as to argue that the good communist armed with TMTT is more powerful than an atomic bomb. The contradiction is more apparent than real. Under the emphasis given by TMTT and the CCP, the individual can only achieve his full measure of importance by reaching that point where he can follow his own desires without transgressing the party line, without questioning TMTT as the fount of all truth. Thus there took place the campaign during 1963 in mainland China to learn from Lei Feng. Lei Feng was an ordinary young soldier who died in an accident and whose diary in praise of Chairman Mao was miraculously found to contain just those slogans and ideas which suited the purposes of a campaign under way in China at that moment. Lei Feng allegedly wrote in his diary during April 1962: "A man is like a cog in a machine. . . . A cog may be small but its value cannot be overestimated. Forever I want to be a cog, well kept and clean, that will not rust."[8] Lei Feng also noted that because of his frugal living and his attitude of blind obedience to Chairman Mao's directives, he was frequently called an "idiot." The following year Lei Feng's remarks on this score were being recalled for the whole nation: *People's Daily* (February 7, 1963) cited him, as writing: "I want to become an idiot. The revolution needs such idiots. The construction of a country requires such idiots. I have one desire: to be all for the Party, all for Socialism, all for Communism."

Within this area of communist emphasis on TMTT, one is back to pristine Marxism with its belief that human will and labor are everything.[9] Mao, who is relatively ignorant of the material forces released by modern science, prefers to believe that revolutionary will is decisive, though only when it accepts and corresponds with the will of that most valid embodiment of the will of the masses, the leadership of the Party. Thus a slight contradiction between the belief in the masses and in the individual human will can be resolved. The CCP has said that it wants more "idiots" like Lei Feng: unquestioning, simple, "poor and blank."

A final area upon which TMTT tends to place more emphasis than the stream of Marxist-Leninist orthodoxy is in the field of revolutionary violence. From the outset Peking has stressed the need for violence and warfare. In an atomic age the outside world has hardly been comforted by communist China's insistence that weapons do not change the necessity, indeed the desirability, of war. In the polemical exchanges with the Soviet leadership and in their attempts to revolutionize the entire Chinese populace through the "everyone a soldier" movement, the disciples of TMTT have quoted again and again passages from the works of the supreme Chinese Marxist-Leninist which argue that revolutionary violence and war are necessary, desirable, inevitable, and "push history forward." Mao's approach is perhaps best summed up in his conclusion that "the central task and highest form of revolution is to seize political power by force, to solve problems by war." Says Mao: "Political power grows out of the barrel of a gun."

By its emphasis on these four general areas of Marxism-Leninism the Chinese communist leadership does not reject other fundamentals. In fact, Peking remains far more committed than Moscow to the Leninist theory of imperialism, which helps to underpin its policies toward the developing areas of Asia, Africa, and Latin America. What is important to note in the Chinese communist belief that Marxism-Leninism as embodied in TMTT remains the only correct foundation for a communist state is that the Chinese approach, filtered through its native experience, its Stalinist heritage, and its single major interpreter, Mao, is more dogmatic, less flexible, and certainly too simplified to be acceptable by people capable of independent thought. As the communist revolution in China has become frozen, this ideological underpinning has also moved toward dogmatic stagnation. Here has been one of the major problems of communist rule over a diverse and often very sophisticated people.

(2) The Method: Struggle

The second magic formula in which the Chinese communists have placed great faith has been their method for politicizing the masses. This method can in many respects be boiled down to one word: "struggle." In line with the apocalyptic Maoist vision of a final great contest between the forces of evil, reaction, revisionism, and darkness (represented by all who disagree with the current leadership in Peking) and the upright, clean, progressive forces of truth (represented by TMTT), all life in communist China is interpreted in terms of struggle. During the course of almost twenty years of communist rule the word "struggle" has come to dominate the thinking of the people. It is one of the most frequently used terms in the controlled press. The small study groups inside and outside the Party hold struggle meetings, where any who lack enthusiasm or commitment or seem to show any doubt about following Party directives are "struggled against." Every major policy or directive, plans for industrialization, teaching programs in the schools, and even the simple functions of life in a family are approached within the framework of necessary struggle. The key element in struggle, of course, is the task of identifying the enemy and struggling against him. The enemy is any thought, any person, any group, or any obstacle which stands in the way of implementing the directives of the CCP or TMTT. During 1958, for example, those peasants who resisted the implementation of the "people's communes" became enemies who were the objects of struggle meetings. By definition, within Peking's simplistic view of the world, they were agents or tools of the camp of the enemy, "U. S. Imperialism."

The struggle approach to politics helps to bring about a militarization of life within mainland China. Reflective of the historical background of the CCP and of Mao's own thinking, military terms and concepts dominate the approach even to the most nonmilitary aspects of Chinese society and economy. Campaigns to increase literacy, for instance, are conducted like military operations with "shock troops" and "brigades of literacy workers and soldiers." In such a campaign the "enemy" of illiteracy must be "attacked" and careful "strategy" and "tactics" worked out.

Through the method of "struggle" the CCP seeks to bring every facet of existence into the framework of communist ideology, to stress the necessity for militancy, and to relate events and problems within China to the outside world. Struggle also serves to justify the important position of the military within China, which has been sustained and actually increased during the course of communist rule. Struggle has also been used by the communist leadership as a method for attacking some of the traditional values of harmony and accommodation associated with China's historical past.[10] It is necessary to understand Peking's belief in the methodology of struggle in order to appreciate the seriousness of the campaign in 1964 against the Party philosopher Yang Hsien-chen. What at first glance appeared to the outside world as a silly bit of philosophical quibbling over whether "two combined into one" or "one divided into two" became a major ideological question related to the Sino-Soviet controversy, to struggle within China, and to the Chinese historical and philosophical tradition. Maoists maintained, of course, that since "imperialism" had not disappeared from the world scene, contradictions exist everywhere (that is, "one divides into two") and that the class struggle continues in a manner which allows for no compromise. The theory that "two combines into one" was associated with the Soviet strategy of "peaceful coexistence" and with traditional Chinese values of compromise, which from the Maoist viewpoint would have undercut the necessary continuing struggle within China and on the world scene.[11] In Peking's view, "Only through struggle can there be hope, only through struggle can there be method, only through struggle can there be victory."[12]

(3) The Instrument: Mobilization and Organization

Perhaps nowhere has the efficacy of mobilization and the power of organized masses been stressed as much as in communist China. It would be tempting to say that this is because there are more people in China to mobilize and organize, particularly since Peking so emphasizes its great population and asserts that the mobilized masses of the Chinese people constitute an invincible source of strength.[13] But it is more likely that the leaders of the CCP are impressed with the organizational instrument that they have fashioned. They have managed to extend the Leninist-Stalinist military-style organization into almost every facet of Chinese society so that practically no one escapes being swept up into one or more organizations which operate under the rigorous discipline of "democratic centralism." The key to the organizational breakthrough which Mao Tse-tung and his comrades made is the "study group." Within small "study groups," to which everyone in communist China belongs, mutual responsibility, criticism and self-criticism help to guarantee obedience.[14] From these organizational cells up through the prefecture and province chains of command to the national capital, uniformity and compliance have been secured through many nationwide functional and propaganda organizations.

Of course, mass organizations carrying out drives led by *agitprop* activists have been a common feature of communist regimes everywhere, but the Chinese mode of operation is distinctive in its intensity and in the extent to which it relies on mass mobilization for the implementation of national policies. Mass organizations, from the outset of Mao's rule in 1949, have been employed as a style of government execution and administration in movements and drives which have followed upon, overlapped, and coincided with one another in fatiguing succession. Instead of adopting and then implementing and following up a policy, as is frequently the case with other communist regimes, Peking's style has been almost as frequently to pass the laws and regulations after the mass movement has swept the country. Mass movements have been geared to Mao's faith in the mass line and have been associated with practically all aspects of communist rule, whether purges, economic policies, battles against nature, conservation, collectivization, and domestic or foreign policy problems.[15] The outside world has gazed over the years with wonderment at the procession of periods of mass mesmerism which have followed each other across the vast Chinese land-mass.

Mass movements can and do serve a number of purposes in the Chinese communist political system. They help to channel away energies which might otherwise express themselves in opposition and dissatisfaction or provide a source for closer relations between the cadres and the people at large. They impress upon the individuals their own impotence to oppose the "line of the masses" and tend to encourage the type of submission and concession which finds expression in becoming, like Lei Feng, "a cog, well kept and clean, that will not rust." The mass drives and demonstrations feed the confidence of the leaders, promote solidarity in the ranks of the leadership, divert attention from troublesome problems and failures, and add dimensions to the militarization and mobilization of society. Through the years of the CPR, mobilization and organization of the Chinese people through never-ending drives have borne the distinct stamp of Mao Tse-tung, frequently deriving their names and contents from his slogans and writings: the "Hundred Flowers" movement, "Learn from the People's Liberation Army" campaign, the drive to "Implement the Three-Eight Working Style," or the "Great Proletarian Cultural Revolution."

(4) The Leader: Mao Tse-tung

For its first two decades, communist rule in China was associated with the name of one man: Mao Tse-tung. Peking has stated in stentorian tones that the key to communist success lies in correct leadership and that in China the people have been blessed with the greatest communist leader. In general, however, there has been too little attention paid to the manner in which Mao, who admitted he had much to learn in 1949, changed and hardened over the years as the cult of personality developed around him. With each passing year the flattery, the sycophantic practices, and the hourless exaggeration through which Mao has been elevated to an almost godlike figure played an increasing part in communist China's politics and policies. Several criticisms, and especially those from the Soviet Union, have been particularly caustic (and with good reason, given the Stalin experience) about Mao's personality cult and arbitrary rule. It is difficult to portray the full extent to which the cult of Mao and the religious fervor attached to TMTT had developed by the time the "great proletarian cultural revolution" linked to TMTT was launched in 1966, but perhaps the following excerpt from the *Liberation Army Daily* (May 30, 1966) can serve as an illustration:

Revolutionary people the world over ardently love Chairman Mao and his thinking, because he has intellectually, creatively, and comprehensively developed Marxism-Leninism.

Mao Tse-tung's thinking is the acme of Marxism-Leninism and the highest and most creative Marxism-Leninism in our time, the powerful ideological weapon against imperialism, modern revisionism, and all reactionaries, and the common truth applicable everywhere.

Because of the existence of Mao Tse-tung's thinking, the world revolution will be successful, and the oppressed and exploited people the world over will stand up and stand up forever. Great Mao Tse-tung's thinking is the banner of revolution and also the banner of victory. . . .

Mao Tse-tung's thinking is the Red sun in our hearts and our lifeline. We deeply love and always adhere to Mao Tse-tung's thinking. It is the duty incumbent upon every revolutionary fighter to study, propagate, and defend Mao Tse-tung's thinking. We will hold still higher the great banner of Mao Tse-tung's thinking, march forward valiantly, and develop his thinking from one generation to another and forever. Whoever dares to oppose it, we will strive against to the end. We will crush all the ogres and monsters and bourgeois "authorities." Long live invincible Mao Tse-tung's thinking.

Such statements evoked a Soviet demand in a *Pravda* editorial (November 28, 1966) that in the world communist movement "the attempt to distort Marxism-Leninism and replace it with the ideology and practice of Mao Tse-tungism be overcome."[16]

Although Peking proclaims that the ever-correct leadership of Chairman Mao, who by 1966 was being dubbed "the great teacher, great leader, great supreme commander and great helmsman of the Chinese people" has been a constant source of strength and success, there is reason to wonder. It remains true that there had been a façade of legend and perfection built around the leader and that it was hard to penetrate, but there is also ample evidence that with the passing of time the cult of personality and the exercise of unrestrained power had been having a debilitating effect on the man and his domain. Unfortunately many of the scholars in the outside world who have studied Mao have not had an opportunity to observe at first hand the impact of power on the man. They have tended, rather, to rely heavily on Mao's published writings, many stemming from earlier years when he was a guerrilla leader, to assess his conduct of CPR affairs.[17] But in the course of the past years the parallels with the reign of other despots long in power, such as Louis XIV or Stalin, argue that the factor of human change should not be overlooked in the rule of Mao.

Far from being the benign father figure pictured in Chinese communist propaganda (in the same manner that Soviet propaganda for twenty years pictured so deceptively for the outside world "Uncle Joe" Stalin), Mao had already become by the late 1950's increasingly impatient, irascible, intolerant of criticism, arbitrary, and in fact a paranoiac. This was reflected in his conduct of affairs in the Chinese communist party, in which the parallels with the arbitrary rule of Stalin during his later years were sufficiently alarming that *Pravda* (April 23, 1964) detailed them for the outside world. This editorial noted that "during the past thirty-five years only two CCP congresses have taken place." [The figure has increased to thirty-nine at the time of this writing.] The purge in 1966–8 reordered the structure of the CCP and the rankings and membership of its Central Committee and Politburo without consulting members of the Party. The Soviet criticisms of 1964 remained valid, within the framework of communist practices, as *Pravda* stated:

> The absence of a program, the refusal to convene party congresses regularly, the acceleration of the decisions of the congresses, and the creation in this connection of the impression that the decisions are not binding, have little in common with Marxism-Leninism. It is peculiar to a party leadership which places the personality cult above everything, which has embarked upon the road of revisionism. It is precisely under these conditions that it becomes possible to alter, by directives formed under such and such impressions, the program and the collective will of the party and the principles which are common to the entire Communist movement.[18]

By 1968 the CCP chairman, in his seventy-sixth year according to Chinese age reckoning, was clearly ailing. Yet the characteristics of one-man rule in his later sclerotic years were reflected in the mode of the power struggle and purge of the "great proletarian cultural revolution." In dealings with the Chinese people, as well as foreigners, Mao and those who acted in the name of TMTT became increasingly arrogant, intolerant of even minor reservations or disagreement, and blinded to possibilities that any policies or actions of the Maoists might be in error. As one observer has pointed out:

> One-man rule provided Stalin with the power to demand "socialist realism" in literature and art, just as it now provides Mao with the power to insist on an even cruder "socialist revolution" in literature and art. One-man rule enabled Stalin to establish a bibliolatry in the name of the CPSU *Short Course;* Mao learned from his Georgian mentor how to erect a new bibliolatry in the name of the *Selected Works.* The Chinese leader's craving for adulation is even more demanding than was Stalin's and its influence on foreign and domestic policies overwhelming. . . . The cult of Mao has now reached heights of irrationalism that put even Stalin's exercises in self-adulation to shame. But it was Stalin, not Lenin, who showed Mao the way to institutionalize—in the period *after* the revolution—the cult of self-idolatry, the distortion of party history, the ruthless destruction of small farmers (erroneously depicted as "kulaks" by Stalin in the late 1920's and "landlords" by Mao in the early 1950's), and the ritualistic purge within the party which has come almost two decades after the Communist victory on the mainland. The parallels are not always exact, and, to be sure, Mao has innovated in all these matters, but whether the innovations represent a continuation or a divergence from Stalinism is a point for academic dispu-

tation. We may quarrel about the precise degree of Mao's originality in applying the ritual of forced confession to CCP officials today, but it is an analytical blunder to ignore the crucial Stalinist heritage of this insensate policy.[19]

While it is true that Mao, in building his own cult, borrowed many of the techniques which were associated with the rule of Stalin, much of the phenomenon has been a standard pattern of megalomania among aging autocrats and therefore is institutionally based. On the other hand, there are aspects of the rule of Mao and the theology of TMTT which lend a distinct Chinese coloration to the political process in China, and here the intensity in fanaticism of the leader cult and its mass expressions command attention.

(5) Foreign Policy: World Revolution

In its claims that revolutionary people all over the world "ardently love Chairman Mao," Peking indicates that it views Chinese communist leadership in world revolution as yet another important formula in its pattern of rule. The view of the CPR, the CCP under Mao, and TMTT, leading the forces of revolution against "imperialists and modern revisionists," gives added dimension to political life within China. As the self-proclaimed "correct Marxist-Leninists" the Chinese communists have with increasing vehemence asserted that they are guiding the forces of revolution among the underdeveloped countries of Asia, Africa, and Latin America. The communiqué[20] following the 11th plenary session of the CCP's 8th Central Committee (August 12, 1966) proclaimed that "Mao Tse-tung's thought is Marxism-Leninism of the era in which imperialism is heading for total collapse and socialism is advancing to world-wide victory." The Chinese people are reminded that "Comrade Mao Tse-tung requires us revolutionaries not only to serve the revolution of the Chinese people and carry the Chinese revolution to the end, but also to serve the liberation of the people of the whole world and carry to the end the revolution of the people in the whole world."[21]

From the first day of the CPR the Chinese people were told that (1) theirs were sacred international revolutionary obligations, (2) they had the sympathy and support of the "people of the world" and were opposed by only a handful of reactionaries, (3) the situation in the whole world was becoming ripe for revolution and the world-wide victory of socialism, and (4) the oppressed peoples of the world looked to China as leader and as a model for carrying through their own revolutions. The last of these points is particularly important in that the line of CCP leaders has appealed to Chinese pride and tended to support the thesis that after decades of humiliation China had indeed "stood up." The *People's Daily* (June 4, 1966), for example, devoted a full page to stories from all over the world reporting on how the "people" everywhere were looking to China for revolutionary leadership. The accompanying article stated: "People throughout the world, and particularly the Asian, African, and Latin American peoples, are passing through different stages of revolutionary struggles. They see in the brilliant example of the Chinese revolution their own future and firmly believe that Mao Tse-tung's thought is the guide to world revolution."[22]

Such statements are reinforced within China by propaganda displays of Chairman Mao meeting with delegates from throughout the world to discuss and share revolutionary experience. Peking also buttresses the belief in its world revolutionary role by providing training in China for revolutionary cadres from Asia, Africa, and Latin America and by the export of training missions and arms abroad in support of revolution.[23] The African monthly *Drum* reported in the fall of 1966 on the activities of Chinese communists in Ghana, brought to light after the Nkrumah government fell. It pointed out how complicated equipment for subversive purposes had been shipped to Ghana as "medical supplies" and went on to state that

> Chinese instructors also showed students how to make a hand grenade out of a coconut, how to manufacture gunpowder and a variety of other deadly explosives.
>
> The main textbook used by the Chinese in their work was Mao Tse-tung's essay on "Methods of Leadership" which explains in minute detail a wide range of guerrilla operations, including "how to destroy an airport," "how to lay different types of mines" and "the work of a guerrilla commander."
>
> The Chinese also gave their student subversives lessons in Mao Tse-tung's version of the theory and practice of Communism. When soldiers of the Ghana army took over the camps after the *coup d'état* in February, they found student notebooks containing test exercises on how to plan assassination, how to make contacts with African countries and how to exploit a person's weaknesses to blackmail him into helping in spy work.[24]

The epitome of the Mao cult's assertion that communist China had a central world revolutionary role and one related to internal Chinese experience and the most eloquent testimony of the distorted and oversimplified view of the world reflected in TMTT came with the publication of Lin Piao's *Long Live the Victory of People's War!* on September 3, 1965. In this essay the man who rose to become "Comrade Mao's closest comrade in arms" a year later, spelled out Peking's version of grand world strategy, extolled the correctness of TMTT, and re-emphasized the Maoist belief in the efficacy of violence and that the Chinese revolutionary experience was of world-wide significance. The new geopolitics outlined by Lin Piao was significant as evidence of the intense derangement at the top levels in communist China, even a year before the "great proletarian cultural revolution." Lin stated that the Chinese communist strategy on "the establishment of rural base areas and the encirclement of the cities from the countryside is of outstanding and universal, practical importance." He went on to assert, in a statement which has been quoted widely throughout the world but which nevertheless deserves reproduction here, the following:

> Taking the entire globe, if North America and Western Europe can be called "the cities of the world," then Asia, Africa, and Latin America constitute "the rural areas of the world." Since World War II the proletarian revolutionary movement has for various reasons been temporarily held back in the North American and West European capitalist countries, while the people's revolutionary movement in Asia, Africa, and Latin America has been growing vigorously. In a sense, the contemporary world revolution also presents a picture of the encirclement of cities by the rural areas. In the final analysis, the whole cause of world revolution hinges on the revolutionary struggles of the Asian, African, and Latin American peoples who make up the overwhelming majority of the world's population. The socialist countries should regard it as their international duty to support the people's revolutionary struggles in Asia, Africa, and Latin America.[25]

Lin Piao's grandiose statements regarding the strategy of people's wars, Chinese communist activities around the world, and the constant attention to building strength and military power in China for China's "international duty"—all indicate that within the unique frame of reference to Mao Tse-tung's concepts of guerrilla warfare and people's wars, world revolution is an important formula in the political life of communist China.

(6) The Pattern: Tension and Relaxation

Communist leaders have frequently used such terms as "waves and troughs" in applying their dialectical process of analysis to the ebb and flow of their political fortunes, and certainly modern totalitarian leaders have been especially effective with the old carrot-and-stick approach to rule. But in the case of rule in communist China the pattern of alternating periods of tension and relaxation has been regular enough to suggest that this is a strategy or operational code in the political process. Outside observers, usually asked to assess a mass movement or mood in communist China at a particular period, have seldom commented on the manner in which periods of internal tension and relaxation have followed one another. It is worth noting also that in broad terms these periods have had concomitant expression in foreign policy. This has been commented upon.[26]

The initial period of consolidation in mainland China during 1949 and 1950, despite the violence in the final battles of the war against the Nationalists, was characterized by the promises of the united front and lenient treatment for those who cooperated with the regime. But during 1951 and 1952, linked with Chinese communist participation in the Korean war and with the final stages of consolidating CCP rule, the line turned hard. The campaign against counterrevolutionaries, the Three-Anti and Five-Anti Movements, and the initiation of vast programs of "reform through labor service" spread terror throughout China. In 1953 with the start of communist China's First Five-Year Plan, and 1954, with the beginnings of the period of the *panch shila* or "Five Principles of Peaceful Coexistence" in foreign policy, which were to culminate in Chou En-lai's "reasonable" performance at Bandung (April 1955), the general atmosphere was one of relaxation. But internally during late 1954 with the campaign against Hu Feng and in 1955 with the drive for collectivization initiated by Mao, tension once again was built up and a new "rectification" campaign launched. In 1956 and early 1957 Mao Tse-tung issued a call for relaxation in order to "let the Hundred Flowers Bloom," and once again it seemed to the outside world that perhaps totalitarian controls in China were loosening up. But this was followed in June 1957 by an intense "Anti-Rightist Campaign" and the following year by the even more stringent measures of the "people's communes" and the "great leap forward." The disastrous consequences of the "great leap" carried into 1961, when once again peasants were beginning to till their own small private plots. For a year, from mid-1961 until mid-1962, there seemed to be a relaxation of stringent controls in the intellectual and artistic sphere. From then on, tension has mounted to the frenzied extremes of the "great proletarian cultural revolution" of 1966–8.

This is, to be sure, broad-brush generalized surveying, and it should be noted that the various rectification campaigns against the intellectuals did not necessarily coincide with drives to tighten controls over the country-side or to reimpose discipline in the artistic world. In most cases tension accompanied and grew with the drives and campaigns by which the Chinese communists conducted their rule, and the seeming relaxation stemmed from stopping a campaign after it had passed the point of diminishing effectiveness or had provoked passive resistance. Each new campaign or period of tension has tended to result in an extension of control, and even when there has been a relaxation, the retreat never goes back to former levels. Thus, although the regime retreated from the draconian measures of the "people's communes" of 1959 and allowed postage-stamp-size private garden plots in 1961, regimentation of peasants could be maintained at a much higher level than under the 1958 "agricultural producers' cooperatives" before the commune movement started.

Though it is difficult to prove that this pattern of tension and relaxation is indeed a calculated strategy (I personally believe it to be so), it can be discerned that this has proved a useful psychological technique for consolidation and extension of control. The period of the "Hundred Flowers" enabled the regime to identify the opposition, and in the rectification movement which followed "poisonous weeds" were mowed down. During periods of tension in the drives and campaigns, energies are mobilized, elements of opposition silenced, Party cadres put on the alert, and tentacles of the regime extended into new fields of control. During periods of relaxation, cooperation is given in hope of preventing yet another frenetic drive, potential opponents attempt to accommodate the regime in order to avoid being targets of the next drive, and new controls can be consolidated. But after an extended period of such cycles, with tension and relaxation alternating, does the regime not find that a saturation point has been reached?

The Dynamics of Disillusionment

Surely the most intense of all Peking's drives, associated with the greatest period of tension and the one which called into full play all six of the formulas for political control in communist China, was the "great leap forward" launched by the second session of the Chinese Communist Party's 8th Congress in May 1958 and linked with the program of establishing "people's communes" confirmed by the Central Committee of the Party the following August. In terms of mass mobilization, organization of people's militia, grandiose economic plans, and wild promises, nothing like it had ever been attempted before. The Chinese people were promised that they were on the heaven-scaling ladder to a communist paradise and would be surpassing all of the advanced countries of the world, including the Soviet Union and the United States, in record time. The results were disastrous and were enough to kindle doubts in the minds of even some of the most ardent Party stalwarts. The magnificent organizational structure which Mao and his comrades had erected was utilized to bring the economy and the Chinese people near to disaster.

In the period of starvation that followed, particularly during 1960 and 1961, Mao and his flatterers insisted that the "great leap forward" and the "people's communes" had been an unqualified success.[27] But the secret archives of the People's Liberation Army (PLA) *Work Bulletin* for 1961, released to the world by the U. S. Department of State in 1964, confirmed not only the hunger but the disillusionment among many of the Party leaders and their criticism of Mao himself.[28] These issues of the *Work Bulletin* also indicated that the top Party leaders knew they had brought the country to the brink of ruin. Yet the cult of Mao had developed already to such an extreme that facts were hidden or distorted and the infallibility of the "great helmsman" maintained at all costs. It was in the wake of the "great leap" disaster that the CCP and the PLA launched their campaign to study TMTT.

The "great leap forward" accelerated a process of disillusionment which had been developing, particularly among the intellectuals and some students, as the pattern of tension and relaxation had proceeded. Totalitarian rigors had gradually been eroding the support and the energies of many people who would be necessary for the regime's continuing verve and élan. During the brief month in which the "Hundred Flowers" bloomed in 1957, the Chinese communist leadership discovered that it had lost the effective support of most intellectuals, who in 1949 had joined the United Front with enthusiasm.[29] The "Anti-Rightist Movement" which followed only tended further to alienate Chinese intellectuals, even though it silenced them. The "great leap" sowed major doubts among the peasants and even within the PLA itself. Furthermore, it occasioned dissatisfaction among the minority nationalities in China's western regions, particularly in Tibet, where a flaring revolt ended in the flight of the Dalai Lama and continuing guerrilla warfare against the regime by Tibetan tribesmen.[30]

As the purge of 1966–7 reached full dimensions, the story of the aftermath of the "great leap" began to emerge, and it focused on Peking: the old capital and the revolutionary center of the twentieth century, where the May 4th Movement started, where Mao Tse-tung and many of his colleagues first learned their Marxism, where the leading intellectual centers—particularly Peita (Peking National University) and Yenching—attracted the top thinkers and scholars of the land, and where the atmosphere practically demanded that bureaucrats and government officials be urbane, sophisticated, and well-read. To Peking, when it replaced the Nationalist capital of Nanking as the center of governmental gravity, had flocked the leading figures of the United Front, leading Chinese intellectual and artistic figures. Peking set the tone and the pace for the CPR.

In the atmosphere of Peking the disillusionment after the "great leap" spread like a contagious disease, and it penetrated into the ranks of Party intellectuals centered in the capital city. While Lin Piao was tightening discipline and reorganizing the morale and authority of the PLA elsewhere in the land (and the issues of the *Work Bulletin* tell of his work on this score), there occurred between August 1961 and September 1962 an intellectual loosening-up in Peking which in due course spread to other centers of learning in China.[31] During this time, which to a certain extent constituted another "Hundred Flowers" blooming period, a sort of "cultural renaissance" took place in Peking. Attention was turned to Chinese history, to the philosophy of former dynasties, to the stage, and to literature.[32] What outside observers failed to note, however, was that this restored interest in Chinese culture (possibly in part because of the nationalism attendant upon the sharpening Sino-Soviet dispute) was being used by Peking intellectuals, and particularly by those who had risen to top ranks in the CCP, as an opportunity to question the authority of the Party hacks, of Chairman Mao, of basic policies, and of communism itself. They did this in a manner only too familiar in the Chinese tradition: by innuendo, by historical analogy, and by spoofs. The revulsion of Peking intellectuals against the stupidities of the "great leap," against the Party dogmatism, against the personality cult, against the slogans and drives, and, in fact, against practically every aspect of totalitarianism in China, expressed itself in a subtle manner which found the urbane Chinese intellectuals in and out of the Party laughing up the sleeves of their long scholars' gowns and poking fun. So high-ranking and prestigious were those involved that the counterattack had to be carefully planned, for it would involve a major purge in the highest levels.

The Party's determination to reimpose uniformity, discipline, and orthodoxy took the form of an anti-intellectual drive, and the purges beginning in 1966 were its culmination. It began with the decision of the 10th Plenum of the Central Committee in 1962 to launch a "socialist education movement." This was followed in 1964 by a drive to force the intellectuals into the countryside so that they would learn from the workers and peasants, combined with a reinvigoration of the "half-work, half-study" system in the schools. In 1964 the Party launched a new drive to "learn from the People's Liberation Army," in an attempt to regain the lost élan and to apply to the whole country remedial measures Lin Piao had found successful for the PLA. And then in late 1965 came the beginning of attacks on Party intellectuals by name. The wrath of the Mao cultists was great!

The list of those denounced between the end of 1965 and mid-1968 and subsequently removed from their positions (particularly in the Peking government) reads like a roll call for the company of leading intellectuals who had given their talents and devotion to the cause of communism in China over more than three decades. Mao Tun (Shen Yen-p'ing) was quietly relieved in late 1964 from his position as Culture Minister. Then in November 1965 the playwright Wu Han, who had been Deputy Mayor of Peking for more than sixteen years, was attacked for writing a play that uses historical analogy to denounce the authoritarian aspects of CCP rule. Playwrights T'ien Han and Meng Chao, Culture Minister Chou Yang, writers Hsia Yen and Liao Mo-sha, and even Propaganda Minister Lu Ting-yi were among the prominent leaders "struggled against," denounced with full venom in the Party press, and purged. Army Chief-of-Staff Lo Jui-ching and Peking Mayor P'eng Chen were removed from their positions.

What had these people actually been saying or countenancing in the intellectual circles of Peking? Perhaps the case of Teng T'o can be used best for illustrative purposes. He was a Party stalwart who had served from 1953 to 1958 as editor-in-chief of the official *People's Daily*. In 1961–2 he joined with Wu Han and Liao Mo-sha in publishing a series of articles in *Front,* the fortnightly journal of the Peking CCP Committee, and in the *Peking Daily* and *Peking Evening News*. It should be noted that these latter two newspapers, like other local newspapers, were not permitted to circulate outside of China. Hence it was difficult for the "China-watchers" to procure copies in Hong Kong and elsewhere. Teng and his colleagues published their series under the titles "Night Talks on Yen-shan" and "The Three-family Village." By June 1966 a monumental campaign against Teng T'o, his "Three-family Group," and his "black gang" filled the press and radio in mainland China.

The *People's Daily* (May 9, 1966) published a long denunciation by six authors entitled "Teng T'o's 'Night Talks on Yen-shan' Are Shady Articles against the Party and Socialism." Upon examination it seems quite clear that Teng T'o was indeed quite guilty of the charges his accusers leveled at him. What he had written was a series of facetious analogies to denounce the Party and its chairman. Obviously referring to Mao and the Party hacks in an article entitled "Big Talk" appearing in *Front* in 1961, Teng wrote: "Some persons are very eloquent and can talk on and on without stopping in any place. . . . They do not know what they are talking about after half a day of talking. Their explanation further confuses things or is as good as no explanation. This is the characteristic of big talk." After an obvious reference to Mao Tse-tung's "scientific dictum, 'The East wind prevails over the West wind'" [the six authors of the denunciation of Teng use the term "scientific"], which Teng characterized as "hackneyed," his concluding advice was the following: "Read more, think more, and talk less. When you want to talk, go to take a rest and don't squander away the time and energy of yourselves and other people."[33]

In another article which he wrote for *Front* in 1962 entitled "Amnesia" references to Mao Tse-tung were even clearer. Said Teng: "People suffering from this disease . . . often go back on their words and do not keep their promises. They even make people suspect that they play the fool and are unworthy of trust." The article, in what was possibly a reference to Mao's growing senility, noted that people suffering from serious amnesia "will either become crazy or turn into an idiot" and that the disease is characterized by an "uneasiness and tendency to lose one's temper." Among the treatments Teng T'o recommended for someone suffering from amnesia were these: "He must promptly take a complete rest. He must not talk or do anything. If he insists on talking or doing anything, he will get into a lot of trouble."[34] Citing other articles by Teng T'o, written in a similar metaphorical manner, the six authors of the *People's Daily* denunciation stated that he "slurs our great leap forward as 'trumpet-blowing' and 'big talk' which has emerged with 'a bleeding nose' under the impact of facts. . . . He slurs our cause of building socialism as having 'collapsed.' . . . He frenziedly shouts a demand that our Party quickly retire 'to take a rest.' "

The materials published in 1966 and 1967 allowed little doubt that in 1961–2, that brief year of relative relaxation, in Peking a great number of important communist leaders were having serious doubts about the pattern of communist rule in China. They were disillusioned and bitter about Mao Tse-tung and were advocating changes which would redirect some of the regime's basic policies and necessitate the admission of error. This would not be an easy task for any government, but it would be hardest of all for a messianic one. The aftermath of the "great leap" and the continuing problems in the countryside were compounded during the following years by other failures which were equally impossible to hide. The year 1965, for instance, was an especially bad one for the Chinese communist leadership on the world scene. The Afro-Asian summit meeting in Algiers failed to materialize—a strong source of embarrassment; relations with Castro's Cuba deteriorated into antagonism and bitter recrimination; the U.S.S.R. proceeded with its proposed conference of communist parties, despite Peking's threatening demands that the meeting be called off; North Korea and North Vietnam, as well as the Japanese communist party, turned away from Mao's leadership; and the attempt at a *coup* in Indonesia, in which the Maoists were clearly involved, backfired.

By 1967 eighteen years of applying the formulas of rule associated with Mao Tse-tung's version of Marxism-Leninism had imposed controls which resulted in ever more mammoth displays of human masses bending to the will of the Maoists, but the contradictions between promises associated with each drive and the realities of nonfulfillment had started a descending spiral of disenchantment. In search for support of the masses and in their attempt to capture enthusiasm and allegiance the Maoists had to turn to the teen-agers. College students and older cadres were probably cynical. Time after time, they had been caught between the demands of the rulers and the protests of the masses. In China it did not take much intelligence to know that when the *People's Daily* proclaimed on October 1, 1966, that "under the wise leadership of the Central Committee of the Communist Party headed by Comrade Mao Tse-tung, the people of our country have won victories by leaps and bounds," this bore little relationship to reality.

The Purge

The dynamics of disillusionment and, as indicated above, particularly the alienation of Chinese intellectuals constituted major background factors for the "great proletarian cultural revolution" which in the years 1966–8 became a major purge and power struggle.[35] In many respects the struggle in communist China was between those with brains and those who derided them, between sophistication and TMTT, between those who think and the Lei Feng-type "cogs," between those who were willing to "surrender their hearts to the Party" and accept its interpretations of events even when such interpretations did not correspond to facts and those who could no longer ignore reality in China and the outside world, between those who accepted TMTT and those who now realized that TMTT was not enough.

But the purge of 1966–8 is obviously more than that. It is also quite clearly a power struggle for the mantle of Mao. That the firmness of the old man's hand was weakening became evident in a number of ways. Since becoming CCP Chairman in January 1935, Mao had been able to sit on the diverse talents of the top communist leadership and preserve unity, particularly among those who had made the fabled 1934–5 "Long March" in China. The split within the ranks of the "long marchers," when combined with a number of other items, represented clear evidence of the "great helmsman's" fading powers. Mao's protracted period of absence between November 1965 and July 16, 1966, the day on which he finally surfaced in the Yangtze River, and the rather erratic pattern of his appearances in the preceding years, was such an item.[36] Then, too, the build-up of the frenzy of praise for Mao and TMTT seemed clearly to be in his name rather than under his direction. But an even more interesting index indicating that Mao's health was a serious enough factor to touch off a power struggle, could be seen in the manner in which Peking "doth protest too much" that the chairman was in the best of condition. Day after day at the time the CPR celebrated its 17th anniversary Radio Peking and the New China News Agency thought up new ways to remind the world *and* the Chinese people that Mao's health was excellent.

Item: In describing the one and one-half million strong anniversary parade on October 1, NCNA described Mao and Lin Piao as "both in glowing spirits and excellent health."

Item: The following day NCNA reported how pleased the Soviet people were to learn of Mao's July swim in the Yangtze. A Soviet citizen was reported to have said to his Chinese comrades: "It's excellent! It's your fortune as well as ours that Mao Tse-tung is in such good health."

Item: On October 3 NCNA reported: "Red Guards of Peking University expressed their joy at Chairman Mao Tse-tung's good health." The dispatch went on to quote a veteran worker: "Chairman Mao is as healthy as he was eight years ago. This is our greatest happiness."

Item: On October 4 NCNA quoted foreign visitors as saying: "The fact that Chairman Mao and Comrade Lin Piao were so healthy and energetic . . . is the greatest happiness."

Item: October 5, NCNA dispatch: "On hearing that Chairman Mao and his close comrade in arms Comrade Lin Piao were in such good health and so active. . . ."

There were other developments in China which argued that a major power struggle must be under way. The manner of buildup for Lin Piao[37] as the "closest comrade in arms" of Chairman Mao was not in keeping with the pattern under which Mao's fellow provincial, Liu Shao-ch'i, had been carefully elevated in the late 1950's. The resultant downgrading of Liu and reordering of the Party hierarchy, without even a meeting of the Central Committee, bespoke a struggle of rather serious proportions. Then, too, the *People's Daily,* which since the beginning of the CPR had been the pace-setter in establishing the official line in communist China, suddenly took a back seat to the *Liberation Army Daily* in the month of May 1966: another indication of a struggle between the head of the Liberation Army, Lin Piao, and some of his comrades on the Politburo.[38]

There were obviously many other factors converging at one time to encourage the purge and the power struggle in communist China. An important one involved the Sino-Soviet dispute. It would seem that some of those who were purged had indeed advocated modification of Peking's rigid line in the interest of national reconciliation. They were accused of being "revisionists." Some of the purged Party intellectuals also apparently had been urging a more flexible stance in other areas of the world, particularly after the disastrous results of the attempted *coup* in Indonesia during September 30–October 1, 1965, and the overthrow of the Nkrumah regime in Ghana during February 1966, with resultant embarrassing revelations.

Then there were the persistent problems of the Chinese scene. The country was slow in recovering from the "great leap" fiasco. The Soviet leadership in its November 28, 1966, broadside against what it called "Mao Tse-tungism" claimed that "China's industrial and agricultural output has sharply dropped and is only now attaining the level of 1957-1958."[39] But the intervening decade had seen mainland China's population increase by perhaps more than 150 million, as it now approaches 800 million. In connection with the mobilization of the Chinese people during 1966–67, once again the students of TMTT were imposing new demands on the Chinese peasants and attacking such tendencies toward "capitalist outlook" as the small private plots.

The purge, involving as it did a new mass movement of the Red Guards, was an almost instinctive Maoist method for calling into action once again the magic formulas which were the only method of response known in the experience of the CCP. But with the Red Guards and the "great proletarian cultural revolution" the bottom of the barrel had been reached. Where could the devotees of TMTT turn after the teen-agers had lost their élan?

Meanwhile the pattern of tension and relaxation may have run its course. Mainland China by mid-1968 was divided and in disarray as never before under communist rule. Party organizations were under attack.

Communism had lost its appeal and had demonstrated its inability to cope with the problems of a populous and historically rich China. Military power and the fanaticism of the mobilized youth seemed the only forces left, and as the Red Guards were sent home, it was the military that increasingly moved into control. Perhaps the seriousness of the demoralization which had set in, as Lin Piao and the other Maoists made a frantic attempt to revive support, is best symbolized by the new Lei Feng-type hero, Tsai Yung-hsiang, whom the press and radio were propagandizing. NCNA reported on November 18, 1966, that "on 10 October eighteen-year-old Tsai Yung-hsiang, a soldier on guard duty at the Chientang River bridge in Hangchow, laid down his life to save a trainload of Peking-bound Red Guards and the steel structure of the bridge itself. He was killed when clearing away a big log of wood laid across the rails in the path of the oncoming train by elements of the class enemy."

Not surprisingly the authorities found a diary in which Tsai had recorded his love for Chairman Mao and TMTT. But the report represented one of the first admissions that this type of sabotage was going on. It was not revealed who had placed the log on the tracks. This was the beginning of disorder and armed clashes approaching civil war proportions in mid-1967 and continuing through 1968. The leaders of the cult of "Great Mao" clustered around Lin Piao and attacked and all but destroyed the national and provincial Party organizations. Although these groups fought back, they were eventually submerged in the Revolutionary committees that were organized at the provincial level to bring about a military rule with the colleagues of Lin Piao in control.

The unity that Mao's magic formulas had brought to China in the early years had vanished by 1968. No one seemed to command the respect and attention or to have an adequate grasp of China's growing problems to rekindle the spirit of optimism which had accompanied the proclamation of communist rule in 1949. Then everything in China was "new," and the outside world was bombarded with ebullient claims about the "New China." In 1968 one could search in vain for any reference to the "New China," as old men continued to cling to power and carry out their last struggles with one another.

As a troubled world watched the internal struggles while Mao's powers faded in China, as it puzzled over the shifting fortunes of the top élite in the purge and counterpurge of the "great proletarian cultural revolution," as it hoped that reason and sophistication would return and that China could move peacefully and cooperatively into the mainstream of world affairs, as it lamented the fetish for secrecy and the Chinese communists' introspection and isolation, it could only pray that the Maoists would not attempt to recapture unity and élan through Mao Tse-tung's recommended method of solving problems: war.

Notes to Chapter 8

1. See the *Peking Review,* Oct. 7, 1966.

2. Dun J. Li, *The Ageless Chinese* (New York, 1965), p. 543.

3. Jen Li-hsin, article on "The Most Brilliant Example," *Jen Min Jih Pao,* Nov. 27, 1966.

4. See the "Introduction" to Boyd Compton, *Mao's China: Party Reform Documents, 1942–4* (Seattle, 1952).

5. This point is stressed in Arthur A. Cohen's perceptive essay "The Man and His Policies," in "Maoism: A Symposium," *Problems of Communism,* XV:5 (Sep.–Oct. 1966), 8–16. Other contributors to the symposium take issue with Cohen.

6. Communiqué of 11th Plenary Session of the 8th Central Committee of the CCP, Aug. 12, 1966.

7. Translated in *Survey of the China Mainland Press* (Hong Kong), No. 3622, pp. 6–8; henceforth cited as *SCMP.*

8. *China News Analysis* (Hong Kong), No. 506 (Feb. 28, 1964), p. 5; henceforth cited as CNA.

9. Arthur A. Cohen, *op. cit.,* which has provided many leads and suggestions for this brief summary of TMTT, argues that rather than being pure Marxism, this belief in the will of man over the material conditions is more closely associated with the views of Lenin, Trotsky, and Stalin. But pushed back to fundamentals, Marxism—in its early stages, at least—argues that the labor of man is entirely responsible for those material conditions.

10. For a valuable and important discussion on Chinese communist utilization of struggle, see Arthur F. Wright, "Struggle versus Harmony, Symbols of Competing Values in China," *World Politics,* VI (1953–4), 31–44.

11. On the Yang Hsien-chen affair see CNA, No. 535 (Oct. 2, 1964).

12. *Shih-chieh Chih-shih* (Peking), No. 5 (Dec. 1960).

13. This was demonstrated, for instance, in June 1966 when the official line on China's population shifted from 650 million to 700 million in mainland publications. (The Albanians, probably not without reason, given their small numbers, had been using the larger figures in hailing their ally for more than a year.) With the shift came a whole new stream of editorial assertions that China's great numbers constituted a major force and source of strength for revolutionaries around the world.

14. H. F. Schurmann, "Organization and Response in Communist China," *The Annals,* CCXXI (Jan. 1959), 51–61, remains one of the most important discussions of the role of the "study groups." Cf. also my *China Under Communism: The First Five Years* (New Haven, 1955), ch. iii, "Psychological Control."

15. John W. Lewis, *Leadership in Communist China* (Ithaca, N.Y., 1963), pp. 70–100, elaborates on the earlier work of H. Arthur Steiner in a valuable discussion of Chinese communist mass line tactics.

16. From excerpts given in *The New York Times,* Nov. 28, 1966.

17. Stuart R. Schram, *The Political Thought of Mao Tse-tung* (New York, 1963), for example, gives little attention to the impact of power on the

man, his thought, and his action, nor does Schram see much personality change. Jerome Ch'en, *Mao and the Chinese Revolution* (London, 1965), wisely terminates his study with the proclamation of the CPR. Schram, Benjamin I. Schwartz, and Joseph R. Levenson are all students of the thought and politics of Mao Tse-tung. They tend to project the image of an unchanging Mao, linked to the liberal image of "the Chinese Revolution" and characterized by "a curious mixture of humanism and totalitarian motives," to quote Schram. See "Maoism: A Symposium" cited in n. 5 above. Many Western writers have relied heavily on the works of Edgar Snow, who first helped to create the legendary Mao and retains his deep admiration for the "old warrior." See, for example, his "Interview with Mao," *The New Republic,* Feb. 27, 1965, pp. 17–23.

18. *Pravda,* Apr. 28, 1964; as quoted by TASS, Apr. 29, 1964.

19. Arthur A. Cohen, "Concluding Remarks," *Problems of Communism,* XV:5 (Sep.–Oct. 1966), 25–6.

20. The full text of the communiqué together with pictures demonstrating the new extremes of the cult of Mao are given in the special issue of Peking's international propaganda publication *China Pictorial* (Sep. 1966).

21. SCMP, No. 3586 (Nov. 29, 1965), p. 2.

22. New China News Agency, on Peking Radio, June 4, 1966.

23. For an interesting account about the Peking training of an African, see Emmanuel John Hevi, *An African Student in China* (New York, 1963).

24. The article from *Drum* is reproduced in *Atlas,* XII:6 (Dec. 1966), 20–2.

25. Lin Piao, *Long Live the Victory of People's War!* (Peking, 1965), pp. 47–9.

26. See V. P. Dutt, *China and the World: An Analysis of Communist China's Foreign Policy* (New York, 1966).

27. For some revealing documents on the extent of starvation connected with the "people's communes" as well as a general summary of developments in the two crucial years, see my "Letters from the Communes" and "Hunger in China: Letters from the Communes—II," special sections of *The New Leader,* June 15, 1959, and May 30, 1960.

28. Important articles from the 29 issues and over 900 pages of the *Kung-tso T'ung-hsun* have been published in a large volume edited by J. Chester Cheng, *The Politics of the Chinese Red Army* (Stanford, Cal., 1966). The editor of CNA has done his usual remarkable job of summarizing all of the materials in three issues: 510, 511, and 512.

29. For some of the texts of denunciation of the CCP and of Mao himself, together with analysis, see Roderick MacFarquhar, *The Hundred Flowers* (London, 1960).

30. George Patterson, "Tibet," *The Reporter,* March 25, 1965, pp. 31–3, gives an account of the continuing guerrilla activities of the Khamba tribesmen.

31. These dates are selected by Donald J. Munro in his valuable summary "Dissent in Communist China: The Current Anti-Intellectual Campaign in Perspective," *Current Scene* (Hong Kong), IV:11 (June 1, 1966). He points

out that the dates for the "period of dissent" are "a convenience and not absolute."

32. See the issue of CNA, No. 404 (Jan. 19, 1962), entitled "Cultural Renaissance."

33. *Current Background,* No. 792 (June 29, 1966), contains the full text of the article; published by the U. S. Consulate General, Hong Kong.

34. Although the article in the *People's Daily* does not commit the impropriety of saying that Teng was talking directly about Mao Tse-tung in his "Amnesia" piece, the *Liberation Army Daily* on May 26, 1966, pointed out that the "Amnesia" article proved that "Teng T'o and his gang hate . . . Chairman Mao with the most intense class hatred" (Peking Radio broadcast, in Mandarin, May 27, 1966).

35. For a discussion of the purge and its relationship to the divisions at the top levels of the Party, see Harry Gelman, "Mao and the Permanent Purge," *Problems of Communism,* XV:6 (Nov.–Dec. 1966), 2–14, and Theodore Hsi-en Chen, "A Nation in Agony," pp. 14–20. Chen's article stresses the regime's problems with the intellectuals.

36. Michael Freeberne, "The Great Splash Forward," *Problems of Communism,* XV:6 (Nov.–Dec. 1966), 21–7, gives a delightful interpretation of Mao's 1966 swim and its "tidal aftermath."

37. On the rise of Lin Piao see CNA, No. 618 (Jul. 1, 1966), and No. 620 (Jul. 15, 1966).

38. CNA 612 (May 20, 1966), pp. 1–3, discusses the affair of the *Liberation Army Daily* versus the *People's Daily.*

39. *The New York Times,* Nov. 28, 1966.

Discussion
ARTHUR S. Y. CHEN

Historically, the communists came to power in mainland China through force and the effective mobilization of the massive discontent felt by Chinese peasants, the *bourgeoisie,* and intellectuals. The Chinese communists had identified themselves with a bitter, resentful nationalism bred among the masses for over a century of humiliation and foreign domination. The record shows that they had profitably exploited postwar conditions in order to create what they called a "revolutionary situation," a situation most favorable for pressing on with their struggle for power.

In brief, the revolutionary processes of Chinese communist consolidation were initially and primarily politico-military, then economic and xenophobic in nature and scope. One of the most important achievements during the war years as well as in various phases of the "united front" involved a revitalization of the Chinese Communist Party (CCP) under the personal leadership and domination of Mao Tse-tung. As a Marxist-

Leninist inspired party, the CCP was obliged to adjust its programs and tactics to conditions of a backward and semicolonial China that had to undergo drastic transformations before the "ultimate victory" of the socialist-communist revolution could be attained. In the past Maoism or the Chinese brand of communism, which served as a creative formula for continuing the revolution both at home and abroad, became incalculably important for the Chinese communists. Mao had been exalted as "the brilliant exponent of Marxism-Leninism in the Chinese context"; Maoism with its agrarian strategy and tactics, as Marshal Lin Piao sees it, should be the model for guiding the communist movement among the oppressed and inexperienced Asians, Africans, and Latin Americans.

From the introductory portion of Professor Walker's chapter on "The Elusive Élan" one cannot but note that after eighteen years of authoritarian control over the mainland the quality of Maoist rule has changed dramatically. By 1968 the Maoist regime appears to be divided and in disarray, not to say on the verge of a civil war. A mystified world, communist and noncommunist, looks on Red China in bafflement. Professor Walker analytically surveyed the harassing problems of political control by the Peking regime under six headings. They include (1) Maoist dogmatism that despises Soviet revisionism; (2) the emphasis on the continuing struggle as a means of political control among the Han and non-Han dissident Chinese; (3) the employment of mobilization and organization in endless drives or campaigns for further consolidation; (4) Chairman Mao, the incomparable leader, and the cult of personality built around him; (5) Peking's insidious policy with its insistence on exporting revolutions or "people's wars of liberation"; and (6) the alternate application of astute tactics of "tension and relaxation," or "zigzag," or "ebb and flow," as a psychological weapon for the consolidation and extension of control. One has to read the entire chapter in order to appreciate more the keen-sighted and interrelated analysis.

The aging Chairman Mao has had an uneasy apprehension of what will happen after he passes from the scene. His unalterable stand maintains that Maoist ideology remains all-important to keep the revolutionary spirit aflame. In his view Maoism should be the guide to China's future, not the "revisionism" of the Soviet Union which has developed since Stalin's death. In mid-August 1966 rules applied by the "great proletarian cultural revolution," the official name for the current convulsion wracking the mainland, imposed the necessity to eradicate the "four olds": old ideas, old culture, old customs, and old habits. The fact is that this "cultural revolution" implies the use of ruthless power to supress all the forces of dissidence and disaffection within Red China.

Among these forces are Party bureaucrats, economic technocrats, intellectuals, scientific and military professionals who have found in Maoism a contradiction between ideology and practice, between dogma and necessity. Some of them have dared to speak out; others used allegories; both groups have been purged. Reportedly even some of the peasants and workers, who have been reluctantly acquiescent, now fight against the Red Guards and emotionally complain about massive repressions and pervasive controls by the regime. Opposing the Mao-Lin group and its inflexible policies are the pragmatists and the moderates. Those realists who witness the terrible waste, inefficiency, and incompetence attribute the nation's manmade calamities (in the rural commune system and the "great leap forward") as the products of Mao's errors. The "infallible" and inflexible Maoist ideology has become far removed from reality and a fantasy to them. The moderates blame deservedly the absurd extremism of the regime for the detrimental results of deteriorating relations with Moscow, the "great slide backward," and various diplomatic rebuffs. Their hostility stems from a mounting conviction that the regime has been running the nation very poorly.

Domestically and internationally in 1968 it is increasingly apparent that the Maoist revolution not only has become outmoded but also is opposed by top leaders within the party apparatus. The rigid Maoist thinking is outmoded in the sense that the pattern of austere Yenan life during the 1930's and the somewhat successful strategy of firmly establishing power in the 1950's are not applicable to the problems of the late 1960's. After eighteen years Maoism has proved to be a fiasco and not the panacea for China's many ills. The vision of monolithic Maoist power is now exposed to the world as a myth. It has become fractured because Maoism in practice made colossal blunders. It should be underscored that the anti-Mao elements, including such personalities as President Liu Shao-chi and Party secretary-general Teng Hsiao-ping, are having considerable influence on the Party apparatus at the province and municipal levels. A large part of the Party machine is of President Liu Shao-chi's own creation, and some Party leaders still in key positions at different levels are Liu's protégés.

The continuing rampage of the supermilitant Red Guards is being identified as a *coup,* designed by the Mao-Lin faction and its newly selected Party leadership to wipe out all opposition inside and outside the CCP. Under the red banner of the "great proletarian cultural revolution" the activities of the teen-age Red Guards reportedly have disrupted the educational system, the transportation network, the economy, and stability in major Chinese cities as well as in some rural areas. This "cultural revolution" which does not seem to be ending quickly, has brought cries of bewilderment and dismay from communists around the world who had once been so enchanted by Mao's new China.

No one would attempt to predict what will take place tomorrow or next week in Red China, which now represents a very complex chaos, a profound crisis with no clear end in sight. Combing the reports, some of which conflict, and reassessing the war of posters between the Red Guards and the "Red Rebels," one wonders if the era of Mao Tse-tung is approaching its finale. In any event, China-watching is a subtle art. As one diplomat has put it, it is like peeping through a window into a dark room full of fighting black cats on a dark night. One has little idea which cat is winning or losing. In brief, the "great proletarian cultural revolution" does not merely consist of antifeudalism, anti-imperialism, or antirevisionism; it is a struggle for power in the politico-ideological sense of the term.

9

economy and foreign trade of mainland china

CHU-YUAN CHENG

When the communists assumed power in October 1949, they appealed to the Chinese people to develop their country from a backward agrarian nation into a modern industrial giant. To achieve this proclaimed goal, two major measures were undertaken during the past eighteen years. On the one hand, the regime commenced a series of institutional changes to undermine the traditional socio-economic structure and to establish a new order following the Soviet model. On the other hand, in 1953 a rapid industrialization program was launched in an attempt to build up modern industry within a short span of time.

In the process of this industrialization drive, foreign trade has been playing a significant role. Although the regime set autarchy as one of its long-run economic targets, communist China has heavily relied on foreign countries in supplying many required items of equipment and raw materials. Quantitatively the share of foreign trade in Red China has ranged from 6.2 per cent in 1953 to 8.8 per cent in 1959, roughly comparable to that of the United States and the Soviet Union but much lower than that of Western Europe and Japan.[1] However, imports constitute a vital channel for Red China to obtain not only equipment but also new technology which has become the driving force of China's modernization and industrialization. Without international trade China's economic growth in the first decade would have been much slower than achieved.

The progress of industrialization and the performance in foreign trade during the past nineteen years, however, were not carried out in a steady manner. During the first Five-Year Plan period (1953–7), in close collaboration with the Soviet Union, trade with the communist Bloc expanded rapidly. More than a hundred major industrial projects were built or expanded. A fairly high rate of economic growth was maintained. Beginning in the summer of 1958, the regime suddenly decided to launch the "great leap forward" movement and substantially altered the schedule of the existing plan. The entire program functioned in an abnormal climate which not only undermined the planned economic system but caused a total breakdown of the national economy. The disastrous effect became further aggravated by the ill-conceived commune system, three consecutive years of natural calamities, and the sudden suspension of U.S.S.R. economic assistance. During 1961–2 trade with the Soviet decreased by 50 per cent. By 1963 the total volume of Chinese foreign trade declined to a level like that in 1952.

In order to alleviate the economic crisis the regime since 1961 has adopted a series of new policies. Capital investment for heavy industry has been curtailed appreciably; high priority has been placed on agricultural development; trade with noncommunist countries has been expanding constantly; and a new campaign for birth control has been in full swing. The new policies brought about a steady yet slower recovery of agriculture and industry. By 1965 output of food grains was slightly higher than the 1957 level, while industrial production still had not reached the peak year of 1960. Although foreign trade recovered faster than agricultural production during the past four years, its 1966 volume was still 4 per cent below the 1959 level.

In the long-range prospect communist China's economic growth and foreign trade may be regarded as a function of the state in food and agriculture. A stagnation in the agricultural sector will hamper the expansion of foreign trade and prohibit any high rate of economic growth. Unless Peking's rulers can maintain a balanced development between food supplies and population growth, the Chinese economy will always be confronted with a vicious cycle and a rapid industrialization program will become impossible to fulfill.

The Major Socio-Economic Reforms

To accelerate the industrialization program the leaders in Peking conceived of a dramatic change in socio-economic institutions as a prerequisite. Such a consideration was based on two fundamental grounds. First, in the ideological aspect, it was deeply felt by the new Chinese leaders that until the final attainment of the communist paradise, the whole of society would be composed of people belonging to conflicting classes. They represent different class interests. The more advanced class is the proletariat, which becomes the leading group in the revolution and the driving force toward a communist society. Opposed to the proletariat are those classes comprising landlords, *bourgeoisie,* and petty *bourgeoisie.* To build a new socio-economic order as well as to consolidate the so-called "proletariat dictatorship" it was indispensable to wage a fierce class struggle. Second, in the economic aspect, the new Chinese leaders followed the Soviet model by creating a central planning and control system. Without nationalization of industry and commerce as well as collectivization of agriculture and handicraft a high degree of central planning could not function. With these considerations in mind since 1949 a series of radical reforms in rural and urban areas had been undertaken.

Land Reform

The most important move to change Chinese rural society was the land reform, carried out during 1949–52. According to the Chinese communist basic plan, land reform meant more than just land redistribution. It actually is an effective weapon for conducting a "class struggle" against the ruling group in rural areas and for consolidation of Party control over the peasants. Land reform becomes an extremely complicated process which includes three basic stages.[2]

In the first, or preparatory, phase the chief task was to awaken the poor peasants by stirring up their hatred toward the landlords. To obtain support from the poor peasantry the rent paid by tenants was decreased. The "positive elements," selected from among the poor peasants, were organized to wage the struggle against landlords. In the second stage the rural population was divided into six classes: landlords, rich peasants of semilandlord type, rich peasants, well-to-do middle peasants, poor peasants, and farm laborers. Each class was then subdivided into many strata. After the differentiation according to class status, land and houses as well as all belongings of landlords and semilandlords were confiscated. This was accompanied by mass trials and executions. In the course of the land reform it has been estimated that some ten million households of landlords, rich peasants, and "reactionaries" were liquidated. The last stage involves redistribution of land. According to an official report, "about 300 million peasants have received economic benefits from the land reform. Some 700 million *mou* [one *mou* equals one sixth of an acre] of land have been distributed."

The Cooperative Movement

Immediately following the land reform the Central Committee of the Chinese Communist Party (CCP) in 1952 adopted a decision to collectivize the peasants through the "cooperative movement." This program embraced three steps: establishment of mutual aid teams, organization of elementary cooperatives, and the formation of collective farms. Beginning in 1951, two kinds of mutual-aid teams had been promoted in the rural areas. The simplest comprised the seasonal team with three to five households. It operated during the busy seasons only. The advanced type was the year-round, or permanent, mutual-aid team, which consisted of six to eight or more households. Some teams accumulated common property such as implements and cattle. Both types of mutual-aid teams were organized on the foundation of private property. The Chinese communists regarded them as a kind of "embryonic socialism."

In 1953 the elementary cooperatives were introduced. The new system was characterized by pooling of land under a unified management. Each cooperative contained from fifty to a hundred households. Ownership of land and other principal means of production continued to remain in private hands. Income distribution depended on two sources: the amount of land a member possessed and the number of work-days he contributed to production. Since land and the principal means of production were still privately owned, this system was regarded as only semisocialist in nature.

The advanced cooperatives or collective farms did not appear until the latter half of 1955. They represented a higher type of collectivization, similar to the Soviet *kolkhoz*. Each collective farm had an average of 158 households. When a peasant became a member, his land and other principal means of production were transferred from private to collective ownership; all payments on his part were abolished. By the end of 1957 China's 120 million peasant households had been organized into 752,113 cooperatives.

The Commune System

In April 1958 a more radical program known as the "people's commune" was launched in rural areas. Within a five-month period, that is, by the end of September 1958, some 90 per cent of the advanced cooperatives had been merged into 24,000 communes. Each commune on the average consisted of over 5,000 peasant households, a membership about twenty times that of the agricultural cooperatives. A commune also differed from the cooperative in its function, ownership relations, income distribution, and manner of peasant life. In the early stage the commune was proclaimed by the regime as a ladder to the communist paradise. Peasants were required to surrender to the commune all of their property and belongings, including the small garden plots of land. They were ordered to eat together in public mess halls, place their children in communal nurseries, and work under central management. However, after one year of experimentation the system proved unworkable. During the past ten years a series of revisions have been adopted.[3] The size of the commune was reduced to only one third of the original, and the number of communes increased from 24,000 in September 1959 to 74,000 in October 1964. The small garden plots have been returned to the peasants since 1959. Mess halls were suspended, and the peasants were allowed to retain their private kitchens. The authority over and ownership of the commune was shifted first from the commune itself to the productive brigade (a unit equivalent to the former advanced cooperative) and then to the level of the smaller productive teams. The whole system has swung full circle to a position similar to that which prevailed before 1958. Although for political reasons the name commune has been retained, its substance has in fact been completely changed.

Private Industry and Business

The transformation of the private sector into a state-operated sector was conducted by means of a more complex process in the urban areas. It consisted basically of two main steps: the first transformed capitalism into state capitalism, and the second converted state capitalism into socialism. In early 1952 the Chinese communists launched the so-called "Five-Anti" *(Wu-fan)* campaign to curb the growth of the private sector. The official justification for this was to combat the five evils of bribery among government workers, tax evasion, theft of state property, cheating on government contracts, and stealing economic information from the government. Its real purpose, however, was to confiscate the liquid assets from private enterprises. During this campaign more than 340,000 private firms were involved.[4] These enterprises were ordered to pay large fines, determined by the local governments. As a result of this action most private firms virtually exhausted their working capital. Taking this opportunity, the regime began to implement an advanced form of state capitalism known as joint state-private management. By the first quarter of 1956 some 92 per cent of all private industry and 75 per cent of private business were transformed into joint state-private enterprises. Thus the old private ownership, which had lasted several thousand years, was changed into a system of public ownership.

Handicrafts and Peddlers

Apart from the private enterprise in urban areas, there were more than 2.4 million private business units in rural areas and some 20 million handicraftsmen in the cities and countryside. To lead them along the path of collectivization the regime adopted measures such as amalgamating their shops into joint companies or organizing them into mixed state-private stores. By the end of 1958, in terms of membership, about 37 per cent of the handicraft cooperatives had been transferred from collective ownership into ownership by the whole people; only 28 per cent retained their collective ownerships as cooperative factories; and the remaining 35 per cent were handicraft cooperatives in rural areas under the supervision of people's communes.

The Urban Commune

While the high tide of the commune movement swept over the rural areas in 1958, urban communes were also established in some cities. By the end of June 1960 over a thousand units, comprising 52 million people, had been established. In organization the urban commune differed somewhat from its rural counterpart. There was no unified pattern: some were formed on the basis of street residence; others centered themselves on factories or mines; still others were organized in government offices and schools. Urban communes have had different sizes, depending upon local conditions. For instance, in Shenyang commune membership ranges from fifty to eighty thousand. In Harbin eight communes have more than 1.27 million people, about 150,000 members per unit. After 1962, however, most of the urban communes were dissolved.

The Industrialization Program

The original plan for industrialization adopted by the Chinese communists will take a fairly long time to complete its fundamental task. The constitution of communist China adopted by its first National People's Congress (NPC) in September 1954 states: "From the founding of the People's Republic of China to the attainment of a socialist society is a period of transition. During this transition the fundamental task of the state is step by step to bring about the socialist industrialization of the country." Planners of communist China expect that to implement such a plan would involve three five-year plans in addition to the three years of rehabilitation from 1950 to 1952. At the same time they recognized that industrialization in any full sense would require a much longer period and that it would be forty to fifty years before China could become "a powerful country with a high degree of socialist industrialization."[5]

The First Five-Year Plan

By the end of 1952 the government had announced that the period of rehabilitation was coming to an end and that the first Five-Year Plan for development of the national economy would begin in 1953. However, the final plan was not submitted until July 1955 to the second session of the First National People's Congress and approved by it the end of that month. Over-all targets under the first Five-Year Plan revealed the emphasis placed on industrialization and the proposed high tempo of economic growth. National income in the five-year period was to increase by 50 per cent. Gross industrial production was to be doubled, whereas gross agricultural production would rise by 25 per cent. The total amount allocated for capital investment was 42.7 billion yuan. Of this amount a sum of 24.8 billion yuan, or 58.2 per cent of the total, was devoted to industrial development. Only 3.3 billion yuan, or 7.6 per cent, was for the agricultural sector. The ratio between investment in industry and in agriculture was 7.5 to one (see Table 13).

TABLE 13

State Investment in Capital Construction of Mainland China (1953–7)
(in billions of yuan)

Category	Targets	Percentage	Actual	Percentage
Industry	24.850	58.2	27.608	56.0
Agriculture	3.260	7.6	4.043	8.2
Transport	8.210	19.2	9.219	18.7
Trade, banking & stockpiling	1.280	3.0		
Urban Pub. Utilities	1.600	3.7	7.430	17.1
Other items	460	1.1		
Cultural, Education & Public Health	3.080	7.2		
Total	42.740	100.0	49.300	100.0

SOURCES: (a) *First Five-Year Plan for Development of the National Economy of the People's Republic of China 1953–1957* and (b) Communiqué on the Fulfillment of the First Five-Year Plan, *Peking Review,* April 21, 1959, p. 28.

Of the total capital investment the major part was allocated for 1,600 above-norm projects,[6] of which 694 were industrial. Among the latter the cornerstone was laid for the 156 industrial projects to be built with Soviet aid. These U.S.S.R. aided projects included modern iron and steel complexes, nonferrous metallurgical plants, coal mines, oil industry installations, heavy machinery plants (including automobile, tractor, and aircraft factories), chemical works, and power stations. Within the first Five-Year Plan work had begun on 145 of these 156 projects. However, with the rapid increase of investment in 1956 the tasks for capital construction set in the plan were reported to have been fulfilled. A communiqué on the fulfillment of the first Five-Year Plan declared that

> The overwhelming majority of the construction projects scheduled under the first Five-Year Plan were completed and many new items were added. In these five years, work went ahead on more than 10,000 industrial and mining projects, of which 312 were ferrous metal projects, 599 were power projects, 600 were coal projects, 22 were petroleum projects, 1,921 were

metal processing projects, 637 were chemical projects, 832 were building materials projects, 253 were paper-making projects, 613 were textile projects, and about 5,000 were foodstuffs processing and other projects.

Among the more than 10,000 industrial and mining projects under construction, 921 were above-norm projects, an increase of 227 projects over the number set by the Plan. Of these above-norm projects, by the end of 1957, 428 had gone into full operation and 109 into partial production. Of the 156 major construction projects to be built with the help of the Soviet Union, 135 were already under construction by the end of 1957, and 68 were fully or partially completed and in operation.[7]

With the large number of newly-built and expanded enterprises completed during the first Five-Year Plan, the production capacity of the major industrial units developed to a considerable degree (see Table 14).

TABLE 14

Annual Increase in Production Capacity Under the First
Chinese Five-Year Plan (1952–7)

Item	Targets (thousands)	Claimed Results (thousands)
Pig iron	2,800 tons	3,390 tons
Steel	2,530 tons	2,820 tons
Electric Power	2,050 KW	2,469 KW
Coal	53,850 tons	63,760 tons
Metallurgical & Mining Machines	70 tons	8.7 tons
Power-generating equipment	800 KW	n.a.
Lorries	30	30
Chemical fertilizers	280 tons	n.a.
Cement	2,360 tons	2,610 tons
Cotton spindles	1,650 spindles	2,010 spindles
Paper	95 tons	250 tons
Sugar	428 tons	620 tons
Petroleum	n.a.	1,312 tons

SOURCES: For targets, see *The First Five-Year Plan, op. cit.;* on claimed results, see *Communiqué on the Fulfillment of the First Five-Year Plan, op. cit.*

The fact that priority in development was given to heavy industry is seen in the high rate of increase set for production of capital goods under the first Five-Year Plan. Total value of industrial output in 1957 reportedly exceeded the original plan by 21 per cent and was 141 per cent higher than in 1952. According to the original plan, the average annual rate of increase would be 14.7 per cent. Actually it reached 19.2 per cent.[8] Targets for most of the heavy industry products were fulfilled or overfulfilled. But those for the consumers goods industry, such as cotton yarn, cotton cloth, edible oils, sugar, and cigarettes, all failed. This clearly indicates that communist China has developed her capital goods industry at the expense of consumers goods (see Table 15).

TABLE 15

Major Chinese Industrial Output
in the First Five-Year Plan (1952–7)

Item	Unit	1952	1957 (Target)	1957 (Actual)	Increase
Steel	1000 tons	1,350	4,120	5,350	296%
Pig iron	1000 tons	1,930	4,674	5,940	208%
Electric power	million KWH	7,260	15,900	19,300	166%
Coal	1000 tons	66,490	112,985	130,000	96%
Crude Oil	1000 tons	436	2,012	1,460	235%
Cement	1000 tons	2,860	6,000	6,860	140%
Timber	10,000 cub. met.	1,120	2,000	2,787	149%
Sulphuric acid	1000 tons	190	——	632	233%
Soda ash	1000 tons	192	476	506	164%
Caustic soda	1000 tons	79	154	198	150%
Chemical fertilizers	1000 tons	181	504	631	249%
Power-generating equipment	1000 KW	——	227	198	——
Metal-cutting machine tools	1000 units	13.7	12.7	28	104%
Locomotives	units	20	200	167	735%
Railway goods wagons	units	5,792	8,500	7,300	26%
Motor vehicles	units	——	——	7,500	——
Merchant vessels	1000 tons	16	——	54	338%
Internal combustion engines	1000 hp	27.6	260	609	2,107%
Cotton yarn	1000 bales	3,620	5,000	4,650	28%
Cotton cloth	million meters	3,830	5,583	5,050	32%
Paper	1000 tons	540	655	1,220	126%
Edible oils	1000 tons	980	1,552	1,100	12%
Sugar	1000 tons	451	686	864	92%
Salt	1000 tons	4,945	5,932	8,277	67%
Cigarettes	1000 cases	2,650	4,700	4,460	68%

SOURCES: For 1957 targets, see *The First Five-Year Plan, op. cit.*; on figures for 1952 and 1957 (actual), see *Communiqué, op. cit.*

To cope with industrial development, attention has also been paid to transportation. Under the Plan it received 18.7 per cent of the total state investment for capital construction. One of the primary tasks under this branch is the development of a transportation network in the northwestern and northern regions of China, where the natural resources are still under-developed and conditions remain very primitive. The proposed investment of almost 5.7 billion yuan for capital construction in railways constituted 72 per cent of the total investment for capital construction in transportation. The Plan proposed building slightly more than four thousand kilometers of trunk and feeder lines. Actually almost five thousand kilometers of new railroads had been built by the end of 1957.

The weak link in the first Five-Year Plan was in the agricultural sector. Investments in rural areas were far below those for industry and transportation. In 1957 the gross output value of agriculture and subsidiary agricultural occupations registered only 25 per cent above that of 1952, with an annual average increase of only 4.5 per cent. Production of food grains reached 185 million tons in 1957, providing an increase of 20 per cent over 1952 at an annual rate of 3.7 per cent, which is just slightly higher than the natural increase per year of population at 2.2 per cent during the same period. The total amount of cotton was 1.64 million tons, representing 26 per cent above 1952 and giving an annual increase of 4.7 per cent. For other crops, such as soya beans and tea, the actual outputs in 1957 all failed to reach their targets. Great setbacks were also registered for livestock products. The picture of the agricultural sector as a whole recorded failure instead of success in the first Five-Year Plan.

Second Five-Year Plan and the "Great Leap Forward"

Proposals for the second Five-Year Plan (1958–62) were presented at the 8th National Congress of the Chinese Communist Party (CCP) held in Peking during September 15–27, 1956. The plan remained in sketch form until it was discarded in 1958. The formal plan has never been published. The guiding principles of the second Five-Year Plan do not differ substantially from the first. The central task of the second Plan was to give priority to development of heavy industry, and particularly the steel and machine-building industries. A fairly rapid rate of growth of the national economy was envisaged. An increase of 51.1 per cent in the total value of industrial and agricultural output was expected during the first Plan, and a further increase of about 75 per cent by 1962 was envisaged, as compared with 1957. The value of industrial production by 1962 would nearly double the figures set for 1957, and agricultural output would increase by about 35 per cent.

Under the first Plan the producers goods accounted for 38 per cent of the total value of industrial output in 1957. During the second Five-Year

Plan the proportion of producers goods was to rise from 38 to 50 per cent, representing an increasing emphasis on capital goods and a de-emphasis on consumers goods. National income in the second Five-Year Plan period was to grow by about 50 per cent. With an expansion of state revenue the amount of capital investment during this period would roughly double that of the first. The proportion of state capital construction investment in industry was to be raised from 58.2 to about 60 per cent. The share devoted to agriculture, forestry, and water conservation was to be increased from 7.6 to 10 per cent[9] (see Table 16).

TABLE 16

Targets for Main Chinese Industrial Output (1957–62)

Items	Units	Targets for 1957	Targets for 1962
Electricity	million KWH	15,900.0	40,000–43,000
Coal	million tons	113.0	190–210
Crude oil	million tons	2.0	5–6
Steel	million tons	4.1	10.5–12
Aluminum ingots	1,000 tons	20.0	100–120
Chemical fertilizers	1,000 tons	573.0	3,000–3,200
Metallurgical equipment	1,000 tons	8.0	30–40
Power-generating equipment	1,000 KW	164.0	1,400–1,500
Metal-cutting machine tools	1,000 units	13.0	60–65
Timber	million cu. m.	20.0	31–34
Cement	million tons	6.0	12.5–14.5
Cotton yarn	million tons	0.9	1.5–1.6
Cotton piece-goods	million meters	5,583.0	8,595–9,509
Salt	million tons	7.6	10–11
Edible oil	million tons	1.8	3.1–3.2
Sugar	million tons	1.1	2.4–2.5
Paper	million tons	0.7	1.5–1.6

SOURCE: *Handbook on People's China* (Peking: Foreign Languages Press, 1957), p. 115.

It was stipulated that during the period of the second Five-Year Plan, vigorous efforts would be made to expand the machine-building industry and to continue development of metallurgy. At the same time special attention was to be paid to electric power, coal mining, and building-materials industries as well as to strengthening backward branches, such as the oil, chemical, and radio-equipment industries. Besides, communist China expressed the ambition to establish factories utilizing atomic energy for peaceful purposes.

In order to cope with the needs of industrial production it was necessary to build from 8,000 to 9,000 kilometers of new railways in these five years. The trunk lines from Lanchow to the Sino-Soviet border, from Paotow (the new iron and steel base in northern China) to Lanchow, from Nei-chiang (in Szechuan province, southwest China) to Kunming (Yunnan province, in southwest China), from Chungking to Kweiyang (in Kweichow province), and from Lanchow to Tsaidam (Chinghai province in the northwest) were to be completed. In addition, some 15,000 to 18,000 kilometers of trunk highways should have been constructed or reconstructed in these five years. Although agriculture drew more attention during the second Five-Year Plan, the increased targets for food grains and livestock still appeared very limited (see Table 17).

TABLE 17

Goals for Agriculture in the Second Chinese Five-Year Plan (1957–62)

Products	Unit	Targets for 1957	Targets for 1962
Grain	million tons	181.59	250.0
Cotton	million tons	1.64	2.4
Soya-beans	million tons	11.22	12.5
Cattle	million head	73.60	90.0
Horses	million head	8.30	11.0
Sheep and Goats	million head	113.00	170.0
Pigs	million head	138.30	250.0

When the second Five-Year Plan was proposed in September 1956, the economic situation in mainland China did not appear as good as had been expected. Since the beginning of the first Five-Year Plan, as a result of overinvestment in capital construction, commodity shortages had become a perpetual phenomenon. Strict rationing of essential consumers goods did not ease the situation. In 1956 a sharp increase by 59 per cent in capital investment over the preceding year pushed the tension of the commodity market to a new peak. Inflationary pressure made the economic leaders aware of their mistake in overinvestment. A considerable reduction in the development-plan goals was adopted by the Peking government in the spring of 1957. Capital investment in 1957 registered a reduction of 7.4 per cent from the preceding year. Industrial production increased by only 6.9 per cent, the lowest attained during the first Five-Year Plan. Targets for agricultural output in 1957 were also reduced. The draft capital investment plan for 1958, the first year of the second Plan, set by the State Planning Commission in May 1957 was lower than the level for 1956. Targets in agricultural output for 1958 were put at a level only 5 per cent above those for 1957. Industrial production increased by only 10 per cent, which was far below the proposed annual rate established under the second Five-Year Plan. A pessimistic outlook prevailed throughout the whole communist party. If this trend could not be reversed, the major targets of the second Plan mentioned above could hardly be fulfilled.

The all-round setback on the economic front also caused a rise in unemployment, both in the urban districts and in the countryside. As capital investment dropped in 1957, demand for labor also declined. The new labor force remained mostly unemployed. In the first half of 1957 a birth control campaign attained full swing. Prohibition of peasant migration to the city was enforced. All this meant that the industrial development had reached a bottleneck. In order to change this situation Mao Tsetung in October 1957 called for an "anti-rightist campaign" within the Party. A new drive known as the "great leap forward" began to be implemented.

The "great leap forward" drive started with the expansion of water conservation projects on an unprecedented scale. According to official statistics, from the winter of 1957 to the middle part of April 1958 some 100 million peasants had been assigned to work on water conservation projects, where they reportedly built 56 billion cubic meters of earth and stone work, using more than 13 billion labor days. In other words, at that time almost every peasant household in China contributed one full-time labor force for a period of over three months.[10] Such a large-scale mobilization of rural manpower finds no parallel in Chinese history.

In May 1958 the second session of the 8th National CCP Congress adopted a new policy, labeled "the general line for socialist construction." This embraced a set of directives to accelerate the development of industry. The most important policy involved the advocacy of local, small-scale enterprises with indigenous methods of production. Prior to 1958 the development plan emphasized modern, large-scale, and capital-intensive industrial projects. Much pride was taken in advanced and up-to-date machinery and techniques of production that had been introduced into the factories. Under the new line, labor-intensive techniques assumed the leading role. According to Liu Shao-chi, CPR chairman, small enterprises had an advantage over large businesses: they required less investment and could more easily absorb funds from scattered sources; they required less time to build and produced quicker results; they could be designed and equipped locally; they could be established over a wide area so as to facilitate industrialization of the country as a whole. Moreover, it was easier for leaders to make flexible use of the manpower available in the countryside.

With this new approach a drastic drive to build up small factories and mines, using indigenous methods in production, swept the whole country. Some sixty million persons became involved with the so-called "back-yard blast furnaces" drive. These back-yard furnaces were built in every neighborhood, not only in rural areas but also in urban centers. They were made of crude clay and bricks. Raw materials included all kinds of scrap, ore and coal the government could lay its hands on, including cooking pots and pans which people were forced to donate. Besides, hundreds of thousands of small coal pits, oil refineries, power stations, cement plants, fertilizer factories, farm-tool manufacturing and repair plants, as well as food-processing factories were set up in the vast rural areas.[11]

The new drive increased the output of iron and steel at a considerable speed. In August 1958 the CCP Political Bureau called an enlarged meeting to adopt a resolution for "taking steel production as the core to achieve a comprehensive leap forward." This statement revised 1958 targets for industrial and agricultural output, set by the State Planning Commission in February 1958, and approved the establishment of people's communes in rural areas. It required that steel output in 1958 reach 10.7 million, coal 270 million, grain production 375 million, and cotton 3.35 million tons. These new targets all doubled the original ones adopted in February. Then in December 1958 the 6th Plenum of the 8th CCP Central Committee further decided that during 1959 China's steel output would reach 18 million tons, an increase of 200 per cent compared with 1957 and a 60 per cent increase over 1958. Coal output would be 380 million tons, also 200 per cent over 1957 and 40 per cent above 1958. Such a high rate of increase for industrial and agricultural output was unprecedented in the world.

However, this fantastic "great leap forward" proved abortive. The facts of economic development in mainland China remained far divorced from official claims. For instance, although Chinese communists claimed a bumper harvest in 1958 by doubling the food grain produced in a single year, the supply of food grain showed no improvement in 1958 or 1959. According to Chou En-lai, premier of communist China, in areas constituting about 5 per cent of the country, food grain was in serious short supply during the spring of 1959. According to another official report, in Hopeh province the per-capita ration of food grain in rural districts was reduced from 0.6 to 0.4 kilograms per day.[12]

Great strain has also appeared in the market, due not only to the shortage of consumers goods but of producers goods as well. These facts shook the people's confidence in official claims and caused a fierce debate within the Party. On August 26, 1959, the Chinese communists finally admitted that all the previously released figures concerning achievements in 1958 and planning targets for 1959 were inflated to a great extent. The new revised figures placed the 1958 output at only 250 million tons for food grains, 2.1 million tons for cotton, and 8 million tons for steel. Compared with the original claim, the revised figures show a 50 per cent drop. A corresponding decline was also admitted for the 1959 targets. Nevertheless, even the revised figures concerning the annual rate of industrial and agricultural output in these two years were still remarkable. Their reliability is doubtful. For the sake of propaganda, the Party issued a communiqué announcing that the major items of planned targets for 1962 envisaged in the second Five-Year Plan had been reached by the end of 1959. The Chinese communists thus proclaimed that the second Five-Year Plan had been fulfilled three years ahead of schedule (see Table 18).

TABLE 18

Major output of Industry and Agriculture in China (1959)

Product	Unit	Targets for 1962	Production in 1959
Steel	million tons	10.5–12	13.35
Coal	million tons	190–200	347.80
Electricity	million KWH	40,000–43,000	41,500.00
Metal equipment	million tons	0.03–0.04	0.205
Power-gen. equip.	million KW	1.4–1.5	2.15
Metal-cutting machine	million units	0.06–0.065	0.07
Timber	million cu.m	31–34	41.20
Cement	million tons	12.5–14.5	12.27
Cotton yarn	million bales	8–9	8.25
Cotton cloth	million meters	7,290–8,060	7,500.00
Grain	million tons	250	270.00
Cotton	million tons	2.4	2.41
Soya-beans	million tons	12.5	11.50

SOURCE: Li Fu-chun's Report on 1960 Economic Plan, *op. cit.*

Economic Adjustment

Although the regime announced success in industrialization, the country's agricultural production dropped sharply in both 1959 and 1960.

Grain output was estimated at about 180 million tons in 1959 and declined to about 150 million tons in 1960, which was 35 million tons below the 1957 level. Famine spread into many parts of the country.

While the national economy suffered a great setback as a result of the agricultural failure, the Soviet government in the summer of 1960 suddenly suspended all economic assistance to Peking. This contributed to a great stress on the already weakened economy. During the first Five-Year Plan, U.S.S.R. assistance represented the most important source of support. The 156 major projects, which constituted the backbone of the first Plan, were constructed totally through Soviet aid. The expansion of the iron and steel, power, coal, and oil industries as well as the establishment of automobile, aircraft, and heavy machine-building industries during the 1953–9 period were all accomplished because of large-scale U.S.S.R. aid. Suspension of Moscow's aid and the decline in Soviet supplies of machinery and equipment forced Peking to revise its program for economic development. The most significant change involved the slowdown in tempo of industrialization so as to concentrate all available resources for agricultural recovery. A "whole country support agriculture" movement was initiated in 1960. During 1960–1 about 20 million laborers and city dwellers as well as government functionaries and students were sent back into the countryside to reinforce the agricultural front.

The shift of economic forces from heavy industry to agriculture and suspension of the "great leap forward" marked an over-all retreat of the Party line. To a certain extent the changes are quite similar to the New Economic Policy introduced by the Soviet communists after the darkest period of War Communism (1917–20) and marked a new era in economic development on the Chinese mainland.

During the next five years (1961–5), since the nation's available resources had been devoted to the agricultural sector and as a result of revisions in the commune system, agricultural output registered slow improvement. Grain production officially reached 185 million tons in 1957. In 1958, the year of the "great leap," it reportedly was 250 million tons but, according to independent estimates, really amounted to about 200 million tons. Grain output declined to 180 million tons in 1959 and then sharply dropped to about 150 million tons in 1960. It then showed a slight increase to 160 million tons in 1961. Output for 1962 was estimated at 175 million tons and for 1963 at 180 million tons. The 1964 grain output, according to Chou En-lai, already surpassed the 1957 level. The official Chinese figure for 1964 was 190 million tons.[13] The 1965 grain production claimed a 5 per cent increase over 1964 or about 200 million tons. Output for 1966 was estimated by Western experts at 195 million tons because of drought in northern China.

Another major agricultural product is cotton. The official figure for

1957 production claimed 1.65 million tons. It was reported as 2.1 million tons in 1958 and 2.4 million in 1959. An independent estimate gave 1.9 million tons for 1958 and 1.8 million tons for 1959. Production dropped to 1.55 million tons in 1960, then 1.45 million tons in 1961, and 1.5 million tons in 1962. Although an official report claimed a 50 per cent rise in cotton output for 1963 as compared with 1962 and a 37 per cent increase in 1964,[14] the absolute quantity in this last year was said to be only higher than that in 1957. It is reasonable to assume that 1964 output of cotton was about 1.9 million tons, the same level as the estimated output for 1958. Thus roughly one can conclude that by 1964 Chinese agricultural output could only have regained the level achieved in 1958.

On the industrial front comprehensive national reports on production since 1961 have been extremely scanty. Steel output, officially reported to have reached 18 million tons in 1960, dropped to about 8 million tons in 1962.[15] When the American expatriate woman reporter Anna Louise Strong interviewed Po I-po, chairman of the State Economic Committee, in early 1964, he indicated that "we believe that 8 million to 10 million tons of fine steel of different varieties are much more useful than 18 million tons of ordinary steel."[16] This statement implies that steel output in 1963 was still within the 8 to 10 million-ton range. In 1964, according to Chou En-lai, production of steel was 20 per cent higher than that in 1963 and would therefore have reached 10 million tons. Output for 1965 was estimated at 12 million tons and for 1966 at 14 million tons.

So far as electric power is concerned, scattered reports show that 30 billion kilowatt hours were produced in 1962 and 33 billion in 1963. Output during 1963 was only 80 per cent of the 1959 output and accounted for 70 per cent of the 1960 output. Production in 1964 and 1965 was estimated at 36 and 40 billion kilowatt hours, respectively. Both figures are still below the 1959–60 level.[17] The 1966 output was estimated at 50 billion kilowatt hours, slightly surpassing the 1960 level.

During the five years from 1961 to 1965 only three sectors of industry registered any substantial progress. The first item is petroleum. According to an official report, the output of petroleum rose by 50 per cent in 1963. By 1964 communist China claimed self-sufficiency both in crude oil and petroleum products. It means that by 1964 China's petroleum output might have reached 6 to 7 million tons. This represented a great achievement in the industrial front.

The next sector involves chemical fertilizers. According to official data, between 1959 and 1962 output rose by 200 per cent.[18] Total use of chemical fertilizers in 1964 was estimated at about 6.5 million to 7 million tons, but only half of this could be produced in China. In 1966 chemical fertilizer production was estimated at 6 million tons, a ninefold increase when compared with 1957.

The third sector is agricultural machinery. According to Chou En-lai, tractors for agricultural use in 1964 numbered four times more than in 1957. The total amount of irrigation equipment in terms of horsepower had increased twelvefold. It was estimated that in 1963 communist China produced 16,000 to 18,000 tractors (in terms of standard 15 HP units), and in 1964 it could have turned out 20,000 units.

Although no one can be certain as to how much steel, chemical fertilizer, and petroleum were really produced in 1964 and 1965, one point becomes quite clear as far as industrial output is concerned. Except for the three items mentioned above, most of the basic industrial output was still below the 1959–60 level. After 1961 no official statistics concerning economic performance have been released. The year 1965 was regarded as the last period of economic adjustment, and the new third Five-Year Plan began in 1966. But up to the end of 1967 no information about agriculture, industry, or foreign trade had been disclosed. This probably means that economic progress during the past five years is still too limited to be publicized.

Changing Trend and Pattern of Foreign Trade

Volume of Foreign Trade

During the past nineteen years foreign trade in communist China progressed commensurate with general economic growth. When the national economy achieved steady improvement between 1950 and 1959, the volume of foreign trade registered a 180 per cent increase. Following the collapse of the "great leap forward" in 1960, trade dropped sharply in 1961 and 1962. As the national economy started its slow recovery in 1963, foreign trade again regained its upward trend (see Table 19).

The steady increase of trade during the 1950–9 period depended upon two basic factors. First, in the early fifties Red China received a 1.3 billion dollar loan from the Soviet Union to import capital goods and military equipment. The U.S.S.R. loan was repaid after 1956 by means of exporting Chinese products. Soviet financial assistance played a significant role in the expansion of Chinese trade with the U.S.S.R., which took up more than half of China's total trade volume during 1952–6. Second, during the "great leap forward" period (1958–60) Red China imported a sizeable amount of producers goods. In 1958, for instance, communist China received from the Soviet Union more than 9,300 motor vehicles, some 8,000 trucks and 2,000 trailers, plus 500,000 tons of petroleum. In order to pay for these imports, Red China had to increase its exports. Since exchange with the U.S.S.R. represented the mainstay of China's foreign trade until 1960, the sharp drop in Sino-Soviet trade after 1961 brought down the total volume in 1962 to the level of 1955. A part of the sharp decline has been compensated by China's purchase of food grains from Western countries during the next five years (1961–5). Her 1965 trade turnover was estimated at $3.7 billion, still 24 per cent below the 1959 level. By 1966 foreign trade recovery was just about completed, with an estimated total turnover of $4.1 billion and approximately reaching 1959 peak levels.

TABLE 19

Chinese Imports and Exports (1950–66)
(in millions of U.S. $)

Year	Exports	Imports	Total
1950	694	849	1,543
1951	917	1,030	1,947
1952	871	890	1,761
1953	1,039	1,107	2,146
1954	1,119	1,260	2,379
1955	1,345	1,321	2,666
1956	1,612	1,465	3,077
1957	1,615	1,391	3,006
1958	1,911	1,865	3,776
1959	2,221	2,011	4,232
1960	2,010	1,912	3,922
1961	1,571	1,414	2,985
1962	1,597	1,139	2,736
1963	1,699	1,271	2,970
1964	1,592	1,189	2,781
1965	——	——	3,600
1966	——	——	4,100

NOTE: There are diverse calculations regarding Communist China's foreign trade volume. One series is compiled by the United Nations and published in various issues of the *U.N. Yearbook of International Trade Statistics;* a second series is compiled by the U.S. Government and published in the *Mutual Defense Assistance Control Act of 1951 (17th Report to Congress for 1964),* issued by the Department of State; a third series is compiled by Prof. Alexander Eckstein, *op. cit.;* and yet a fourth by Prof. Feng-hwa Mah. Since the respective methods, coverages, and exchange rates between dollars and Chinese currency are different, the results are not identical. The data for this table are mainly from Table 4–1 of Prof. Eckstein's book (pp. 94–5), with the exception of those for 1950–1 and 1964–5.

SOURCES: 1950–1, from Prof. Feng-hwa Mah's paper (to be published), p. 40. 1964–5, *Far Eastern Economic Review* (Jan. 27, 1966), pp. 123–5. 1965, estimated. 1966, Chu-yuan Cheng, "The Cultural Revolution and China's Economy," *Current History,* LII, No. 313 (Sept. 1967), p. 152.

Direction of Trade

In the precommunist era China's foreign trade was mainly oriented toward Great Britain, Japan, and the United States. Trade with Russia was negligible. After 1949, under the "lean-to-one-side" foreign policy, the traditional trade pattern was sharply reversed. By 1954 China's trade with communist countries accounted for about 80 per cent of the total. During the years 1950–2 Red China's total turnover rose by one fourth. Her trade with noncommunist countries, nevertheless, dropped by more than half (see Table 20).

The year 1956 marked a new turn in China's trade orientation. Partly due to the dwindling of Soviet financial assistance and because of relaxation in Western restrictions on China's trade, turnover with Japan, Hong Kong, and Southeast Asia grew rapidly. By 1957 China's trade with noncommunist countries reached its former level in terms of absolute amount although the relative share was still less than 40 per cent. The exacerbation of relations between Peking and Moscow effected a new orientation of China's international trade. Within the short span of six years, from 1959 to 1965, Sino-Soviet trade dropped from over one half to about one quarter of the total. Simultaneously China's trade with noncommunist countries rose from less than one third of the total in 1959 to nearly two thirds in 1965.

By 1963 among communist China's major trading partners the Soviet Union was still leading, and yet its importance had declined drastically. Hong Kong had advanced to the second position and become the most important source of China's foreign exchange. A total trade surplus of 1.3 billion dollars was achieved with Hong Kong during 1959–64. Australia ranked third, being the chief supplier of food grains to China since 1961. In 1966 Japan topped the Soviet Union as China's leading trade partner. Sino-Japanese trade in 1966 reached 621 million dollars. China's trade with Hong Kong reached second place during 1966. In the years to come Japan and Hong Kong will become the most significant partners in Chinese foreign trade.

Composition of Commodities

The composition of commodities traded between Red China and foreign countries has also undergone substantial change through different periods. In the field of imports the most significant items until 1960 were equipment, machinery, ferrous metals, and petroleum. Imports of consumers goods were kept at a minimum level, about 6 to 7 per cent of the total for most of the years from 1952 to 1960.

The picture becomes clearer when one examines the structure of the commodities which China imported from the Soviet Union. By the end of 1957 the value of equipment delivered amounted to almost one half the

TABLE 20

Directions of Chinese Foreign Trade (1952–63)
(percentages)

	1952	1953	1954	1955	1956	1957	1958	1959	1960	1961	1962	1963
Imports												
Communist countries, Total	79.4	82.6	82.5	78.3	72.2	63.5	60.0	67.6	65.0	47.7	40.5	33.5
Soviet Union	62.2	63.0	60.2	56.6	50.0	39.1	34.0	47.4	42.7	25.9	20.5	14.3
Eastern Europe	(16.1)	(18.0)	(19.8)	17.9	18.0	(20.4)	22.0	16.2	17.8	11.6	6.8	(6.9)
Asian Communist countries	(1.1)	1.6	2.4	3.8	4.1	(4.0)	(4.0)	(4.0)	(4.4)	(10.2)	(13.2)	(12.2)
Cuba	—	—	0.1	negl.	—	—	0.2	negl.	1.7	6.5	7.8 }	66.5
Noncommunist countries, Total	20.6	17.5	17.4	21.6	27.9	36.5	39.8	32.4	33.4	45.8	51.7 }	
Exports												
Communist countries, Total	66.7	66.0	72.8	69.1	66.1	66.7	66.5	71.5	64.7	57.2	53.4	45.1
Soviet Union	47.8	45.8	51.7	47.8	47.4	45.7	46.1	49.5	42.2	34.9	32.3	24.2
Eastern Europe	(16.9)	(17.6)	(17.2)	17.2	14.7	(15.4)	15.4	15.9	15.7	10.4	9.2	(9.1)
Asian Communist countries	(2.1)	2.6	4.0	4.1	4.0	(5.6)	(5.0)	(6.1)	(6.9)	(11.9)	(11.9)	(11.8)
Cuba	—	—	—	—	—	—	—	—	0.5	5.3	6.1 }	54.9
Noncommunist countries, Total	33.3	34.0	27.2	30.9	33.8	33.3	33.5	28.5	34.7	37.5	40.5 }	

SOURCE: Alexander Eckstein, *op. cit.*, p. 98.

total value of all Soviet exports to Red China. The relative share climbed to 62.6 per cent in 1959 and declined slightly to 61.7 per cent in 1960. It then dropped sharply to 29.4 per cent in 1961 and only 11.7 per cent in 1962. The second major item China imported from the Soviet Union during 1950–62 included petroleum and petroleum products, which totaled about 12 per cent during the first Five-Year Plan (1953–7) and surged to 33 per cent in 1961 and 35 per cent in 1962. The third important item imported from the Soviet Union was ferrous metals. During the first Five-Year Plan it ranged from 6.3 per cent to 11 per cent of the total, and its relative importance grew from 5 per cent in 1959 to 12 per cent in 1962 during the second Five-Year Plan. These three items together accounted for 60 to 70 per cent of China's imports from the Soviet Union during the years 1952–62.

China's exports from 1950 to 1960 were basically composed of food, food products, nonferrous and alloy metals. Roughly speaking, in the first decade of communist control about 70 to 75 per cent of China's exports was still composed of raw and processed agricultural commodities, with only 25 to 30 per cent made up by industrial and mining products. The export pattern reflects clearly its similarity to the traditional pattern, despite Red China's one decade of efforts to industrialize.

However, in the 1961–5 period the export pattern underwent a drastic change. After three consecutive years of crop failure, from 1959 to 1961, the relative weight of farm products on the export list diminished considerably from a high of 70 per cent in 1952 to a low of 20 per cent in 1961. The decline of agricultural products was compensated by the increase of textile products, whose relative share in the export list advanced from 17 per cent in 1955 to 45 per cent in 1961 and now has become China's leading export commodity.

In addition to agricultural products and textiles Red China also exported pig iron, tungsten, tin, salt, and nonferrous metals. Their percentage averaged at about 10 of the total Chinese export during the 1953–63 period (see Table 21).

Balance of Payments

During the entire period from 1950 to 1964 Red China achieved a rough balance in its trade accounts. China's trade balance with the Soviet Union and the balances with the noncommunist countries have followed completely different courses during the past nineteen years. Until 1955 Red China's imports from the Soviet Union exceeded exports by a sum of 100 million to 220 million dollars annually. By the end of 1955 China's cumulative trade deficit with the U.S.S.R. had reached 933 million dollars. But in the same period China's trade with noncommunist countries maintained a surplus of about 500 million dollars.

TABLE 21

Commodity Structure of Chinese Imports
and Exports by Category (1950–8)
(percentages)

Year	Imports		Exports		
	Pro-ducers goods	Con-sumers goods	Agricultural Products		Industrial & Mining Products
			Raw	Processed	
1950	87.2	12.8	57.5	33.2	9.3
1951	83.1	16.9	54.6	31.4	14.0
1952	90.6	9.4	59.3	22.8	17.9
1953	93.0	7.0	55.7	25.9	18.4
1954	92.8	7.2	48.3	27.7	24.0
1955	94.5	5.5	46.1	28.4	25.5
1956	92.4	7.6	42.6	31.3	26.1
1957	92.7	7.3	40.1	31.5	28.4
1958	93.7	6.3	35.5	37.0	27.5

SOURCE: State Statistical Bureau, *Ten Great Years* (Peking: Foreign Languages Press, 1960), p. 176.
N.B.: The agricultural products include "products of agricultural side occupations."

The trend has been reversed since 1956, when Red China began re-payment of the early trade deficit with the Soviet Union, starting with a moderate sum of about 30 million dollars in 1956 and reaching approximately 250 million dollars in 1958 and 185 million dollars in 1961. In 1962 China sharply cut back her imports from the U.S.S.R., while only slightly reducing her exports, and thus achieved a huge trade surplus of 283 million dollars. Through this growth in exports over imports during the 1956–62 period China not only paid off the total trade debt to the Soviet Union but also registered a surplus of 123 million dollars by the end of 1962[19] (see Table 22).

When China built up a trade surplus with the Soviet Union, her trade balance with the noncommunist countries turned into a deficit. In the three years of 1958, 1959, and 1961 China's total trade deficit with noncommunist countries amounted to 179 million dollars, which slightly exceeded the four-year surplus of 163 million dollars achieved in 1957, 1960, 1962, and 1963. But taking the entire period 1950–63 into account, Red China still gained a total trade surplus of nearly two billion dollars from her noncommunist partners which enabled her not only to pay off all of the Soviet debt but in the same time to conduct a foreign aid program. Up to the end of 1964 Red China committed close to two billion dollars in foreign aid, of which more than one billion dollars have been drawn upon.

TABLE 22

Balance of Sino-Soviet Trade (1950–62)
(millions of U.S. $)

Year	Annual Figures	Cumulative Total
1950	−197	——
1951	−147	−344
1952	−140	−484
1953	−223	−707
1954	−181	−888
1955	−105	−993
1956	+ 31	−962
1957	+194	−768
1958	+247	−521
1959	+146	−375
1960	+ 31	−344
1961	+184	−160
1962	+283	+123

SOURCE: Chu-yuan Cheng, *Economic Relations Between Peking and Moscow 1949–63* (New York: Praeger, 1964), p. 68.

Foreign Trade and Economic Growth

During the period from 1952 to 1959 communist China's export and import share in GNP ranged from 6.2 per cent in 1952 to 8.8 per cent in 1959. Although the ratios are not so impressive as those in Great Britain and Japan, foreign trade has played a significant role in the development of the Chinese economy. The importance of foreign trade to the industrialization program is clearly illustrated by the dependence of capital goods on foreign supply. During the first Five-Year Plan 40 to 45 per cent of the machinery, 27 to 32 per cent of forging equipment, 24 to 40 per cent of metal-cutting tools, 15 to 28 per cent of transformers, 14 to 55 per cent of steel, and 44 to 65 per cent of petroleum products required by the national economy were imported from foreign countries.[20] Without foreign supplies it would have been impossible for China to lay the foundation of a modern industry.

In the aftermath of the "great leap" foreign trade performed another new function by supplying China with five to six million tons of food grains per year. The foreign food stuffs help Peking to maintain the minimum food ration for its urban population and reduce the impact of famine to a certain extent.

In the years to come China's foreign trade will continue its current trend in shifting from the Soviet Bloc to the noncommunist world. Japan,

Hong Kong, and Western Europe will resume their traditional role in China's international trade. The composition of commodities is also expected to undergo substantial change. Light industrial products and textiles as well as some machinery will outweigh the agricultural products. Precision machinery and capital equipment will replace the common machine in leading the Chinese import list. The changing trend and pattern of Chinese foreign trade may also produce a new impact on the world market.

Appraisal and Prospects

Economic development on the Chinese mainland during the past nineteen years of communist control has registered both achievements and mistakes. Considering the whole process of institutional transformation, the Peking regime was successful in eliminating the middle class and in transforming private industry as well as commerce into state capitalism. Within a short span of five years (1952–6) the three million private firms were completely absorbed into state control, without rousing any chaotic disturbance in production. Collectivization of agriculture succeeded during the period of land reform but encountered great difficulty in its latter stage, when the peasants lost their lands again. The commune system dealt heavy blows to the incentive of peasants and was the basic reason for crop failures during the past five years.

In the course of industrialization the Chinese communists progressed substantially during 1953–7. The increase on heavy industrial production was impressive, and facilities for transportation were also greatly expanded. Nevertheless, the deterioration of agriculture and the subsequent emergence of a famine offset a great deal of the previous achievement.

One significant accomplishment is the regime's ability to maintain a high rate of capital investment. With a low level of national income and an increasing population growth, the rate of saving should be very low, if there were no radical change in the socio-economic structure. During the first eight years of communist control the regime, by means of drastic changes in economic institutions, absorbed a great part of assets from the agricultural and private sectors at fairly regular intervals and transferred them into the state treasury for effective utilization, thus bringing about a high rate of capital formation.

In the course of land reform (1949–52) almost all assets of landlords and wealthy farmers, including their personal belongings, jewelry, and art collections, were confiscated. During the "Five-Anti" campaign of 1952 the regime reaped an additional windfall from private enterprises totaling the equivalent of 1.7 billion U.S. dollars, which was the chief source of capital investment for the first Five-Year Plan. In 1958 despite the poor crops of the previous year the state was able to place property previously owned by cooperatives and private individuals at the direct disposal of local government by establishing rural communes. The capital investment of 1958 registered a 93 per cent increase over the 1957 total. Facts such as these clearly prove the direct influence of institutional change on capital formation during the first eight years of communist control.

Another source for the increase of savings stems from the strict ration system of consumers goods. The living standard was lowered to a minimum level. For the period 1949–58, when official statistical data were available, the relative share of consumers goods in the total industrial output of communist China declined constantly from 73.4 per cent in 1949 to 62.7 per cent in 1953 and 42.7 per cent in 1958. The ratio of consumption in the national income during 1952–6 also dropped from 81.8 per cent in 1952 to 77.5 per cent in 1956. However, the sharp decrease in agricultural production since 1959 forced the regime to abandon the high rate of savings in order to alleviate the economic crisis. The rate of capital formation during 1960–5 was much lower than that of the previous years.

Probably the foremost mistake that Peking's leaders have committed during the past nineteen years was to follow exactly in Soviet footsteps, without regard for the different economic conditions or stages of economic development. The fact alone that the U.S.S.R. possesses about 1.5 times more arable land than China, yet has only one third of China's population, should have prevented Peking from directly imitating Moscow. It is far more profitable for the Soviet Union than for China to carry out agricultural collectivization and mechanization because the former possesses vast tracts of virgin land. Nor can the U.S.S.R. pattern of squeezing the agricultural sector to feed heavy industry be applied by China. To build the country's economy on a solid base Peking from the very beginning should have made agriculture her economic foundation. The allocation of 58.2 per cent of capital investment to industry and only 7.6 per cent to agriculture in the first Five-Year Plan apparently involved a misguided decision. Peking's hurried establishment of the commune system was also a critical mistake. After the completion of collectivization in 1956, had the Chinese leaders sought ways and means to consolidate the existing system by leaving some leeway for individual subsidiary jobs and providing the minimum incentive for the peasants, the agricultural sector would have enjoyed steady progress and the tragic famine following the wake of the communes might not have occurred.

The "lean-to-one-side" policy, which led to close Sino-Soviet economic collaboration from 1950 to 1959, also had mixed effects on communist China's economic development. U.S.S.R. assistance did spur China's economic growth during the first ten years of communist control, yet China was isolated from the Western world. Had the Chinese communists adopted a middle-of-the-road stand, as India did, they would have been eligible for economic assistance from both East and West, and the CPR's present economic situation would be entirely different. By cooperating only with the Soviet Bloc, China actually placed herself under Soviet control. Since half of China's foreign trade was previously with the U.S.S.R., the sudden interruption of Soviet deliveries of machinery and equipment dealt a serious blow to the economy of the CPR. The sharp decline of industrial output during 1961–3 is partially a result of the Soviet economic sanctions.

Although the national economy has embarked since 1963 upon a path of slow recovery from the "big leap" failure, the regime is in fact caught in several dilemmas. The first difficulty is the choice between the advancement of peasant incentive and maintenance of ideological dogma. The former is one of the vital factors required for national economic advancement. It is now clear that the crop failures of 1959–61 were due partly to natural calamities, but more seriously to the killing of peasant initiative under the commune system. During the years 1961–5, the regime has gradually become aware of its mistake and considerably revised the commune system to stimulate peasant incentive. Some of the measures, such as the return of the small plots of land to private use and the encouragement of peasants to engage in sideline production, have proved very successful. In many communes in the coastal provinces, although the private plots account for only 5 per cent of the total cultivated land, their products were more than 20 per cent of the total output. Peasant willingness to work these small plots undoubtedly has been enhanced. Their incentive for collective production, however, is still very low. Unless the regime gives further autonomy to individuals and lets them enjoy more fruits of their labor, peasant incentive cannot be effectively promoted. Under the impact of the current cultural revolution there has been an increasing tendency toward tighter control over the rural areas. The Chinese communist leaders' adherence to the dogmas of agricultural collectivization will damage peasant incentive and make any substantive improvement of agricultural production impossible.

The second problem involves competition between the military and the civilian production for scarce resources. Red China is striving desperately to become a nuclear power with long-range missiles and hydrogen bombs. In recent years the regime has spent more than 400 million dollars per annum for nuclear weapons development.[21] Of the eight machine-building industrial ministries, six are believed to be specializing in defense production. The concentration of a substantial amount of financial and technical manpower resources for this nonproductive purpose will produce adverse effects on the industrialization program.

The third problem is the regime's attitude toward the Vietnam war and its desire to carry out a new Five-Year Plan. On the one hand, the Peking leaders made every effort to prevent any peaceful negotiation of the Vietnam conflict and thus created great uncertainty for the development plan, since any long-run economic plan will automatically become invalidated if a war should involve China. On the other hand, the regime has expressed its wish to launch a third Five-Year Plan but, in view of the Vietnam uncertainty, has been forced to operate only annual plans. Therefore, although the new Five-Year Plan officially started in 1966, it seems that the details of that plan have not been worked out. As long as the Vietnam conflict continues, no rigid economic plan can be implemented.

The future of economic development on the Chinese mainland will depend on three basic conditions: control over population growth, substantial improvement of agricultural production, and the adoption of a reasonable and realistic policy.

The population in communist China was estimated at 750 million in 1966. If the past natural rate of increase stays unchanged, the estimated population in China will reach the one billion mark by the end of 1980. This would mean greater pressure for economic growth as well as on the living standard. During the past six years (1961–6) the regime has become aware of this population pressure and adopted a more realistic attitude toward population policy. Measures for birth control, including contraception, late marriage, abortion and sterilization, have been allowed and even encouraged. Early in 1962 importing of contraceptive devices and medicine from Hong Kong registered a great increase. Nevertheless, since the base of the population in China is extremely huge (a one per cent increase means 7.5 million more people annually, and a 2 per cent increase means 15 million), and since the rural population in China is still traditionally oriented and considers a big family desirable, the continuous growth of the Chinese population is expected unless the regime enforces some effective measures. With a rapidly growing population it would be difficult enough for the economy to maintain a subsistence level. Capital formation would be even more difficult, and the rate of economic growth would probably be very slow.

The importance of agriculture for China's economic growth is self-evident. Up to the present the economic foundation of the Chinese mainland still involves agriculture. Of the total population, rural inhabitants account for 85 per cent; more than 50 per cent of the state revenue comes from agriculture; over 70 per cent of the commodities exported consisted of farm products or processed farm products. During 1952–8 available statistics showed a close relationship between economic growth and agricultural production. A bumper harvest in the preceding year is always followed by an upsurge in industrial production, capital investment, and foreign trade. Unless the agricultural output can keep pace with the population growth, Red China has to spend a great part of her foreign exchange to import foreign food stuffs, which would definitely hinder her general economic growth.

The improvement of agricultural production not only demands a constant increase of investment in the agricultural sector but also requires that the regime abandon many of its ideological dogmas. Under the present commune system, wherein the major share of production must be surrendered to the government and peasants receive only a subsistence ration, no incentive can be further promoted. Since Chinese agriculture still relies too heavily on human labor rather than on mechanization, incentive is the central problem of agricultural production. Unless the regime allows the peasants more privacy, a substantial increase in agricultural output would be unlikely.

In the years to come, with the continuous increase of investment in defense industry, Red China's capability for manufacturing nuclear weapons will rise steadily. However, under the dual pressures of the agricultural stagnation and the population explosion, the tempo of the industrialization program will be much slower than that in the first decade of communist control. It seems that to transform China into an industrial giant the Peking government should plan from now on for another twenty to thirty years of effort—provided that there is no major war and that the leaders will adopt reasonable and realistic policies.

Notes to Chapter 9

1. Alexander Eckstein, *Communist China's Economic Growth and Foreign Trade* (New York, 1966), p. 122.

2. For a detailed discussion, see Chu-yuan Cheng, *Communist China's Economy 1949–62: Structural Changes and Crisis* (South Orange, N. J.: 1963), ch. iv.

3. Chu-yuan Cheng, "The Changing Pattern of Rural Communes in Communist China," *Asian Survey* (Nov. 1961), pp. 3–9.

4. Po I-po, "The Three Years of Achievements of the People's Republic of China," in *New China's Economic Achievements 1949–52* (Peking, 1952), pp. 152–3.

5. Report by Li Fu-chun, chairman of State Planning Commission, in *Jen min Jih pao* (Sep. 29, 1955).

6. Any construction project, whether it is new, rebuilt, or restored, is classified as "above-norm" or "below-norm" according to whether its invested capital is above or below the "norm." In industry, for example, the investment norm for the iron and steel, motor vehicle, tractor, and shipbuilding industries is 10 million yuan. For textiles it amounts to 5 million yuan, and for other light industries 3 million yuan. The official rate of exchange is one U.S. dollar for 2.355 yuan.

7. "Communiqué on the Fulfillment of the First Five-Year Plan," *Peking Review,* Apr. 21, 1959.

8. Official figures concerning the rate of growth in industry during the first Five-Year Plan were highly inflated. According to independent estimates, the rate of growth was 13.7 to 14.2 per cent per year. Chao Kang, *The Rate and Pattern of Industrial Growth in Communist China* (Ann Arbor, Mich., 1965), pp. 88 and 96; Liu Ta-chung and Yeh Kung-chia, *The Economy of the Chinese Mainland: National Income and Economic Development, 1933–59* (Princeton, N. J.: 1965), pp. 66, 146, and 573.

9. See "Proposals of the 8th National Congress for the Second Five-Year Plan for Development of the National Economy, 1958–62," supplement to NCNA (New China News Agency) release.

10. *People's Daily,* May 3, 1958.

11. Communiqué on the Development of the National Economy in 1958, issued by the State Statistical Bureau, Apr. 14, 1959.

12. Chou En-lai, "Report on the 1959 Economic Plan," *Peking Review,* Sep. 1, 1959; *Hsin-hua Pan-yeh-kan* (Peking), No. 6 (1959), p. 24. From 1953 communist China adopted a strict food rationing system. The amount of the ration is always an indicator of the country's grain output.

13. The United States government estimated 194 million tons in 1958 and only 168 million tons in 1959, according to "Agriculture in China 1963," *Current Scene,* XI:27 (Jan. 15, 1964); Mao Tse-tung personally told British Field Marshal Montgomery that the grain harvest in 1960 was 150 million tons and the forecast for 1961 was for 10 million tons more, according to *The Sunday Times* (London), Oct. 15, 1961, p. 25. The 1964 figure is from *The New York Times,* Dec. 13, 1964.

14. *Ta Kung-pao,* March 23, 1964.

15. According to the *Far Eastern Economic Review,* Apr. 16, 1964, p. 160, the output of steel in 1962 was in the range of 6.7 to 7.7 million tons. The *United Nations Statistical Yearbook, 1963,* p. 283, gave 12 million tons for 1962. In view of Po I-po's statement, 8 million tons was more likely.

16. *Ta Kung-pao* (Hong Kong), Jan. 15, 1964.

17. For the 1962 and 1963 figures, see *Far Eastern Economic Review,* Apr. 4, 1963, p. 6, and Apr. 16, 1964, p. 160. For the 1964 and 1965 figures, see U.S. Congress, Joint Economic Committee, *An Economic Profile of Mainland China* (Washington, D.C.: 1967), p. 293.

18. *Ta Kung-pao* (Hong Kong), Jan. 15, 1964.

19. Chu-yuan Cheng, *Economic Relations Between Peking and Moscow, 1949–63* (New York, 1964), pp. 66–68.

20. *Tung-chi Kung-tso,* No. 13 (Jul. 14, 1957), p. 30.

21. Chu-yuan Cheng, "Truth About Red China's Bomb," *U.S. News and World Report,* Dec. 28, 1964, pp. 28–32.

Discussion

Arthur S. Y. Chen

The chapter by Dr. Chu-yuan Cheng adequately covers the subject matter, and its last part on "Appraisal and Prospects" is both objective and searching. However, one has to re-examine the thirty-year Sino-Soviet treaty of February 14, 1950, in order to appreciate fully the developmental stages of communist China's economy and its related problems. The said alliance was supposedly based on a convergence of interests, one of which included economic "mutual assistance." Prior to 1957 it functioned rather well, as everyone expected it to. Minor strains and stresses were quietly settled behind the scenes. Subsequently the limited and grudging nature of Soviet economic assistance became one of the latent causes for a divergence of mutual interests, resulting in the current deterioration of relations between Moscow and Peking.

In the early stage of economic development the Chinese communists aspired to restore immediately and quickly the Manchurian industrial base within a period of five years. Moscow insisted on having a three-year rehabilitation period (1950–2), to be followed by the first Five-Year Plan (1953–7), which, according to the Soviet advice, should lay the groundwork for China's socialist construction. Economic planning during this period was patterned after the Soviet model as part of the transition, with special emphasis on heavy industry. The development of heavy industry in China then centered on a nucleus of Soviet aid projects manned by Soviet advisers and technicians. Soon Peking realized that the U.S.S.R. was weighing its preferred forms of economic aid so as not to nurture a potential rival or dissipate its own resources. Other irritants included lengthy sessions for trade negotiations (deliberately kept low), the slow level of Soviet deliveries, and rigid requirements either for exchange of Chinese farm products or expenditure of Soviet credits. With this background one can better understand why Red China had wanted to escape from the U.S.S.R. influence and total reliance on Soviet aid and get into trade with the noncommunist Bloc.

Dr. Cheng's chapter also discusses the second Five-Year Plan, which was supposed to cover the period 1958–62. Officially there was no draft plan ever submitted to the State Council, let alone its supervisory body, the National People's Congress. There existed only five *ad hoc* annual plans during that period. At best, one can say that because of moderate successes achieved toward the end of the first Five-Year Plan, the Central Committee began to prepare for launching a second plan for national economic development. What actually happened was Mao's initiation of the "great leap forward" (1958–60) in conjunction with the rural commune adventure. Both, despite lofty and inspiring thoughts of Mao, foundered in a sea of incompetence. Having managed to raise itself from the economic bottom into which the regime fell as a result of the "great leap," the top Chinese communist leaders are now talking about "love of leaping" as one of the touchstones of the true revolutionary. Whether they will be able to eliminate their colossal blunders, before they leap again and assume an eager pace of industrial growth, remains to be seen. The much postponed "third Five-Year Plan," which was originally scheduled for the period 1963–8, will have as its basis the development of agricultural production.

As Peking shifted from its early "lean-to-one-side" (to Moscow) to its ultimate aim of autarchy, or national economic self-sufficiency, which the antiforeign Red Guards are now advocating, it appears that Maoist ideology may be Red China's most serious single obstacle to fostering economic growth. Without any change of policies the goal of rapid industrialization and a food–population balance is distant from what the grandiose Maoist ambitions may envisage.

Dr. Cheng has pointed out that "official statistical data were available for the period 1949–58." In those days communist Chinese juggling of production figures made the latter notoriously unreliable and was later exposed to mockery. Their top planners never came down to stern realities but placed the blame on the cadres and the vagaries of weather. For example, gross national product for fixed investment in 1957, prior to the "great leap," claimed a 16 per cent increase. This was an exaggerated figure. Western analysts estimated that the rate of GNP growth in Red China averaged about 6 per cent per annum between 1952 and 1960. They also revealed that even if the 1957 figure of 16 per cent increase were not inflated, it roughly corresponded with that for Japan during the 1930's. When the reader comes across such a statement as "the capital investment of 1958 registered a 93 per cent increase over the 1957 totals," he will find it meaningless and difficult to use as the basis for an objective appraisal.

10

problems of the chinese communist armed forces

JUERGEN DOMES

The armed forces of communist China developed into a civil war army from original guerrilla units. If one accepts August 1 as the day on which the People's Liberation Army *(Jen-min chieh-fang chün)* was founded, it would be correct philologically to relate this to the uprising by the communist-infiltrated units within the army of the Chinese nationalist party *(Kuomintang)* at Nanch'ang, the capital of South China's Kiangsi province. This took place on August 1, 1927. The united front of the Kuomintang and the Communist Party of China during 1923–4 resulted from an alliance between the Chinese nationalist leader, Dr. Sun Yat-sen, the U.S.S.R., and the Communist Internationale.

This collapsed in April 1927, when the leader of the Nationalist center group, Chiang Kai-shek (and in July of that year the left wing of the Kuomintang also), broke with the communists. At that time the struggle against the communists began. During the period of cooperation between both parties the Chinese communists succeeded in infiltrating a number of nationalist army units with their trusted cadres. The first among these included the 11th and 20th Army Corps, led by the communist party members Yeh Ting and Ho Lung. At the end of July 1927 military units under communist control comprised a total of about 16,000 men.[1] It was possible for them to seize the city of Nanch'ang on August 1, where they were able to halt the swiftly approaching units of the Nationalist army for five days. Then they were driven away but escaped in the first "Long March" into the southern Chinese coastal province of Kwantung. Here finally it was possible for the nationalist general, Chu Tê, who had defected to the communists, to assemble in October 1927 about a thousand men dispersed in the mountains.

At the same time a member of the Chinese communist party's Central Committee, Mao Tse-tung, during September and October 1927 led the communist-controlled peasant militia and two regiments of KMT troops in Hunan province in the so-called "autumn-harvest uprising," which also failed. It was possible for Mao to retreat with the rest of his followers, about 2,000 in all, into the mountains along the border of Hunan province, where he spent the winter. In the spring of 1928 the remainder of Chu Tê's troops and the dispersed peasant militia of Mao united in the Chingkangshan mountain range. Here, they formed the "4th Army Corps of the Red Workers' and Peasants Army."

In the course of bitter guerrilla warfare against the nationalist army as well as against troops of regional warlords, the Red Army succeeded by the end of 1931 in controlling a territory with about sixty million inhabitants. The guerrilla units, on constant alert, at the time when the Chinese Soviet Republic was established in November 1931 totaled about 250,000 men.[2] The cadres in this army were mainly composed of professional soldiers with many years of experience, who had deserted the nationalist armed forces. Only after 1930 were they preponderantly strengthened from among tenant farmers and agricultural workers. One can accept only with great reservations the statement that the Red Chinese armed forces had their origin among groups of "insurgent peasants." Two annihilation campaigns by the Nationalist army, under the personal leadership of Chiang Kai-shek, inflicted heavy losses on the strength of the Red Army. By the end of 1934 only about 100,000 men had been compressed into a narrow area in the south of Kiangsi province. Here the communists succeeded finally in breaking out of the nationalist encirclement.

On October 16, 1934, the legendary "Long March" by about 90,000 guerrillas began. This is the heroic period in the history of the Chinese communist party. In the course of one year the Long March took the Red Army across 11,000 kilometers and involved fighting with troops of the nationalist army, units of regional warlords, and wild native tribes through the provinces of Hunan, Kweichow, and Szechwan, across eastern Tibet, the Gobi desert, Kansu, and finally into the area of Yenan in North Shensi. Of the 90,000 men who had started out, a scant 20,000 reached their destination in the fall and winter of 1935–6. One should realize that this was a revolutionary elite which had been hardened by all conceivable privation.

Despite their newly-acquired sphere of influence in northwest China, the communists soon felt insecure. After an interruption, because of a conflict with the local warlords which led in December 1936 to his temporary imprisonment, Chiang prepared himself to exterminate the communist guerrillas. However, on July 7, 1937, the Sino-Japanese war broke out, and this saved the Chinese communists from complete annihilation. By then they had again some 100,000 guerrillas at their disposal.

Under the impact of foreign aggression an armistice took place between Chinese nationalists and communists. During a new united-front period, which lasted eight years, communist positions in the north and northwest could be considerably strengthened. Only in the first two years of the war did the communists participate with all of their forces in the defense against Japan. Afterwards they started only occasionally to take guerrilla action and occupied themselves mainly with construction of bases in the front and to the rear of Japanese lines. It seems that after 1942 some kind of tacit truce was established with the Japanese. At the same time the nationalist forces struggled with heavy losses in the southwest of China against great Japanese offensives.

At the time of the Japanese surrender in the Pacific in August 1945, the Red Army had more than 600,000 soldiers and about one million militia under arms. The Chinese Communist Party simultaneously included almost one million members, and at the end of World War II it controlled a territory with about ninety-five million people.[3]

Thus during the period between 1934 and 1940 a unity developed between the Party and the party-army which determined the future of the People's Liberation Army (PLA). Nearly all Party leaders at one time served as officers or as political commissars in the PLA. The army generals, as a result of this, even today consist in great part of men who at the same time participated in political functions of the Party. Originally civilian members of the Party found their way in large numbers into leadership positions of the armed forces. During the same period Mao Tse-tung developed his theory of the "revolutionary war of liberation," which the leader of Chinese communism discussed in three important essays during 1936 and 1938.

In this respect the PLA received theoretical and practical training. It started a new offensive in the winter of 1945–6 against the nationalist government which by 1949 brought about the victory of communism on the Chinese mainland. The civil war, with an interruption between 1937 and 1941 (theoretically until 1945) in effect had lasted some twenty-two years. It came to an end at the beginning of 1950. At this time the PLA numbered about 3.5 to 4 million soldiers. Equipment, strategy, and tactical principles were most suitable for the conduct of a civil war in an underdeveloped country. However, for defense in a modern war between states this was hardly appropriate.

Experience derived from twenty-two years of struggle considerably influenced the theory of the Chinese communist party and the structure of the PLA. Mao Tse-tung's version of Marxist-Leninist ideology concedes to the armed forces a more important place than does Soviet revolutionary theory. Already in December 1939 the leader of Chinese communism declared: "No matter where the army of the Chinese communist party arrived, it always established for Marxism-Leninism a communist party and a communist government. It is rifles and cannon that build the party, culture, and even the world!"[4]

Should one accept this proclamation literally, one would come to the conclusion, not that Marxism-Leninism establishes the armed forces, but that the revolutionary armed forces alone create the Party. Later Mao did not go quite so far. Even to this day one finds the long identification of the Party with the armed forces in the collapse of Chinese revolutionary theory. According to the Chinese interpretation, it is not the automatic economic and social developments which are correctly understood and furthered by the Party as the motive forces of the revolution. Rather the "revolutionary" or "national" liberation war represents the most important force of the revolutionary process. One understands this to mean the guerrillas and later also regular fighting units. Less important are strikes, infiltration, and agitation.

Since revolutionary war represents the decisive factor in a revolutionary process for the Chinese communists, the correct ideological orientation of the armed forces remains one of the essential weapons for internal and external conflict. The PLA is an important part of the apparatus which serves to extend and secure control. It is more than just an instrument for protection. It also plays a decisive role in the revolutionary process of social and political transformation.

The PLA Role in Revolutionizing the People

The importance of the PLA as an instrument to implement the leadership imperative of the Party center has grown considerably since 1960. The breakdown of the "great leap forward" policy and the people's communes movement during the years 1959–60, following various economic crises, led to a disintegration of the regular Party mainly in the villages of the south and central regions of China. Because of this Peking could no longer trust the command channels to the same extent as it used to until 1958. Here, especially since the taking over of the defense ministry by Marshal Lin Piao (a doctrinaire adherent of Mao), the PLA became a substitute. Already during 1961–2 one often pointed to the duty of the armed forces to serve in the name of the Party as an example for the people in revolutionizing society:

> When the combat duties of the party are accomplished, the army always stands in the most advanced lines . . . as it now approaches the glorious task to build and develop the fatherland, the troops overcome difficulties,

they must consciously and with constant discipline transform themselves. Their communist ideological consciousness must agree with the teachings of Chairman Mao, and this they strive to accomplish without interruption. So that they may become energetic young people and Red fighters of the revolution, who are capable of accomplishing every revolutionary task, of accepting each command, and of overcoming all difficulties. This is what the party and Chairman Mao demand from young soldiers.[5]

While the Party has attempted since the summer of 1963 with the help of a "socialist education movement" to recover from years of crisis which had damaged the infrastructure in the villages, members of PLA were prepared for assuming their tasks through a comprehensive indoctrination campaign. These functions they were supposed to perform in the government, within the Party, and in the mass organizations.

Principles for this campaign were established after preparatory work at an enlarged plenary session of the Central Committee's military commission in 1960 and at three conferences on political work in the PLA during March 1961, February 1963, and January 1964. Obligatory guide lines for political indoctrination and also for the regular educational process in the PLA were required to be in consonance with these principles, the study of Mao Tse-tung's works, "and the frequent practical application" of the latter. Thus "the way of thinking of Mao Tse-tung" serves "as the strongest and most effective weapon of the PLA." Through the use of meaningful and brief slogans one tried to enlighten soldiers on what the leaders in Peking expected of them. Of particular importance, in this connection, is the slogan: "Four things come first":

1. In the relationship between weapons and men the human factor comes first;
2. Even though military activities (education, technology, logistics, etc.) are of great importance, political work comes first, since it represents the "soul" of the PLA;
3. In political work itself ideological education takes precedence over any routine work;
4. In ideological education practical knowledge supersedes any "book knowledge" (theoretical knowledge); the soldiers must be prepared ideologically to endure every life situation.[6]

After intensive preparations the experiences which first had been used for indoctrination of the military forces were applied to the civilian sphere at the beginning of 1964. On February 1 of that year a lead article appeared in the central organ of the Chinese communist party, the Peking *Jen-min jih-pao* (JMJP) in which the "whole country" was called upon to "learn from the PLA." The population was challenged to consider the above-mentioned "four points" also in the economy, education, and civilian Party work. In proportion to the growth of the power of Defense Minister Lin Piao in Party and state life since the beginning of 1965, calls to apply the works of the PLA as an example for all aspects of revolutionary activity have become more frequent. Already since November 1965, but even more emphatically since April 1966, the PLA organ *Chieh-fang-chun pao* has become the mouthpiece of the Central Committee and for some time nearly replaced *JMJP* as the official newspaper for internal communist propaganda. Here first appeared the fundamental position of the currently governing power group in the form of "the great proletarian cultural revolution." Only later was it expressed by other party newspapers.

This also pertains to an editorial by Mao, the origin of which was not recognized at the time but which was cited on August 1, 1966, in the military newspaper. It stated that in order to build a communist society step by step, everybody in China had to recognize henceforth these manifold tasks. Above all, the army should be concerned with politics, culture, the economy, and industry. It should become "a great exclusive school for the people." The factories, people's communes, commercial associations, and schools must be organized in a military fashion and become active in political and cultural affairs. Factory workers must help during the harvest. Small factories are to be established in the villages. Students must engage in productive agricultural and industrial labor. In this fashion Mao thinks that all differences between factory and field, village and city, physical and spiritual work should finally disappear so that a homogeneous communist society will become reality.

It seems as if these thoughts of Mao and his collaborators, which are similar to but not so precise as those back in 1958, refer to the previous theory of the Chinese communists regarding the transformation of society. The importance of the PLA outweighs that of the regular Party. The youth organization of the "Red Guard" *(Hung-sê hsien-fêng pao-wei-ping)*, which has been the bearer of the "cultural revolution" in many parts of China since 1966, is dependent on the leadership of the PLA. It seems as if the Party units are also being replaced gradually by the PLA. Domestic political tasks with which the PLA is faced today are of such magnitude that they should be capable of absorbing a considerable part of the army's energy.

Control over political education in elementary and high schools and universities belongs to the PLA, which is also connected with the paramilitary training of large groups of adults in the "militia" as well as supervision over the work of many civilian Party organs and the establishment of regular directives concerning production in factories and people's communes. In such a manner the PLA wins more and more influence in communist China. Because of this it is at the same time more important to be informed about the membership strength, organizational structure, and military problems. Should one want to form a picture about events which are taking place on the Chinese mainland, the foregoing is imperative.

Strength and Organization of the Armed Forces

Statements were made by the Chinese communists in 1959 according to which Red China then had over 170 million militiamen at its disposal. The fact that at least 120 million or maybe even 150 million men of military age lived on the Chinese mainland, led temporarily to an exaggerated estimate in the Western world regarding the military strength of Peking. In this respect one did not take into consideration that the country even today cannot implement even the most primitive logistic requirements to make one fourth of this population available to fight. If one accepts only one tenth of the above mentioned number, i.e., about 12 to 15 million men, this would require weapons, munitions, transportation facilities, and buildings to such an extent that the Chinese people's economy could hardly support this effort. Should these limitations be considered, then one attains a more realistic estimate of China's fighting forces, which are still quite impressive but appear in comprehensible numbers. Estimates by the nationalist Chinese and Western press media lead to the conclusion that the country disposes of about 8.3 million militarily trained reserves which already have fulfilled their active duty.[7] They form the backbone of the militia *(min-ping),* which should embrace altogether about 15 million members. In 1963, according to communist sources, however, the latter comprised only about 12 to 15 million men. If the militia is counted as part of the armed forces, then one can divide the military power of Red China into three groups: (a) the People's Liberation Army (PLA), including active military units, whose strength according to various trustworthy sources vacillates between 2.5 and 3 million men; (b) the "Security Forces," which are similar to GPU or NKVD military units during the Stalinist period in Russia or the units of the *Waffen SS* in Germany until 1943; these are confined to barracks and number about 200,000 men subordinated to the public security ministry; and (c) the "militia." Differences regarding the strength of the PLA can be traced to the fact that certain observers include the "Security Forces" in their figures. I will now attempt to summarize the fairly reliable and current estimates on the strength and organization of these armed forces.

The Army

The personnel strength of the army is given between 2,150,000 and 2,540,000 men. Samuel B. Griffith, one of the leading experts on the military potential of Red China, considers that the ground forces are divided into 40 field armies, of which each corresponds to an army corps and comprises 3 divisions. An infantry division includes about 11,000 to 12,000 men and is broken down into 3 infantry regiments plus one motorized regiment. A regiment has 3 battalions of 3 companies each.

In the spring of 1961, according to a secret document of the PLA which fell into Western hands, an infantry company comprised a total of

87 men, of whom 9 were officers and 18 noncommissioned officers. In this typical company 18 soldiers belonged to the Chinese Communist Party; 33 were members of the Communist Youth League; 62 came from poor and 24 from middle peasant families.[8] A publication of the nationalist Chinese intelligence in July 1964 spoke about 36 "infantry armies," 6 independent tank divisions, 3 cavalry divisions, and 5 independent infantry divisions, to which a number of special units belong.

These data agree on the whole, should one compare numbers with those of Griffith. It can be assumed that the army of Red China numbers today about 110 to 125 divisions. Of these only six or seven are completely motorized. Some 95 per cent of the units obviously consist of infantry which has only a limited number of tanks and artillery. In case of war it seems that the army will be divided into six "fronts," of which each will have the equivalent of one army group.[9]

At this time the units of the army are dependent upon the commanding officers of the thirteen military districts in the country. Of these, ten (Shenyang, Peking, Chinan, Nanking, Fuchow, Canton, Wuhan, K'unming, Ch'engtu, and Lanchow) were organized in June 1954, whereas three (Inner Mongolia, Tibet, and Sinkiang) were only later formed. (In November 1967, Inner Mongolia was again included as part of the Peking military district.) Information from nationalist Chinese sources in July 1964 about the distribution of army units is shown in Table 23.

TABLE 23

Distribution of Chinese Army Units (1964)

Military Districts	Provinces	Strength
1. Shenyang	Liaoning, Kirin, Heilungkiang	480,000
2. Peking	Hopei, Shansi	321,100
3. Chinan	Shantung	139,500
4. Nanking	Anhui, Kiangsu, Chekiang	453,800
5. Fuchow	Fukien, Kiangsi	178,500
6. Canton	Kwangtung, Kwangsi, Hunan	393,300
7. Wuhan	Hupei, Honan	109,100
8. K'unming	Yunnan, Kweichow	160,000
9. Lanchow	Kansu, Shensi, Ch'inghai	66,100
10. Ch'engtu	Szechwan	47,900
11. Inner Mongolia	——	9,900
12. Sinkiang	——	21,400
13. Tibet	——	71,800
	Total	2,451,400

SOURCE: *Handbook of Chinese Communist Affairs* (Taipei, 1964), p. 76.

In this connection the estimates for Inner Mongolia, Tibet, and Sinkiang seem too low. Besides, since the summer of 1964 extensive regrouping has taken place as a result of an intensification in the Sino-Soviet conflict, escalation by the United States in Vietnam, and the Chinese position regarding the war in Kashmir during August–September 1965. See Table 24, based on reports from observers in Hong Kong, Nationalist China, India, the Soviet Union, and the West.

TABLE 24

Deployment of Chinese Troops (Summer 1966)
(estimated)

Territory	Provinces	Strength
1. Facing the USSR		740,000
Manchuria	Liaoning, Kirin, Heilungkiang	450,000
Inner Mongolia	——	40,000
Sinkiang	——	250,000
2. Facing India		
Tibet	——	180,000
3. North of Vietnam		410,000
On the Mainland	Yunnan, Kwangsi, Kweichow	250,000
Island of Hainan	——	160,000
4. Facing Taiwan		
	Chekiang, Fukien, Kwangtung	780,000
5. The Interior	Other provinces	250,000
	Total	3,510,000

The heavy weapons of the army leave much to be desired. Tanks are either of U.S.S.R. origin (currently almost half of the heavy equipment dates back to the time of the Korean War) or they were built in China according to Soviet models in 1958. Most of the tanks which were produced in China come from a factory in T'aiyuan, Shansi province, which in 1963 had an annual capacity of 300 to 400 tanks.[10] Since then, however, this plant has increased its production. In general one would not err to estimate the number of tanks ready for action in the Chinese Red Army to be somewhat over 3,500. Of these only about 600 are T-54's. A large number of heavy, stationary artillery pieces with a 12.5 cm. caliber are located across from the nationalist Chinese–occupied island groups of Kinmen (Quemoy) and Matsu. A total of about 5,000 field artillery and heavy guns should be available. This heavy equipment and also the motorized vehicles are absolutely insufficient for an army of 2.2 to 2.5 million soldiers. In the meantime only about 8 to 10 per cent of the armed forces has been equipped with modern weapons. Certain elite units, like the six tank and two parachute divisions, correspond to modern conventional warfare requirements. However, over 90 per cent of the Red Chinese ground forces still comprise up to now lightly armed infantry units. Here, in the area of light weapons, Red China has attained autarchy. This already led in the fall of 1965 to the modernization of all such arms, except for machine guns, in more than half of the army.[11]

On the other hand, considerable deficiencies are evident in transportation. Even in October 1964 over two thirds of the railroads in China were single-track. The all-weather highway network is likewise insufficient for rapid movement of large units, just as the number of trucks is inadequate. The fact that especially in southern China the traffic network is extremely vulnerable adds to the problem. The elimination of a bridge over the Yangtze River at Wuhan, of a viaduct along the Fukien-Kiangsi railroad at Yenp'ing, and some of the smaller bridges along the north-south coastal highway would destroy the logistic system for units stationed south of the Yangtze. The same applies to the Tibetan Highway, leading to Lhasa, and the Kansu-Sinkiang railroad.

The above-mentioned weaknesses have led to a recognition by the PLA, especially since Lin Piao became defense minister in the fall of 1959, of those traditions acquired during the period of guerrilla warfare. This type of war represents the basic area of Mao Tse-tung's military theory. Here the PLA has had the most experience in combat. The large terrain and physical characteristics of China also play a part in this connection. Because of this it would be wrong to regard the pronouncements by Mao Tse-tung and, above all, by Lin Piao concerning the tactics of a "human ocean" and about the "struggle of world villages against world cities" only as pure propaganda. The statements of Foreign Minister Ch'en Yi at a press conference in Peking on September 29, 1965, deserve to be taken quite seriously in this respect.[12]

Despite the six successful nuclear tests in October 1964, May 1965, May 1966, October 1966, and December and June 1967, the strategy of the Chinese communists leans obviously, as heretofore, on the planned development of a large-scale guerrilla war against a possible aggressor. This guerrilla war should be supported by "national liberation wars" in Asia, Africa, and Latin America as well as by massive propaganda campaigns sponsored through adherents and fellow travelers of communist China abroad, even in the country of the probable aggressor. In such a manner the strength of the enemy will be splintered and the morale of his fighting men undermined. The leadership in Peking considers the Vietnam war to be of exemplary significance in this respect.

The Navy

The weakest part of the PLA is without a doubt the navy. Even though it includes a total of 1,251 units with a displacement of about

290,000 tons, most of these comprise armed and motor-propelled junks, transport ships, small coast-guard vessels, and many ships which are over forty years old. Only 127 of them can be classified as combat ready and effective fighting vessels. Four of these are destroyers, 6 frigates, 34 submarines (according to other sources, 40 to 50), 16 gunboats, 39 escort vessels, 12 mine sweepers, 10 coast-guard vessels, and 3 auxiliary boats.[13] Of lesser importance are the 168 small torpedo boats and 36 landing craft. The size of the Red Chinese navy is only insignificantly larger than that of nationalist China, which has modern and up-to-date equipped units. The Red Chinese navy is divided into three fleets: (1) the North Sea Fleet, with 203 ships of all types, including 15 warships, stationed at Ch'ingtao; (2) the Eastern Sea Fleet, with 750 ships of all types, including 49 warships, located at Shanghai; and (3) the South Sea Fleet, consisting of 264 ships of all types, including 29 warships, stationed at Canton.

Submarines are under a special command. There are various estimates about the number of submarines which are at Red China's disposal. Whereas most sources speak of 32 to 34, the commanding officer of the U. S. Seventh Fleet in 1962 gave the number as 50. This number was also thereafter corroborated by nationalist Chinese sources.[14] The submarine fleet represents without a doubt the strongest part of the Chinese communist navy. At least five ships are large enough to carry short-range missiles, and at least one is capable of firing medium-range missiles. Beyond this, the submarines of Red China are able to further the infiltration of all islands in Southeast Asia, and presumably they have been already used as such.

Otherwise the navy can be employed in the best way as defense for coastal areas. Since it lacks supply units and repair ships, on which it must depend at sea, the fleet is tied to its land bases. Besides, it has very little experience in actual combat. Many of the naval officers come from the army and have insufficient training. Out of the four sea battles in which the Chinese communist navy engaged with nationalist China since 1964, the former were able to win only one and this with greatly superior forces. In the other three they were badly defeated. Red China's navy, except for the submarines, represents hardly any real menace to its neighbors. In combatting domestic unrest it can be used only under certain conditions.

The Air Force

The Red Chinese air force astonished the Western world during the Korean War with its fighting power and capabilities. Its fame as being "unbeatable" evaporated when thirty-seven MIG-17 jet fighters were shot down in the battles off Kinman (Quemoy) in September and October 1958. Simultaneously the nationalist Chinese lost only three Sabrejets. Until 1958 the air force of Red China developed very rapidly and consistently. At that time it belonged among the largest in the world. Whereas the country disposed of 515 aircraft in 1950 (among these 60 were jets), by 1958 it had already reached 3,332 aircraft, of which 2,614 were jets.

As a result of the Sino-Soviet conflict, U.S.S.R. spare parts have failed to arrive since 1962. The withdrawal of Soviet technicians was also responsible for great deficiencies. Some aircraft had to be cannibalized in order to provide parts for others. Because of the fuel shortage, training hours for active-duty pilots were shortened by about 45 per cent during 1963. This also led to a decline in the quality of pilots. By the summer of 1963 about two thirds of the aircraft had been used for more than 1,000 hours in overtime beyond specifications.[15] In the meantime the number of aircraft has declined to 2,732 planes. Some 2,354 had jet engines, and of these 1,884 were fighters.[16] Only about 290 have been built since 1960. About 470 are more than seven, 340 over eight, 240 more than nine, 260 over ten, and 340 more than eleven years old. In November 1964 some 1,400 jet fighters needed a complete overhaul, which evidently could not be accomplished. Individually the Chinese communist air force in December 1966 consisted of the types detailed in Table 25.

TABLE 25

Numerical Strength and Types of Chinese Aircraft (1966)

Utilization	Types	Number
Combat squadrons	MIG-19 and 21	296
	MIG-15 and 17	1,588
Bomber squadrons	TU-2	86
	TU-4	12
	TU-16	2
	IL-28	270
Transportation squadrons	IL-12, IL-14, IL-18, LI-2, AN-2	232
Reconnaissance squadrons	IL-28	8
	MIG-17	38
Navigation squadrons	IL-12, IL-14, IL-18, and LI-2	22
Naval Air Force	IL-10	36
	MIG-15	152
	BE-6, M-14	50
	Total	2,792

SOURCE: Oral statements by the director of the Institute for Political Research (Taipei), Pao Chin-an, in conversation with me during December 1966.

These aircraft are located at more than 51 air bases: 11 in the military district of Shenyang, 3 in Inner Mongolia, 7 in the Peking district, 2 in Wuhan, 9 in the district of Nanking, 9 in Fuchow, 7 in the district of Canton, and one each in Lanchow, Chengtu, and K'unming.[17]

Evidently Red China has thus far not developed its own aircraft models. It seems, however, that two factories are producing MIG-17, MIG-19, and MIG-21 planes according to Soviet designs. In the summer of 1962 Red China again received a supply of sixteen MIG-21's from the U.S.S.R., but since then no further delivery is known to have been made. The six successful nuclear tests since October 1964 seem to have motivated the Red Chinese air force to prepare itself for a change to nuclear armaments. In this connection the development of missile technology has acquired considerable importance. The successful testing of a long-range guided missile with a nuclear warhead in October 1966 brought Red China a long way ahead. Also the supply of atomic bombs should have increased in the meantime to about twenty. Nevertheless presumably it will be necessary for Red China to spend five to ten years before it can realistically join the circle of nuclear powers that are taken seriously.

Security Forces

The strength of the security troops *(Kung-an-tui)* is estimated at about 200,000 men. They are officially subordinated to the ministry of public security, although it seems that they receive their operational orders as a rule from the defense ministry. Organized into forty brigades, each with about 5,000 men, they are to a great extent motorized and have at their disposal (under Red Chinese army conditions) very modern equipment which also comprises light field artillery and armored vehicles. One deals here with mobile units which have proved very valuable since 1959 during the suppression of spontaneous uprisings and resistance movements.

The Militia

During the "people's commune" campaign in summer 1958 there occurred a transition in China. Younger citizens were organized into militia formations in order to concentrate and train them in the use of light weapons (without allowing them live ammunition, as a rule). According to communist statements, already by December 1958 a total of 170 million men belonged to the militia. Soon it turned out that these units were anything but reliable. During the years 1960 and 1961 there were many reports about participation by militia units in uprisings. In July 1961 the government was forced to introduce measures which were supposed to guarantee better control over the militia.[18] They were now subordinated to the defense ministry, and officers of the PLA were delegated as commanders for local militia formations. Evidently even this was not sufficient to overcome difficulties with the militia. Besides, maneuvers had a detrimental effect on farm and industrial production. Therefore the leadership evidently decided in 1962 to curtail substantially the training of the militia. Since May 1965 an attempt has been made to revive the organization. Success or failure of these efforts is thus far little known.

Today one can distinguish between two categories of militia: (1) basic militia, which embraces men between sixteen and thirty-two years old who in case of war would be called upon to re-enforce the PLA; and (2) regular militia, which theoretically comprises the bulk of citizens from sixteen to fifty years of age. In reality two thirds of the militia seemingly includes trained reserves which from time to time conduct field exercises. The equipment is outdated (for the most part this includes weapons captured from 1937 to 1949), and the ammunition supply manifests considerable deficiencies.[19]

During the course of October 1966 a number of reports appeared in the Chinese mainland press from which one can determine that at least parts of the Red Guard were being armed. It is possible that the Peking leadership wanted to build up the Red Guard instead of the militia as auxiliary troops, but after the "cultural revolution" met with widespread resistance in 1967, this idea obviously has been abandoned. On the whole it can be ascertained that the militia experiment did not proceed as Mao and his coworkers had hoped it would. The militia manifests the characteristics of a mass organization rather than of a military unit. In case of war it might serve, nevertheless, for protection of bombing targets and construction work. In this respect it could relieve the regular army considerably.

A comprehensive survey of Red Chinese strength in armed forces leads to the conclusion that thus far (and probably also for a number of years to come) they will be unable to achieve victory in a military conflict with one or both of the two world powers. They can, however, without doubt serve as a means of political pressure on China's weaker neighbors in the east and south of Asia. Their offensive capability, of course, meets with a barrier in the spectrum of protective alliances with non-Asian powers. To the extent that the United States and possibly also the U.S.S.R. are ready to provide security guarantees to the neighbors of mainland China, the chances for expansion of Red China diminish.

Command Structure

During the first years after the communist seizure of power on the Chinese mainland, between 1949 and 1954, the party leadership was characterized by features of a military dictatorship. The "Revolutionary Military Council" *(Kê-ming-chün-shih wei-yuan-hui)* was perhaps the most important source for the provisional government which stood at the head of the country until the constitution of the People's Republic of China could be introduced. To it belonged, under the personal leadership of Mao

Tse-tung, the most important commanders of the large Red Army units. Today they are regarded as the almost legendary six field armies. Under the direct leadership of the Military Council stood the entire armed force of Red China. A defense ministry or an independently organized general staff did not exist. Besides, the country had been divided into six large military districts, which served simultaneously as overlapping administrative areas. Each of these districts was subordinated to a veteran of the "revolutionary war" who usually ruled arbitrarily within his own sphere of authority.

Manchuria remained under the control of an old-time communist, Kao Kang, who had a good relationship with the military. Northwest China was dominated by the commander of the First Field Army, Marshal P'eng Tê-huai. East China had Marshal Ch'en Yi as commander of the Third Field Army. In central and south China the commander of the Fourth Field Army was Marshal Lin Piao. In southwest China the command over the Second Field Army remained with Marshal Liu Po-ch'eng. In the immediate vicinity of the capital, command was held by Marshal Nieh Jung-chen. In the province of Kwangtung, finally, Marshal Yeh Chien-ying enjoyed a considerable measure of autonomy under the supervision of Lin Piao.

The extent to which the central government had become stabilized was reflected in the civilians around Mao who ruled at Peking, especially Liu Shao-ch'i, Chou En-lai, Ch'en Yün, Tung Pi-wu, and Teng Hsiao-p'ing. They began to fear the disproportionate power of the regional military commanders. In the first half of 1954 they commenced to introduce countermeasures. Kao Kang was accused of mobilizing the military within the Party against the civilian leaders. In Manchuria he allegedly wanted to build his own "kingdom." On the basis of these charges he was liquidated. The other regional commanders were transferred to high positions in the capital where one could exert better supervision over them. In place of the six administrative regions, henceforth twenty-eight provinces or "autonomous regions" and large cities were formed (whose administrative chiefs could be controlled more easily from Peking than the distinguished general from the civil war). Simultaneously a fundamental reorganization of the army was introduced.

Then it was decided to replace the revolutionary volunteer army with a modern-equipped compulsory army. The core was supposed to include long-term and well-trained professional soldiers. At first the top echelon of the armed forces underwent transformation. With the new constitution of 1954, in place of the hitherto all-powerful Revolutionary Military Council, a "National Defense Council" *(Kuo-fang wei-yuan-hui)* was constituted but with a strongly limited competence. This group included, following its last reorganization on January 3, 1965, a total of 119 members. Among these were all the well-known leaders of the Red Army units from the civil war period and some generals who had defected in 1949 to the communist side from the former Kuomintang.[20]

The Defense Council evidently does not possess real power of command but performs essentially a consultative function. The official commander-in-chief of the armed forces is the chief of state, the Chairman of the "People's Republic of China." In his name and on his orders the armed forces are led by the minister of national defense. This office since September 1959 remains under the control of Lin Piao. Immediately under the supervision of the minister and his eight deputies (since January 1965) are the general staff; the general political department; inspectorate-general for training of the armed forces; headquarters of the air force, navy, security troops, artillery, tanks, engineer troops, and transportation units. A separate high command of the armed forces does not exist. Commanders of the twelve military regions are subordinated moreover directly to the chief of the general staff who, in time of peace, in reality possess *de facto* authority. The power of command is reserved to the defense minister.

Already during the reorganization in 1954 the general political department of the PLA assumed special importance. All political branches in military units and individual political commissars in the PLA were placed under its authority. It maintains at its disposal a direct chain of command down to the lowest level within the armed forces. Since the take-over of the defense ministry by Lin Piao in 1959 the position of the political department has been further strengthened so that today it represents an independent organ. It is now coequal with the general staff.

Of utmost importance to the leadership of the PLA is the "Military Commission of the Central Committee, Chinese Communist Party" *(Chung-kuo Gung-ch'an-tang chung-yang wei-yüan-hui chün-shih wei-yüan-hui).* Although one deals here with a strictly Party organization, nevertheless it possesses in practice authority to issue directives to the National Defense Council, the defense ministry, and all ranks within the PLA. Until 1965 Mao himself occupied the chairmanship of the Military Commission; after the spring of 1966, however, Lin Piao has been identified as *de facto* head of this group.[21] This position without a doubt has considerably strengthened the power of the defense minister, who recently has been designated as successor to Mao Tse-tung.

The reorganization in 1954 did not proceed without opposition. The old heroes of the PLA, who had been linked personally to their soldiers, were superseded in active command posts by younger and less-known generals. However, one could not immediately replace substantially the influence of the old communists among the military with that of the "civilian" Party leaders. In order to attain this goal Mao, Liu Shao-ch'i, and Chou En-lai (at that time evidently still in complete harmony) proceeded indirectly by issuing a proclamation on the army of "experts." Instruction methods were developed which stressed military technology stronger than the promotion of "revolutionary consciousness." In this manner, however, a threat arose to the Party. Under the leadership of Defense Minister P'eng Tê-huai and the director of the general political department, Marshal Lo Jung-huan, a group of old veteran military communists united with younger "military technicians." They utilized the slogan of the "modern army" to defend themselves against rule over the military by political commissars. Their endeavors were unsuccessful, however. Since the spring of 1956 the Party leadership succeeded again in reasserting the rule of the political commissars over the military officers.

At the 8th Party Congress of the Chinese communist party in September 1956 Lo Jung-huan did not deliver the report about the political work in the army. This was done by his deputy, T'an Cheng, who at that time still represented the Party line against the professional military. Later he also joined the group of P'eng Tê-huai. In December 1956 Lo was relieved of his post because he had advocated "a purely military point of view."[22] T'an assumed in his place the top position over the general political department.

Political leadership over the armed forces was definitely asserted when in the late summer of 1959 Peng Tê-huai, T'an Cheng, and the chief-of-staff, Huang K'ê-ch'eng—all of whom were considered to be "right-wing deviationists"—were relieved of their posts. Supported by the organization of the political commissars, Lin Piao now began to establish his rule over the PLA. The conflict between professional officers and political commissars continued. It led in 1965 to grave differences in the leadership of the Red Chinese armed forces.

Problems of Sociological and Political Structure

The PLA since March 1955 has been based on compulsory military service in the People's Republic of China. The general principles of military service at first involved two, then three, and after May 1965 up to five years of active duty. In fact, however, this military service represents a paper obligation. Among the 2.5 million troops, some 1.2 million are professional soldiers. The number of potential draftees, each year six to seven million, cannot be absorbed. Hence only 10 per cent of them can be called to service. The remaining 90 per cent at best can go through militia training. Thus the Party leadership is able to draft reliable communists and in this way strengthen the ideological reliability of the armed forces.

According to reports in July 1962, 36.8 per cent of the soldiers were members of the Party and 41.9 per cent belonged to the Communist Youth League. Only 21.3 per cent were not full members of any communist organization, but among these almost half were candidates for membership in the Youth League.[23] Since then the figures may have changed in favor of the Party. This could lead to the conclusion that the PLA politically represents an extraordinarily reliable instrument of the Peking leadership. In reality, however, the situation obviously looks different.

Complaints about the "missing revolutionary spirit" in the armed forces between 1956 and 1964 appeared daily in Red Chinese domestic propaganda. Even today they have not completely disappeared. The difficulties which have occurred in this area result above all from the sociological structure of the PLA. Since the majority of members in the communist party derive from the peasantry (in 1961 this category amounted to 69.8 per cent of all party members), most of the soldiers come from villages. Since 1956 the increasing opposition by the farmers to collectivization of agriculture did not remain without effect on the army. The attachment of soldiers to their families at home still appears to work effectively against communist indoctrination.

The differences between the old cadres who had come from the revolutionary army and the younger officers trained since 1950 add to this problem. General Yang Ch'eng-wu, who was acting chief-of-staff from July 1966 to March 1968, had written eleven years ago: "Old cadres who were derived from the workers' class and the peasantry, swell with pride and arrogance. They wear their merits proudly on their chests and treat others with contempt. The most important for them are military rank, promotions, salary, pleasure, and an easy life."[24] The "new cadres" held up to the veterans again and again that modern military knowledge was more important than political orthodoxy.

As a result three substantial problems have been present for a long time in the PLA which cause great difficulties for the party leadership: (1) the discontent by a majority of soldiers, who are peasants, with Peking's agricultural policies; (2) differences between officers and enlisted men, which until May 1965 had involved privileges for the officers; (3) contradictions between the old revolutionary veterans and younger career officers as well as enlisted men. These contradictions erupted openly during the period of the "hundred flowers' movement" in the spring of 1957 and led to the discharge of several prominent younger professional officers. In November 1957 the director for training in the PLA, Marshal Liu Po-ch'eng, was also accused of "purely military thinking" and spreading dogmatism in the army. A month previously he had already accused himself in a "self-criticism article" of "deviationist tendencies" and promised to "surrender his heart to the Party." In this article Liu, who until that time obviously had supported the criticism by "technicians" against "politicians," suddenly stressed the necessity "to place the army completely under the political leadership."[25] This admission and repentance preserved his high position in the Political Bureau. His merits during the civil war saved Liu at that time from a total purge. He was only demoted from chief of training to the less influential position of commander at the Military Administration Academy.

The training branch itself, which had become the center for opposition to the political indoctrination of the army, was dissolved and its functions transferred to the general staff. With the purge of the "right-wing deviationists" in September 1959 it was possible to destroy a strong residue of opposition in the top ranks of the PLA against the policies of Mao. The new course was clearly formulated by Lin Piao already on September 30, 1959, as he plainly expounded in a directive-giving article: "Forward, under the red banners of the party's general line and the teachings of Mao Tse-tung!" Thus he made clear in which direction the PLA would proceed henceforth: "It is our principle that the armed forces are subordinate to the command of the Party and not the Party to the command of the armed forces. . . . The relationship between the individual and the Party must be clearly defined: the individual must submit to the absolute leadership of the Party. Individuals may not pursue any ambitious plans which contradict the interests of the Party!"[26]

The victory of the political commissars for control over the leadership of the army did not resolve, however, the weighty political problems within the PLA. It is true, no doubt, that the top positions were largely occupied by personal followers of Mao, but in the lower ranks a threatening crisis developed after 1958. The wave of collectivization in Chinese villages and the ensuing food difficulties led to a situation, where those soldiers who came from peasant families made their complaints loudly known to the Party leadership. Thus *Chieh-fang-chün pao* in an editorial comment on July 1, 1958, stated the following: "Young soldiers who come from farm areas bring with themselves antirevolutionary feelings into the army." And in October 1960 Lin Piao reported to the Military Commission of the Central Committee: "The right-wing deviationists in the armed forces behave skeptically regarding the general line of the Party, the Great Leap Forward, and the peasant communes. . . . When they encounter difficulties, they strongly criticize present conditions. Yes, some people in the army move with counterrevolutionary action openly against the policies of the Party and of the state."[27]

The spreading criticism of Peking policies, which even increased during 1960, reached threatening proportions in the spring of 1961. This was confirmed by those issues of "Work Bulletin" *(Kung-tso t'ung-hsün)*, published by the general political department between January and May of 1961, which came into the hands of Western news services the following year. Finally, during the summer of 1963 they were published. From these documents the extent of opposition in the armed forces becomes clear.

Sometimes the opposition even exploded into violent action. During one day alone, May 6, 1960, the above mentioned "Work Bulletin" revealed reports from the political departments of the 28th Army Corps, the 20th Army Corps, the 13th Artillery Regiment, and from the military court in the PLA city headquarters at Nanking about three suicides and murder committed by a soldier on two officers and one political commissar. Characteristic of the situation prevailing at that time is also the following quotation from the same publication: "Comrade Hu Chen-ts'an, who entered the army in 1958, voiced a loud cry during a discussion about the people's communes. He had just received a letter from his family which informed him that for fifteen days no rice had been issued."[28]

As the Party leadership established the extent of the opposition and resistance within the PLA, it immediately introduced energetic countermeasures. From the summer of 1960 and into the year 1964 a movement for "improvement of work style" and ideological training in the army replaced all other movements in rapid succession. The goals for these campaigns were determined through principles of the political leadership. These were decided upon at an enlarged plenum of the Military Commission of the Central Committee during the summer of 1960 and in the course of conferences on political work in the PLA during March 1961, February 1963, and January 1964. They assumed special importance because Mao, Lin Piao, and their faction now strove in the campaign for the "great proletarian cultural revolution" *(Wu-ch'an chieh-chi wen-hua ta-ke-ming)* to expand it into all areas of politics, administration, and agriculture throughout Red China.

These principles determine that the study of Mao Tse-tung's works and "its use in practice" will serve as the obligatory guide line in political work and also in the indoctrination of the army. "The Thoughts of Mao Tse-tung," so it is said, are the "strongest and the most effective weapon of the PLA." Next to ideological correctness, and above all simplicity of living, flexibility and "good military ability" are worthwhile virtues for which to strive. It was recommended for the political commissars, and today also for the whole nation, to acquaint themselves with the above mentioned "Four Things Come First."

As a result of these principles, already during 1960 and 1962 different "movements" within the PLA began to point in the direction that the armed forces also in the lower ranks would again be in the hands of the Party. In 1960 Mao had formulated the "work style of the PLA" in the form of "three statements and eight ideograms." The "three statements" demanded a correct political orientation, hard work and simple living, as well as flexibility in strategy and tactics. The "eight ideograms" represented the Chinese concepts for unity, energy, seriousness, and liveliness. From these formulations of Mao, at the end of 1960 the "three-eight movement" grew. Within its framework, the attempt was made on the basis of the above principles to conduct indoctrination work in the PLA.

Already after one month, at the turn of the year 1960–1, the "three-eight movement" was enlarged to the "five-good-soldier-movement." In the latter one was concerned to make clear to the soldiers of the PLA that they had to be "five times good": good in political thinking, good in military training, good in "three-eight work style," good in execution of tasks, and good in physical training.[29]

In the summer of 1961 a further campaign began which was intensely activated by the end of 1964 and called the "four-good-company-movement." Emphasis was placed on the significance of company-level political education and indoctrination. It called upon the troops to be "good in political thinking, good in the three-eight work style, good in military training, and good in style of living." In connection with this movement, since September 1961 contests between individual companies and platoons have taken place. Repeatedly particular units receive the designation "four-good-company." This usually involves financial premiums for officers and enlisted men as well as augmentation of rations for the unit concerned. This example generally has played a major role in the PLA indoctrination campaign since 1961.

The brave soldier Lei Feng was glorified in March 1963. His short life (he had died in an accident) which, astonishingly had been followed by photographers throughout, was so "great" because he lived with the works of Mao Tse-tung. During the summer of 1963 the "Good 8th Company in Nanking Street at Shanghai" heroically resisted all temptations of a metropolis, reactionary insinuations, girls, and opium because it found protection in the teachings of Chairman Mao. In January 1964 the brave company commander Kuo Hsing-fu was publicized as an expert in explaining, lecturing, teaching, and leading in ideological works.[30] The political commissar Wang Chieh in the spring of 1966 helped poor farmers very much. Repeatedly these examples of real or fictitious good conduct in social or ideological life were portrayed before the eyes of the soldiers in the PLA.

The long duration and results from different individual actions during the indoctrination campaign from 1961 until 1964 permit one to conclude that the Party leadership had to fight against increasing difficulties in order to overcome crises in the PLA. This crisis apparently went deeper than generally had been accepted at that time in the West. Nevertheless Mao and Lin Piao did not remain without success. They were able publicly until the summer of 1965 to strengthen the position of the Party and, above all, that of the political apparatus. The extension of universal military training and abolition of military ranks in May 1965 mark the victory of the radical faction within the army. Mao and Lin had in their hands through the PLA an instrument which could render great service to them in any conflict with their opponents within the Party leadership.

Whereas between 1954 and 1964 the conflict involved securing mastery by the Party over the army, now a faction strove with the help of the army to conquer power in the Party. Before that time Mao and Lin had been prepared for any action against their opponents in the Party leadership; they now once again had to be concerned with breaking up an opposition group within the PLA. In the course of the year 1965 the chief of the general staff, Lo Jui-ch'ing, apparently organized a group among the military which protested against the predominant influence of the political commissars and the overemphasis on political education work. It is unknown whether he had any immediate contact with the men in the party apparatus around Liu Shao-ch'i and Teng Hsiao-p'ing. The latter were soon in open conflict with Mao and Lin. It would appear that the radical faction around Lo and some of his coworkers had been directly threatened. Lin Piao and his followers, the political commissars and officers from the old Fourth Field Army, are asserting themselves again. Concerning Lo nothing has been heard since November 27, 1965. In July 1966 it was reported that Lin's old comrade in arms, Yang Ch'eng-wu, had assumed the office of acting chief of the general staff, which he held until March 1968.

Summation and Trends

There can hardly be any doubt that the PLA plays an extraordinarily important role in the struggle for power. It began with the proclamation of the "great proletarian cultural revolution" in April 1966, and conflict openly erupted within the Peking leadership. The political commissars of the army, as is known today, since May 1966 trained the cadres of the "Red Guards." The PLA supplied this youthful militia of Mao and Lin with its logistic apparatus. In many places army officers frequently stood at the head of the "Red Guards." Their maintenance and equipment often was guaranteed by the PLA.[31]

But the "Red Guards" obviously did not represent an adequate instrument to promote Mao's new way of revolution. When they started a general offensive against strongholds of the opposition in administrative and economic areas at the beginning of 1967, they met with such widespread and intense resistance that their onslaught soon proved to be a failure. On January 23 the Party center was forced to issue an order of the day, imploring the PLA to support the "left wing," if necessary with direct military action against the "new general attack of the reactionary capitalist line."[32]

The response by the PLA, however, was rather ambiguous. In Peking and Shanghai as well as in the provinces of Heilungkiang, Shansi, Shantung, and Kweichow the army command and military units came out unreservedly in support of the Maoist faction. The same is true regarding the majority of troops in certain vital areas of Hopei, Hupei, Kiangsi, and Fukien. There occurred, furthermore, some verbal support for Mao and Lin Piao by the commanding officers in the province of Kwangtung and the Autonomous Regions of Kwangsi and Inner Mongolia.

On the other hand, PLA units in Chekiang, Yünnan, Ch'inghai, Kiangsi, Anhui, Sinkiang, and Tibet remained more or less neutral. Eager only to keep "peace and order," they turned against organized resistance groups as well as against the activities of the most radical pro-Mao organizations. In the provinces of Kirin, Liaoning, Honan, Shênsi, Hunan and Ssuch'wan and in the Autonomous Region of Ninghsia—areas in which nearly one third of the Chinese population lives—commanders and troops obviously did not bother very much about orders from the central authorities.

When, after a period of comparative lull, the leftist extremists in the Peking leadership tried to start a new "general offensive" against the opposition, military units in Wuhan (July 20, 1967), Canton (August 1967), and several other centers turned openly against the Maoist organizations, among which a number of splits occurred. Lin Piao, however, was able to generate a compromise with the regional military leaders. The most outspokenly anti-Maoists among them were dismissed, while, on the other hand, Lin Piao and Chou En-lai started a drive against the extreme left in the central leadership.

Since October 1967 the "Red Guards" have been tightly disciplined by the PLA; the military, for all practical purposes, has taken control of nearly all regional Party and administrative organizations. By mid-April 1968 "Revolutionary Committees," substituting for the former administrative and Party leadership, had been established in 19 among the—by now—29 administrative units of Communist China. Among the 102 leading cadres on these committees, 62, or more than 60 per cent, are military men.

Hence, regional military power emerges more and more and, although great efforts have been made to achieve military unity again—efforts to which the basic ideas of Mao's cultural revolution seem to have become a casualty—it still remains to be seen whether the future trend will go toward centralized and highly militarized rule, or whether a new period of military regionalism, though qualitatively different from the one China experienced between 1850 and the 1930's, will begin.[33]

One fact, however, is certain: the PLA represents today, without any doubt, the most important power factor for China domestically and also for the policy of Communist China toward its Asian neighbors. One has to be aware of the fact that in a few years it might also become a serious threat to the other great powers in the field of nuclear strategy.

Nevertheless the PLA suffers from structural weaknesses which considerably diminish its potential effectiveness. The morale of the troops has been impaired by the conflict between military officers and political commissars, and even more so by the breakdown of Party unity in the course of the recent crisis. Should the Chinese mainland suffer another economic setback like that of 1960–2, new tensions in addition to those which affected the Chinese armed forces at that time—and probably of an even more serious nature—would have to be expected.

(Translated from the original German
into English by Jadwiga M. Staar)

Notes to Chapter 10

1. "Protocol of the 23rd extended plenum of the Standing Committee, KMT Executive Committee on Aug. 5, 1927 at Wuhan," KMT *Archives* Taichung, Taiwan. Cf. also Warren Kuo, *Analytical History of the Chinese Communist Party* (Taipei, 1966), I, 281.

2. *Chung-kuo kung-ch'an-tang chih t'ou-shih* ("Behind the Scenes of the Communist Party in China"), published by the Central Organization Department of the KMT (1935; 2nd edn., Taipei, 1962), pp. 267ff.

3. Mao Tse-tung, "Report at the 7th Party Congress of the Chinese Communist Party" (English version), *Selected Works of Mao Tse-tung* (New York, 1955), IV, 253ff.

4. Mao Tse-tung, *Chung-kuo ke-ming-te wen-t'i* ("Problems of the Chinese Revolution"), (Yenan, 1939), p. 7.

5. *Chung-kup ch'ing-nien pao* ("Chinese Youth Newspaper"), (Peking) Jul. 31, 1962.

6. Compare in this connection, *China-Analysen* (Frankfurt am Main), (April 1964), pp. 18ff.

7. Tai Kao-hsiang, "The Chinese Communist Conscription System," in *Issues and Studies* (Taipei), II:4 (Jan. 1966), 14ff.

8. *Kung-tso t'ung-hsun* ("Work Bulletin") of the General Political Department of the People's Liberation Army, according to *China News Analysis,* (Hong Kong), No. 510 (Apr. 3, 1964), p. 7.

9. Peter Christian Hauswedell, "Die Volksbefreiungsarmee," in *Politik und Herrschaft in Rotchina,* ed. Jürgen Domes (Stuttgart, 1965), p. 93.

10. *Ti-ch'ing yen-chiu* ("Studies of the Opposition Situation"), (Taipei), Volume B/28 (Aug. 1963), p. 14.

11. Cheng Chih, "Peking's Military Situation in Recent Years and Its Future Development," *Issues and Studies* (Taipei), II:8 (May 1966), 26ff.

12. New China News Agency (NCNA), in English on Peking Radio (Sep. 29 and 30, 1965).

13. *Handbook of Chinese Communist Affairs* (Taipei, 1964), p. 80; henceforth cited as *Handbook*.

14. *Hongkong Tiger Standard,* April 5, 1962. Compare also Liu Chi-chuen, "Peiping's Submarine Force," *Issues and Studies* (Taipei), I:9 (June 1965), 14ff.

15. *Chieh-fang-chun pao,* Jul. 16, 1963.

16. *Handbook,* p. 82.

17. *Ibid.,* pp. 3–5.

18. *Chieh-fang jih-pao* (Shanghai), Dec. 22, 1958; "Regulations Governing Militia Work," as published by Ministry of National Defense at Peiping (July 1961); *Issues and Studies* (Taipei), II:1 (Oct. 1965), 45–52.

19. *Kung-tso t'ung-hsün* ("Work Bulletin"), (Peking), No. 5 (Jan. 17, 1961).

20. *Who's Who in Communist China* (Hongkong, 1966), pp. 727–30.

21. *Chieh-fang-chün pao,* March 28, 1966.

22. *Ibid.,* Dec. 23, 1956.

23. *Ibid.,* Aug. 4, 1962.

24. Article in *Chung-kuo ch'ing-nien* ("China's Youth"), Feb. 1957.

25 *Jen-min jih-pao* (Peking), Nov. 14, 1957; and *Cheih-fang-chün pao,* Oct. 16, 1957.

26. *Jen-min jih-pao,* Sep. 30, 1959.

27. *Chieh-fang-chün pao,* Oct. 21, 1960.

28. *Kung-tso t'ung-hsun* ("Work Bulletin"), May 6, 1960.

29. *Chieh-fang-chün pao,* Sep. 16, 1960.

30. Radio Peking (domestic service), Feb. 17, 1964.

31. Compare the report over the German service of Radio Peking, Dec. 21, 1966, at 7:00 and 9:00 p.m.

32. *Chieh-fang-chün pao,* Jan. 25, 1967; English translation in *Background on China,* No. 30 (Jan. 30, 1967).

33. For this paragraph, cf. Juergen Domes, "The Cultural Revolution and the Army," *Asian Survey,* VIII: 5 (May 1968).

Discussion

KENNETH R. WHITING

The platitude, long believed in the Western world, that the Chinese have a supreme contempt for the military hardly bears up under close scrutiny, and it is certainly not true on either the mainland or Taiwan today. Over half a century ago Yuan Shih-k'ai seized the revolution from Dr. Sun Yat-sen and maintained power by virtue of his control over the best military force in China. After Yuan local military chiefs ruled their respective satrapies contemptuous of the writ from Peking; in brief, the curse of warlordism was visited upon the land. Even when the completion of the Northern Expedition in 1928 made it possible to establish a Kuomintang government at Nanking, the unity of China remained only "nominal." Chiang Kai-shek constantly engaged either in bribing warlords to pay at least lip service to Nanking or in bitter conflict with them in his bid for supremacy. This resulted in a "militarization" of the Kuomintang regime.

For the communist movement itself military power and the Red Army became the *sine qua non* of political power. By the mid-1930's—the exact year is still in dispute—the leadership of the Chinese Communist Party passed to Mao Tse-tung, mainly because he had control over military power. Between late 1927 and late 1949 the Chinese Red Army grew from a few thousand to almost four million soldiers. During that period of twenty-two years a relatively small group of political-military leaders dominated the movement and engaged in almost constant combat. This road to power should be contrasted with communist seizure of authority in Russia. In this case a spasmodic *coup* brought a political group to power, and the politicians have never shared their power with the military. At least up to now there has been no real question in the Soviet Union about the dominance of the political leaders. Even a hint of the "man on horseback," e.g., Trotsky, Frunze, Tukhachevsky, or Zhukov, led to the elimination of the potential offender.

Dr. Domes quite rightly points up this difference in the Chinese revolutionary experience and thus accounts for the fact that Mao gives the armed forces such an extremely important place in his revolutionary theory. Mao's well-known statement that "political power grows out of the barrel of a gun," once counterbalanced by the assertion that the political must always control the military, seems mild in comparison with the quotation cited by Dr. Domes that it "is rifles and cannons that build the Party, culture, and even the world!" This little gem from the brow of Mao, if it represents his present thinking at all, could have tremendous implications for the future development of China; that is, if the Mao–Lin Piao team should win. As Dr. Domes mentions, since the ousting of P'eng Teh-huai in 1959 Mao has come to depend more and more on the PLA as the instrument best fitted to maintain the revolution on the path he desires. Apparently Mao feels that if China has to be "militarized" to keep it from lusting after the fleshpots of "goulash communism" *à la* U.S.S.R., then "militarized" it must be.

It is just possible that students of communist affairs have been mesmerized by the Soviet model. The political leaders in Moscow have kept their military machine under control; ergo the communist system means political control over the military. But the communist political leaders in Russia did not come to power in an environment similar to that inherited by their

Chinese comrades and were not called upon to rule a people that had been bossed by military leaders, be they warlords, Japanese, Kuomintang, or Red Army, for half a century. That underdeveloped China, frustrated in the creation of even the preconditions for economic take-off, should revert to military rule would hardly be a strange phenomenon in a world where one of the outstanding features of economically underdeveloped nations seems to be the prevalence of military dictatorships.

If the PLA, however, becomes the main pillar of power in China, how long will it remain satisfied with Mao's guerrilla–mobile warfare military doctrine? Is there not a great probability that other P'eng Teh-huai's will come to the fore, that is, military leaders who want a PLA equipped with both modern weapons and a suitable doctrine for their use? Dr. Domes's description of the PLA of today is that of an army still organized and equipped to fight the 1946–9 civil war but hardly the type of a military machine fit to challenge either the United States or the Soviet Union. Mao's "cultural revolution" seems not only determined to alienate outside sources for the modernization of the PLA, the U.S.S.R. in particular; but it is also doing its best to frustrate industrial development within China, not to mention its hostility toward an efficient educational system so necessary in the training of skilled personnel required to operate the industrial structure. One wonders how long the professional military officers will put up with such a state of affairs.

Dr. Domes could hardly have selected a time in modern Chinese history when the future looks murkier, and one can only admire his courage in outlining possible future developments. Any one of his guesses may turn out to be correct, but there are so many other possibilities that conjecture at this point in time, especially given the paucity of reliable information emanating from China, would seem a fruitless game. Vague reports from Sinkiang, Inner Mongolia, Manchuria, and other outlying areas could be used as data for predicting that a new era of warlordism might be just over the horizon. The situation could deteriorate to such an extent that even the return of Chiang Kai-shek to the mainland might be a possibility, although hardly a probability. But whatever the scenario used, Dr. Domes is correct in pointing out that conditions within the PLA will be of extreme importance. A united PLA should swing the balance; a divided PLA might result in civil war; a neutral PLA might permit chaos.

Finally, it is puzzling to read that the Red Chinese Air Force attained a reputation of being "unbeatable," a fame which Dr. Domes says it lost when the nationalists slaughtered it in 1958 over the Taiwan Strait. The ratio of kills in "Mig alley" during the Korean war was so highly in favor of American pilots that the Red Chinese Air Force could hardly have taken unto itself the term "unbeatable" at that time. And that was the last real conflict in which it has been engaged to date.

Part V
Other Asian States

11

the mongolian people's republic since world war II

WILLIAM B. BALLIS

In discussing the political, economic, and military developments of the Mongolian People's Republic since 1945 one should first of all give a summary of what happened before that period in the oldest Soviet satellite. The Mongolian People's Republic was the first of these dependencies to be classified as a people's democracy. The Red Army entered Outer Mongolia in 1921 and laid the military basis for the "people's revolution" which had been engineered on U.S.S.R. soil. Involvement in World War I, the Bolshevik Revolution, and the civil war contributed to a weakening of Russia's position before 1921, although even the tsars had been interested in Outer Mongolia prior to 1914. While Russia was in the throes of revolution and counterrevolution, Outer Mongolia was also experiencing similar struggles. In the period 1919–21 Moscow-oriented Mongol revolutionaries began to join indigenous elements demanding radical change. The Mongolian revolution of 1921 resulted partly from these centripetal forces of the growing Mongolian revolutionary movement, which was diffused and varied.

While it is true that all the segments of the Mongolian revolutionary movement wanted to drive Chinese influence out of Mongolia, all the Mongolian revolutionary groups were not united in deferring to Russian communism for leadership. In 1919 the Mongolian revolutionaries who were communist-oriented and located at that time in the Buryat area of Siberia, which was under Soviet control, met and organized the Mongolian People's Revolutionary Party. The approximately one dozen Mongolian nationalists who formed the prototype of this party swore an oath to maintain iron discipline, secrecy, and a communist party type of organization.

As long as the Chinese controlled Outer Mongolia and were in possession of the capital at Urga, the U.S.S.R. did not move into Outer Mongolia. When Chinese power in Outer Mongolia collapsed, at first the White Russian forces moved in to set up their authority in Outer Mongolia. Ungern-Sternberg's invasion of Outer Mongolia brought anti-Bolshevik troops, which moved against Urga in the fall of 1920 and in early 1921 captured the city. Several months after Ungern-Sternberg's invasion the Mongol revolutionaries who had organized in Siberia joined with the Red Army and occupied Urga on July 6, 1921. Ungern-Sternberg was captured and executed in the fall of 1921.

Early in 1921 the Mongolian People's Revolutionary Party, which had been established in Siberia in 1919, met with representatives of the Soviet communist party at the Mongolian border city of Kiakhta. The guiding force in the Comintern, the organization directing this revolution, was the head of its Far Eastern Secretariat, a certain Shumiatsky.[1] The Comintern had established close relations with the Mongolian People's Revolutionary Party, which at that time was still a very small organization and only later admitted into the Comintern. In late 1920 and early 1921 Shumiatsky met with the Mongolian revolutionary leaders and decided to send some of them to Moscow for further training. Other Mongol leaders, such as Sukhe Bator, the "Lenin of Mongolia," and Choibalsang, the "Stalin of Mongolia," stayed in the Siberian city of Irkutsk, where they commenced their studies in the military school.

The Soviet communists through the Comintern supported the Mongolian People's Revolutionary Party. At a conference in March 1921 at Kiakhta the two groups agreed to regard each other as "the only lawful government" on its own territory. The Mongolian People's Revolutionary Party as a result of this conference became a formal member of the Communist International and sent delegates to the 3rd Congress of the Comintern in the summer of 1921.

On April 10, 1921, the provisional revolutionary government of Mongolia, which was established at the Kiakhta conference, requested Soviet military assistance. This brought the Red Army into Outer Mongolia. An official U.S.S.R. account of this period says: "The Soviet government, having accepted the invitation concerning the joint liquidation of the White bands in Outer Mongolia, aided the Mongolian partisans and army in liquidating the bands of Ungern and having remained, at the request of the Mongolian Government, in the country up to 1925, helped to wipe out finally the remnants of White Guardism."[2]

When the Red Army came into Mongolia, the authority of the Russians transcended that of the Mongols. As the American consul in Kalgan, Inner Mongolia, at that time reported in a dispatch of October 10, 1921, "There may be a Mongolian government but the authority is the Russian Soviet Commandant. He issues orders for the release of men even if they have been arrested by the Mongols." At Urga the titular head of the state was the Living Buddha, Bogdo-Gegen. The Red forces allowed him to rule in name as long as he lived, which was until 1924.

George F. Kennan has described this period in the following way:

Outer Mongolia lay close to the vulnerable part of this line [the trans-Siberian Railway] that bends to the south around Lake Baikal. To remain inactive would have been to invite penetration and domination of the area by the Japanese, acting in association with anti-Bolshevik Russian forces. This was particularly dangerous, because the part of Siberia just west of Baikal contained, itself, a large Mongolian population. If the Mongols in the South remained under Japanese and White Russian influence, this could become a source of disaffection for the Mongols within Siberia proper.

Faced with this problem, the Russian Communists acted in the best Asian tradition. They arranged the establishment of a puppet government in Outer Mongolia, got it to request their military assistance, intervened with military force, and restored, in effect, the old Tsarist protectorate—an arrangement which has endured to the present day.[3]

When I myself presented in more detail a similar argument on the development of Soviet colonialism in Outer Mongolia in a paper read to the 25th World Congress of Orientalists at Moscow in August 1960, Soviet scholars severely criticized it. In an article on the Congress, published afterwards, B. G. Gafurov (director of the Institute for Oriental Studies at the U.S.S.R. Academy of Sciences and also a member of the Central Committee of the Communist Party of the Soviet Union) wrote: "After noting a number of correctly stated facts about the history of the Mongolian People's Revolutionary Party and the Mongolian People's Republic, Puntsuk-Norbo [a Mongolian scholar who attacked my paper] exposed the slanderous character of Ballis's statement concerning the 'export of revolution to Mongolia.' "[4]

The Soviet government and the provisional government of Outer Mongolia (the Mongolian People's Republic was not formally established until the death of the Bogdo-Gegen in 1924) signed on November 5, 1921, at Moscow their first treaty. This treaty provided for the recognition of both countries and established a legal basis for Mongolian-Soviet relations. The year before, in 1920, at the 2d Congress of the Comintern, Lenin had stated his theory of economic and political development in backward countries as follows: "It would be incorrect to say that the capitalistic stage of development is inevitable. With the help of the proletariat of the more advanced countries, backward countries can switch over to the Soviet structure and arrive at communism through special stages of development, avoiding the capitalist stage all together."[5]

This statement made by Lenin forty-eight years ago established the theoretical basis for the Asian people's democracies. Lenin was thinking of those countries which were not yet industrialized nor capitalistic and which could escape capitalism and therefore become socialist states without having to experience first an industrial revolution. The significance of this for Outer Mongolia was that the basis of the economy involved nomadic livestock raising. There could be very little industrial development, as the economy was of a simple pastoral and basic exchange character.

A leading Soviet writer on Outer Mongolia has provided an official description of Lenin's interview with the Mongolian representatives at this time.

> Comrade Lenin widely developed for our delegation the idea of the possibility and necessity of a noncapitalist development of the Mongolian People's Republic. The main condition which would guarantee this transition on the path of noncapitalist development is the strengthening of the work of the People's Revolutionary Party, and of the government; cooperatives would grow, new forms of economic and national culture would increase and the *arats* [Mongol nomad herdsmen] would be joined around the Party and the government for the economic and cultural development of the country. Only from the little islands from the new economic order created under the influence of the Party and government will the new noncapitalist economic system be formed in *arat* Mongolia.[6]

In this early period of the history of Outer Mongolia there occurred a power struggle involving leading Mongol personalities after the death of Sukhe Bator in 1923. The first successor was supplanted by Choibalsang, who took over the leadership of the new state and Party and held it until his death in 1932. Choibalsang was in turn succeeded by Tsendenbal, who had been deputy prime minister in the government and general-secretary of the Mongolian People's Revolutionary Party. Since 1952 Tsendenbal has been the dominant political personality.

When the nominal head of Outer Mongolia, the Bogdo-Gegen, died in 1924, the Mongolian People's Revolutionary Party led by Choibalsang established a new formal government of the Mongolian People's Republic. On November 8, 1924, the Great Khural, which is the Mongol equivalent of the Supreme Soviet in the U.S.S.R., adopted a constitution patterned after the one in Moscow.

On the basis of this constitution of 1924 the old propertied interests, such as the clergy and nobles, were divested of political rights and their property taken over by the state. With the promulgation of the constitution the old theocratic state was abolished and changes began to develop in the nature of the economy. In the twenties there was very intense political conflict in the new Mongolian People's Republic between the left wing and the right wing of the party. By the end of the twenties the right wing had been eliminated and the left wing started the process of collectivization in 1929. This was synchronized with collectivization in the U.S.S.R.

Comintern representatives in the Mongolian People's Republic directed the forced collectivization in that country. This measure proved very disastrous for the economy. There was not only a decline in the standard of living but also a widespread famine—results similar to those in the Soviet Union. The Mongolian people expressed their opposition to the Comintern policies of the government by revolting. A strong center for the revolts was in the western part of the country.

Revolts included not only the nomadic herdsmen but also young members of the Mongolian People's Revolutionary Party and their young people's organization, the Revolutionary Union of Youth, as well as some detachments of the Mongolian People's Army. The rebellion got out of hand so much so that the U.S.S.R. sent in detachments of the Red Army with airplanes and tanks to quash the uprising. This event, widely known at the time by foreign residents of the Soviet Union and also by observers in Outer Mongolia, has never been officially admitted by U.S.S.R. authorities.

To correct the mistakes made by the "left deviationists" in the party during 1931–2, an extraordinary plenum of the Central Committee of the Mongolian People's Revolutionary Party met in July 1932. This "marked out the part for further development of the Mongolian People's Republic, in conformity with the problems which confronted Mongolia as a bourgeois-democratic republic of the new type."[7] Despite this new course elements opposing the Soviet direction of Outer Mongolia continued to express their discontent. In November 1934 new revolts broke out even in Ulan-Bator, the capital. Soviet troops in the country successfully put down these uprisings.

In the Soviet Union at this time there were changes taking place among top personnel of the Comintern. Many of its leaders who had been associated with Trotsky were eliminated. It is possible that the chief Comintern representative in Mongolia, Amagaev, was caught in the midst of the Trotskyite purges. As a result of this upheaval Choibalsang, the minister of war and chief-of-staff for the Mongolian army, became deputy prime minister and minister of internal affairs. He convinced Soviet authorities that he was "their man" in Ulan Bator. By 1939 he had become the equivalent of Stalin in Outer Mongolia, holding all the leading posts in the Party and government.

Politics: Party and Government

As in the U.S.S.R., where the Communist Party of the Soviet Union (CPSU) is the guiding hand, the Mongolian People's Revolutionary Party (MPRP) is also the directing force behind the government at Ulan Bator. The Mongolian Constitution of 1940, in Article 95, states that the MPRP is "the leading core of all organizations of workers, both public and state."[8]

Rules for membership in the MPRP are similar to those for membership in the CPSU, and in many instances the same language is used. Admission to the Party, like the CPSU, is from the age of eighteen; but if applicants are under twenty, they must join it through the *Komsomol* as in the U.S.S.R. and the *Revsomol* (Revolutionary Union of Youth) in the Mongolian People's Republic. In both parties members must serve a probationary or candidacy period: in Mongolia it is six months, and in the U.S.S.R. it is one year. Candidates for the MPRP have to be recommended by two individuals who have been Party members for at least two years and who have worked with the candidate for one year, if the latter is a "worker", an *arat* herdsman, or engaged in intellectual work, or is coming from the ranks of labor.

The bylaws of the MPRP in Article 6 provided that "persons from the nonlaboring population, children and relatives of feudal lords, former members and lamas [Mongol priests], who have transferred to socially useful labor, unless formally excluded from the Party, must present . . . three recommendations from members of the Party who have had Party membership of not less than three years."[9]

The same bylaws also exclude certain persons from Party membership. Article 6, paragraph 2, states: "Higher lamas, former feudal lords, and high-ranking members of the feudal class and people living on unearned incomes, and also other exploiting elements, wasters of state and public funds, leaders of counterrevolutionary organizations and their active coparticipants, are not accepted in the Party."

Like the bylaws of the CPSU, those of the MPRP in Article 15 provide for Party discipline over members: "Warnings, reprovals, reprimands, strong reprimands, and re-reprimands with warning of expulsion from the ranks of the Party, and in case of repeated offenses, transfer to Party candidacy for a period of six months to one year, and in an extreme case for more serious acts unworthy of any one in the Party ranks, expulsion from the Party." As is true for expulsion of CPSU members, the procedure in the MPRP must be approved by the next higher Party committee.

The structure of the MPRP copies the CPSU. Beginning at the bottom are the primary Party organizations or cells. Article 47 of the MPRP bylaws states that "Party cells are organized in *somons, bags,* institutions, state farms, industrial combinats, hay-making stations, schools, enterprises, and so forth, when there are at least three members of the Party present."

This is taken almost verbatim from the CPSU. When there are more than eighty members in the MPRP primary organization (in the Soviet Union, more than 100), further cells may be established with the approval of the next higher Party committee. In the Mongolian People's Republic this would be the *aimak* (province) or city committee. In the Soviet Union approval is given by the rural *raion* or city committee. If there are more than 300 Party members in one of these units, then a factory or institutional Party committee can be established.

The organizational structure of the MPRP, like the CPSU, is comparable to a pyramid. Forming the base are the delegates elected to the MPRP Congress, which should meet every three years (in the U.S.S.R., every four years). Delegates to this Congress are chosen by numerical ratio in respect to the number of members in a Party conference. The Party conferences exist at intermediate levels between the party Congress and the lowest party organizations. The MPRP Congress elects a Central Committee and also a Central Inspection Commission, as is the case in the Soviet Union. The MPRP's Central Committee should convene at least once a year (in the Soviet Union, once every six months), and it elects agencies to carry out its work.

Article 35 of the MPRP bylaws states that "the agency for political work is the Political Bureau, which is the agency for the general direction of organizational work. For current work of an organizational executive character is the Secretariat and for checking on the execution of party decisions and decisions of the Central Committee of the Mongolian People's Revolutionary Party is the Commission on Party Control." The Central Committee of the MPRP (Article 27 of the bylaws) specifies the following departments: organization and instruction, cadres, propaganda and agitation, livestock raising and agriculture, industry, transport, and trade.

Committees of Party organizations in the *aimak* and cities convene Party conferences at least every eighteen months. These conferences hear reports and elect members of the *aimak* and city Party committees, which in turn elect bureaus of seven to nine persons and their secretaries. These secretaries must have been members of the Party for at least three years. The conferences also elect Inspection Commissions, which, according to Article 46 of the bylaws, have the following functions: to check on the correctness and speed with which work is done by the *aimak* and city Party committees and to check the accounting and financing of these committees.

Lower party organs or cells, according to Article 50 of the MPRP bylaws, serve as links "between the broad masses of workers, laboring *arats,* and intelligentsia and the managing organs of the party." This passage is translated from the Party bylaws of the CPSU. Other similar functions of the primary Party organization cells of the MPRP include explaining government and Party directives, recruiting new members of the Party, implementing decisions of the *aimak* and city Party committees, participating in the economic and political life of the country, organizing and conducting educational work among the workers, and mobilizing the masses "in enterprises, state farms, *arat* combines, and so forth, for the fulfillment of the production plan, the strengthening of labor discipline, and the development of revolutionary competition." It is interesting to note that in the bylaws of the CPSU the provision on the function of the primary Party organizations reads as follows: "mobilization of the masses in industrial enterprises, state farms, collective farms, and so forth to fulfill the production plan, strengthen labor discipline, and develop socialist competition."

The bylaws of the MPRP in Article 51 assign to the "party cells and productive enterprises in state farms . . . responsibility for the condition of the work of enterprises, the right of control over enterprise-managements." This was almost directly copied from Article 58 of the CPSU bylaws. Another parallel provision is the article that deals with Party cells in ministries, which may not exercise controlling functions but can transmit their comments on shortcomings in their ministries to the Central Committee of the MPRP.

Party cells with more than ten members elect bureaus of three to five persons, and each bureau elects the cell secretary from among its own membership. If the cell has from three to ten members (in the U.S.S.R., three to fifteen), then only a secretary is elected. He must have belonged to the Party for at least one year. Unlike in the CPSU, the MPRP bylaws do not specify that Party secretaries are approved by the next higher Party committee, but it is safe to infer that in a membership as small as that of the Mongolian People's Revolutionary Party (48,570 in June 1966) all the secretaries would be approved by *aimak* or city committees, and all *aimak* or city Party secretaries would be approved by the Central Committee.

The relationship between the MPRP and the Mongolian government is a close one. The two are inextricably interwoven, so that it is difficult to ascertain where the Party ends and where the government begins. The same phenomenon occurs in the Soviet Union. The fact that all key Mongolian government officials belong to the MPRP, and many of them hold leading positions in it, represents an indication of the close relationship between the two.

The structure of the MPRP follows closely the structure of the Mongolian People's Republic government and vice-versa. The structure of the government is described in the constitution. The Mongolian People's Republic has had three such basic laws: in 1924, 1940, and 1960. The basic structure of the government under the 1924 constitution paralleled to a large extent the system of the U.S.S.R. before 1936.

The Congress of Soviets, which had over 2,000 members and met only once a year, served as a model for the Great Khural, or Mongolian equivalent. The Central Executive Committee of the Congress of Soviets under the U.S.S.R. constitution was the pattern for the Little Khural. This body acted for the Great Khural when the latter was not in session. The Central Executive Committee in the Soviet Union did not meet continuously but operated through an elected Presidium. The Mongolian constitution of 1924 provided for a Presidium of five members elected by the Little Khural.

The 1940 Mongolian constitution included several provisions which its 1924 predecessor did not have. These included a detailed bill of rights, an economic and educational plan, with material on the state planning commission, and sections on the judiciary and local administration. More detail was given on higher governmental organs. The basic pattern of government in the Mongolian People's Republic under the 1940 constitution appeared similar to that outlined in the 1924 constitution. There were, however, some minor differences.

Instead of having the Great Khural elected annually and convening once a year, as provided before, the Great Khural was elected for an unspecified term and convened only once in three years except for extraordinary sessions. The size of the Little Khural was increased from five members to seven members, and powers of the Council of Ministers were extensively enumerated for the first time. The 1940 constitution, before amendments in 1949 and 1952, incorporated the main features of the Soviet constitution of 1918. In 1949 the constitution was amended by decree of the Presidium of the Little Khural to grant electoral rights to all "with exception of the insane and persons deprived of political rights by the Court." Restrictions on voting in the U.S.S.R. were eliminated by the 1936 Soviet constitution. The 1949 amendment provided a new basis for voting in the Mongolian People's Republic, which had been on a *viva voce* basis. The 1936 U.S.S.R. constitution introduced the secret ballot and direct elections, and the 1949 amendment in Mongolia did the same.

Members of the Great Khural had been elected from the *aimak* and urban khurals. These two were in turn elected by the *somon* khurals and the latter by the *bag* khurals. This method of indirect election was similar to the system of elections for town, province, and national soviets under the U.S.S.R. constitution of 1918. The February 1949 amendment in Mongolia "democratized" the electoral system. This took the form of calling all organs of state power "khurals of workers' deputies" and having direct elections to the Great Khural on the basis of one deputy for every 25,000 people.

The 1960 constitution,[10] which is the current basic law of the Mongolian People's Republic, has changed the electoral ratio in the Great Khural to one deputy for every 4,000 people. Under the 1960 constitution the Little Khural has been replaced by a larger Presidium of the Great Khural. This Presidium numbers nine members. Under the 1960 constitution there is a new structure of local organs of power. The Mongolian People's Republic is still divided into *aimaks* and towns. The *aimaks* are subdivided into *somons* and the towns into *horons*. Each of these units has a khural with its own deputies. One can see that there is a parallel structure between the Party hierarchy and the government, because in each level of government there is a corresponding Party echelon which watches very carefully over the activities of the former.

The present constitution has some new theoretical features. The 1960 document, as commented upon by Mongol leaders, is constructed on the theory that the Mongolian People's Republic is now building socialism and moving toward establishment of a communist society. The current constitution formalizes the economic relationship under which private property has been eliminated and the socialist sector of the economy expanded.

Article 81 of the 1960 basic law stresses the equality of Mongol citizens in their right to "participate in the administration of the state and society" and to vote. This document also implies a unity of the communist Bloc and the position of the Mongolian People's Republic as a people's democracy, operating under a common ideology as part of the socialist camp. The preamble to the 1960 constitution states that "the supreme duty of the Mongolian People's Republic and the most vital prerequisite for ensuring its all-round prosperity and further consolidation of its independence is to work constantly for the complete unity and solidarity of the peoples of the socialist countries on the basis of Marxist-Leninist principles."

Article 5 of the 1960 constitution states that the basic principle of organization and activity for all organs is democratic centralism. This was also part of the 1940 basic law. The promulgation of the 1960 document occurred at the same time as new constitutions for Czechoslovakia and the Democratic Republic of [North] Vietnam. This may indicate a plan for the Soviet Bloc to have as much as possible of a common constitutional principle which involves "the establishment of close political and economic relations between all nominally independent communist states."

The 1960 constitution admits the importance of support by the Soviet Union in the creation and development of the Mongolian People's Republic. The first paragraph in the preamble to this document states: "The Great October Revolution, which laid the foundations for the transition of humanity from capitalism to communism, was the turning point in a century's long liberation struggle of the Mongolian people and made possible the creation of its sovereign and independent people's democratic state."

This preamble goes on to say that "the Mongolian People's Republic grew up and got its strength through the brotherly help of the Soviet Union and as a result of the consolidation of its economic and political independence and its harsh fight with imperialist aggression and internal reaction, because of the ability to overcome the evil results of the formal national and social oppression and because of the elimination of the feudal class and the establishment of a socialist culture and economy."

Returning again to the role of the Party in the process of transmitting the doctrine of socialism through the government into the economy, one should mention the impressive developments which have occurred during recent years in the government field. "In order to insure the correct implementation of the proposed program of building socialism in Mongolia, the State and Party leadership has, therefore, been obliged to take direct participation in local affairs, political as well as economic, and to assume a formal role in administrative matters in all levels of government from the district councils to the central ministries."

This same writer goes on to say that "with the reduced size of the elected bodies of government, the increasing concentration and administrative apparatus, in the proliferation of diverse interlocking directorates, the newly renovated and strengthened Mongolian People's Revolutionary Party, only lately emerged as a powerful factor on the local scene, has gradually been able to consolidate and secure its hold on the Khurals, where hitherto its role has been quite nominal and primarily in the form of an ideological guide rather than a concrete control. Judging from the doctrinal formulas enunciated in the preamble to the new constitution this process may only be expected to persist in the coming years and indeed to gather speed with the passage of time."[11]

Though the Mongolian People's Revolutionary Party seemingly has just begun to assume a more controlling position in local affairs, it nevertheless traditionally exercised a very strong directing force on national political activities. In the thirties the congresses of the MPRP possessed considerable authority and represented the center of power. Since then the locus has moved to the Central Committee of the Party and specifically to its Political Bureau as well as Secretariat, which interlocks with the Politburo.

At the present time the Politburo numbers some nine members and the Secretariat has five. All five of these secretaries are also members of the Politburo, which thus comprises an even more extensive interlocking directorate than in the CPSU. While the principle of democratic centralism is proclaimed for the operation of the Party, yet actually the appointment of

Party officials is done on a cooption basis by the top leadership, which selects them from lower Party bodies.

The key personality today in the operation of the Party as well as the government is Tsendenbal, prime minister and also first secretary of the Party. Choibalsang, who had been undisputed ruler of the Mongolian People's Republic in the 1940's and early 1950's, died in 1952. His successor, Tsendenbal, has continued many of the policies of his predecessor. When Stalin was denounced, beginning with the 20th CPSU Congress in 1956, Tsendenbal followed shortly thereafter in not only denouncing Stalin but also in 1962 by denigrating the rule of Choibalsang. Choibalsang's transgression was that he fostered, like Stalin, the "cult of personality" in all spheres of life.

In the top leadership of the Politburo and Secretariat there has been in the last nine years some reshuffling and actual purging, but Tsendenbal has continued to be the top ruling personality. In late 1957 and early 1958 Tsendenbal's position in the top leadership was challenged by Damba, a Party secretary, but Damba's political career at the summit did not last long. He was dismissed in March 1959 for "lack of principle and dishonesty before the Party, stupid idealist-political backwardness, conservatism and inertia, egotism and faulty self-criticism, opportunistic conciliation, with distortions and defects in work."[12]

In September 1962 Politburo member Tomor-Ochir was purged. The charges specified that he had gone too far in denouncing Choibalsang. They stated:

> As is well known, the Mongolian People's Revolutionary Party vigorously condemns the development in the country and Party of the cult of personality of comrade Kh. Choibalsang as a development alien to Marxism-Leninism, opposed to our social order, and has carried out and continues to carry out the logical measures for liquidation of its traces, in order to end finally the possibility of reappearance of the cult of personality. Nevertheless, our Party does not forget nor ever will it forget the great revolutionary merit of Comrade Choibalsang nor the founders of our Party and the Mongolian People's Democratic State, fighting advocate of the international friendship of people, a man who gave all his strength to the struggle for freedom and independence, for the triumph of socialism in our country.[13]

This controversy was precipitated when the Mongolian People's Republic celebrated the 800th birthday of Genghis Khan, with Tomor-Ochir eulogizing him. The Russians attacked this celebration, referring to Genghis Khan as an unsavory and evil individual.

Shortly after the purge of Tomor-Ochir another top MPRP member, Tsende, was removed from the Politburo and the Central Committee for not fulfilling his Party duties, for intrigue, for deceit, and "cunningly supporting nationalist ideas."[14] It has been suggested that his removal was not related to the Chinese support involved in the earlier removal but might have been due to career politics in which Tsende had posed a threat to Tsendenbal.

While the Politburo and Secretariat are the two top bodies of the Central Committee, the Party Control Commission, which is also under the Central Committee, represents an important agency for checking on Party affairs. It has its counterpart in the U.S.S.R. in the old CPSU Control Commission.

In addition to these bodies the MPRP also maintains agencies for mass control, like the Mongolian People's Revolutionary Union of Youth, the Mongolian Profintern, or Trade Union Congress, and a monopoly over all media of mass communication such as the press, radio, theater, and so on.

Regarding the course of development for the MPRP, some clues were given at the 15th Congress of the Party, which commenced on June 7, 1966. At this gathering the MPRP adopted a new Party program. It intends to secure the "full victory of socialism."[15] The new Party program takes the position that the rate of development toward a socialist society will not be as rapid as before but that the Party should concentrate on increasing the per-capita consumption in the country, so as to bring the level of the Mongolian People's Republic up to that of other socialist states. This is very much the Moscow rather than the Peking line.

The Economy

As has been mentioned previously, the basis for the economy of the Mongolian People's Republic is livestock. Herds were tended traditionally by nomadic herdsmen, some of whom had their own herds, whereas others cared for herds owned by princes and lamas before Mongolia became a people's democracy. In the 1920's, as a result of the Mongolian revolution, all the herds became property of the herdsmen. Absentee herd owners were liquidated. By 1929 the number of livestock approximated 22 million.

As already pointed out, the government, following the course of events in the Soviet Union, decided in the early thirties to collectivize the herds. As a result of this forced procedure, the number of livestock dropped to approximately 14 million in 1932. Similar to the *dekulakization* in the U.S.S.R., many Mongol herdsmen, when forced to go into the collectives, either killed their cattle or neglected to give them proper care. This depletion of livestock resulted in a less stringent effort on the part of the Party and government to collectivize the herds.

By 1959 it was claimed by the regime that almost all the livestock was owned either by collectives or state cattle farms. The collectives vary in degree of independence allowed their members. In some the members tend the herds as if they were personal property, while in others they are much more jointly administered. On the state farms the herds are tended by employees of the state. At the present time almost 80 per cent of the livestock is under the control of state livestock farms and the remaining 20 per cent in collectives. There is still a very small number of herds which are privately owned.

As in the Soviet Union, the livestock picture in the Mongolian People's Republic is not a very optimistic one. As a matter of fact, Mongolia is dependent primarily on livestock for its economy, whereas the Soviet Union is not. It is interesting to note that at the beginning of 1964 the number of livestock in the Mongolian People's Republic had reached approximately the same level as in 1929, before collectivization started.

While the Mongolian People's Republic has been in some ways a socialist state ever since its beginning in 1924, it did not use state planning until after World War II. The first five-year plan commenced in 1948 and lasted until 1952. It set targets for increasing livestock production and also the industrial output of the country. The principal industrial product was coal, and in addition there was some gold mining and small manufacturing.

The second five-year plan lasted from 1953 to 1957 and attempted to increase the numbers of livestock over the previous period. This could not be accomplished. Other goals involved increasing the coal production as well as the output of flour mills and the fishing industry.

The next plan lasted three years, from 1958 to 1960, and called for increasing the numbers of livestock and also the percentage of livestock to be collectivized. While Mongolia did succeed in collectivizing more of the livestock, it failed to increase in any appreciable way the number of animals.

Since 1960 other plans have been underway, and the Mongols are now at work planning for the seventies. Mongolia has recently completed its third five-year plan, from 1961 to 1965. This was to attain the stage of development in which industry would surpass livestock production. This goal, however, has not been attained. As one student of this subject has put it:

> The Mongolian People's Republic has thus made some gains during its period of planning. Industry has grown up, where little existed before. Schools and hospitals have been constructed. Ulan Bator begins to look like any Soviet Russian provincial center. But in the matter of agriculture the MPR has not been fortunate, although it might have profited much from the relationship with the Soviet Union due to the very low level of investment techniques in the pastoral nomadic economy. It has been least of all successful in expanding output in stock raising. This lack of success may well be one of the necessary prices which the MPR must pay for

Soviet tutelage for, of course, the Soviet Union still has to solve its own agricultural problems.[16]

Planning the economy of the Mongolian People's Republic is at present closely interwoven with the Council for Mutual Economic Assistance (CEMA, also known as COMECON), with its headquarters in Moscow. Mongolia joined this Soviet Bloc trading organization in the summer of 1962 as a full member. The Mongolian People's Republic is the only Asian member of the CEMA organization, which included all of the East European satellites of the U.S.S.R. as charter members. CEMA operates on the principle of an economic division of labor to the maximum benefit of the Soviet Union. It probably is safe to infer that since the economic division of labor which gives the Mongolian People's Republic the most productivity is livestock and livestock products, Mongolia will continue to remain in the dependent relationship economically to the U.S.S.R. and the East European Bloc.

The industrial development of the Mongolian People's Republic has been directly correlated with the degree of aid given by the U.S.S.R. and the Soviet Bloc. There has been considerable economic assistance from these sources. Most of the agreements between the Soviet Union and the Mongolian People's Republic have concerned economic and cultural relations. When Mongolian Premier Tsendenbal was in Moscow during May 1957, he and Soviet Prime Minister Bulganin made a joint statement in which they said that almost one billion rubles in credits had been given to the Mongolian People's Republic and that Moscow was extending further credits of over 200 million rubles over the following two years and that over 100 million rubles had been given as gifts to the Mongolian People's Republic.[17] In 1964 new Soviet aid agreements were made. These involved large projects as well as the shipment of goods to Mongolia.

Since 1954, after the death of Stalin, U.S.S.R. economic aid to underdeveloped countries started on a large scale. The experience gained in assistance to Mongolia had undoubtedly some effect on the philosophy and nature of Soviet foreign aid projects. It is worth noting that the pattern for economic assistance and trade between the U.S.S.R. and the Mongolian People's Republic has considerably set the pattern for aid and trade with other Asian and African states.

With a population of little more than one million, the Mongolian People's Republic allegedly boasts of the highest amount per capita of Soviet economic assistance of any country which the U.S.S.R. has been aiding. One can say, therefore, that the economy of the Mongolian People's Republic has become exceedingly dependent upon the benevolence of the Soviet Union. On April 19, 1965, the U.S.S.R. signed with Mongolia an economic and technical assistance agreement for the period 1966–70. This treaty gave the Mongols more than a half billion rubles in credit and another 200 million rubles (one ruble officially equals U.S. $1.10) in extended credits.[18] This will make up approximately one third of the capital outlay in Mongolia during the period 1966–70.

It is obvious, therefore, that the Soviet Union is not only the principal foreign trade partner but also the main banker for Mongolia. In recent years the East European states have assisted the economy of the Mongolian People's Republic. Czechoslovakia has extended considerable help in technical and industrial assistance, and Bulgaria, along with Poland and East Germany, contributed significant numbers of specialists to Mongolia.

Military Affairs

The Mongolian People's Revolutionary Army has been an important force in stabilizing communist rule. Always coordinated with the Red Army of the U.S.S.R., the army of the Mongolian People's Republic from its very inception has had a large degree of Soviet assistance in the form of advisors, technicians, doctrine, and weapons. It has been pointed out previously that Soviet troops entered Mongolia in the early twenties and later withdrew. They returned in the thirties to help the Mongolian People's Republic put down a rebellion. U.S.S.R. troops later withdrew again and formally in 1937 returned "on the initiative of the MPR government in accordance with a treaty of mutual aid between the U.S.S.R. and the MPR."[19]

During World War II Tsendenbal held the rank of lieutenant general. The present commander of the Mongolian People's Revolutionary Army is Colonel General Lkhagbasuren. Since Tsendenbal is a lieutenant general, and a colonel general is higher, one might infer that Lkhagbasuren outranks Tsendenbal. However, for all practical purposes Tsendenbal is the top commander, since he is the senior Party official and clearly commands the army as well as the Party.

Party control over the army is very close; 90 per cent of the officers are members of the Party. Like the Soviet army, the Mongolian counterpart has the system of political officers. By the year 1945 the Mongolian People's Revolutionary Army had some 80,000 troops with modern tanks and airplanes. This was the greatest expansion of the army, as a result of the Soviets capturing the Mukden arsenal from the Japanese and turning over to the Mongolians a large amount of material from it. In 1961 the Mongolian Society for the Promotion of the Army was established and numbers almost 100,000 members. It has also been reported that there is a Soviet lieutenant general who serves as advisor to the Mongolian People's Revolutionary Army. Article 89 of the 1960 constitution states that "military duty is required of all citizens of the Mongolian People's Republic."

On March 19, 1966, *Novosti Mongolii* printed a speech by Mongolian defense minister Colonel General Lkhagbasuren at a rally held in Ulan

Bator commemorating Mongolian Army Day. He referred to assistance from the U.S.S.R. as follows: "Thanks to the spontaneous aid of the Soviet Union and its armed forces, the Mongolian People's Army has now turned into a powerful motorized army which possesses technical equipment ranging from submachine guns to modern rockets and radio equipment."

Very little material has been published on the number of U.S.S.R. troops in the Mongolian People's Republic. There are supposed to be construction battalions in Mongolia helping to build large industrial projects. With the presence of construction troops it is quite obvious that there would be regular Soviet army troops stationed there also. Aside from this kind of military assistance the U.S.S.R. had provided the Mongolian People's Republic with extensive training facilities. Mongolian pilots are trained in the U.S.S.R. to fly Soviet MIG's. It is possible that an independent Mongolian People's Revolutionary air force has been set up.

The fact that there was considerable space devoted in the Soviet press to the celebrations on behalf of the Mongolian army on its forty-fifth anniversary (March 18, 1966) is an indication that the Soviet Union is very much concerned with the Mongolian army. In view of the crisis with China the U.S.S.R. must make sure of the good staff and equipment in Mongolia. At the Ulan Bator celebration of Mongolian Army Day, Soviet Marshal A. L. Leonov spoke of the Mongolian army as being "equipped with modern weapons and war materials for modern warfare." Mongolian General Tsend-Ayush spoke on March 11, 1966, in regard to the Mongolian army becoming "an army equipped with the most modern fighting machinery and armaments."[20]

Later on at this celebration Colonel General Lhagbasuren described the modern armaments of the Mongolian army as consisting of rockets. The current concern of the Soviet Union over the border questions with China and the need for having the Mongolian People's Revolutionary Army act as a buffer between the Soviet Union and the Chinese communists is most likely the reason for this intense U.S.S.R. interest at the present time in the Mongolian army.

There has been considerable speculation over the presence of Soviet troops in the Mongolian People's Republic. It is believed that a secret protocol to the twenty-year mutual assistance pact between the U.S.S.R. and the MPR signed on January 15, 1966 (see below) provided for the stationing of Soviet troops in the MPR.[21]

Before terminating this summary of the current military situation, one should emphasize the connecting role of the Mongolian People's Revolutionary Army in contributing to the leadership cadre which directs the Mongolian People's Republic. As one Soviet expert on Mongolia puts it: "The *arats* with past service in the MPRA and transferred to it from the reserve were the first representatives of the people's intelligentsia. . . .

The MPRA instructed the *arat* youth to handle bayonet and knife, machine gun and cannon, airplane and tank; it taught it the national language and converted the soldier into a culturally and politically aware soldier-citizen, a guide in the progressive ideas of the people's democracy and a leader of the masses in the task of social-economic reconstruction of society."[22]

Foreign Relations

Until World War II the foreign relations of the Mongolian People's Republic (MPR) were exclusively with the Soviet Union. Since China did not recognize Outer Mongolia as a sovereign state, Peiping had no formal foreign relations with the MPR. World War II brought the Mongolian People's Republic closer militarily and logistically to the U.S.S.R. Not only were the two states allied militarily by treaties, but also MPR was an important source for Soviet war supplies. Meat, animal products, and horses were given to the U.S.S.R. in larger numbers. As a result of the strategic bargaining position which the Soviet Union gained at the Yalta Conference, Stalin's agreement to join in the war against Japan was in part granted "on condition that the *status quo* in Outer Mongolia (Mongolian People's Republic) shall be preserved."

This agreement was signed on February 11, 1945, by Roosevelt, Churchill, and Stalin. The independence of Outer Mongolia was eventually recognized by China in the Sino-Soviet treaty of August 14, 1945, on the condition that the people of Outer Mongolia express the desire for independence by plebiscite. The plebiscite was held on October 20, 1945, and the result was "in favor of the independence of Outer Mongolia by a vote of 98.4 per cent."[23]

The next formal documents between the U.S.S.R. and the Mongolian People's Republic were the Treaty of Friendship and Mutual Assistance and also the Economic and Cultural Convention, both signed on February 27, 1946. In the following June the MPR applied for membership in the United Nations but was refused. Again it applied in 1947 and a third time in 1955. Finally, in October 1961 membership in the UN was secured by the Mongolian People's Republic.

At this time the question of MPR recognition by the United States and West European countries was closely studied in connection with admission to the UN. Great Britain recognized the MPR. American recognition, however, has not yet been forthcoming. It comes up repeatedly, and only in late 1966 was there a discussion in the press advocating that the United States recognize the Mongolian People's Republic. The main objection to an exchange of diplomatic missions by the United States and the MPR comes from the nationalist Chinese government on Taiwan.

Relations between the Chinese communist regime and the MPR have continued for sixteen years. On February 14, 1950, Peking and Moscow signed a treaty guaranteeing the independence of the Mongolian People's Republic. Two years later, on October 4, 1952, the Chinese communist government signed a treaty with the MPR for economic and cultural co-operation. This was preceded by an agreement to build a railroad connecting Ulan Bator, the MPR capital, with China proper.

The country with which the Mongolian People's Republic has the closest relations, next to the U.S.S.R., has been until recently communist China. In May 1955 a new development occurred in the MPR with the arrival of Chinese workers in Mongolia. In the period from May 1955 to May 1957 the Soviet Union cooperated in allowing the communist Chinese to play a larger role in Outer Mongolia. For this short time it looked as if Chinese ascendency might be returning to Outer Mongolia. But this came to naught when Tsendenbal went to Moscow in May 1957. The Bulganin-Tsendenbal joint statement, already mentioned, reasserted the importance of the Soviet Union for the Mongolian People's Republic. Chinese workers, however, continued to come to Outer Mongolia during 1958, when some 2,400 laborers were sent there in addition to the 10,000 that had already arrived before.

During the beginning of the Moscow-Peking break in 1959–60 it seemed that the Chinese were still trying to woo Outer Mongolia away from the Soviet Union. During May and June of 1960 Chou En-lai and Chen Yi went to the Mongolian capital of Ulan Bator and announced a Chinese loan of 200 million rubles to the Mongolian People's Republic for the years 1961–5. The Chinese made an agreement with Mongolia in September 1961 providing for a supply of Chinese workers to Mongolia. This prompted the U.S.S.R. to announce a loan of 615 million rubles for 1961–5.

Beginning in 1962 Chinese laborers, whose numbers had exceeded 10,000, began to return to China. Tension existed in Mongolia between Chinese laborers and Mongols, and relations had been strained. Although diplomatic missions in Peking and Ulan Bator have continued, the Mongolian People's Republic has protested to the Chinese embassy about propaganda activities concerning the Moscow-Peking controversy and attacking the U.S.S.R. In the Sino-Soviet dispute the Mongolian People's Republic has almost always gone along with the U.S.S.R. ideological and organizational position in the dispute, believing that Moscow rather than Peking is the center of the communist world and that the doctrines of the men in the Kremlin concerning the means for establishing communist states are to be followed rather than the teachings of Mao Tse-tung.

Mongolian relations with the Soviet Union are firmly entrenched. The significant development in 1966 was the signing in Moscow on January 15 of the Treaty of Friendship, Cooperation, and Mutual Aid between the

U.S.S.R. and the Mongolian People's Republic.[24] This treaty extended the 1946 Treaty of Friendship and Mutual Aid and the agreement on Economic and Cultural Cooperation, which had twenty-year durations. The treaty was signed on behalf of the U.S.S.R. by Brezhnev and for the Mongolian People's Republic by Tsendenbal. The whole hierarchy of the Politburo and the Party Secretariat in the MPR as well as other members of the Mongolian government párticipated in this ceremony at Moscow.

In his speech Tsendenbal said: "The talks that have taken place have again demonstrated the unity of views and actions of the MPRP and the CPSU and of the MPR and the U.S.S.R. governments on questions of socialist and communist construction in their countries, the development of Mongolian-Soviet relations, and the contemporary international situation and the world communist movement. . . ."[25] This obviously means that the Mongolian People's Republic aligns itself with the U.S.S.R. on the Sino-Soviet situation as well as other aspects of world politics.

Tsendenbal's speech also referred to help during the next five years, 1966–70, by the Soviet Union for all phases of the Mongolian economy. In Brezhnev's speech commemorating the signing of the treaty he referred to the close relations between the U.S.S.R. and the MPR, attested to by the number of Mongols who are presently studying in the Soviet Union (2,500). In commenting on the statement of Tsendenbal that the Mongolian People's Republic supports the policy of the Soviet Union in Vietnam, Brezhnev added that "despite the absence of a common frontier and Vietnam's remoteness from the Soviet Union, our country is giving the Democratic Republic of Vietnam every increasing aid in repelling the American aggression."[26]

It is apparent from reading the joint Soviet-Mongol communiqué as well as the speech of Brezhnev that the U.S.S.R. and Mongolia are completely coordinated in their foreign policies and in their position regarding the international communist schism. As the communiqué states in its last sentence: "Both delegations expressed a determination to continue their efforts aimed at overcoming the difficulties that have arisen in the international communist movement, at strengthening the solidarity and unity of the countries of the socialist commonwealth, and at achieving the goals and tasks worked out jointly by the fraternal communist and workers' parties set forth in the 1957 Declaration and the 1960 Statement."[27]

While the Mongolian People's Republic still has diplomatic relations with China and with all members of the Asian communist Bloc, including North Korea and North Vietnam, as well as with the East European communist Bloc, the MPR also maintains missions in some West European states, such as Austria and Great Britain. It is recognized also by certain Middle Eastern and south Asian countries, e.g., the United Arab Republic and India. Though an Asian country, the MPR is tied closer to the U.S.S.R. and Eastern Europe through COMECON than to other Asian countries.

The foreign relations of the Mongolian People's Republic are still inextricably bound up with those of the U.S.S.R. In its more than forty years of history as a people's democracy the MPR gives every indication of continuing its very close dependence on the Soviet Union. Economically, culturally, militarily, and politically the Mongolian People's Republic is closely identified with the U.S.S.R. Perhaps one can say that among all Soviet satellites the Mongolian People's Republic appears to be the most loyal and devoted. One could speculate on whether being so close to the Soviet Union, the MPR might be absorbed outright into the U.S.S.R., as was its sister people's republic but smaller Mongol territory of Tannu-Tuva.[28]

Tannu-Tuva, which borders on the Mongolian People's Republic, once held the status of a theoretically independent people's democracy, having a common frontier with the Soviet Union. On October 13, 1944, Tannu-Tuva became an autonomous *oblast* within the Russian Socialist Federated Soviet Republic (RSFSR), the largest of the fifteen republics forming the U.S.S.R. Adjoining the Mongolian People's Republic to the north is the Buryat Autonomous Republic of the Soviet Union, whose inhabitants are also fellow Mongols. The Buryat Autonomous Republic is very much a part of the RSFSR.

The question of whether or not the Mongolian People's Republic will be absorbed by the Soviet Union can be answered by saying that if it were the wish of Moscow to do so, Moscow would have done it already. Apparently it is the desire of the U.S.S.R. that the Mongolian People's Republic be kept in its legal position separate from the Soviet Union.

At one time in its history Mongolia remained a vassal of China. The return of Mongolia to this vassalage seems most improbable, especially in view of the Soviet-Chinese split. Recent events indicate that Moscow is doing everything it can to strengthen its frontiers against the Chinese People's Republic. This undoubtedly means a build-up of Soviet military positions in the Kazakh, Kirghiz, and Tadzhik Republics of Central Asia as well as along the Amur and Ussuri Rivers in eastern Siberia.

The Mongolian People's Republic has an even longer common frontier with China. This provides the MPR with a very valuable role as a buffer between China and the U.S.S.R., which Moscow can use in times of tension against China. The presence of a highly sovietized Mongolian army, battle-trained in World War II, does strengthen the military position of the U.S.S.R. *versus* the Chinese People's Republic. Therefore it seems most unlikely that Moscow will ever allow the Mongolian People's Republic in the future to become once more a part of the Chinese Inner Kingdom as it was before World War I.

The Mongolian People's Republic serves well the new foreign policy of the Soviet Union toward the third, or underdeveloped, world. Since the death of Stalin and the new ideology of the Kremlin concerning the role of the U.S.S.R. in helping underdeveloped countries eventually to become socialist countries, the Mongolian People's Republic represents a valuable showcase for the U.S.S.R. to demonstrate to the third world the value in staying close to a Moscow orientation.

Tsendenbal at the 14th Congress of the Mongolian People's Revolutionary Party stated: "The fraternal relations between the MPR and the U.S.S.R. are based on the great principles of proletarian internationalism and are models of the equality and mutual assistance between large and small states. The MPR's experience in this field, in noncapitalistic development, has a very great international significance especially now that the backward people of Asia and Africa have been liberated from the imperialist's yoke, and the problem of forms and methods of reorganization of their socio-economic life and the course of their future development are becoming even more urgent. Soviet assistance created favorable conditions for liberation of the Mongolian economy from the domination of foreign capital and for development of Mongolia's economy in an orderly manner."[29]

Summary

The Mongolian People's Republic, though not technically a communist state according to the U.S.S.R. formula, is the oldest Soviet satellite. It is also the closest satellite. Its Party, constitution, and government are all based on U.S.S.R. models. Its economy approximates that of the economy of some of the Asiatic republics within the Soviet Union. Its army is in reality a branch of the Soviet Army. The Mongolian People's Republic has or will receive by 1970 about two billion rubles in Soviet aid, not counting military assistance. Its foreign relations are mostly influenced by Moscow, and it can be called the U.S.S.R.'s most reliable puppet. Originally set up as a bulwark against Japanese imperialism in Asia, it has developed into an armored bastion of resistance to the increasing threat of Chinese communist expansion.

Notes to Chapter 11

1. For a fuller discussion of these events, see my article, "The Political Evolution of a Soviet Satellite: The Mongolian People's Republic," *The Western Political Quarterly*, IX:2 (June 1956), 293–312.

2. *Bolshaya sovetskaya entsiklopediya*, XL (Moscow, 1957), 81.

3. George F. Kennan, "Stalin and China," *The Atlantic*, CCVII:5 (May 1961), 36.

4. *Vestnik Akademii Nauk SSSR,* No. 10 (Oct. 1960), p. 6.

5. V. I. Lenin's report to the Commission on Nationality and Colonial Questions, in *Sochineniya,* XXV, pp. 351ff.

6. I. Ya Zlatkin, *Mongolskaya Narodnaya Respublika* (Moscow, 1950), p. 135.

7. S. Viktorov and N. Khalkin, *Mongolskaya Narodnaya Respublika* (Moscow, 1936), p. 28.

8. For an English translation of the 1940 Constitꞏtion, without the 1949 and 1952 amendments, see *Soviet Press Translations* (Seattle: University of Washington), III (Jan. 1948), 3–13.

9. Party bylaws were adopted by the 11th MPRP Congress in Dec. 1947 and were first published in Mongolian in 1949. The Russian translation is in *Mongolskaya Narodnaya Respublika: sbornik statei* (Moscow, 1952), pp. 373–84.

10. For an English translation of the 1960 Mongolian constitution, see Robert A. Rupen, *Mongols of the Twentieth Century* (Bloomington, Ind., 1964), Uralic and Altaic Series, XXXVII, Part 1, Appendix II, pp. 413–26.

11. George Ginsburgs, "Local Government in the Mongolian People's Republic, 1940–1960," *The Journal of Asian Studies,* XX:4 (Aug. 1961), 507.

12. *Pravda,* Apr. 1, 1959.

13. *Ibid.,* Nov. 1, 1963.

14. Rupen, *op. cit.,* p. 322.

15. Christian Duevel, "Mongolian Party Congress to Adopt New Party Program," Radio Liberty Bulletin (Munich), No. 2255 (May 31, 1966).

16. George G. S. Murphy, "Planning in the Mongolian People's Republic," *The Journal of Asian Studies,* XVII:2 (Feb. 1959), 258. See also his *Soviet Mongolia: A Study of the Oldest Political Satellite* (Berkeley and Los Angeles, 1966), pp. 204–5.

17. *Mongolia Today,* III (Nov. 1961), 6.

18. Robert A. Rupen, "The Mongolian People's Republic," *Bulletin of the Institute for the Study of the USSR* (Munich), XIII:3 (March 1966), 33.

19. Robert A. Rupen, *op. cit.,* p. 231.

20. *Novosti Mongolii* (Ulan Bator), March 19, 1966.

21. *The New York Times,* Mar. 16, 1966; and Robert A. Rupen, "The Mongolian People's Republic: The Slow Evolution," *Asian Survey,* VII:1 (Jan. 1967).

22. I. Ya Zlatkin, *Die mongolische Volksrepublik* (Berlin, 1954), pp. 228–9; footnote in R. A. Rupen, "The Mongolian People's Republic and Sino-Soviet Competition," ch. viii in *Communist Strategies in Asia,* ed. A. Doak Barnett (New York, 1964), p. 283.

23. I. Ya Zlatkin, *Mongolskaya Narodnaya Respublika* (Moscow, 1950), p. 267.

24. *Pravda,* Jan. 16, 1966.

25. See *The Current Digest of the Soviet Press,* XVII:3 (Feb. 9, 1966), 3.

26. *Ibid.,* p. 6.

27. *Ibid.,* pp. 9, 44.

28. See my article, "Soviet Russia's Asiatic Frontier Technique: Tannu Tuva," *Pacific Affairs,* XIV (March 1941), 91–6.

29. Cited in M. T. Haggard, "Mongolia: The First Communist State in Asia," in *The Communist Revolution in Asia,* ed. R. A. Scalapino (Englewood Cliffs, N.J., 1965), p. 108.

Discussion

EDWARD D. SOKOL

In the historical summary with which Professor Ballis opens his chapter, he writes of the Mongolian People's Republic as the oldest Soviet satellite. Other writers (see his footnote 29, for example) call it the first. This is a common misapprehension. Actually the Far Eastern Republic (FER) set up under Soviet auspices east of Lake Baikal during the years 1920–2 was the first U.S.S.R. satellite. Though nominally independent, with all the trappings of a bourgeois democracy and with the Bolsheviks only a minority in the assembly, the FER remained under Soviet control from its inception, as U.S.S.R. historical accounts unfeignedly admit. Only Soviet economic aid enabled it to make ends meet; only the U.S.S.R. officially recognized it in the two and a half years of its existence. Considerations of space do not permit a detailed examination of the reasons impelling the Soviet Union to set up a satellite state on historically Russian territory, but in any event, once it had fulfilled its functions, it was liquidated. Professor Ballis speaks of Red Army units intervening during May–August 1921 in Outer Mongolia together with Mongolian revolutionaries organized in Siberia to crush Ungern-Sternberg and his White Guardists. He might also have added that troops from the FER fought alongside Soviet and Mongol units (*Bolshaya sovetskaya entsiklopediya,* 2nd edn., Vol. XXVIII, p. 224).

Professor Ballis states that early in 1921 the Mongolian People's Revolutionary Party (MPRP) met with representatives of the Russian Communist Party "at the Mongolian border city of Kiakhta." Actually Kiakhta lies on the U.S.S.R. side of the border, a point which in effect buttresses the author's presentation of the MPRP as a Soviet-sponsored and originated entity. Despite Russian patronage, however, the Party program drawn up reflected a pan-Mongol nationalistic bias. Clause 2 read: "In view of the fact that the peaceful existence of the Mongolian tribes and their links with the culture and knowledge of the enlightened peoples requires the formation of an independent self-governing Mongolian national state and not enslavement and oppression by foreign imperialists, our People's Party strives for the ultimate goal of a union of all Mongolian tribes in one single, autonomous state" (Walther Heissig, *A Lost Civilization: The Mongols Rediscovered* [London, 1966], p. 185).

In his comments on the collectivization drive Professor Ballis indicates that it was launched by Outer Mongolia in conjunction with the one in the U.S.S.R. He goes on to mention the revolts which broke out in Outer Mongolia against collectivization and adds: "A strong center for the revolts was in the western part of the country," i.e., the area near the then Soviet protectorate of Tannu-Tuva. He then states that the revolt "has never been officially admitted by the Soviet authorities." This is not quite correct. A recent history of Tuva provides the following: "In the Mongolian People's Republic the deepening of the antifeudal revolution caused a sharpening of the class struggle. . . . In the spring of 1930 the counter-revolutionaries raised an armed revolt in the Ubsu Nur *aimak,* directly bordering on Tuva" (*Istoriya Tuvy* [Moscow, 1964], Vol. II, p. 138). Later, speaking of similar revolts which broke out in Tuva at this time, the same Soviet source prefaces this with a statement that "it is characteristic that the slanderous propaganda of the insurrectionists in Tuva coincided literally with the demagogic calumny of the Mongol counterrevolutionaries" (*Ibid.,* p. 139).

Professor Ballis states that "World War II brought the Mongolian People's Republic closer militarily and logistically to the USSR." In fact this had occurred earlier, prior to the war, in the face of the Japanese threat from Manchukuo (Manchuria). "In May 1939 Japan began military operations against the MPR in the district of the Khalkin-Gol River [located in the easternmost projection of the Mongolian People's Republic]. The Soviet army and the Mongol National-Revolutionary army routed the Japanese army" *(Malaya sovetskaya entsiklopediya,* Vol. VI, col. 152.) The fighting came to a crescendo when on August 31 General (later Marshal) Zhukov, leading Soviet and Mongol forces, defeated important Japanese units at Khalkin-Gol. These military actions, it should be noted, lasted several months. While Mongol troops did participate with Soviet forces against the Japanese in the Inner Mongolian Autonomous Region and in Northeast China at the very end of the war in 1945, the whole activity was over in several days—hardly much time for the Mongol troops to become "battle-trained" in Word War II, as is claimed elsewhere by Professor Ballis.

He notes that the U.S.S.R. in 1962 was nettled because of celebrations prepared in the MPR to honor the 800th anniversary of Genghis Khan's birth and that the Soviets referred to the latter "as an unsavory and evil individual." Two points should be made here. Genghis Khan is the national folk *hors de pair* under whom the Mongols found unity. (Parenthetically, of the more than three million Mongols in the world, only slightly more than one million live in the MPR. Some 750,000 reside in the

U.S.S.R. and over 1,750,000 in China, mainly in the Inner Mongolian Autonomous Region). The Soviets, who are resolutely anti-pan-Mongol in their policies, are quite naturally against any glorification of this Mongol national hero. But there is another aspect, namely, that glorification of Genghis would detract from the U.S.S.R. line in the writing of history. In the Soviet view Russia, by its manful and tenacious resistance to the Mongol hordes, so weakened them that although they did proceed on to Eastern Europe, they could not sustain their advance and had to turn back. The Russians were the saviors of Europe from the yoke of the Mongol-Tatars. In 1948, for example, in a typical effusion one Soviet source stated: "Thus the resistance of Rus' to the Mongols destroyed the plans of Batu [Genghis Khan's grandson] to conquer Europe. Rus' took the blow itself and prevented the Mongol-Tatars from conquering Europe" (B. A. Rybakov in his chapter on "The Struggle of Rus' Against Batu," *Narod-Bogatyr', IX-XIII vv.* [Moscow, 1948], p. 55). The controversy over Genghis remains a not unimportant ingredient in the current Sino-Soviet dispute. The Chinese People's Republic (CPR) in a bid for Mongol support has fostered the glorification of Genghis despite the fact that China, too, suffered grievously from the hordes of this conqueror. In 1955 the CPR inaugurated a memorial museum at Ejen Khoro on Chinese territory, housing the putative remains and relics of Genghis Khan. Since that time, every three months formal ceremonies have been performed in honor of his memory (Heissig, *op. cit.,* p. 13). The CPR, in undertaking this action, must have known that it would offend the U.S.S.R., in view of Soviet susceptibilities with regard to Genghis.

To say, however, that in the U.S.S.R. view Genghis is unqualifiedly "an unsavory and evil individual" is to present matters too simplistically. In the Soviet presentation Genghis's reign may be divided into two periods: the first, lasting up until 1206, when he unified the Mongol tribes, may be viewed as progressive; after 1206, when Genghis spent the rest of his life in foreign conquests, "Genghis Khan played a negative role" (I. Maiski, "Chingis Khan," *Voprosi istorii,* No. 5 [1962], p. 83). On balance, however, the activities of Genghis are seen as having "brought very great harm to the matter of human progress," both for the Mongol people and the peoples of Europe and Asia. This view of Genghis is the one officially propagated now in Mongol schools (Owen Lattimore, "Mongolia Revisited," *Royal Central Asian Journal* [Jul.–Oct. 1962], p. 294).

Incidentally, if the Soviets wanted to use the cult of Genghis in a bid for Mongol support, they would have an advantage over the Chinese communists. The relics of Genghis at Ejen Khoro are generally regarded by scholars as spurious. There is good evidence to believe, on the other hand, that Genghis was born on what is today U.S.S.R. territory, in the Chita region east of Lake Baikal. At least this is the view held by one of the foremost living authorities on the early history of the Mongols (J. A. Boyle, "Genghis Khan," *The Encyclopaedia of Islam,* new edn. [Leiden and London], Vol. II, Fasc. 23, p. 41).

Professor Ballis notes the signing on January 15, 1966, of the Treaty of Friendship, Cooperation, and Aid between the U.S.S.R. and the MPR as a significant development in the furtherance of Mongol-Soviet relations. The treaty was signed in Ulan Bator, not Moscow, as is averred by Professor Ballis. More importantly, Professor Ballis neglects to point out the military implications of the treaty. Article 5 of the pact, the text of which is given on the front page of *Pravda* (January 18, 1966), states that the cosignatories "will jointly undertake all necessary measures, including military, for the purposes of securing the safety, independence, and territorial integrity of both countries." Since the MPR shares a boundary only with one other country, the Chinese People's Republic, there can be little doubt against whom the treaty is directed. Earlier the same article states that the cosignatories "will render mutual aid in the securing of the defensive capabilities of both countries." On August 17, 1966, Harrison Salisbury reported in *The New York Times* persistent though unsubstantiated rumors "that a division or more of Soviet troops has been brought into eastern Mongolia adjacent to the Chinese borders." He added that no foreigners were being admitted into the area nor into the adjacent city of Choibalsan.

Though the MPR was officially recognized as an independent socialist state after the Chinese communists came to power, vacillations in CPR statements on Outer Mongolia can give the Mongols little ground for complacency (see *Communist Affairs* [Sep.–Oct. 1964], p. 20). But what of Soviet intentions? Most scholars are of the opinion that at present the MPR is more convenient as a buffer state to the U.S.S.R. than as an integral part of the latter. Yet there are grounds for uneasiness. Reports have it that in 1958 the Soviet Union pressured the MPR into ceding to it a small area abutting Tuva which contains newly-found mineral deposits. Much more ominous, perhaps, was the up-grading in 1961 of Tuva from an autonomous oblast to an autonomous republic (ASSR).

In a discussion on the history of national units in the U.S.S.R. during 1966 in the leading Soviet historical journal, the author of an article stated that almost all of the up-grading of "lower" to "higher" units took place before the adoption of the 1936 constitution still in force in the U.S.S.R. The author then continued with the following significant statement: "Beyond the limits of this period there emerge only three reorganizations of this type—the Karelian ASSR into the Karelo-Finnish Republic (1939), the Moldavian ASSR into the Moldavian Union Republic (1940), and the Tuva Autonomous oblast into the Tuva ASSR (1961)" (*Voprosi istorii,* No. 7 [1966], p. 80). The Moldavian ASSR was up-graded, it may be noted, after including within its boundaries most of Bessarabia, taken at that time from Romania and transforming a minuscule republic into a measurably larger unit. The Karelian ASSR was up-graded to the Karelo-Finnish SSR at the time of the Soviet attack on Finland, and lands annexed from the latter were incorporated into the new unit. As one author remarked percipiently: "The Karelo-Finnish Republic and the Moldavian Republic were designed to play yet another role in Soviet diplomacy—that of a reverse *irredenta*" (V. Aspaturian, *The Union Republics in Soviet Diplomacy* [Geneva, 1960], p. 80). In view of this, did the up-grading of Tuva mean that the Kremlin had territorial designs on the MPR? One can only speculate. The Soviet line has been that the people of Tuva have Turkic antecedents, that in the past only Tuvinian reactionaries claimed that the people of Tuva came from the same stock as the Mongols (*Istoriya Tuvy*, op. cit., p. 113). This line, the object of which was to undercut Mongol claims to Tuva, could be reversed. There is, in any event, a small minority of Tuvinians living today in the MPR who could be used for pressing any irredentist claim.

Some exception must be taken to Professor Ballis' contention that the MPR is leechlike in its loyalty to the U.S.S.R. Soviet preeminence in the MPR has been secured, not only by massive injections of economic aid in which members of the communist Eastern European Bloc have taken part, but by wide-ranging purges since 1961 within the MPRP of elements suspected of pro-Chinese orientation or excessive nationalism. (For the dimensions of this purge see *The New York Times,* Aug. 17, 1966.) The MPR, despite its landlocked geography, has expanded its diplomatic relations with other countries so that by the end of 1966 it had such ties with thirty-three countries. In 1963 the MPR signed tourist-exchange agreements not only with the (East) German Democratic Republic but with Japan, its erstwhile enemy. Mongol leaders have made it known that they would welcome recognition by the United States. American tourists have been welcomed to the MPR, along with those from Western Europe, despite lack of formal recognition. Afton Tours, Inc., of New York City, as well as Cosmos, advertises tours in United States newspapers. The Mongol authorities have also encouraged scholarly contact. The formation of an Anglo-Mongolian Society under the chairmanship of Lord Furness was announced at the annual dinner of the Royal Central Asian Society held in December 1965 at London, the president of the Society adding that "Lord Furness is in that country at the moment at the invitation of the Mongolian government" (*Royal Central Asian Journal* [Feb. 1966], p. 96). In 1963 the MPR applied for and received a technical grant from the United Nations in the amount of $300,000. There are other earnests of Mongol independence. Though Choibalsan, the "little Stalin" of Mongolia, was dutifully denounced in 1962 in the wake of the de-Stalinization campaign in the U.S.S.R., his body was not removed from the mausoleum he shares with Sukhe Bator, "the Mongol Lenin." Two statues of Stalin still stand publicly in Ulan Bator, certainly a rarity today in countries which follow Soviet bidding. At the meeting of seventy-four communist party delegations to the Bulgarian Congress at Sofia, held in November 1966, Mongolia as well as North Korea, North Vietnam, and Cuba ignored the Soviet call to endorse a preliminary motion for a conference to read the Chinese out of the world communist movement.

These are admittedly small gestures. The economic dependence of the MPR upon the U.S.S.R. is even stronger now that Chinese aid has been phased out and the rail link connecting Irkutsk with Ulan Bator and Peking has been cut, from which, among other things, the MPR had derived transit tolls. The presence of Soviet troops on Mongolian soil also serves as a deterrent to any more outward show of independence. Yet there is ample reason to believe that the Mongolian leadership is deeply concerned lest it be smothered in the embrace of the Russian bear.

12

north korea: emergence of an elite group

DAE-SOOK SUH

More than two decades have passed since the end of World War II, when Korea was divided and the Japanese made their exit from that country, and the subsequent cold war helped perpetuate the division of the country. Today, even though the nature of the cold war has substantially changed, Korea is still divided under two disparate political regimes, each concerned with consolidating its own position. However, apart from the division of the country, there have been some significant political changes in both the northern and southern parts of Korea. Paradoxically the Japanese have recently returned to the southern half, and economic progress in the northern half has surpassed the estimates of many analysts. One of the more obvious yet important transformations has involved the political leadership, including the emergence of new elite groups.

Like the elites in so many other states that have arisen since World War II as a result of withdrawal by the former colonial rulers, the political elites in postwar Korea comprise those who contributed in some capacity to the anti-Japanese revolutionary movement during the years when the country was under Japanese occupation. Although their revolutionary activities contributed little to the ultimate defeat of Japan, many of these men, whether of nationalist or communist inclination, claimed a place of political eminence by advertising their role in the anti-Japanese struggle. Much of the official political socialization process during the first decade after the liberation was directed toward glorification of this revolutionary struggle, although a few individuals could advance to the status of authority without this background.

The process of change in South Korea is conspicuous because a complete transformation in leadership from those who led and participated in the revolutionary movement to those who can claim no relationship to the movement has occurred. This transformation has been both violent in nature and productive of political instability. Since 1948 South Korea has witnessed three republics, a student revolution, and a military *coup*. The combined effect has been to transfer ascendancy from the traditional revolutionary elite to the new military elite, some members of which would prefer to forgo identification of their prewar activities.

In the North, however, the process of change has been less dramatic. Aside from an initial setback caused by the Korean conflict, a substantial degree of political stability accompanied by rapid economic progress has been achieved. The process of political socialization is not only continuous but also enhanced by firm control and consolidation as well as confinement of authority to a traditional revolutionary elite and its subgroups. It is misleading, however, to assume that political stability in the North can be attributed to the absence of struggle among various revolutionary groups or to the lack of any change among the elite. On the contrary, the stability and perpetuation of political power in the North during the past 23 years can be attributed to the systematic advancement of one particular group of revolutionaries and the successful elimination of all other competing traditional elites. This particular dominant group is led by Kim Il-song, the present North Korean premier and chairman of the Workers' Party of Korea (WPK). It has been referred to by such names as "Russian-Koreans" or "Soviet-Koreans," the "notorious Manchurian bandits," and the Kapsan clique.[1]

Primarily because of the nature of the Korean revolution, which scattered the bases of various groups from Moscow to Washington, without a central coordinating and controlling organ, there has been a general lack of communication among the revolutionaries. This created, among other things, a situation conducive to factional differences. The communist groups that returned to the North are thus identified by such labels as Yenan, Russian, Japanese, Manchurian, and domestic. Most studies on the political development of North Korea deal with these factional groups and the process of eliminating them and attribute the consolidation of power to one man, Kim Il-song.[2]

Although the consolidation of Kim's power is a fact, purges of these various groups were not systematic; members of different groups were at times eliminated concurrently, and there was no uprooting of one particular group after another in orderly succession. The elites that replaced the purged ones reveal a systematic pattern of consolidation by a group of revolutionaries who shared in the common anti-Japanese revolutionary struggle with Kim Il-song.

This process of change can be seen through various organs in the North. During the 1st and 2d WPK Congresses, Kim's group contributed only two members (Kim Il-song himself and the late Kim Ch'aek) to the fifteen-member Standing Committee. Today, however, Kim's group dominates this organ by contributing nine of the eleven members (now called the Political Committee). All but two of the nine candidate members are part of Kim's group. The chairmanship of the Standing Committee of the Supreme People's Assembly (SPA) also has been transferred from the Yenan (Kim Tu-bong) to the Kim group (Ch'oe Yong-kon). The post of secretary-general of the SPA Standing Committee, held by a leader of the domestic group (Kang Yang-uk and later Pak Mun-kyu) is now held by Kim's man (Im Ch'un-ch'u). The rise of Kim's group can be seen more conspicuously by the changes in cabinet posts. Under the premiership of Kim, the first vice-premier (Kim Il) and ranking vice-premier (Kim Kwang-hyop) are members of his group. More noticeable are the changes in a few of the more important agencies, such as foreign affairs (from Pak Hon-yong and Nam Il to Pak Song-ch'ol) and national security (from Pak Il-u and Pang Hak-se to Sok San). The Ministry of National Defense has never been headed by anybody other than a Kim supporter (Ch'oe Yong-kon, Kim Kwang-hyop, and Kim Ch'ang-pong). However, the pattern of political development in North Korea does not consist merely in the replacement of discontented factional leaders with those subservient to Kim's authority. More significantly, it reveals the rise of an elite group that shares a communist revolutionary experience upon which the main emphasis of present indoctrination is based.

The purpose here is to analyze political developments in North Korea, with special attention to the rise of a new political group which shares a common revolutionary past in the anti-Japanese partisan struggle. Attention will also be given to evaluation of the political influence exercised by these elites in effecting rapid economic progress and to an examination of the control over the military by the new political elites.

The Partisan Group

The controlled political socialization process in North Korea today is heavily oriented toward the revolutionary experience of the partisan group. The essential materials used for general political indoctrination relate to this past anti-Japanese revolutionary activity. The 1.7 million WPK members and 400,000 troops in the Korean People's Army (KPA) are instructed in this revolutionary past, and partisan traditions are widely extolled in literary writings and the arts. A large museum has been built to house the historic relics of the partisan group, and there are numerous monuments in the northeast glorifying the partisans as they allegedly appeared during their revolutionary days.

However, for many Koreans and even communist revolutionaries the partisans' past remains enigmatic. Their anti-Japanese revolutionary activities appear to be of a dubious nature. Some of this suspicion has resulted because they have not divulged a complete account of their revolutionary background.

The essential history of the partisan group, however, is known, and those portions of it that have been made public are grossly exaggerated. Partisan activities were short-lived and under the direction of non-Korean revolutionary groups. In contrast to other communist revolutionaries, this group began to operate long after Korea's loss of independence and was defeated before the fall of Japan. It was led by relatively unknown young men who participated, not as a unit subordinate to Korean revolutionaries, but as individuals in a separate although unmistakably communist and anti-Japanese revolutionary group. The credentials of this enigmatic group seem even more dubious to fiercely anti-communist groups because of their distaste due to its subsequent accession to power. The major operations of the partisan group in Manchuria during the 1930's are known, and the majority of the present North Korean political elite which claims to have participated in this activity can be traced back to these anti-Japanese communist revolutionary activities.

The main body through which this partisan group operated was called *Tung-pei k'ang-Jih lien-chun* (Northeast Anti-Japanese United Army), organized in the northeast (Manchuria) to agitate against the Japanese after the establishment of Manchukuo and commanded by a Chinese communist named Yang Ching-yü. More accurately, this army was controlled by the Manchurian Province Committee of the Chinese Communist Party, and a few Koreans did participate in the Army. The military operations of this group extended from 1933 to 1939, at which time the army was defeated and virtually disintegrated. The remaining partisans retreated to the Russian Maritime Province.[3] Some of the Koreans who participated in this army later emerged in the North as an elite group under the leadership of Kim Il-song. Throughout several reorganizations of this army the Koreans were heavily concentrated in the Second Army and later in the First Route Army. Kim Il-song ultimately became perhaps the most famous member of this army.

The ranking Koreans who survived and returned to Korea today hold important positions. Among them the more obvious include Ch'oe Yong-kon, titular head of the Democratic People's Republic of Korea (DPRK) and chairman of the SPA Standing Committee, who was a deputy commander of the Seventh Army; General Ch'oe Hyon, of the armed forces, a member of the WPK Political Committee, who served as fourth division commander in the Second Army; former Vice-Premier (1948–51) Kim Ch'aek, who was a political commissar in the Third Army under a Chinese commander, Shih Kuei-lin. The current vice-premiers, Kim Il and Kim Kwang-hyop, were also members of this army. Kim Il-song served as third division commander in the Second Army (later sixth division commander in the First Route Army) and Second District commander just prior to his retreat to Khabarovsk in early 1940.

Primarily because of a lack of proper understanding the partisan group is known under many inaccurate as well as ludicrous names. The various designations can be explained. Although the Manchukuo police together with the military gendarmes of the Japanese garrison army in Manchuria defeated the partisan group, the inhumane actions and notoriety of the partisans led to their designation as "notorious bandits." The majority of the group retreated to Khabarovsk after its defeat and was said later to have joined the Soviet army. There are a few eyewitness reports of the return to Korea after the liberation, together with that army and in its officers' uniforms. Hence, they were called "Russian-Koreans" or "Soviet-Koreans." However, the inadequacy of this appellation became obvious when some of the Russian-Korean leaders who did not share a partisan background were later eliminated (e.g., Ho Ka-i, Pak Ch'ang-ok, Ki Sok-pok).

The name "Kapsan clique" comes from one of the more successful campaigns of the partisan group, which involved a raid on a Korean border town, Poch'onbo, executed with the cooperation of a small group in Korea known as *Kapsan kongjak wiwon-hoe* (Kapsan Operation Committee).[4] Of the important leaders of this group (Pak Tal, Kwon Yong-pyok, Yi Che-sun) only one has survived and participated in politics, Pak Kum-ch'ol, presently fourth ranking member of the WPK Political Committee as well as vice-chairman of the SPA Standing Committee. Most of these names were invented by anticommunist groups in the South to identify factional affiliation of communists, and none represent a satisfactory designation for the partisan group.

The 1st and 2d Party Congresses

When the partisans returned after World War II, their status and fame as Korean revolutionaries was negligible compared with other communist groups. However, this obscurity could be offset by the fact that the partisans were meshed with the Russian-Korean group, and it returned home with the tacit blessings as well as under the direction of the Soviet occupation forces. Compared with the leaders of groups that had based their communist activities within Korea and those that based their revolutionary activities in China (the Yenan faction), the leaders of both the partisan and Russian-Korean groups were almost totally unknown to the Korean masses. Far more popular than any of these four communist factions was perhaps a nationalist organization represented in the North by Cho Mansik, but his popularity was irrelevant and did not last beyond December 1945.

The position of the partisan group was further enhanced by strife between the domestic and Yenan factions. Furthermore, those leaders of the domestic group who had emerged in the North were not only disenchanted with the Yenan group but also appeared to be leaders of local prominence. The majority of the nationally known old communist revolutionaries were in Seoul, attempting to re-establish a nationwide Korean Communist Party (KCP). It was at this weak position that the leaders of the partisan faction, allied with the Russian-Korean group, directed their first blow.

After the liberation, Party organization activities in the North were begun first by the domestic faction. However, the main preoccupation was with the central leadership organ of the KCP in Seoul. In conformity with what they considered an important communist principle, namely, "one party, one country," the domestic group in the North organized a North Korean Bureau of the KCP soon after the liberation. On October 23, 1945, the Bureau was recognized by the KCP in Seoul as the legitimate representative of the Party in North Korea. During the short period before Kim Il-song's takeover of the Bureau at its third plenum during December 17–18, 1945, he successfully eliminated two leaders of the domestic group who had headed the Bureau: Hyon Chun-hyok and Kim Yong-bom.

Hyon, the first Bureau chairman, was assassinated on September 28, 1945. Although Kim's elimination of Hyon seems to be a fact, the reported circumstances and plot to assassinate Hyon are hardly convincing. The original story, from which the currently accepted version of the assassination emanates, appeared in a violently anticommunist popular magazine published in the South. The article implicated not only Kim but also Major General Romanenko and a colonel (Ignatiev?) of the Soviet occupation forces, as well as certain leaders of the domestic faction, including Kim Yong-bom, Pak Chong-ae, Chang Shi-u, and a Russian-Korean named Yu Chae-il. The alleged plot is difficult to believe, for it involved the ranking Soviet occupation officers in the assassination of a local communist and also allegedly pitted local communists against one another, there being no evidence to support such an allegation. Kim Yong-bom, who succeeded Hyon as chairman, was unseated by Kim Il-song, Kim Yong-bom is reported to have died from a "premature" operation for cancer in September 1947.[5]

Kim succeeded in gaining the Bureau leadership but received little support from members of the domestic group. However, Kim and the partisan faction, acting together with the Russian-Koreans and utilizing the party organization built by the domestic group, now faced the Yenan faction. The latter had returned to Korea from China[6] in December 1945 and transformed their revolutionary group into a political party, *Shinmintang* (New People's Party) on February 16, 1946.

The coalition of the North Korean KCP Bureau and the New People's Party led to the meeting of the 1st Congress of the Workers' Party in the North. Thus four leading groups were brought together into a single political movement. The groundwork for the coalition is said to have been laid in July, and the first congress convened at Pyongyang during August 28–30, 1946. It has been reported that Party membership numbered 366,000 at the time of the coalition. Given the short period since the liberation, this figure appears extremely large, especially when one recalls that the leadership consisted primarily of little-known revolutionaries from abroad. The 818 representatives who participated in the initial congress were probably more influenced by the domestic faction than any other group.

The leadership of the Yenan group expressed extreme caution and contempt toward the coalition. Kim Tu-bong, the head of the Yenan group, in his speech at the founding congress made it clear that one of the important reasons for the coalition was to balance the lack of intelligentsia in the leadership of the KCP Bureau in the North.

The Congress elected the first Central Committee, consisting of sixty-six members. In turn, the latter chose a seven-man Political Committee and a fifteen-man Standing Committee. Kim Tu-bong, the leader of the Yenan group, was elected Party chairman. The two vice-chairmanships were divided between the partisans (Kim Il-song) and the domestic faction (Chu Yong-ha). Party organization affairs were controlled by a Russian-Korean (Ho Ka-i) and the official newspaper was placed in the hands of another Russian-Korean (T'ae Song-su). The seven-man Political Committee was similarly divided: the Yenan faction contributed three men, the Partisans two, the domestic group and the Russian-Koreans one each. The composition of the fifteen-member Standing Committee included four from the Yenan group, three each from the partisans and domestic group, and five from the Russian-Koreans.

Although the partisans did not dominate the 1st Congress, they succeeded in both asserting their position and in gaining recognition in Korea. Perhaps the most important effect involved the subsequent decline of the domestic faction. The KCP in Seoul failed to unite the leftist groups in the South. It was not until after the formation of the Workers' Party in the North that the leftist groups in the South established a Workers' Party in South Korea. When this took place, however, the communists in the South were divided into two factions which contested the merit of following the

North Korean pattern.[7] Furthermore, the division within the KCP yielded the leadership of the Workers' Party in South Korea to a moderate leftist, Ho Hon. The former KCP chairman, Pak Hon-yong, shared the vice-chairmanship with yet another moderate.

The effects of these developments were strongly felt in the North during the 2d Congress of the Workers' Party, held during March 28–30, 1948. In his report to the Congress on behalf of the Central Committee, Kim Il-song condemned certain local leaders of the domestic group who had constantly reiterated their loyalty to the "central party" in Seoul. He stigmatized such a man as O Ki-sop as "a frog in the well who knows nothing beyond the bounds of the well." No significant changes in the composition of the Political and Standing Committees took place between the 1st and the 2d Congresses. Most were minor in character, and those reprimanded (all members of the domestic group) were later reinstated.

The continued division of the country and subsequent consolidation of noncommunist revolutionaries in the South under the aegis of the American occupation authorities made communist activities in the South extremely difficult. Consequently many of the members as well as leaders of the Workers' Party in the South fled to the North. Although the steady influx of nationally known communists was feared by the partisan group, the communists from the South were disunited and their participation in North Korean politics rather small. Only a few took part, and most of them expected a dramatic fall of the "unknown revolutionaries" in the partisan group. Unification of the country became more an aspiration than anything else when the two disparate Korean governments were established. Political power of the partisan faction was steadily consolidated in the North, despite the presence of "famous and known" communists from the South.

The decline of the communists from the South can be traced to the fusion between the Workers' Party of North and South Korea. Procedures for forming a coalition were discussed on June 11, 1949, at the sixth *ad hoc* meeting of the Workers' Party Central Committee, which established a joint unification committee. The fusion that resulted on June 24, 1949, appeared more like an incorporation of the Workers' Party of the South into the Workers' Party of the North than a unification of the two. A national congress was not called for this purpose, although major changes were made in the Party. Chairman Kim Tu-bong, of the Yenan group, who earlier had been elected chairman of the SPA Standing Committee, was replaced by Kim Il-song, of the partisans. The latter headed not only the Political Committee but also the Organization Committee of the Party. Pak Hon-yong, head of the communist groups from the South, became vice-chairman. Ho Ka-i, of the Russian-Korean group, headed the Secretariat. Thus by June 1949 Kim Il-song, leader of the partisans, had become premier of North Korea as well as chairman of the ruling party.

The Korean War and Communists from the South

Much has been written about the origin of the Korean war. Most of the studies seek to explain it by analyzing the external influence which caused the North Korean leadership to launch the attack. It has been concluded generally that the North Korean leaders would not have embarked on such an undertaking without the prior consent and approval, if not an express order, of the Russians. Chinese involvement in the original decision-making has been termed "problematical."[8]

The magnitude of participation in the Korean war, which may have been incidental, forces one to seek the explanation elsewhere than in the international sphere. The complicated power struggle among the various groups within North Korea cannot be dismissed simply under the generalization of their common desire to unify the country. The hope for a unified Korea, to be sure, was common not only among the communists in the North but also among the nationalists in the South.

There are several studies seeking to account for North Korean politics, both before and after the war, by analyzing foreign influences and particularly those existing since the Sino-Soviet confrontation within the communist bloc. The advancement of a few members of the Russian-Korean group, such as Ho Ka-i and Pak Ch'ang-ok, was interpreted as a clue to the dominant influence of the Soviet Union. The prominence of the Yenan faction (Kim Tu-bong and Ch'oe Ch'ang-ik) was seen as an indication that the Chinese were in control. However, past revolutionary activities of these persons show that there is little to support such conjecture. Members of the Russian-Korean group had been prominent in neither the Comintern nor the Communist Party of the Soviet Union. There is, for example, no known relationship between Ho Ka-i and Stalin or any other influential Comintern official, such as Otto Kuusinen, who was particularly interested in the Korean communist movement. The relationship of the Yenan group to the Chinese communists in Yenan appears to have been not as close as alleged. The extent of Mao Tse-tung's guidance, if any, for Kim Tu-bong in Yenan is not known.

The record of Kim Il-song and the partisan group with prominent Chinese and Russian communists during their revolutionary period remains equally obscure. Kim's relations with both the Russians and the Chinese were confined to military leaders. In the former case he may not have advanced any higher than Generals Chistiakov and Shtykov. The Chinese who guided Kim and the partisan group during their activities included Yang Ching-yü, commander-in-chief of the Northeast Anti-

328 / ASPECTS OF MODERN COMMUNISM

Japanese United Army; Second Army commander Wang Teh-t'ai, Kim's immediate superior; and perhaps the most intimate were Wei Chi-min, political commissar and later commander of the Second Army, and Ch'en Han-chiang, a fellow division commander. None of these men lived through World War II. Surviving Chinese guerrilla officers who knew of Kim Il-song and the partisans include: Second Route Army commander Chou Pao-chung, who after the war became deputy commander of the Chinese Northeastern Democratic Allied Army under the command of Lin Piao; and Li Yen-lu, commander of the Fourth Army, who is now a member of the Standing Committee of the Third Chinese National People's Congress.[9]

Thus when a separate government was established in the North, the ambassadors to the Soviet Union and later to communist China were neither Russian-Koreans nor members of the Yenan group. Rather both were from the domestic faction: Chu Yong-ha in Moscow and Kwon O-jik in Peking.

The prominence of Russian influence in the North prior to the Korean war is a truism, for the People's Republic of China did not come into existence until October 1949. Although the important positions attained by the Russian-Koreans were immediately noticeable, their subsequent decline and relatively short period of prominence are seldom analyzed.[10] Of more immediate concern, perhaps, should be the analysis of political conflict within North Korea, including power relations among the four groups and the complication stemming from the influx of more "prominent" communists from the South.

The steady migration of communists to the North enhanced somewhat the position of the domestic group; four of the nine-man WPK Political Committee, the second and third secretaries on the WPK Secretariat, and the first SPA chairman, Ho Hon, were all members of the domestic faction. However, these attainments fell short of the role anticipated for themselves by the "prominent" communist revolutionaries from the South, who regarded with contempt the paltry revolutionary past of the partisans. After evacuation of the Soviet army from the North the position of the partisans became somewhat debilitated, although numerous Russian advisors did remain and Kim managed to have General T. F. Shtykov kept on as ambassador from the Soviet Union. The unification problem was more important to the domestic group than any other, and it stood to benefit the most from a unified Korea. Not only were the members better known throughout Korea, but they also would have regained the large number of Workers' Party members left behind in the South. A united country would have enhanced their political position greatly.

At the third plenum of the Central Committee (the so-called *Pyol-o-ri* conference), which convened on December 21, 1950, a large-scale re-examination of the conduct of the war took place. Those eventually reprimanded for insufficient loyalty and lack of due diligence included, from the partisans, Kim Il, the current first vice-premier; Im Ch'un-ch'u, the SPA secretary-general; and Ch'oe Kwang, the Korean People's Army commander-in-chief.[11] Others came from the Yenan group (Mu-jong) and the Russian faction (Kim Yol), but none from the domestic group.

However, by the time of the fourth plenum on November 1, 1951, the tide gradually turned against the domestic faction. Those earlier reprimanded were reinstated, and a new item on the agenda involved discussion of irregularities in admission of new members to the Party. The person charged with this serious error was Ho Ka-i, the ranking member in the Russian-Korean group, who held third place in the Party. Ho allegedly had favored admission of communists from the South without the usual investigation of their qualifications, while establishing a far more rigid standard for applicants from the North. Ho was accused of exercising favoritism and practicing *Kwanmun chu-i.* The extent of Ho's involvement with the domestic group, if any, is not really known, for he committed suicide.[12]

Because Chinese intervention had produced a stalemate in the Korean war, the unification expected by the domestic faction did not materialize. The tension existing within the Party, between the communists from the South and the partisan group, became obvious. Kim Il-song at the fifth plenum of the Central Committee in December 1952 pointed out the disharmony among Party members and initiated a campaign to eliminate all factionalists and bureaucrats, most of whom were communists from the South.

The campaign to purge the domestic group began in January 1953. At the sixth plenum of the Central Committee on August 3, 1953, only a week after the conclusion of the Korean war by truce, the domestic faction including Pak Hon-yong, the wartime ambassadors to both Russia (Chu Yong-ha) and China (Kwon O-jik), and other leaders were expelled from the Party.[13]

Subsequently a military trial was held for twelve conspirators, all members of the domestic faction, who were charged with attempting to overthrow the North Korean regime in order to institute a new government, a government which would have been headed by Pak Hon-yong. The seriousness of this treason charge is reflected in the judgment of the military tribunal, which sentenced ten of the twelve accused to death. Although Pak was implicated in the plot, he was tried only later on a separate charge and executed in 1955.

The extent to which the domestic group became involved in the origin of the Korean conflict is difficult to ascertain, but it is clear that their effort to attain hegemony in the North began and ended with that war.

The partisan faction emerged triumphant. Large-scale political indoctrination by the partisans, extolling their past anti-Japanese revolutionary activities, began after the purge of the domestic group. The official political biography of Kim Il-song was published for the first time after the Korean war, together with numerous materials praising the revolutionary past of the partisans. With the elimination of the domestic faction all public socialization processes in the North were controlled and guided by the partisans, who began a more systematic political indoctrination program concerning their revolutionary past.

The 3rd and 4th Party Congresses

By the time the execution of Pak Hon-yong was announced on December 5, 1955, the dissident elements of the domestic faction, especially those from the South, had been almost completely eliminated. Those who remained found it expedient to pledge fealty to the ruling group within the Party. At the 3rd WPK Congress (April 23–9, 1956), Kim was eloquent in denouncing the treasonable acts committed by the domestic faction. In contrast to the latter, the steady rise and emergence of the partisans as a dominant power became quite disturbing to the Yenan and Russian-Korean groups. Glorification of the partisans' revolutionary past, which began to appear in abundance, reached beyond the limit of the other groups' tacit approval, even though rewriting of revolutionary history included only anti-Japanese activities. To those members of the Yenan group who had fought under the Chinese communists against the Japanese and whose accomplishments were deliberately ignored by the partisans, the new history included only half-truths grossly exaggerated with falsified events.

After denunciation by the partisans of the purged Ho Ka-i, Party membership increased by more than 50 per cent (from 700,000 at the time of the merger between North and South Korean Workers' Parties to 1,165,000 members at the 3rd Congress), which strengthened the partisan faction. Those who replaced the purged leaders of the domestic group in the Party were drawn from various factions, but most of the more important positions were filled by partisans. The majority of the new eleven-member Standing Committee, elected at the 3rd Party Congress was drawn from the partisan group, signifying openly its dominance. Numerous cabinet posts were also filled by partisans: Ch'oe Yong-kon and Kim Il both became vice-premiers. Although a Russian-Korean, Nam Il, succeeded Pak Hon-yong in the Ministry of Foreign Affairs, the ambassadors to the Soviet Union and communist China were both partisans (Im Hae and Han Ik-su, respectively). Military leaders, particularly veterans of both the anti-Japanese struggle and the Korean war, made conspicuously rapid advances.

The 3rd Congress demonstrated the dominance of the partisan faction because at that juncture it seemed clear that no group or combination of groups could successfully challenge its position. Although the leaders of other factions occupied a few important positions, they probably saw that the changes taking place within the Party were to their disadvantage. Subsequently a few leaders of the Yenan group attempted to check the rise of the partisans through a conspiracy with some leaders among the Russian-Koreans. It has been reported that the conspirators planned an outright armed *coup* during the absence of Kim Il-song, who left in June 1956 for a tour of the Soviet Union and Eastern Europe. The conspirators allegedly confided their plot to the Russian ambassador in North Korea, V. I. Ivanov, in an effort to win his support for the *coup*. The plotters reportedly stressed the dictatorial character of Kim's rule and his "cult of personality" to Ambassador Ivanov in an effort to capitalize on the de-Stalinization campaign begun after the 20th Congress of the Communist Party of the Soviet Union.[14]

Curtailing his trip, Kim Il-song returned on August 19 and immediately called a meeting of the Central Committee for August 30–1, 1956. The leaders of the Yenan and Russian-Korean group are said to have argued their position eloquently, concentrating their attention on three specific issues: Kim's dictatorial character and the alternative of collective leadership; the economic policy of prolonged concentration on heavy industry, enslaving the peasants and workers; and the preferential treatment of military personnel in the Party. However, the partisans controlled the Central Committee. They easily defeated the opposition groups and later purged their leaders, charging them with treason against the state.

The process of eliminating all dissident elements went slowly, lasting until the end of 1958, when Kim Tu-bong was finally demoted and sent to the *Sunmok-jang* collective farm. The partisans not only successfully purged the opposition but also exploited the situation to the fullest by instituting a "self-criticism" campaign throughout the country. This began with Party members and advanced to a collective investigation of dissident elements from local to national levels. During this campaign the second general election was called (the first one took place on August 24, 1948), and the second SPA was convened during September 18–22, 1957. At this SPA Kim reorganized his power structure and announced his second cabinet, which was dominated by partisans.

The chairmanship of the SPA Standing Committee, formerly held by Kim Tu-bong, of the Yenan group, was awarded to the partisan Ch'oe Yong-kon. The ranking vice-premiership, previously in the hands of Ch'oe Ch'ang-ik, of the Yenan group, was given to the partisan Kim Il, who is currently first vice-premier. A few members of the dissident group survived the purge and actively participated in the second cabinet, such as

Vice-Premier Pak Ui-hwan and Minister of Justice Ho Chong-suk. However, they were replaced by the partisans before the formation of the third cabinet in October 1962.[15]

When the 4th Party Congress convened in September 1961, a number of significant changes within the Party were evident, not so much because of the elimination of any one dissident group, but rather because of the more obvious pattern in the rise of the partisans. Some 146,000 new members had been admitted since the 3rd Party Congress, and the number of Central Committee members increased from 71 to 85 after the 4th Congress. The changes in the composition of the Central Committee were striking. The chairman and 3 out of 5 vice-chairmen of the Central Committee came from the partisans. The majority of the Political Committee and 14 out of the first 26 members on the Central Committee were chosen from the partisan group. All of these officials traced their revolutionary past to anti-Japanese activities with Kim Il-song in Manchuria.

Among others only a few who had remained aloof from any factional struggle or sided with the partisan faction in condemnation of other groups kept their official positions. These included Pak Chong-ae and Chong Il-yong (both members of the WPK Political Committee) and also Vice-Premier Yi Chu-yon and Finance Minister Han Sang-du (both candidate members of the WPK Political Committee) from the domestic faction. From the Yenan group Vice-Premier Kim Ch'ang-man (a member of the Political Committee who had vigorously condemned another Yenan comrade, Ch'oe Ch'ang-ik) and President of Kim Il-song University, Ha Ang-ch'on (candidate member of the Political Committee), survived; and from the Russian-Korean group Vice-Premiers Nam Il and Yi Chong-ok (both members of the Political Committee) also remained.

However, all of the foregoing individuals were eliminated from the Party leadership at the October 1966 meeting of the Central Committee.[16] The significance of this most recent purge and the circumstances surrounding it are not yet apparent. There were some indications that a few members, such as Pak Chong-ae and Nam Il, would fall. Other cases are as yet difficult to analyze. The only conjecture that can be made is that the purge resulted from the unsuccessful operation of the current seven-year economic plan, which has been extended for another three years. The announcement of the extension and of the purge came concurrently.[17]

For the purpose of this analysis, however, the circumstances surrounding the dismissal are of only marginal value because all of these men were replaced by the members of the partisan group. Those advanced to the Political Committee included such partisan leaders as Kim Ch'ang-pong (minister of defense), Pak Song-ch'ol (minister of foreign affairs), Sok San (minister of internal security), Im Ch'un-ch'u (secretary-general of the SPA Standing Committee). Others included mostly army generals:

Ch'oe Hyon, Ho Pong-hak, Ch'oe Kwang, O Chin-u, Kim Tong-kyu. All of these men have one thing in common, namely, anti-Japanese guerrilla activities in Manchuria during the late 1930's.

At the conclusion of the October 1966 plenum only two persons not identified as partisans remained on the eleven-member WPK Political Committee: Yi Hyo-sun and Kim Ik-son. The identity of Yi Hyo-sun is difficult to ascertain, but Kim Ik-son is of native origin and has long served in various judicial posts for the Party. However, regardless of these two, it can be said that the consolidation of power by the partisan group in North Korea is complete.

Zungsan Campaigns and Economic Development

More readily discernible than the rise of the partisan group has been the rapid pace of economic development. More advanced economically than the South, the North's superior economic status seems particularly impressive because of the corresponding difficulty and failure to sustain comparable progress in the South. Regardless of whether the pattern of economic planning has been copied from the Soviet Union or based on the experience of communist China, the economic strides that the North has made through "socialist construction" are important. Whatever the means utilized to achieve progress both in industry and in agriculture, the result is phenomenal. Those who understand the progress have praised it most highly, and one observer has even called it a "Korean miracle."[18]

Although significant economic progress has been recorded, the North has neither achieved any substantial measure of economic affluence nor come close to surpassing Japan's industrial production per capita as has been prophesized. Economic planning has not all ended in success. Although the rate of development may appear miraculous, the rapid progress was in part due to economic backwardness. Current difficulties in the seven-year plan, launched on the basis of a relatively advanced and stable economy, is indicative of this fact.

In all, however, the rapid economic progress already achieved is a remarkable success, and the potential for further progress in the North is realistic.[19] One of the important characteristics is the rapidity with which state economic planning has been instituted. This began as early as 1947, soon after the liberation. Two one-year national economic plans were instituted in 1947 and 1948, and these were followed by a two-year plan in 1949. After the conclusion of the Korean war a new economic plan to rehabilitate and develop heavy industries began almost immediately.

At the sixth plenum of the Central Committee in August 1953 a detailed economic plan in three stages was adopted. The first stage, devoted to reconstruction and rehabilitation of the economy, was to last from six months to a year; the second stage provided for a three-year plan to regain prewar economic levels; the third stage was designed as a five-year plan which would lay the basis for industrialization.[20] The three-year plan that ended in 1956 was immediately followed by the five-year plan, 1957–61, and the current seven-year plan was to end in 1967.

A more important characteristic of the rapid pace of economic development involved the role of political indoctrination and mobilization of the workers to promote successful completion of assigned targets. Political indoctrination reached such a stage that at one point it claimed that the high productivity came from enthusiasm for work rather than excessive toil. Such political campaigns, like the *Zungsan* (Increase-Production), became more numerous as the economic plans increased in duration from one- or two-year plans to five- and seven-year plans. These campaigns, accompanied by so-called "maximum thrift" campaigns, took various forms as time progressed.

They began with the Ch'ollima movement in 1956, soon after the conclusion of the three-year plan. Toward the end of the five-year plan, another campaign known as the "Ch'ongsan-ri method" or "Ch'ongsan-ri spirit" was instituted. This was followed by still another, the "Dae-an working system." Today there continues to be numerous efforts to utilize political disturbances in the South by encouraging the workers to attain a production level which will also fulfill the share of revolutionaries killed in the South.

The Ch'ollima movement began in 1956 before the start of the five-year plan, which, like the preceding three-year plan, stressed "the development of heavy industry, simultaneously developing light industry and agriculture." The movement emphasized high production with minimum costs and demanded maximum mobilization and efforts by the workers. As a result, the goals of the five-year plan were reported to have been completed in less than three years. The Ch'ollima movement was later modified and took the form of groups known as the Ch'ollima Workers' Corps.[21] These first ones began in March 1959 at the Kangsan Steel Mill and later developed into an honor program competitively attainable through excessive effort and hard work.

The next exertion of political influence for increased production took the form of an intensive analysis of the role played by the lower-level organs of the Party machine in the direction of the economy. Subsequently these Party organs were reorganized so that increased production could be achieved through greater attention and efforts by Party members to their task of economic guidance. This campaign began with a fifteen-day field trip by Premier Kim Il-song himself to a village known as Ch'ongsan-ri during February 1960 (hence the name "Ch'ongsan-ri spirit" or "Ch'ongsan-ri method"). Kim Il-song went to the lowest unit among Party organs and dealt directly with the workers, personally guiding the work and correcting the mistakes of local Party leaders. This, it is said, not only aroused the workers to a higher pitch of efficiency but also reorganized the Party management organs to increase production in both agriculture and industry.[22]

The Dae-an work system is a further elaboration of the *Zungsan* campaign. Under this system each working corps was to introduce or learn "one or more new methods of production each month" in an effort to revolutionize the technology of production. This movement began in early 1963, when two young workers (Yi Chong-kun and Yi Yun-kwang) of the Dae-an Electrical Machine Factory attempted to revolutionize production methods by helping other work groups in "specialization, mechanization, and automation techniques." This was popularized in factories throughout North Korea.[23]

In addition to these campaigns the latest outburst of *Zungsan* involves exploitation of numerous disturbances in the South. This began with the members of a Ch'ollima Working Corps of Kaesong, led by Kim Chae-yol, who was enraged by the brutal death of a South Korean student, Yi Yun-sik, during a student demonstration against the ratification of the treaty between Japan and South Korea. The additional lathe which the Corps produced was named for "Yi Yun-sik." Many other factories followed the example and increased production, naming the extra production after South Korean students, towns, regions, and factories which they anticipate building or assisting in the future. Some recent labels are indicative of future ambitions in the South; the "unification sheet metal," the "reunion issue," the "Honam plain" pump, and others.[24]

The inauguration of each new economic plan has coincided with a political purge in the Party. This fact was most obvious during the three- and five-year plans. The announcement in October 1966 of a three-year extension to the seven-year plan also accompanied significant changes in the composition of the Party's Central Committee. Although some disagreements among the elites on the various economic plans were obvious, the extent to which economic issues were utilized by the partisans to consolidate their power is not clear. The consequences of the removals from the Political Committee in October 1966 are not yet known. Signs that the current seven-year plan would fail had been evident for some time. When Kim Il-song spoke at the Aliarcham Academy of Social Sciences in Indonesia on April 14, 1965, he indicated the possibility that the seven-year plan might not be fulfilled and attributed the difficulties to external factors, particularly political disturbances in the South and the uneasiness which they created. He claimed that the military *coup* in the South had forced the North to devote more of its resources to military preparations.[25]

The use of political indoctrination methods by the partisans, as manifested in the *Zungsan* campaigns, has contributed significantly to the rapid rate of economic development in the North. Excessive work may in fact represent a function of patriotic enthusiasm, but it is through such political exploitation of toil by the partisans that economic progress has been effected.

The Military and the Partisans

The most clearly manifested control by the partisan group has been exercised over the military, i.e., the Korean People's Army (KPA). Unlike the situation in the Party, the partisans have managed to dominate the military from the very beginning. Their guerrilla background and Soviet occupation contributed to this uniquely advantageous position, and the Korean war strengthened it by helping some of the younger members to achieve positions of prominence in the army. Control over the army by the partisans has never been challenged seriously.

On February 8, 1958, the KPA tenth anniversary, Kim Il-song declared the armed forces to be both the direct and the only successor to the anti-Japanese guerrilla activities of the partisans, thereby rejecting other contentions that the army had been created by the united front of past revolutionary struggle. Kim emphatically denied any claim by other groups to KPA ancestry and repudiated the traditions of the Yenan group's military units, the "Independence Army," the "Volunteer Army," and others, pointing out their non-Marxian character and irrelevance.[26]

At the time this statement was made, the partisans had succeeded in eliminating the last remnant of the Yenan group from the KPA through the purge of Lieutenant General Chang P'yong-san, the deputy commander-in-chief. Kim's emphasis on the partisan tradition and the link between revolutionary guerrilla activities and the KPA, becomes even more striking when it is compared with the address that he made to celebrate the establishment of the KPA.[27]

After the liberation the only group that had any capacity to challenge the position of the partisans in the army was the Yenan group. The domestic faction engaged primarily in political struggle and had no military units at its command. Prominent members of the Russian-Korean group also engaged in political rather than military organizations in the North. The military contingents of the Yenan group are reported to have met with some difficulties when they attempted to enter the North as an organized formation.[28] However, the Yenan faction initially did manage to gain some important positions, primarily because of a few experienced communist military leaders who had accompanied it into Korea. The most prominent person of this group, Mu-jong, is reported to have fought under the communist Chinese General P'eng Te-huai. Others included Pak Hyo-sam and Pak Il-u, the latter becoming minister of interior in Kim's first cabinet.[29]

Despite the presence of these men the initial group of military leaders to emerge after the formation of the Party had all been partisans. Ch'oe Yong-kon, the first minister of national defense, and An Kil, as chief of the general staff, were assisted by Kim Il. Both Ch'oe Yong-kon and Kim Il advanced in rank and were succeeded by still other members of the partisan faction. An Kil, perhaps the closest associate of Kim Il-song during his guerrilla days, died of illness before the Korean war.[30]

During the Korean war the partisans dominated the Military Committee by virtue of having more members on it than did the Yenan or any other group. That conflict ended with the loss of Kim Ch'aek, perhaps the most important comrade of Kim Il-song. During the initial stages of the war a few of the partisans had been purged, but this did not affect their over-all control of the KPA. A more significant postwar event was the reinstatement of those purged members of the partisan group. The purged military leaders of other factions were not rehabilitated, however.

An interesting observation can be made concerning the dismissal of Mu-jong. Mu-jong's association with General P'eng Te-huai (the former Chinese minister of defense, who was himself later purged) during World War II in China has been widely reported. Nonetheless there is no evidence of any real concern by General P'eng over Mu-jong after the Korean war, even though General P'eng had commanded the Chinese Volunteer Army in support of the North Korean cause during that conflict. In light of this the allegation that General P'eng made a special "secret" trip to the North in support of the Yenan group (Ch'oe Ch'ang-ik or Yun Kong-hum) in 1956 seems highly unlikely.

Following the Korean war the Military Committee was dissolved and its personnel incorporated into the national defense ministry. General Kim Kwang-hyop, a member of the partisan group, replaced Ch'oe Yong-kon in the second cabinet in September 1957; General Kim Ch'ang-pong, another partisan, was appointed to the third cabinet in October 1963. Today the entire KPA command is drawn from the partisan faction: the marshal, Kim Il-song; the vice-marshal, Ch'oe Yong-kon; the minister of defense, Kim Ch'ang-pong; the director of the KPA political bureau, General Ho Pong-hak; and the commander-in-chief, General Ch'oe Kwang. These men participated in guerrilla activities of the Northeast Anti-Japanese United Army. The other young generals are also partisans and include O Chin-u, Chon Mun-sop, Im Ch'ol, O Paek-yong, among others. The rise of these men who participated in guerrilla activities with Kim Il-song is conspicuous.

The relationship between these generals and the Party is quite obvious, for the partisans with military backgrounds also advanced most rapidly within the Party. Of the twenty-five members in the partisan group who now hold membership on the Central Committee, only five have not served in the KPA. Almost all of these persons advanced directly from the KPA into the Central Committee. There is little need to evaluate the relationship between the Party and the army, because the majority of KPA leaders are all relatively high-ranking members of the Party. Notwithstanding the allegation of an attempted military *coup* led by General Chang P'yong-san of the Yenan group in 1958, it is difficult to believe that this man would have attempted to sieze power against such overwhelming odds.

The control of the army by the partisans has been complete in recent years. Thus the military mission to Moscow in November 1962, which came in reaction to the military *coup* in the South, was headed by Kim Kwang-hyop, who is a former KPA general and minister of national defense as well as a member of the Party's Political Committee. The latest military agreements between China and North Korea and between the U.S.S.R. and North Korea were designed to deal with the military escalation in Vietnam caused by the dispatch of South Korean troops there. The leaders who represented the KPA in negotiating the agreements, Ch'oe Kwang and Kim Ch'ang-pong, are both generals and members of the Political Committee. Most important, however, they are members of the partisan group.

Conclusion

The rise of the partisan faction in the North was slow and difficult, but the pattern is obvious and systematic. The partisans in fact comprise the elite group of the North today. The October 1966 plenum of the Central Committee has enhanced and perhaps completed their absolute hold on power.

A few characteristics of this elite group can readily be stated. Members of this faction share a common revolutionary past in the Northeast Anti-Japanese United Army, and the process of power consolidation in North Korea has had an evolutionary element. Their struggle met with various obstacles. Viewing it from the early 1930's onward, as the partisan leaders do, there are few revolutionary groups that have sustained such a protracted conflict since before World War II. In a way it is the indifference and at times even the pernicious practices of the other contending factions that helped prove the mettle of Kim Il-song and his supporters as successful organizers and masters of the Korean revolution.

The past of the partisan group is no myth or enigma but an avatar of the defeated communist guerrilla forces with which Kim consolidated his political power. Grossly aggrandized at times and deliberately ignored at others, this revolutionary past served well to block other revolutionary groups, whose inability to discern the rising pattern of the partisan faction ended in their ultimate defeat. This rise was difficult but readily apparent, and every faction had an opportunity to challenge it.

Although the partisans received assistance from both Russian and Chinese communists, the impact of external influence on the ultimate emergence of the group did not represent a dominant factor. Such external influence was equally unimportant in the fate of other factions in their struggle for power against the partisans.

Both the Soviet Union and communist China were involved in the affairs of the North at different stages. Although various Korean revolutionary groups shared their past with these countries, foreign involvement in the struggle of these groups for power appears to have been minimal. Although the Russians did help Kim to power immediately after the liberation, their support was equally significant for the Russian-Korean group. If the Chinese communists did prefer the Yenan group, this was not revealed in the struggle.

Furthermore, the relationship of the Russian-Korean group to the Soviet Union and that of the Yenan group to the Chinese communists are as dubious as those of Kim Il-song and the partisans to both Moscow and Peking. The severity of the current dispute between the U.S.S.R. and China has prompted many to analyze the behavior of the North Korean regime, but these analyses must be based on factors other than the revolutionary past of the leaders or their former activities. The relationship that Kim and the partisans have established with both the Soviet Union and communist China since the establishment of North Korea as a state, is far more significant and relevant today than it was during the revolutionary period.

Any meaningful analysis of members within the partisan group is difficult, if at all possible, primarily because not enough information has become available. However, some general characteristics of the members can be deduced from their known political activities over the past two decades.

Members of the partisan faction have all advanced through military organizations. Their guerrilla activities and additional experience during the Korean War in part explain their militarily oriented attitudes. The partisans are aware and at times proud of their past, which may indeed become an important asset in the future of an as yet un-unified Korea. Whether their military partisan past, which they have effectively used as an instrument of political socialization, is truly conducive to a propensity for violence or not remains unclear; but this background is certainly a factor that demands closer evaluation.[31]

Another characteristic is that almost all members of the elite group are relatively young men. Only Ch'oe Yong-kon and Ch'oe Hyon are over sixty. Others, including Kim Il-song, Pak Kum-ch'ol, Kim Kwang-hyop, and Kim Tong-kyu are all in their mid-fifties. Still others are younger: Kim Ch'ang-pong, Pak Song-ch'ol, Sok San, Ho Pong-hak, Ch'oe Kwang, O Chin-u. Some of these men admittedly participated in the guerrilla movement as young boys or as leaders of the youth group. If the military orientation of the partisan faction is important, then membership in the group of relatively young men should indicate vigor, if not relative permanence, for their power positions.

Still another characteristic is the level of education; formally it is low; whatever training they had, was mostly confined to military subjects. Kim Il-song may have finished the twelfth grade before participation in guerrilla activities. Ch'oe Yong-kon is rumored to have attended a military academy in China, and Kim Il allegedly completed a high school (Tonghung Middle School at Lungch'ingtsun in Manchuria). Ch'oe Hyon admits that he did not learn the Korean language until he was in his twenties. Whatever higher education the younger members may have received, occurred under rigid communist indoctrination in the North after liberation.

There are other factors that need to be analyzed, such as social and geographic backgrounds, particular specialties, intellectual inclination, records of past success and failure, but the lack of required data makes it difficult to evaluate such aspects of the partisan group. However, if the hypothesis that political power is passing from specialists in persuasion to specialists in coercion is true, the partisans have not only succeeded in removing the former but, more importantly, have proved their capacity as specialists in coercion. Despite the intensity regarding Sino-Soviet differences and their effect on the increase or decrease in autonomy of North Korean political behavior, the ultimate objective of the young and militant partisan group now in complete control of political power must remain the fulfillment of its permanent desire and primary political objective: the domination over Korea, including the southern half of that divided country.

Notes to Chapter 12

1. Several analysts have labeled this group differently. The names come primarily from Kim's past revolutionary activities in Manchuria and Russia. See U. S. Department of State, *North Korea: A Case Study in the Techniques of Takeover* (Washington, D.C.: 1961).

2. See Koan chosa-cho, *Chosen minzoku tokuritsu undo hishi* ("Secret History of the Korean Independence Movement"), (Tokyo, 1959); Tsuboe Senji, *Hoku-Sen no kaiho junen* ("Ten Years Since the Emancipation of North Korea"), (Tokyo, 1956); Kim Ch'ang-sun, *Puk-Han ship-o-nyon-sa* ("Fifteen-Year History of North Korea"), (Seoul, 1961); R. A. Scalapino, *North Korea Today* (New York, 1963); and F. I. Shabshina, *Ocherki noveishei istorii*

Korei, 1945–1953 ("Outlines of Recent Korean History, 1945–1953"), (Moscow, 1958).

3. For an account of this Army, see the Chinese author Feng Chung-yün, *Tung-pei k'ang-Jih lien-chün shih-ssu nien k'u-tou* ("A Brief History of the Fourteen-Year Bitter Struggles of the Northeast Anti-Japanese United Army"), (Harbin, 1946). In Russian, see Sun' Tsze, *Partizanskaya bor'ba Man'tshurii* ("Partisan Struggle in Manchuria"), (Moscow, 1939).

4. The Kapsan Operation Committee became established in March 1935, much earlier than Kim Il-song's alleged organization of the Korean Fatherland Restoration Association in Manchuria. See the details in Pak Tal, *Choguk un saengmyong poda do kwijung hada* ("The Fatherland is More Precious than Life"), (Pyongyang, 1960).

5. The Korean magazine is *Arirang*. See the details in Tsuboe Senji, *op. cit.,* pp. 36–9; and Kim Ch'ang-sun, *op. cit.,* pp. 65–8. The death of Kim Yong-bom is also traced to Kim Il-song, implying that the operation on cancer conducted by Ch'oe Ch'ang-sok, who later became minister of health in Kim's third cabinet, was premature. (Tsuboe Senji or Tsuboe Hokichi is a lifelong Japanese police officer who made a career at capturing and persecuting Koreans during the Japanese occupation. His postwar works are informative, but his information is often from dubious characters. It is used indiscriminately, often to denigrate Koreans).

6. For the revolutionary activities of the Yenan group, see C. S. Lee, "Korean Communists and Yenan," *China Quarterly,* No. 9 (Jan. 1962), pp. 182–92.

7. See the argument justifying the coalition of Pak Hon-yong, "Minami Chosen ni okeru san minshu seito no godo" ("Amalgamation of Three Democratic Political Parties in South Korea"), *Zen-ei,* No. 13 (Feb. 1, 1947), pp. 11–12.

8. A. S. Whiting, *China Crosses the Yalu* (New York, 1960), pp. 34–46; G. D. Paige, *The Korean Democratic People's Republic* (Stanford, 1966), p. 35; P. E. Mosely, *The Kremlin and World Politics* (New York, 1960), pp. 323–35.

9. For a more comprehensive analysis of this army, see my *The Korean Communist Movement, 1918–48* (Princeton, 1967). For information on others, see Union Research Institute, *Who's Who in Communist China* (Hongkong, 1966), pp. 150–1 and 367–8.

10. For the competition by various factions, see the article of G. D. Paige and D. J. Lee in R. C. Scalapino, *North Korea Today,* pp. 17–29. For Sino-Soviet competition in North Korea, see G. D. Paige, "North Korea and the Emulation of Russian and Chinese Behavior," in *Communist Strategies in Asia,* ed. A. D. Barnett (New York, 1963), pp. 228–58.

11. For the reasons behind these reprimands, see Kim Il-song, *Selected Works* (Korean Edition), III, 138–49.

12. Ho's suicide was first reported on Radio Pyongyang on Aug. 11, 1953. Details are in *T'ong-il Choson yonkam, 1965–1966* ("One-Korea Yearbook, 1965–6"), (Tokyo, 1965), pp. 362–3. See also Kim's accusation of Ho in his *Selected Works* (Korean Edition), VI, 269.

13. For the condemnation of Pak and the domestic group of Kim Il-song as well as Kim Tu-bong, see *The Third Congress of the Workers' Party of Korea: Documents and Materials, April 23–29, 1956* (Pyongyang, 1956).

14. There are several versions of this affair. For example, some state that Soviet-Koreans had written a letter to Khrushchev. However, in general all sources agree on the fact that the Yenan and Soviet-Korean groups challenged Kim's leadership and the partisans. Most of the sources originate in South Korea.

15. For a complete list of cabinet posts as well as a roster of important leaders in North Korea, see *Gendai Chosen jinmei jiten* ("Biographical Dictionary of Modern Koreans"), (Tokyo, 1960).

16. The 5th Congress of the WPK was reported to have been scheduled for 1966 but was not held. Instead, this enlarged Central Committee plenum met in October 1966.

17. *T'ong-il Choson shinmun*, Oct. 15, 1966.

18. Joan Robinson, "Korean Miracle," *Monthly Review*, XVI: 9 (Jan. 1965), 541–9.

19. There exists as yet no comprehensive study of the North Korean economy. Among available sources, see Economic and Law Institute, *Sahoe chu-i kich'o konsol ul wihan Choson nodong-tang ui kyongje chongch'aek* ("Economic Policy of the WPK for the Establishment of the Foundation of Socialism"), (Pyongyang, 1961).

20. Kim Il-song, "On Our Party's Policy for the Further Development of Agriculture," *Selected Works*, English ed. (Pyongyang, 1965), I, 167–8.

21. When it began in 1960, there were 928 Ch'ollima Workers' Corps units with 21,102 workers involved, but by 1964 the number of the Ch'ollima Workers' Corps reached over 22 thousand with involvement of some 3 million workers. For more statistics, see Kim Il-song, *Selected Works*, English ed., II, 161–70.

22. See the details of Kim's trip in his speech to the Party upon his return. Kim Il-song, "On the Lessons Drawn from Guidance to the Work of the Kangso County Party Committee," *Selected Works*, English ed., II, 38–78.

23. Kim Il-song, "On Further Developing the Dae-an Work System," Speech to Enlarged Meeting of the Party Committee of the Dae-an Electrical Machine Factory, on November 9, 1962, *Selected Works*, English ed., II, 375–92.

24. *Nodong Shinmun*, Feb. 1, 1965.

25. Kim Il-song, "On the Socialist Construction in the Democratic People's Republic of Korea and the Revolution in South Korea," *Selected Works*, English ed., II, 510–60.

26. Kim Il-song, *Selected Works*, Korean ed., V. 308–49. See also *Nodong Shinmun*, Feb. 8, 1962.

27. Kim Il-song, "On the Occasion of the Founding of the Korean People's Army," *Selected Works*, English ed., I, 58–65.

28. The Korean Volunteer Army was returning to Korea from Yenan through Manchuria. When it reached the border town of Antung, the army is said to have asked for clearance to enter Korea, but the Russian occupation

authority allegedly disarmed the Volunteer Army. For details, see Kim Ch'ang-sun, *op. cit.*

29. There are few materials available on the Korean People's Army: General Headquarters, *History of the North Korean Army* (Tokyo: Far Eastern Command, July 31, 1952); V. A. Matsulenko, *Koreyskaya Narodnaya Armiya* ("The Korean People's Army"), (Moscow, 1959).

30. Kim's relationship to An Kil is reported in detail in the Japanese Ministry of Justice report on communists in Manchuria (Nov. 1940). An Kil later returned to Korea together with Kim, serving as his close personal aide. See Gitovich and Bursov's account in *My videli Korei* ("We Saw Korea"), (Leningrad, 1948).

31. See an excellent analysis of the Korean communists and their experience with political violence by Glenn D. Paige in *Communism and Revolution,* ed. C. E. Black and T. P. Thornton (Princeton, 1964), pp. 215–42.

Discussion

YOUNG HO LEE

North Korea is in some respects the most communist of all communist-ruled states. Its ratio of Workers' Party members to total population is the highest in the world: 15.5 members per hundred (1961). It remains one of the most tightly and effectively controlled societies. It is also almost totally closed to the noncommunist world. Therefore information on events and developments in that country is both extremely limited in quantity and highly defective in quality. What little information is available can seldom be corroborated. The task confronting a student of North Korean politics is thus much like that of one trying to put together a jig-saw puzzle many of whose pieces are either missing or badly mutilated. He cannot prove much. The best he can hope to do is to suggest some meaningful generalizations or ask questions that may be of help in future inquiry.

The problem of defective information becomes particularly critical when the student attempts, as does Dr. Suh, to analyze the pattern of power struggle among top elite groups. On this particular subject information is even more restricted. Dr. Suh has done remarkably well, particularly in view of the information difficulty inherent in the problem itself.

Throughout this very informative paper one is struck time and again with the amazing amount of information Dr. Suh has managed to obtain and the skill with which he has made so much sense out of such confusing bits of evidence. He has presented a good and detailed description of the process through which the present ruling group has consolidated its power position by eliminating, one by one, leaders of other groups that posed any threat to the partisan faction's supremacy. He has also very ably demonstrated that the ruling elite is not a conglomeration of ambitious communists who happened to side with, or managed to be favored by, Kim Il-song, but that it definitely shares a common "revolutionary" background which can be traced all the way back to anti-Japanese military-political activities in Manchuria during the thirties.

There is, however, one important question which calls for a more vigorous and systematic treatment. What factors can account for the partisan group's ultimate victory over other factions in the prolonged struggle which has occurred throughout the postwar (or postliberation) years? This question seems to have been asked, at least implicitly, in Dr. Suh's paper. But it needs more detailed formulation.

It is widely accepted that Kim Il-song and his group did not have, upon their return to Korea after World War II, the prestige and popularity which, for example, the Yenan or domestic faction enjoyed. Then what other advantages did the partisan group possess that not only counterbalanced these apparent disadvantages but also brought to it what seems to have been a relatively easy victory?

From Dr. Suh's paper one learns who was eliminated from a top power position and who replaced *whom*. But one would like to know the factors and circumstances that made possible the steady rise of this one particular group. In short, Dr. Suh has provided us with a good description of one dependent variable. But we also want an explanation of this other dependent variable—in terms of major independent variables. Probably it is not possible to give a satisfactory explanation. Yet the quest must be pursued, even to attain only a partial answer.

Several explanatory factors are suggested in Dr. Suh's paper. First, it may be hypothesized that Soviet influence was one of the major factors for the partisan group's rise to power, at least during the first postwar years. It must be remembered that most of the important leaders of the partisan group had retreated into the U.S.S.R. after their defeat by the Japanese forces in Manchuria in the mid-thirties and returned to North Korea with the advancing Red Army of occupation. At this time the Chinese communists were largely too preoccupied with their domestic struggle against the nationalists to pay much attention to developments in North Korea. It is likely that the Soviets, who were in the position of decisive influence, did not differentiate the partisan group from other returnees. But by promoting returnees from the U.S.S.R. as a whole, including the partisan group, they may well have laid the first cornerstone in the partisans' eventual power edifice. Second, the group's dominance in the North Korean military may have been one of the deciding factors. Any attempt to follow this line of speculation must also show how the partisan group came to dominate the military in the first place. Here again Soviet influence may have been decisive. Third, the unity and certainty of purpose in the partisan group and the lack thereof in other groups may be considered another contributory factor. Other hypotheses can be added to these. At any rate, propositions must be clearly formulated so that an analytical effort to test them can provide us with more valuable insights into the political dynamics of a new communist-ruled state and also indicate the important gaps in evidence.

This is not a criticism of Dr. Suh's commendable work but merely suggests a next promising step to be taken by any student who may be interested in the subject matter. Dr. Suh could not possibly have done much more than he did in one paper.

There are, however, two other matters which should be mentioned. One concerns Dr. Suh's rather incidental comparisons between North and South Korea. The impression is strongly conveyed that in terms of both economic development and political stability the communist regime has done remarkably well, while the successive regimes in the South have failed. It is not my intention to argue here that such is not the case. But caution should be exercised in any comparison on several grounds. First, in economic development, it must be remembered that North Korea started from a much higher base when the country was divided along the thirty-eighth parallel. Not only was the North much more industrialized than the South, but its population density was less than half that of the latter. It must also be remembered that although the South has been slow in economic progress in the past, it has shown a surprising rate of economic growth during the past few years, with an annual rate of growth in GNP reaching as high as or even beyond the 10 per cent mark. In the long run, therefore, South Korea may catch up with and even surpass the communist North.

Next, in the political sector, it should be noted that political stability may not be desirable under all circumstances. If the Rhee regime had not been destroyed in 1960 but were still in power, would one then not say that such a situation showed a high degree of political stability? If the answer is affirmative, one can ask if such stability is a desirable end. The answer to this question will probably be negative. In this connection one must observe also that political stability with no freedom may be easier to achieve than stability with freedom, even a little freedom. Certainly the successive regimes in South Korea have not been notably free. But each one of them has been at least freer than the communist regime in the North. Since the present regime seems to have achieved a considerable degree of political stability while allowing a relatively high degree of freedom by non-Western standards, in this respect, too, South Korea should not be compared unfavorably with the North.

The other thing which is slightly disturbing involves Dr. Suh's use of the term "revolution" in reference to the Korean nationalist movement against Japanese colonialism. Perhaps "independence movement" is a better phrase. After all, "revolution" is the standard term communists use vis-à-vis the independence struggle.

13

achievement and failure in north vietnam

HOANG VAN CHI

Over the past few years communist parties in various countries have shown individual "personalities," characterized by different attitudes regarding a few problems of common interest: the concept of peaceful coexistence, the dogmatism versus revisionism dispute, the advisability of launching guerrilla warfare in Africa and Latin America, and the problem of war and peace in Vietnam. Divergent and often conflicting attitudes among communist parties signify one fact: nationalism, chauvinism, or even the big-power complex are eroding the doctrinal principle of universal proletarian solidarity. As national consciousness is revived, international unity fades away at the same rate.

The case is, however, not the same for communism in Vietnam, where its process of development has taken the opposite direction: from nationalism to internationalism. It grew out of patriotism and anticolonialism, from which it acquired the power it now holds. Ho Chi Minh himself started his revolutionary career as a nationalist, calling himself for some time Nguyen Ai Quoc, or Nguyen "the Patriot." This is how he explains his conversion from patriotism to Marxism: "In the beginning it was patriotism, and not communism, which induced me to believe in Lenin and in the Third International. Gradually, however, as the struggle progressed and as I combined theoretical studies of Marxism-Leninism with practical activities did I realize that only socialism and communism are capable of emancipating the workers and the oppressed people in the entire world."[1]

As the first Vietnamese convert Ho was naturally entrusted with the task of proselytizing other Vietnamese to the new faith. For that purpose he was dispatched by the Comintern to Canton in 1924. As soon as he arrived in this South China city, where the Vietnamese nationalists for many years had an established headquarters, he contacted the nationalist leader Phan Boi Chau. After a talk with Phan, Ho sent the following report to Moscow:

> He [Phan Boi Chau] knows nothing about politics and ignores completely the techniques of mass organization. I explained to him the necessity for organizing the masses and the futility of unorganized activities. . . . I offered him a plan for organization. He accepted my plan, and I obtained from him a list of ten Vietnamese (in Vietnam) who are presently active in his own movement. I have fixed my choice on five, each one a native of a different province in Vietnam. I am now planning to send a messenger to bring them here to Canton, so that I can teach them the techniques of organization. When they complete their three-month training course, I will send them back to Indo-china for [revolutionary] activities and another group will come here. . . .[2]

By recruiting active members of the nationalist movement to whom he taught revolutionary techniques and a rudiment of Marxism-Leninism, Ho gradually set up an organization of his own, the Association of Vietnamese Revolutionary Youth, a kind of "Marxist nursery" which served him for further propagation of communism in Vietnam. Ho's efforts resulted in the formation of the Vietnamese Communist Party in 1930, the name of which changed the following year to Communist Party of Indochina, and later (in 1951) to the Lao Dong (Labor) Party of Vietnam. Thanks to Ho's skillful leadership and also to the political guidance and financial support of the Comintern, communism continued to grow at the expense of Vietnamese nationalism, which until the present moment remains as unorganized as it had been during Phan's time.

Vietnam, however, has a strong tradition of nationalism, and the fact that communism was "grafted" onto Vietnamese nationalism produces three particular effects:

(1) Ho and all of his aides converted themselves from nationalism to Marxism. Not unlike new converts to any religion, they are more devout and fanatical than others who do not change faiths. This seems to explain why the Vietnamese communists are still intensely devoted to the cause of proletarian international brotherhood and why North Vietnam is permanently ready to bear all kinds of sacrifices for the cause of international communism. It also explains why Hanoi, unhappy with the Moscow-Peking split, cannot take sides either with Soviet Russia or with Red China and is still hoping for a final reconciliation.

(2) Being copiously supplied with patriotism and anticolonialist fervor, communism had a favorable start and achieved brilliant successes "in a relatively short period of time" (*Hoc Tap,* February 1965). These

successes have been summarized as follows by the same source: "As soon as it came into existence (1930), our Party provided the leadership for the Revolutionary Movement of 1930–31 and for the 'Nghe-Tinh Soviet' uprising. At the age of fifteen, our Party succeeded in capturing power through the August (1945) Revolution. At the age of twenty-four, our Party defeated the French and liberated one-half of our country (1954). . . ."

(3) These relatively "precocious" successes in turn, have produced in the communist mind two secondary effects: (a) the communists tend to believe that any future attempt will be equally successful, and, for instance, fighting the Americans will not be more difficult than fighting the French; (b) They imagine that success also will be easily achieved in other domains (the economy, construction, etc.), where anticolonialism has no role to play. It will suffice to hold firmly to the correctness of Marxist-Leninist doctrine.

Hoc Tap has divided the history of Vietnamese communism into three phases, which are listed as follows:

Phase 1: The period of secret activities, leading to the victory of the August Revolution (1924–45);

Phase 2: The Resistance War against the French (1946–54);

Phase 3: The present period, which consists of constructing socialism in the North and wholehearted support for the "liberation" of the South, progressing toward the reunification of the country (under communism).

Phases One and Two have been described by me in my book *From Colonialism to Communism*.[3] The present chapter will review briefly what has been accomplished in Phase Three, the construction of socialism, in its economic and political aspects.

Economic Construction

The transition from colonialism directly to socialism had to be effected in every sphere of human activity, but this brief review of the economic situation of North Vietnam will be limited in its discussion to developments in three areas: agriculture, industry, and trade.

Agriculture

Vietnam was and still is a basically agricultural country, with some 85 per cent of the total population tilling the land. Similar to Red China, the fundamental problem centers on population and food. Communist leaders came face to face with that problem for the first time when they became uncontested masters of North Vietnam after the 1954 Geneva Agreements. Since the country was partitioned, rice could no longer be brought in from South Vietnam. As a result, only a few weeks after the Viet Minh government had come back to Hanoi, food rationing was introduced. The problem did not encompass, however, the magnitude that it does at present. About a half million peasants from the Red River delta in anticipation of communist rule left their unharvested fields and fled South. The killing of hundreds and thousands of "reactionary landlords" during the land reform of 1954–6, on the other hand, further reduced the total population.

Food shortages became, however, more and more acute, so that by 1956 rice had to be imported from Burma in exchange for cement produced in Haiphong. Very soon thereafter Burma refused to accept the cement because of its poor quality. Hanoi then tried to purchase wheat, which the Vietnamese masses had never tasted before, from Australia in exchange for handicraft products, but Australia refused to trade. For some time (1962–5), Hanoi has managed to obtain wheat secondhand from China in exchange for tropical fruit and medicinal plants that are used in Chinese pharmaceutical products. Since 1965, a larger amount of wheat flour has been provided by the U.S.S.R. Accurate figures are not disclosed, but, according to Radio Moscow (July 14, 1967), the chief of the Vietnamese-Soviet friendship delegation stated that "millions of North Vietnamese were living on Soviet wheat."

It should be noted that food production seems to have decreased progressively as collectivization was more and more vigorously enforced. There must be a definite relationship between the two, but as other factors were also interfering (population increase, climatic calamities and epidemics, free aid from other communist countries, etc.), it is not possible to determine with any degree of accuracy the responsibility of collectivization for the decline in food production. The general impression is that these two factors developed on a par: food rations in fact diminished as collectivization extended.

The story of collectivization began with the land reform of 1954–6, the aim of which was to make land ownership equal. The average area of individual plots was about one third of an acre at the time land reform was completed in 1956,[4] but as a result of the population increase at an annual rate of 3.4 per cent, the present average for each member of a peasant's family is perhaps a little smaller.

Progress in collectivization can be represented by the growing number of peasant families joining cooperative farms (see Chart II).

The first two years (1956 and 1957) which immediately followed the land reform were called the "period of economic recovery." During this brief time private land ownership was respected. Each peasant tilled his own plot, which was practically equal in size to that of his neighbors. Villagers were simply advised to help one another by joining some kind of mutual aid team, either seasonally or all year round. This was their first initiation into the collectivist pattern of life and, as it was only an initiation, no strong pressure was applied.

CHART II Development of Collectivization in North Vietnam (1955–1965)

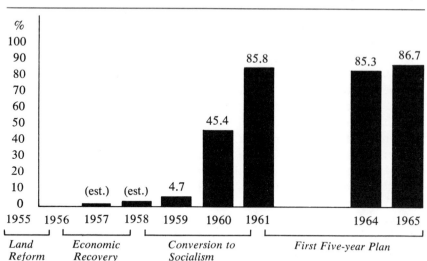

Notes: *Percentage of peasant families joining collective farms in North Vietnam; numbers of cooperatives and total acreage of collectivized lands roughly follow the same trend.*
SOURCE: *Nghien Cuu Kinh Te,* No. 29 (Oct., 1965), pp. 6–7.

Next came the period of "conversion to socialism," which lasted three years, from 1958 to 1960. During this second stage, collectivization of land as well as of labor was drastically enforced. Peasants had to pool their miniscule plots and work in large groups, less for themselves than for the welfare of the communist state. At the end of this period in 1960 some 85 per cent of the North Vietnamese peasants were already regimented into some 30,000 collective farms established throughout the country.

The year 1961 marked the beginning of an important period, that of the first Five-Year Plan, which ended in 1965. The most valuable source of information, *Nghien Cuu Kinh Te* ("Economic Studies") does not produce any figure concerning total collective-farm membership during the initial two years (1961–2) of this Five-Year Plan and, instead, vaguely states: "During the beginning years of our first Five-Year Plan, our agricultural production encountered many difficulties due to natural calamities."[5]

Floods and drought might have had some responsibility, but the fact that *Nghien Cuu Kinh Te* avoids revealing the percentage of peasants working on collective farms during these two years tends to confirm the belief that cooperative membership declined to such an extent that it would have been inconvenient to disclose. As the preceding period of "conversion to socialism" had been similar to a "great leap forward," little attention was paid to cooperative management and technical capabilities. Peasants were not enthusiastic about working in collectives, and the cadres who supervised their work were still inexperienced in agricultural techniques as well as in business management. As a result production sharply declined, and peasant income dropped to such a low level that great numbers had to withdraw their membership from collective farms and resume their former status as independent farmers.

To correct the situation the Party was forced in 1963 to take a few steps backward. Five per cent of the collectivized lands reverted to farmers for private entrepreneurship, but at the same time taxes were made much heavier for independent farmers than for cooperative members. Also, in case of natural calamities, collective farms benefited more readily from tax reduction or even tax exemption. This pliable policy, now termed "economism" by the Chinese, seems to have salvaged the grandiose program of agricultural socialization. At the end of 1963 the percentage of peasants who joined collective farms again reached its former level of 85 per cent. This high figure indicates that collectivization has been practically completed in the densely inhabited areas, the other 15 per cent representing for the most part minority peoples who live deep in the highlands.

New efforts now are being directed toward "improvement of cooperative management and agricultural techniques" with intensive cultivation as a national policy. The target for rice production has been set at five metric tons of paddy a year per hectare (4,494 pounds per acre). This level is said to have been attained in a few areas, while total food production is asserted to have increased at an annual rate of 3 per cent. But as the population increase per year is about 3.4 per cent, food shortages will tend logically to become more acute. To have enough food to feed the nonagricultural population[6] (workers, cadres, troops and city dwellers in general), peasants are not permitted to keep for themselves more than six kilograms (13 pounds) of rice per "mouth" each month. The so-called "surplus" must be sold to the state at a price of approximately U.S. four cents a kilogram, while in the "free market" the same kilogram is sold at a price of U.S. sixteen cents, i.e., exactly four times more. (Le Duan in *Hoc Tap,* June 1965).

As the monthly ration of six kilograms is not sufficient to keep a person alive, farmers have to supplement their diet with anything edible that they can lay their hands on. As Le Loc, a Central Committee member of the Lao Dong Party, recently described, the core of the problem involves the following: "Reality has proved to us that in the Northern part of our country, only the Delta of Tongking and the Delta of the Fourth Zone [Thanh-hoa and Nghe-an] are most fit for rice planting, but these areas are (unfortunately) already overcrowded. . . . At the present moment, the per-capita acreage is not large, and in the future, it will certainly continue to decrease in size."[7]

All of this tends to show that after more than a full decade of rigorous collectivization in general, the North Vietnamese do not live better than before. This is, however, not to assert that a noncommunist regime would be able to solve easily this fundamental problem.

Industrial Development

For a long time now the Vietnamese have firmly believed that their country possesses enormous natural resources, and they blame the French in particular for their unwillingness to exploit these resources and to modernize the country's economy. Next door, Japan always served as an example to be emulated. In the 1930's the question as to "how Vietnam could become an industrialized nation" divided public opinion. The nationalists were confident about the possibility of treading in Japan's steps, but the communists argued that it was too late. International capitalism, they explained, had become too strong and too united for the emergence of another industrialized nation in Asia. The only way to make up the lost time, in their view, was to move toward communism and obtain support from Soviet Russia. Later, after the communists had demonstrated fully their unmatched talent for mobilizing, organizing, and controlling the great masses, their proposition prevailed although their technical capability still remained doubtful. As a consequence a great number of Vietnamese patriots who opposed Marxism as a political doctrine, willingly accepted communism as an efficient means for rapid economic development.

After Dien Bien Phu the communists effectively implemented what they had proposed. Over the past ten years some eighteen million North Vietnamese have tightened their belts and worked "one like two," and reshaped their fields, improved their crops, extracted mineral ores, bought modern equipment, and built new factories.

Communist leaders, however, regard industrial development less as a means to make the country prosperous than as a prestige symbol of socialism. In the new North Vietnamese lexicon the term "industrial construction" is practically confused with that of "socialist edification." At almost any occasion it has been stated over and over again that only communism is capable of building modern factories in Vietnam. There are, in fact, more than one thousand new plants of small, medium, and large size in today's North Vietnam. Such a performance might be judged as quite slow according to Western standards. In the case of North Vietnam, poor, underdeveloped, and almost completely devasted by ten years of war, such an achievement is prodigious.

Most of these plants were established prior to 1960, when machinery, materials, and money were being generously donated by Soviet Russia,

Red China, and the East European countries. Two large complexes have been built, one for metallurgy in the Thai-nguyen area and the other one for chemical products in Viet-tri. There exist also at least two tea factories, two paper and two sugar mills, one plywood factory, one machine-tool plant and many others of lesser importance. The construction of these plants and factories proceeded relatively fast, but time schedules have been too slow for entry into full operation. The metallurgical complex at Thai-nguyen and the chemical combine at Viet-tri were not yet in full production when they were partly destroyed by American bombing; they were then dismantled for evacuation deep into the jungle. Only factories of small size and a few medium ones have entered the stage of operation, providing local markets with the following articles: "Many consumer goods which we previously imported from abroad are now locally produced. These include: cloth, office articles, enameled kitchen wares, bicycle tires, etc."[8]

Such a meager result is obviously not what could normally be expected from huge investments and ten years of tremendous effort. There have been reports of waste due to corruption, red tape, and careless work. Although not admitted, the major blame must be put on the technical incompetence of political cadres as well as on the leaders themselves. Antagonism between technical directors and political commissars has been cited as a contradiction in the new regime, but in the Party's view technical know-how is always less important than the correctness of the political line and the intensity of the "national salvation" spirit which should animate every worker's mind. It will be noted in this connection that, ideologically speaking, North Vietnam is still no less dogmatic than Red China. Discussing any problem, either "how to improve agricultural techniques to increase food production" or "how to improve the quality of theatrical performances," etc., the emphasis is invariably laid on the primordial necessity of further intensifying ideological indoctrination. As reflected in the Party's official newspapers and journals, everything will be perfect and final victory certainly won if all North Vietnam knows how to "hate the American aggressors" correctly.

The almost complete standstill in industrial development of North Vietnam, however, came largely as a result of a certain event which completely escaped Hanoi's control and for which the Lao Dong Party had no responsibility: the Sino-Soviet conflict, with its impacts on Chinese and Soviet aid.

As North Vietnam had received large gifts from both Soviet Russia and Red China during the period of "conversion to socialism," Hanoi tried its best to remain neutral and uncommitted in the dispute between its two giant benefactors. It seems, however, that for some time Hanoi's ambiguous neutrality was interpreted by Moscow as pro-Chinese, and by Peking as pro-Russian. In any case, free assistance from the Soviet Union, China, and also the East European countries stopped altogether during 1961. In this connection *Nghien Cuu Kinh Te* discloses the following information: "Since the beginning of our first Five-Year Plan (1960), the Northern part of our country entered a new phase, that of Socialist Edification. Imports are now greater than ever, but exports have not developed quickly enough. Moreover, we have spent all financial aid given to us free of charge by brotherly socialist countries. The sole form of assistance which still remains available are long-term loans which, being a form of cooperation between nations, must be profitable for both sides, the lender and the borrower countries."[9]

As the program of "socialist edification" had been relatively grandiose, the sudden withdrawal of financial and technical aid by both Soviet Russia and Red China left many industrial projects uncompleted. It seems that when the program of large-scale industrialization was first conceived, the idea in the planners' minds was to produce manufactured goods for export in exchange for imported food. But after ten years reality has proved that North Vietnam's newborn industry still remains a long way off from fully satisfying local demands.

The picture, far from brilliant before 1965, has been worsened by the effect of American bombing. In May 1966 Vice-Premier Pham Hung disclosed the following problems: "The greatest difficulty we have had to face during the past year is the fact that demands of every kind speedily increased and were concentrated in a few areas, while production was lagging. Even worse, as the enemy has escalated the war of destruction, aiming particularly at our means of transportation, it has been difficult for us to receive goods from foreign assistance and to transport local products from one area to another" (*Hoc Tap,* May 1966).

To face the new critical situation, a few urgent measures have been taken. They have the following objectives: (1) to take apart and hide in the jungle every piece of machinery which can be dismantled; for other pieces, which are too big for convenient removal, orders have been given to operate them at maximum output, waiting for possible destruction by American bombs; (2) to decentralize industry and to make every province self-sufficient in basic consumers' goods; (3) the fundamental role of industry is to serve agriculture, making farm tools for the peasants; it is expected that more efficient equipment (irrigation pumps, wheelbarrows with ball-bearings, etc.) will remedy the present shortage of manpower, as more than one million farmers have been drafted for military activities.

Trade

As Vietnam is basically an agricultural country, with a tradition of self-sufficiency at the village level, even local commerce cannot be "prosperous" to any extent. The rigorous application of collectivism makes the situation worse. Over the past two years the disruption of transport by American bombing has reduced the exchange of goods in North Vietnam to an unprecedentedly low level.

Village markets still exist, but they are strictly limited to small-type barter among residents of the same village. Intervillage or interprovince trade is concentrated in the hands of "trading cooperatives," while foreign trade remains exclusively governmental business.

As far as local trade is concerned, the present situation is in many aspects similar to that during the Resistance War (1946–54) against the French. Bombing by the latter interrupted transportation of goods, which in turn created an uneven distribution resulting in scarcity of basic commodities for some areas and a surplus of the same goods for others. It should be noted, however, that during this early period trade still remained free, and private entrepreneurs resorted to individual ingenuity for transporting their merchandise to every part of the country. They encountered great risks, but they were motivated by a desire for large profits. Prices were uneven, but it was precisely this unevenness which assured more or less regular distribution.

Since free enterprise has been suppressed, the distribution of goods now is centralized by a hierarchy of "trading organizations," all of them strictly controlled by the Ministry of Local Trade. It is quite natural that centralization engenders bureaucracy and red tape, which contribute to making the situation even more critical. Priority in distribution is reserved for food, but in this connection *Hoc Tap* wrote as follows: "Our demand for food has sharply increased. The war of destruction waged by American pirates creates a certain number of difficulties in food production and distribution. . . . Every region must try its best to be self-sufficient in food and to satisfy the most essential needs of the local population. Cities also must produce enough rice and part of other foods they need for themselves."[10]

To solve the critical problem of food and adequate distribution the following measures have been taken: (1) decentralization of light industries: machines from large factories have been removed and scattered throughout the country, aimed at producing ordinary and semimechanized tools for agricultural cooperatives; (2) extensive evacuation of nonessential city residents to rice producing areas: included in this category are children, old people, and entire corporate groups of handicraftsmen (shoemakers, tailors, knitters, etc.); (3) transfer of excess population from the overcrowded Red River delta into the highlands: this program started in 1964 and is aimed at "developing the economy and culture of the mountain areas." Unofficially it also aims at "Vietnamizing" ethnic minorities living in these areas and developing "bases for resistance" in anticipation of an eventual attack upon North Vietnam by American ground troops. These same areas served in fact as military bases for the Viet-Minh, during the struggle against the Japanese and later against the French. Up to January 1967 a total of approximately one million inhabitants (4 per cent of the total population) had been evacuated to the highlands.

Difficulties are evidently enormous, but a corresponding effort has been made to match the situation. Apparently, at least, no immediate economic collapse is in sight. A Hanoi radio broadcast on April 16, 1967, disclosed, however, the emergence of rampant inflation due to an excess of demand on production and the unevenness of distribution in food and other basic necessities. This would indicate a collapse of the government plan aimed at self-sufficiency for every locality, which was conceived as an urgent remedy for the almost complete collapse of interprovince trade.

Foreign trade, which includes import and export, seems to be of greater importance, particularly because the former is heavily supported by foreign aid. As disclosed by *Nghien Cuu Kinh Te* (see Table 26), foreign trade has always operated at a deficit over the past ten years.

TABLE 26

Foreign Trade of North Vietnam (1955–64)
(millions of rubles)

Year	Export	Import	Deficit	Export/Import Ratio
1955	27.3	294.4	−267.1	9.2%
1956	81.7	314.2	−232.5	26.0%
1957	163.8	398.0	−234.2	41.1%
1958	204.6	253.2	− 48.6	80.8%
1959	269.2	417.9	−148.7	64.4%
1960	319.6	511.6	−192.0	62.4%
1961	72.5	129.5	− 57.0	55.9%
1962	——	——	——	60.4%
1963	——	——	——	59.1%
1964	——	——	——	74.1%

NOTE: All figures refer to Old Rubles, with the exception of those for 1961, which represent New Rubles. There were 4.44 Old Rubles to the new one.
SOURCE: *Nghien-Cuu Kinh-te* (Hanoi), Dec. 1964.

A careful look at the above table reveals the following facts: (1) exports and imports continue to increase; however, (2) the balance between exports and imports always shows a deficit; and (3) exports cover, on the average, about 60 per cent of imports. It should be noted that for 1962 and subsequent years only export/import ratios are disclosed, not the exact figures for exports and imports or the deficit. Once again the nonpublication of these data provides ground for suspicion that they are too low to be comfortably disclosed. The discontinuance of free Soviet and Chinese aid, previously mentioned, confirms such a view. One may suppose that without renewed aid a deficit in the trade balance cannot be kept at the same level year after year.

Imports consist of most essential food products, industrial equipment, and raw materials (wool for knitting sweaters which are then exported back to Soviet Russia and the East European countries, rubber, cotton, jute, etc.), while exports cover a few items listed in Table 27.

TABLE 27

North Vietnamese Exports (1960)

Type of Item	Percentage
Mineral ores	27.9
Building materials (mostly cement)	8.3
Light industry products	5.2
Handicrafts (Shoes, knitted articles, silverware, rattan products, etc.)	23.1
Agricultural, forestry, animal, and sea products (lumber, chickens, tropical fruits, medicinal herbs, salt, etc.)	31.1
Miscellaneous	4.4
Total	100.0

As can be seen, the two most important articles for export are mineral ores (chrome, tungsten, manganite, etc., which cannot be processed as yet in North Vietnam) and agricultural-forestry products. Among the latter are some "luxury foods," such as chickens and ducks[11] exported to Eastern Europe, canned longans to France, tropical fruits and medicinal plants to communist China.

It should be noted that most of the foreign trade is conducted with countries in the communist Bloc, and figures relating to the period from 1958 to 1960 indicate an increasing volume, as seen in Table 28.

From 1960 to 1965 efforts were made to increase exchange with countries outside the communist Bloc. It has been asserted that in 1965 forty-five countries were trading with North Vietnam, as compared to thirty in 1960: "At the end of 1960 we signed trading agreements with a certain number of Afro-Asian countries, such as Indonesia, Cambodia, Yemen, and we have established foreign trade relations with other countries such as Burma and Ceylon. We have also established foreign trade relations with capitalist markets such as Hongkong, Japan, Singapore, France, West

Germany, Holland, Belgium. At the end of 1960 we were trading with thirty countries, eleven of which are socialist, nine nationalist, and ten capitalist" (*Nghien Cuu Kinh Te,* October 1965).

TABLE 28

Exports and Imports from and to North Vietnam (1958–60)
(in percentages)

	1958	*1959*	*1960*
Export			
With socialist countries	80	80	85
With nonsocialist countries	20	20	15
Import			
With socialist countries	84.6	87	91
With nonsocialist countries	15.4	13	9

SOURCE: *Nghien Cuu Kinh Te* (Hanoi), Oct. 1965, p. 16.

What has happened since October 1965 is not yet disclosed. But simply by taking war conditions into consideration, one can presume that North Vietnam's foreign trade must have declined greatly. The exchange of goods, if it still exists to any degree, would be mostly conducted with countries inside the communist Bloc, and particularly with neighboring China.

Although no figures have been released, there are a few indications relative to a resumption of free aid from Soviet Russia, communist China, and other Bloc countries. There are also grounds to believe that imports from Soviet Russia consist mostly of wheat flour, machinery and military equipment and that communist China is providing light weapons and a notable quantity of rice as well as wheat.

As Harrison Salisbury, the *New York Times* correspondent who visited North Vietnam in December 1966, has correctly observed, the country looks tired without, however, any apparent sign of economic collapse. It is the view of this writer that although American bombing has destroyed almost everything the communist regime had built during the past ten years, the Vietnamese people are always able to get along with the rudimentary economy which has been theirs for centuries. As long as they can obtain any kind of food which provides them some 2,000 calories per day, they can endure the situation almost indefinitely. Even if they receive less than the minimum vital requirement, they still have no means to voice their misfortune or dissatisfaction. And this would testify to the greatest achievement scored by the Lao Dong Party: the population, as a whole, still remains firmly under its political control.

Political Developments

Taken as a whole, the communist leadership in North Vietnam manifests a marked tendency to follow the Chinese line as closely as possible. This is due to geographic proximity, the confidence in effective support from China (considering her vast territory and huge population), and the belief that the two nations, in similar economic and social conditions, are faced with the same problems for which similar solutions are required. But stronger than all these considerations, the factor which firmly attaches Hanoi to Peking is the deep-rooted influence exercised by Chinese culture on the Vietnamese mind, whether it be nationalist or communist.

Imitating China is not something new; for over two thousand years, while continuously resisting Chinese efforts at annexation, Vietnam always tried to mold herself in the image of China. This mental disposition remained unaffected by the impact of Western culture with which Vietnam came into direct contact only during the period of French domination.[12] Proof of this can be found in a statement made by Tran Trong Kim, a contemporary Vietnamese historian (1882–1953). As late as 1928 he wrote: "In the matter of education every one of us still maintains the conviction that anything Chinese is good, is the best of all. In the domain of thinking as well as in practical activities we always look at China as an example. Anyone who succeeds in imitating the Chinese is considered a capable man, and anyone who fails is a worthless person."[13]

The fact that the Vietnamese elite continued to study Chinese classics[14] from the dawn of its history up to 1917 produced a most remarkable effect: although Vietnam had brilliant generals, administrators, and scholars, the country never possessed a philosopher of its own. The situation is still the same at the present moment. South Vietnam is lacking in political thinkers, while in North Vietnam the Lao Dong Party does not have any theoretician worthy of mention.

French education, which includes a tradition of free thinking, with Montaigne's skepticism and Descartes' methodology, could have improved the situation. Started too late, it could not produce any deep and lasting effects. If this fact is true for the Vietnamese elite in general, it is more so for the communist leadership, since with only one or two exceptions communist leaders in Vietnam did not have much French education, if any at all.

It should be noted in this connection that although it is not possible to describe any of the Hanoi leaders as fully pro-Chinese or pro-Russian, there seems to be a certain general rule as follows: the more a Central Committee member is Western-educated, the less he is pro-Peking. The rule has been proved true in at least two extreme cases. Truong Chinh, former Party secretary-general who spent most of his youth in jail, was the one who promoted the implementation of Mao's pattern of land reform in

Vietnam during 1954–6. When this land reform was over, and following the de-Stalinization campaign in Moscow, it was General Vo Nguyen Giap, a university graduate, who officially admitted the mistakes and launched a whole campaign for "rectification of errors."

Hanoi's readiness to accept Mao's thinking and Mao's methods did not, however, solely originate with the traditional attitude of "imitate China." It was also due to the prevailing condition of the moment: China was the first among communist countries which lent Ho Chi Minh a hand and helped him to secure military victory against the French. Comparatively speaking, the Russians came to Vietnam much later. A *Pravda* correspondent was probably the first Soviet visitor to North Vietnam in 1954, but thousands of Chinese advisers had been there since 1951. This means that prior to and immediately after Dien Bien Phu, Chinese influence upon the Lao Dong Party remained practically exclusive. It was during this period of Chinese "monopoly of influence" upon North Vietnam that Mao's program of reforms was carried out in that country. These included political, economic, financial and fiscal reforms, a campaign of "re-education," and a purge of "reactionaries" throughout the country, similar in many aspects to the present "cultural revolution" in China. All these campaigns served to pave the way for the most important and bloody one, which involved the land reform of 1954–6. To confiscate a total of some 1.7 million acres of land from the "landowning class" so as to distribute it among 2,104,100 peasants,[15] hundreds of thousands of "landowners" were killed while an even larger number either committed suicide or died in jail or inside their own houses because of the policy of "isolation."[16]

As an average of one human life was sacrificed for the confiscation of each four acres of land, the reform generated widespread dissatisfaction. Peasants, workers, and intellectuals rebelled together against the regime on the occasion of the de-Stalinization campaign. To remedy this situation the Party had to launch a corrective campaign known as the "campaign of error rectification." The excess of terror used during the land reform and its disastrous consequences produced two major effects: (1) a general disillusionment among "old" Party members who had been attracted to communism because of the idealistic aspects of Marxism, and (2) a sudden collapse of Chinese prestige, as Peking's methods applied in North Vietnam revealed themselves as too "barbarous." At the same time (1957–8) the Soviets, who had started providing North Vietnam with modern equipment and capable technical advisers, began to build up their influence. "Stalinist" leaders like Truong Chinh and To Huu, who had disappeared from the political scene during the brief period of de-Stalinization and "rectification of errors" (1956–7), were, however, not long in returning to power. This situation created a sort of a delicate balance between Soviet and Chinese influence, to be followed a few years later by an attitude of "nonalignment" when the Sino-Soviet conflict broke into the open.

The official policy of strict neutrality adopted by the Lao Dong Party vis-à-vis Moscow and Peking does not, however, imply the nonexistence of a latent conflict between "pro-Chinese" and "pro-Soviet" elements inside the Party itself. The fact that the Lao Dong Party is also contaminated from the ideological dispute between "revisionists" and "dogmatists" has been admitted by Nguyen Luong Bang, former secretary-general, who wrote as follows:

> The fight between the two (different) tendencies inside the international communist movement cannot have no influence upon the rank and file of our Party. Facing such a situation, the absolute majority of our cadres and Party members appears to be completely of the same mind and correctly to accept the Party's line, policy, and strategy. . . . But this does not imply the nonexistence of comrades, irresponsible and undisciplined, who take advantage of the democratization process inside the Party to talk without rhyme or reason. There are also people who make ill use of the Party tribune to make unreasonable remarks, to propagate their personal views which are in contradiction with those of the Party.[17]

The above complaint was made in February 1965. But in September 1966 *Hoc Tap* still referred to the "necessity of fighting against both revisionism and dogmatism."[18]

It should be noted in this connection that Hanoi's nonalignment between Moscow and Peking is essentially political in character. As such, it is not very different from that of India or Burma, which sit on the "political" fence dividing East and West. Ideologically speaking, every communist who respects himself must opt either for "revisionism" or for "dogmatism," as the following question inevitably comes to his mind: "Do the Soviet comrades, or anybody else, have the right to *revise* the doctrine of Marxism?" This presents a real dilemma for every communist, because such a question permits only two answers, either "yes" or "no." Those who reply in the affirmative are undoubtedly "revisionist," and anyone answering with a negative is certainly a "dogmatist." As there is no intermediate ground for this question, there unfortunately can be no room for "ideological neutralism."

Other signs of internal dissension also occasionally appear in the Party press. Le Duc Tho, an influential Central Committee member admitted, for instance, that "conflicts are continuously growing inside the Party."[19] Party secretary-general Le Duan disclosed that "a certain number of comrades are lacking in a solid platform, have failed to grasp the basic policy of the Party, and have become faltering, wavering."[20] Le Duan probably referred to Party veterans who, disillusioned by the meager results after ten years of "socialist edification," have lost almost completely the valiant fighting spirit they had shown during the anticolonialist war. This case is particularly applicable in the Thai-nguyen and Cao-bang areas, which served as guerrilla bases for the Viet Minh during World War II. In this connection General Chu Van Tan, chairman of the Viet-Bac Autonomous Region, wrote: "In Party branches in mountain areas there are a certain number of Party members who appear to be tired, apathetic, whose fighting spirit has decreased and is no longer adequate to the new demands of the revolution. A certain number of well-trained Party members, who have been through the ordeal of the August Revolution [1945] and that of the Resistance War [1945–54], are at present conceited, excessively proud of their past activities, but always lagging behind others in the [revolutionary] movement."[21] As the "old guard" is showing signs of apathy and lassitude, the Party tends to rely on the younger generation, born after 1945 and knowing nothing of the precommunist past. This is the reason why teen-agers are sent to fight in South Vietnam.

Also, as most of the able-bodied men have been sent either to the front or drafted to serve in paramilitary activities in remote areas, work at home as well as in the fields and factories must be assumed by women. They are now enjoying unprecedented attention from the Party. Much more than their male companions, Vietnamese women have a record of courage and endurance. These exceptional qualities are being most highly exalted by the regime. With the exception of the Party Central Committee and the government's cabinet, where all members are males, women are rapidly replacing men in every echelon of public affairs. The most illustrative testimony on this new trend can be found in the most recent election to people's councils in the Hanoi area during April 1967. The number of women elected amounted to exactly 50 per cent of the total seats.

With a growing number of women and youths occupying responsible positions and being admitted into the Party,[22] the Party's control over the population seems to remain firm, if not stronger than before. This does not mean, however, that the whole country is without trouble. In 1965 there appeared the story of a postman who received a citation for having crossed, for the first time in many years, an area in Lai-chau province said to be infested by *t'u-fi,* or Chinese pirates. Lai-chau is in the northwest of North Vietnam, bordering on China and Laos.

In Lang-son, another province adjacent to China, something serious seems to have happened a few years ago. In its issue for November 1966 *Hoc Tap* devoted an eighteen-page article to the so-called "Improvement of the Revolutionary Movement in Lang-son," in which it was admitted that for some time the "revolutionary movement" remained actually at its lowest ebb. The situation in Lang-son was described as follows:

> In the period from 1961 to 1963 . . . the Party section in Lang-son committed serious mistakes in many fields, and because of these mistakes

the revolutionary movement in the whole province sharply declined. The number of peasants joining collective farms went down from 80 per cent of the total to 47 per cent; material and technical edification of socialism was badly conducted; the development of agricultural and industrial production was too slow, the requisition of rice and foodstuffs was inadequate; in free markets, prices—and particularly that of rice—increased sharply; state regulations were not being properly implemented; drunkenness, gambling, and larceny reappeared in many areas; in a certain number of areas bad elements [reactionaries] raised their head [revolted] and imposed their rule over the population; the revolutionary enthusiasm of the masses decreased; many Party branches were in bad shape; many Party cadres were weak . . . incapable of leading the masses. . . .[23]

Not unlike other frontier provinces, Lang-son has an ethnic problem. The Vietnamese are themselves in a minority, while the Nung, who are closer to the Chinese than to the Vietnamese, are in a majority. As disclosed in the following passage from the same article, contacts between these two ethnic groups—Vietnamese and Nung—are poor. "In some areas the [revolutionary] movement slackened because the relationship between the Party and the masses, between one ethnic group and another one, is not good." And in another passage one reads that "the lesson learned from Lang-son teaches us that problems in multiracial areas must be solved with great care, by means of a persevering effort at persuasion. A ruthless or hasty move may result in disastrous consequences."

What transpires from the *Hoc Tap* article might be summarized as follows: During the difficult years of 1961–3, the Party's prestige was low, and popular resentment became widespread in Lang-son province. The local Party section reacted with ruthless repression against so-called "bad elements," who happened to be Nungs—the former Nung tribal chiefs. This led the Nung to revolt more or less openly against the regime. Later, realizing that a racial clash between Nung and Vietnamese seemed in the offing and would lead to disastrous consequences, the Central Committee dispatched a team to Lang-son to investigate and to take the whole affair in hand. After three years (from 1963 to 1966) of "persevering efforts at persuasion" the Party finally succeeded in restoring peace and order. Then the editors of *Hoc Tap* went in a group to Lang-son to study the "Lang-son experience," i.e., the manner in which the Party had successfully "pacified" the area and brought the Nung tribes back into submission. The above-mentioned article serves as a guideline for cadres and Party members working in multiracial areas. The main advice included the following: "The Party section [probably a reorganized section of the Lao-Dong Party in Lang-son province] repeats to its cadres and Party members that extreme caution is required when dealing with problems involving people of different races, [problems] left over by history or recently created by new circumstances."[24]

The advice is wise and easy to understand, but what remains not so perfectly clear are the "new circumstances," which, according to *Hoc Tap,* are susceptible of creating racial conflict between Vietnamese and Nungs.[25] As far as it is possible to guess, these "new circumstances" may include either the recent arrival of Vietnamese in large numbers from the overcrowded delta or some kind of repercussion from what is happening on the Chinese side of the border, namely, the political turmoil created by Mao's "cultural revolution."

To an outside observer the lesson to be drawn from the *Hoc Tap* article is twofold: (1) since what happened in Lang-son from 1961 to 1963 was only revealed in November 1966, it would be correct to suppose that should Hanoi choose to disclose any aspect of the present situation in North Vietnam, it would not do so before 1973; and (2) because it is almost by chance that one learned about the "bad situation" in Lang-son province, such conditions may exist in other provinces.

Also in this connection, it should be noted that while a "Million like One Unity behind our Uncle and our Party" had been permanently claimed, Hanoi quite unexpectedly announced on March 21, 1968, the existence of a special decree directed at some fifteen "counterrevolutionary crimes." This decree is said to have been signed by Ho Chi Minh some time in October 1967, although no explanation was given as to why it had been kept in Ho's drawer for four months. Since the decree lists such crimes as "plotting to overthrow the People's Democratic Power," "armed rebellion," "destruction of defense installations," "murder of cadres and soldiers," "attacking detention camps and freeing convicts," and so forth, one may suppose that somewhere in North Vietnam, and to some extent— still unknown to the outside world—such specific "counterrevolutionary crimes" actually have been committed.

Summary

It is no exaggeration to say that for a whole decade North Vietnam has made a prodigious effort to instill socialism, i.e., to modernize the country according to a collectivist pattern for the economy and for life in general. Brilliant performances have been achieved in many fields, but the basic problem of food and population, instead of being solved, is becoming more acute than ever. The difficulty in this domain has been officially attributed to the fact that North Vietnam had boldly "passed without transition from feudal and colonial backwardness to socialist modernity." This is certainly a great handicap, but a careful analysis would reveal other factors which are no less decisive. These seem to include the high birth rate (which is the normal privilege of any undernourished population), the limitation of natural resources (it has been calculated, for instance, that the low annual amount of sunlight in North Vietnam would not permit that country to have a maximum rice output as high as that of Japan), the incompetence of the Party leadership in technical matters,[26] and the quasi-impossibility of applying modern machinery to rice cultivation in a country where the annual amount of rainfall is too high. These are objective factors to which must be added a few subjective ones, as follows: not unlike the Communist Party of China, the Lao Dong Party of Vietnam is excessively dogmatic; it is being driven by an intense impulse to catch up with and, very soon afterwards, to defeat the "imperialists," and the necessity of justifying the efficiency and superiority of the communist regime so as to preserve and to consolidate the Party's control over the population.

The general picture is far from brilliant, and the question to ask is the following: why does Ho Chi Minh prefer to continue the war when the economic situation of North Vietnam is rather critical? The question is complex, and answers are many,[27] but the most significant one seems to be that although the war causes physical devastation of the country, politically it strengthens the Party's control over the population. As a matter of experience this has happened before: In 1946 Ho Chi Minh purposefully accepted the return of the French and later ordered the Viet-Minh troops to attack them. Ho Chi Minh possesses a kind of boldness very particular to Vietnamese Confucians which is best illustrated by the following anecdote.

In the 1880's Ton That Thuyet was commander-in-chief of the Vietnamese army and regent for the throne. He was known to be the most bloodthirsty of men in recent Vietnamese history. He once ordered the killing of a mother whose baby, by crying at night, had disturbed his sleep. As everybody was frightened at his approach and nobody dared come to see him, a group of Confucian scholars, when joking, expressed the doubt that any among the group was courageous enough to meet Ton That Thuyet face to face. A bet was made, and one scholar calmly accepted the challenge. His name was Xien Ngo.

Xien Ngo waited in front of the general's residential palace until he saw him in a good mood, picking flowers from his garden. Then Xien Ngo went in, bowed in front of the general, who, much puzzled, asked the reason for his unexpected presence. Very humbly the scholar said: "I am a brilliant student, but I always failed in examinations. I do not want to live any longer, and being informed that Your Highness may kill anyone he wants, I am coming to beg a very small service from you. Please kill me so that I may have a better fate in my next life."

The unexpected proposition presented by Xien Ngo placed Ton That Thuyet in a most difficult position. Although he had killed many people, he had never killed anyone on voluntary request. Forced to find an escape for himself, the general said: "You told me you are a brilliant student. Let me check your capability. If you are really brilliant, I will give you a big reward. If not, I will satisfy your request and send you to your next life." He then gave Xien a subject on which to compose a poem immediately. Xien Ngo did not hesitate, and the verses he composed on the spot were so beautiful that he received a large sum of money and went home peacefully.

Ho Chi Minh is not a Confucian, and as a Marxist he is even opposed to the latter. But born into a Confucian family, he certainly has that kind of Confucian boldness in his blood. Ho Chi Minh was bold when he started the war against the French, and he won that war. His principle seems to be that one who risks nothing, has nothing. And not unlike Xien Ngo, he knows that the risk of facing any danger is limited because any power one dares face, regardless of how great it might be, has always some inherent restrictions on its use. This is not to say that Ho has no other sound motives to continue the fight and to believe in "final victory." He simply has too many.

Notes to Chapter 13

1. Ho Chi Minh, article on "The Road That Led Me to Leninism," *Echo du Vietnam* (Paris), Jul. 1960.

2. *Hoc Tap* is the journal of political and ideological studies of the Lao Dong Party.

3. Hoang Van Chi, *From Colonialism to Communism* (New York, 1964).

4. "In the North there are too many people and not enough land [and as a result] after the Land Reform, each poor peasant 'mouth' possesses an average of 1,437 square meters (1,718 square yards), and each middle-peasant 'mouth' has 1,610 square meters (1,925 square yards). In the delta, figures are even smaller." *Nghien Cuu Kinh Te* (Hanoi), No. 29 (Oct. 1965), p. 5.

5. Luu Van Dat, article on "Ten Years of Foreign Trade," *Nghien Cuu Kinh Te,* No. 29 (Oct. 1966), p. 29.

6. There were 3,495,000 nonagricultural people among a total population of 17,922,000 in 1963. The percentage was 19.5 for that year.

7. Le Loc, article on "Correct Solution to the Food Problem in View of Defeating the Americans," *Nghien Cuu Kinh Te,* No. 31 (Feb. 1966), p. 19.

8. Luu Van Dat, *op. cit.*

9. Luu Van Dat, article on "How to Balance Export/Import," *Nghien Cuu Kinh Te,* No. 24 (Dec. 1964), p. 46.

10. Nguyen Van Tran, article on "Goods and Markets at Present in the North," *Hoc Tap* (Nov. 1966). "Cities" like Hanoi are administrative units including a city proper, in the center, and a vast "suburban area" which still remains basically agricultural. This agricultural suburban area is now urged to produce enough food to feed the population in the city proper.

11. Every year each schoolboy or schoolgirl must sell to the government at least two chickens for export.

12. Although the French conquest of Vietnam was completed in 1884, serious efforts to propagate French education started only in 1917.

13. Tran Trong Kim, *Viet Nam Su Luoc* ("Summary of Vietnamese History"), (Hanoi, 1928).

14. In the traditional triennial examinations, which were maintained until 1917, study of Chinese literature, philosophy, and history was compulsory; Vietnamese history was optional.

15. Official figures published by *Nghien Cuu Kinh Te* (Oct. 1965), p. 6.

16. See Hoang Van Chi, *op. cit.*

17. Nguyen Luong Bang, article on "Let Us Heighten Our Sense of Organization and Discipline, Improve Our Unity and Our Party's Fighting Strength," *Hoc Tap* (Feb. 1965), p. 19.

18. "Greater Effort in Ideological Studies," editorial in *Hoc Tap* (Sep. 1966), p. 12.

19. Le Duc Tho, article on "Stronger Criticism and Self-Criticism to Eradicate Intraparty Contradictions," *Hoc Tap* (Feb. 1965), p. 11.

20. Le Duan, article on "Stronger Leadership for the Consolidation of the Economy and the Defense of the North," *Hoc Tap* (Sep. 1965), p. 12.

21. General Chu Van Tan, article on "Improvement of Party Edification in Mountain Areas . . . ," *Hoc Tap* (Feb. 1965), pp. 26–35.

22. "[Only] in the North, our Party counts at present more than 766,000 members, i.e., 153 times more members than at the time of the August [1945] Revolution. . . ." Talk by Ho Chi Minh in *Hoc Tap* (June 1966), p. 9.

23. Investigation team of the *Hoc Tap* editorial staff, article on "Basic Lessons Learned from the Improvement of the Revolutionary Movement in Lang-son," *Hoc Tap* (Nov. 1966).

24. *Ibid.*

25. The problem of the Nungs in Vietnamese history is comparable to that of the Kurds in Iraq. For some time the Nungs revolted against both Vietnamese and Chinese and tried unsuccessfully to establish an independent Nung kingdom.

26. Le Duc Tho disclosed dissension between technical directors and Party representatives in industrial enterprises. *Hoc Tap* (Apr. 1965).

27. See Hoang Van Chi, "Why No Peace in Vietnam," *Viet Nam Seen from East and West* (New York, 1966).

Discussion

DONALD E. WEATHERBEE

Among the Communist-ruled states North Vietnam appears to be in the most perilous circumstances, a condition resulting from domestic failures exacerbated by the strains of international conflict. In attempting to telescope time by proper application of Marxism-Leninism, the Lao Dong leaders have simultaneously endeavored to force modernization through totalitarian methods upon an essentially traditional society, create a socialist state, and "liberate" by force South Vietnam, which has meant in effect war with the United States. The hard choices for Hanoi regarding the establishment of priorities are complicated by what might be called the "objective reality" of scarce resources. The recognition of interdependence between North Vietnamese domestic and international goals provides greater clarity to a perspective of the three aspects of the Vietnamese economy discussed by Mr. Hoang: agriculture, industry, and trade.

Agriculture by any measure is the most important sector of the North Vietnamese economy. Despite the attention to industrialization and heavy investment in nonfarming sectors, just the fact alone that 85 per cent of the labor force works in agriculture (Mr. Hoang's statement) gives it a predominant role now and during the foreseeable future. This contrasts strongly with the pronounced sectional shifts away from farming in the labor forces of the Philippines and Malaya as well as similar trends in Thailand and Cambodia. Perhaps it may represent a useful comparative index to the North Vietnamese march toward "socialism."

Agriculture's commanding position in the economy means, as in most of the Asian countries, that development in the farming sector in terms of greater productivity serves as a precondition for general economic development because it is the rural areas that must generate the capital for investment in industry. An increase in the productivity of North Vietnamese agriculture must come about through the interaction of a number of factors: investment, application of new technology, efficient management of farm units, marketing arrangements that provide incentive, efficiency of the labor force, and others.

In point of fact, however, there has been a relative decline in North Vietnamese agricultural productivity, discernible even before the disruptions caused by extensive American bombings. Mr. Hoang has noted some of these indications. Although the goal remains at five metric tons per hectare, North Vietnam now is probably below the 1957–62 average of 1.7 tons per hectare. This combined with the population growth has meant serious food shortages and of course depresses the entire economy. The organs of government are constantly exhorting the population to solve the food problem. "Waste not, want not" is the motto. Soberly, the people were told (in an article, entitled "Use Food Rationally and Sparingly," *Nhan Dan,* November 2, 1966) the following:

> Solving the food problem is the principal task of agricultural production. This is an indispensable condition for the development of agriculture in a comprehensive manner so that it may serve as a good basis for the development of industries and so that it may serve socialist industrialization.

Under present circumstances the solution of the food problem to insure that our army and people eat their fill in order to fight and defeat the U.S. aggressors while continuing to build material and technical foundations for socialism is a task of very great significance.

The situation has not shown any signs of improvement. The 1966 tenth month harvest, despite claims of bumper local crops, if one reads carefully Hanoi's verbiage, appears to have been quite poor. Nor were the prospects for the 1967 spring harvest any better. Even accepting the occurrence of pestilence, disease, drought, and flood, the continuing failure in agriculture must be related to other factors as well. Obviously the strain of the war has had a deleterious effect. There have been immediate demands on the farm labor supply for nonagricultural and, in the main, nonproductive tasks: military service, transport levies, road and railway repair. The necessary capital investment in farming has had to be deferred in favor of military and defense expenditures. Normal marketing and transport facilities have been disrupted. The dispersal of urban populations has burdened the agricultural hinterlands. In addition, one should add the nonquantifiable psychological demands on the population.

The Party has proclaimed a threefold transformation in agriculture: the revolution of production relations, the technological revolution, and the cultural and ideological revolution (see the article entitled "To Satisfactorily Carry Out the Campaign to Improve Cooperative Management and Agricultural Techniques," *Hoc Tap*, October, 1966). Of these three, the technological one is deemed the most important but is probably most hampered by demands of the war. Moreover, the methods employed by Hanoi planners to force change in a traditional farming society that is resistant to innovation have created tensions in North Vietnam that cannot be passed over lightly. Mr. Hoang, in his conclusions, states: "The Party's control over the population seems to remain firm, if not stronger than before." These words were carefully chosen and speak of Party control over the population, not the population's allegiance to the Party's leadership.

I would suggest that Lao Dong demands upon the population, now made more exigent by the military emergency, have contributed to the agricultural stagnation. Demands have not been accompanied by desirable rewards, and there is evidence that one counterproductive consequence has involved growing dissatisfaction, if not disaffection, on the part of the rural population toward its bureaucratic and Party masters, personified in the lower-level officials who have the unenviable task of translating Hanoi's requirements into reality.

A long article by Le Duc Tho is instructive in this regard (see the article on "The Relationship Between Basic Party Organizations and the Masses Must be Consolidated," *Nhan Dan*, November 7, 1966). It is the lower-level cadre who is the bridge between the Party and the people. If one interprets the criticisms of Le Duc Tho correctly, the bridge needs repair. He accuses the cadres of "bureaucracy," by which is meant lack of association between Party organs on the one hand and workers and peasants on the other, the reluctance of the Party official to perform manual labor, and failure to implement or encourage non-Party participation in the decision-making process at the level of the local economic unit. Then there is "commandism": the use of coercion rather than persuasion on the masses. Finally, there is "individualism" or detachment from the masses of the Party cadres.

Many of the criticisms that have been leveled at the latter, who may be considered members of the modernizing elite, are characteristic of bureaucracies in the other emerging states of Asia and Africa. There is a general bureaucratic attitude that the "masses" are backward, unprogressive, unenlightened. The values held are different. Economic and political change have not found roots in an indigenous political culture. This phenomenon of intellectual alienation from the traditional society by the Party in North Vietnam, what Le Duc Tho called "biased and indifferent" attitudes toward the backward masses, becomes critical when abnormal demands are made upon society. Little wonder that the communist cadres of North Vietnam contend that coercion is necessary to accomplish the goals that have been set for them to implement.

These tensions are inherent in the modernization process, where elites attempt a rapid transformation of political and economic systems. One can endorse Mr. Hoang's caution: it should not be assumed automatically that a noncommunist regime in North Vietnam would have been any better able to solve easily the fundamental problems of development. However, it is doubtful that a noncommunist regime would have so aggravated the problem by pursuing a foreign policy that has led to widespread destruction of the tangible gains over the past decade. Moreover, the gulf between Party and people in North Vietnam may widen as physical hardships increase.

Mr. Hoang gives Hanoi the benefit of the doubt. He argues that despite the tremendous strain of war, destruction wrought by the United States, setbacks in agriculture, casualties, rampant inflation, and war weariness, North Vietnam will not collapse. He states that "the Vietnamese people are always able to get along with the rudimentary economy which has been theirs for centuries. . . . They can endure the situation almost indefinitely." Going along and enduring can not be considered measures of achievement. Certainly one cannot proceed from this conclusion to an assumption that the communist regime will survive or not be threatened. The maintenance of a subsistence level is a far cry from building socialism.

Assuming for the moment a prolongation of the war, what might one expect for the future of communism in Vietnam? Mr. Hoang has answered that "the war causes physical devastation of the country, but politically it strengthens the Party's control over the population." It has been suggested above that there are reasons to add qualifications to this assertion. Furthermore, one would venture the proposition that the Lao Dong in its efforts to minimize real economic loss has taken steps that could in the future cause a reduction in the degree of its control over the population. Measures of economic decentralization which Mr. Hoang has described should be remembered. Economic decentralization, emphasis on autarchic policies in the provinces, dispersal of the urban population, and other steps taken to reduce North Vietnam's military vulnerability may have as an undesirable concomitant, from Hanoi's point of view, a trend toward decentralization of political control.

Mr. Hoang has commented upon the "apathy and lassitude" of the older generation of Party leaders and the increasing reliance being placed upon the post-1945 generations. He has adduced as evidence for his belief that the Party remains firmly in control of the population the fact that women and youth have moved into positions of Party responsibility. On the other hand, the "generation gap" combined with loss of revolutionary élan might work to loosen Party control. One conclusion does appear fairly certain. The Lao Dong will emerge from the war with more than just bridges and factories to rebuild.

In his remarks Mr. Hoang has called attention to certain basic characteristics of North Vietnamese communism that have provided it with both direction and dynamism. In the first place, he reminds us that North Vietnamese communism had its original inspiration in nationalism, which then evolved toward proletarian internationalism. What will be the impact of war in Vietnam on the latter aspect? Mr. Hoang does not comment, but it is necessary to point out the possibility that North Vietnam, caught between the Chinese People's Republic (C.P.C.) and the U.S.S.R., has benefited insufficiently from communist internationalism in terms of defense, economic assistance, and aid in the common struggle against the United States. Forced to turn more and more to excessive demands on its own scarce resources, both material and human, North Vietnam may retrace historical steps and renew its spirit in nationalist as opposed to specifically communist appeals. This, too, will tend to erode the legitimacy of the Lao Dong leadership.

The above thought comes into sharper focus when compared with the second basic characteristic of North Vietnamese communism, i.e., adoption of the Chinese model. Mr. Hoang has termed this "imitating China." But the model probably is not as attractive today. Certainly the C.P.C., beset by its own self-devouring agonies, will not be able to deliver the requisite political and economic assistance that North Vietnam may have expected. Moreover, it is highly doubtful that North Vietnam will follow the C.P.C. to self-destruction. Among all the influences which Mr. Hoang has mentioned to explain the former allure of the Chinese model for the North Vietnamese communists, probably greatest weight should be given to Hanoi's appreciation of China's power and influence in the immediate region. (Conversely, one would assign less importance to cultural affinities than does Mr. Hoang.) If that power and influence were to wane through domestic turmoil, lack of real international capabilities, and re-evaluation by third parties of China's relative power vis-à-vis the United States and the Soviet Union, then is it not reasonable to anticipate, in the light of the other factors discussed and at the same time keeping aware of the many variables involved, a more pragmatic approach by Hanoi to its problems than has been its experience in the past?

I am making, in effect, two conjectural statements. In the first place, existing internal problems, made more serious by the war, combined with the changing Asian international environment, may produce a North Vietnamese policy tied more to national interest than to proletarian internationalism. Secondly, and related to the first speculation, I am less convinced than Mr. Hoang of the capacity of the North Vietnamese communist apparatus to maintain its present level of control.

In most respects the position of North Vietnam, when compared with the other communist-ruled countries, is rather unique. The political and economic circumstances of North Vietnam at independence were more akin to the noncommunist states of Southeast Asia and emergent states elsewhere than with their communist counterparts in Asia or Europe. Space does not permit detailing the differences, particularly between China and North Vietnam. I can merely point out that a number of measures undertaken by the Lao Dong since 1954 may have been undertaken with reference to an appreciation for real economic and social problems confronting the leadership rather than in simple imitation of China or other communist parties in power. The question, of course, is whether proletarian internationalism will give way to nationalism under the pressure of the need to preserve North Vietnam's independence or whether the Lao Dong will continue to sacrifice themselves and their population to an increasingly costly and lonely struggle against "imperialism."

Part VI
Cuba

14

cuban-soviet relations: conditions and constraints

DESMOND P. WILSON, JR.

Competition and conflict between the communist and noncommunist states have created a number of political anomalies throughout the world. Cuba is one of these along with others such as Berlin and the two Germanys, divided Korea, the two Chinas, and a divided Vietnam. With regard to communist Cuba the general question of interest concerns the role of that small country as one of the communist-ruled states, given the conditions which prevail and the constraints which have been imposed by the United States government and the Organization of American States since Fidel Castro came to power.

The significant conditions are those which stem from geography and from the almost complete economic and diplomatic isolation of Cuba within the Western Hemisphere. Not only is Cuba the sole communist-ruled country which does not share a common border with another communist state, but it is also insular and located some 6,000 nautical miles from the Soviet Union, its major protector and extraterritorial supplier. Another condition which shapes the context of Cuban-Soviet relations is the calculated policy of economic and diplomatic isolation of Cuba by the United States and the Organization of American States (hereafter referred to as the U.S./O.A.S.). In the words of Edwin M. Martin, at the time Assistant Secretary of State for Inter-American Affairs, the isolation of

Cuba has the following aims: "we [the United States] are committed to do everything we can to hamper the political and social and economic development and prosperity of the Castro regime in Cuba, to make it more costly to the Soviets and less successful, and to encourage the Cuban people to want to change their regime."[1]

The constraints on Cuba and the Soviet Union concern the introduction into Cuba of offensive strategic weapons and the use of the island as a base for carrying out aggression in the Western Hemisphere. It is U.S. policy forcefully to oppose any externally supported or Cuban-based use of force against any Latin American state. In addition the United States will not permit the introduction into Cuba of strategic military systems of an offensive nature.

Given the above conditions and constraints, the more specific questions to be examined in this paper are the following: (1) short of those actions which would clearly provoke another military confrontation with the United States, what are the alternative courses for the Soviet Union with respect to making Cuba either a more useful or a less burdensome ally? (2) What do the alternative Soviet courses of action imply for the political and economic life of the Castro regime?

There is considerable evidence to support the inference that the Soviet leadership is under pressure to minimize costs or to increase its benefits from Cuba. The costs are quite high. Estimates would place Soviet and East European economic and military aid to Cuba between $2 and $3 billion for the calendar years 1960 through 1966 (see Table 34). Furthermore, the cost to the Soviets appears to be increasing instead of decreasing.[2] The higher expenditures are in large part due to the effectiveness of the U.S./O.A.S. boycott, poor economic conditions in Cuba, low sugar prices, high shipping costs, and bad management on the part of the Havana government.

Comparing only the economic assistance given by the socialist states to Cuba with that provided other major noncommunist recipients of aid, it is clear that Cuba accounts for a relatively substantial amount (see Table 29). The comparison is even more impressive when examined on a per-capita basis and when account is taken of the fact that Cuba did not start receiving aid until 1960.

It appears that there is growing disenchantment and exasperation among some of the Soviet administrators and engineers working in Cuba. One U.S.S.R. engineer recently expressed regret to a Swiss correspondent that his country had put so much money into Cuba because "in the Soviet Union there is more poverty to eliminate than Cuba has ever known."[3] *Business Week* asserted on June 25, 1966, that privately many Russians in Cuba have come to look upon that island as a liability and that many East

European communists regard Castro as a sort of "buffoon." Finally, the Soviets are reported to be stiffening their trade terms with the Cubans.

TABLE 29

Soviet and East European Economic Assistance
to Cuba, Compared with Other Large Recipients (1954–64)
(millions of U.S. $)

	Totals	*Per Capita*
Cuba	1,400	193
U.A.R.	1,664	58
India	1,299	3
Indonesia	740	8

NOTE: Excludes military assistance.
SOURCE: U.S. Department of State, Bureau of Intelligence and Research, Report on "Communist Governments and Developing Nations: Aid and Trade in 1965," RSB-50 (June 17, 1966).

While it is extremely difficult to know just how burdensome the U.S.S.R. leadership regards Cuba, it is clear that costs are substantial and that, compared with other alternative targets which the Soviets have regarded in the past as important, Cuban expenditures are very large indeed. Therefore, it seems reasonable to infer that the U.S.S.R. is interested in cutting costs. If, as it appears, the Soviets are unsuccessful in this effort and, instead, are saddled with constant or rising costs at least for a few years, then they are likely to be under considerable pressure to increase the benefits or effectiveness of Cuba in terms of larger U.S.S.R. interests. In short, they are likely to be pressed to strike some more favorable balance between the costs and advantages from their Cuban "outpost." Short of another attempt to convert the island into a base for direct support of offensive strategic weapons systems, there appear to be three broad alternatives for the Soviets.

These options include: (1) retention of Cuba as a base for an overtly militant form of communist expansionism; (2) retention of Cuba as a base for supporting a variety of U.S.S.R. interests, including subversion and communist expansion, but of a less overtly militant nature; and (3) abandonment of Cuba and the Castro regime. The first two alternatives correspond to the polemical positions of the Chinese communists on the one hand and the Soviets on the other. The first places emphasis on armed struggle as a catalyst in the process of acquiring power. Armed insurrectionists and rural-based guerrilla forces led by a clearly identifiable, communist vanguard is the preferred Chinese strategy. It is also the preferred strategy of Fidel Castro. The second alternative purports to be more pragmatic and contemplates the submergence of communists in united-front political activities, where beneficial, and a generally more cautious approach to the use of force. Revolutionary violence in Venezuela is representative of the first option. Urban-based insurrection and communist identification with legitimate left-wing parties in the 1965–6 Dominican crisis is an example of the second alternative.

The alternatives can be viewed in terms of the preferences of Fidel Castro and his close followers, with the first option being the most preferred, the second being much less preferred, and the third presumably being the least preferred. They can also be viewed in terms of costs and risks to the Soviet Union, with the first alternative being the most costly and involving the greatest risk of a serious confrontation with the United States; the second option would seem to be less so and has more promise of being cheaper than alternative number one; while the third option, Soviet abandonment of Cuba, would seem to be the least costly and least hazardous for the U.S.S.R.

The possibility should be noted that from the Soviet point of view there may well be costs and risks attached to the consequences of an abandonment of Cuba which would exceed the costs and risks of its retention. In this same sense the U.S.S.R. may be likened to the mythical tar baby—stuck with its Cuban involvement. If so, the situation has its analogies with the U.S. Vietnam involvement and the problem of demonstrating credibility to a network of allies.

Although the third alternative is an admittedly remote contingency, it could occur in any one of a number of ways. For example, a sort of global exchange between the Western alliance system and the Kremlin might be negotiated whereby Cuba would be exchanged for some Western concession. A historical analogy of great power manipulation involved the agreement of King George II with France in 1748 to exchange the colonists' hard-won Cape Breton Island in Nova Scotia for French-held Madras in India. Another illustration for this type of manipulation was Khrushchev's proposal in October 1962 of an exchange of Turkish-based missiles for Cuban-based missiles. Incidentally, this offer, along with the suggestion to allow inspectors into Cuba, infuriated Fidel Castro and no doubt made him more aware of his instrumental role in great power politics.

Cuba might be abandoned by the Soviets if it became ideologically too intransigent. There are precedents for this type of U.S.S.R. reprisal. In 1958 the Soviet Union unilaterally terminated economic agreements with Yugoslavia, and in June 1960 with Albania when it sided with the Chinese People's Republic at the Bucharest conference of communist parties. However, unlike Yugoslavia and Albania, there is no apparent economic alternative, other than the Soviet Union, which would allow the Castro regime to survive. The magnitude of even bare subsistence requirements for Cuba would appear beyond the capabilities of contemporary communist China, to say nothing of the merchant shipping required to maintain an island with a population of over 7.3 million (see Table 35). For example, the cumulative total through December 1964 of reported Chinese credits and grants extended to eighteen less-developed, noncommunist countries comes only to $786 million.[4] This is about one third of what Cuba is estimated to have received from the Soviet Union alone.

Finally, the U.S.S.R. may become disillusioned with its situation in Cuba and the lackluster possibilities for furthering Soviet and world communist interests. It simply could terminate all arrangements and withdraw from Cuba, indifferent to the consequences for the Havana government.

Of the three alternatives it will be argued that the second, controlled retention of Cuba, is the most likely course of action for the U.S.S.R. Each of the three would have quite different political and economic consequences for Cuba and the Castro regime.

The Politics of Survival

The central political issues with respect to Cuban-Soviet relations concern the methods for furthering communism in Latin America and the rest of the less-developed world as well as the composition of the Cuban government. The outcome of these issues has profound implications for the future of Fidel Castro and his regime.

The first issue has to do with the above-mentioned role of violence in Latin America. The political identity of Fidel Castro, and perhaps even his physical survival, seems closely tied to the maintenance of high levels of militant, revolutionary ardor and enthusiasm at all levels of Cuban society. Continual focusing on real or imagined threats to the state and on counter-revolutionary tendencies is, of course, a classic device in marshaling support for a regime.

From the Soviet point of view, however, the optimal strategy with respect to Latin America in particular appears to denigrate the role of violence until a more auspicious time. The crucible of experience with violent revolution in Latin America appears to have strengthened, not the Castro and Chinese orientations, but that of the U.S.S.R. The lessons derived from the apparent failures in Venezuela and Colombia, contrasted with the near success in the Dominican Republic, have not been lost on Latin American communists nor on the Kremlin. A pro-Moscow Guatemalan communist noted that revolution in Latin America has become more difficult since Castro's coming to power, not less difficult![5] Interestingly enough, Castro himself is reported by Theodore Draper to have said on one occasion that his 26th of July Movement would never have come down from the mountains of the Sierra Maestra had they identified themselves as Marxist-Leninists before actually taking power. In short, the U.S.S.R. and pro-Soviet Latin American communists recognize that an early and overt identification of dissident revolutionary elements with Moscow, Peking, or Havana will make the task of acquiring political power by communist revolutionaries more difficult. This has become the case since Latin American governments are more alerted to the danger and, in conjunction with the United States, have taken a range of military, economic, and political steps to counter the threat.

It is for these reasons that the U.S.S.R. appears to be adopting a more united-front approach. Communists are apparently being urged to support left-wing political groups and to rely more on democratic as opposed to violent revolutionary slogans. This course of action raises a serious question with respect to the maintenance of Castro's identity and charisma. If this is in fact Soviet policy and if Castro is obliged to adhere to it, his identity and charisma will be threatened to the extent that they are dependent upon the image of a spirited, revolutionary *caudillo*. The logic of U.S.S.R. policy cannot be attractive to Fidel Castro. It implies an eventual role for the Cuban leader not unlike that of a loyal, Ulbricht-type party hack.

Given the extreme dependency of Cuba on the Soviet Union, it is most unlikely that Castro will be permitted to pursue those policies which have not been endorsed by the U.S.S.R., regardless of how Castro and his close followers feel about matters. A number of factors already point to Soviet predominance. Examples include the disappearance and subsequent death of "Che" Guevara, the direction and integration of the Cuban economy within the network of socialist economies, the growing Cuban rift with Peking following the November 1964 secret conference of Latin American communist parties, and the length and content of Castro's speeches. Many of his speeches are now down to two hours instead of the usual five, and he is far more likely to devote time to techniques of raising tomatoes and the like than previously.

A second and related issue has to do with the staffing of the Cuban government. On this issue the Kremlin appears to be moving very cautiously. Castro is successfully resisting the appointment of long-term communist party members, loyal to Moscow, to positions of responsibility, despite the fact that their administrative skills are likely to exceed by considerable measure those of Castro's appointees. According to Castro, the prime criterion for a responsible position is revolutionary zeal. If it becomes a "question of choosing between revolutionary zeal and competence, the former quality must be decisive."[6] Reportedly many of Cuba's administrators at all levels are former workers or peasants whose loyalties to Castro and the revolution are strengthened by their recent accession to positions of privilege and power.

The competition between old-line, pro-Moscow communists and the close followers of Fidel Castro and his 26th of July Movement has been reflected in the types and staffing of the various political and governmental organizations. After coming to power in 1959, Castro ruled Cuba from the Revolutionary Directorate of his Movement with the cooperation of the *Partido Socialista Popular* (PSP), Cuba's communist party. In 1961 Castro's 26th of July Movement was formally merged with the PSP to form the Integrated Revolutionary Organization (ORI). Reportedly, old-line communists from the former PSP began gaining influence and power within the new Party and the government, excluding former Castro followers in some cases. Anibal Escalante, a former PSP member and long-time communist, became a dominant figure in this apparent attempt to control the government. Escalante evidently sought to control the administration through the ORI and, perhaps, to replace Castro's erratic personal rule with a Party-centered collective leadership. He was unsuccessful. Castro denounced him in March 1962, and the ORI underwent a purge and reorganization. It became the United Party of the Socialist Revolution (PURS). PURS was viewed as an interim or transitional organization, in which the influence of the former PSP communists was greatly diminished. It ceased to exist in October 1965, when the Communist Party of Cuba was established.[7]

Veteran Cuban communists and former PSP members are notable by their absence from positions of power in the new line-up of the Communist Party of Cuba. The Politburo, the central and organizational power source, is comprised entirely of individuals whose personal loyalties are first to Fidel Castro. Of the eight Politburo members not one is a veteran communist (see Table 30). Long-term Cuban communists are represented at the top level only by Blas Roca, ex-editor of the daily *Hoy,* now named the *Granma,* and economics minister Carlos Rafael Rodriquez. Both are on the Secretariat.

Suppression of veteran communists whose personal loyalties to Fidel Castro may have been in doubt and periodic public denunciation of them as not having contributed to the revolution, may well be Fidel Castro's only alternative to complete submission to Moscow. He must maintain control over the government of Cuba if he is to retain any freedom of action whatsoever and any significant political identity.

A tenuous compromise appears to have developed between Moscow and Havana on policies and staffing. For the time being, at least, Castro successfully has excluded long-term, U.S.S.R.-loyal Party members from positions of power. On the other hand, the Cuban regime, though comprised of personal followers of Castro himself, is implementing policies acceptable to the Soviet Union. However, the problem remains that the Castro regime is not doing very well in administering the country. Inexperienced and inefficient Cuban officials make mistakes which cost the Soviet Union money. Understandable pressures are being mounted to rationalize the bureaucracy by staffing the administration on the basis of capability and not just revolutionary ardor. Fidel Castro is feeling but resisting these pressures. Although he reportedly hates bureaucracy, offices, and the routine of administering the country, the Cuban leader recently described his island in rather extraordinary terms as entering the "era . . . of the institutionalization of the revolution," which means that "no one man is important any more . . . the revolution would go on under its own power."[8]

TABLE 30

Politburo of the Communist Party of Cuba (1965)

Name	Other position
Fidel Castro	First Secretary
Raul Castro	Minister of Armed Forces; Director of State Security
Osvaldo Dorticos	President; Chairman of the Economic Commission
Juan Almeida	Deputy Armed Forces Minister
Ramiro Valdes	Minister of Interior
Armando Hart	Minister of Education
Sergio del Valle	Armed Forces Chief-of-Staff
Guillermo Garcia	Commander, Armed Forces in Western Cuba

SOURCE: Radio Havana, Oct. 3, 1965.

Regardless of the Kremlin's policies with respect to Cuba's communist leadership, Castro's political future can hardly be described as bright. With time mass support of his revolution seems bound to wane. Poor economic conditions probably will expedite this process. Castro is increasing totalitarian controls, and Cuba reportedly is becoming one of the world's most tightly organized police states along with Albania and the Chinese People's Republic. "Citizens Committees for the Defense of the Revolution" exist throughout Cuba. It is reported that in some localities half the population is organized into such committees to report on the other half. Estimates of the number of political prisoners in Cuba range from 20,000 to 80,000.

Periodic and quite pervasive purges of important bureaucratic organizations such as the ministries for industries and foreign affairs have occurred. Other indicators of disaffection with the revolution are the 350,000 refugees who have fled Cuba and an estimated 800,000 who are listed as wanting to leave. Assuming that those listed as wishing to emigrate represent an approximately correct number, then the total refugees, both actual and potential, comes to over 1.1 million, or about 14 per cent of Cuba's population. Finally, there are the forced labor camps, euphemistically called "Military Units for the Aid of Production," where "unreliable" elements, including teen-age loiterers, are sent to work (usually in the cane fields) for sentences up to five years at seven dollars in monthly wages.

Castro may be in a corner. Those courses of action which would increase his regime's autonomy are likely to prove fatal to his political personality, if not to Castro himself. An effective economy could develop in Cuba under a number of circumstances but probably not under conditions of rigid totalitarianism. The staffing of key administrative posts with persons selected principally on the basis of revolutionary ardor and loyalty to Castro rather than administrative capabilities and the insistence upon violent revolution under Castro-like banners would have to give way to a more effective government and less belligerence in world politics. However a rational administration implies a bureaucracy which cannot be overly concerned with ideology. This has its implications for Castro's *jefatura*. An effective economy appears to depend in large part not only upon the Soviet Union but upon the United States and other Latin American states as well as upon Castro's abandoning his call for violent revolution. A significant shift on any or all of these interrelated issues is likely to speed up the submergence of Castro and Castroism.[9] It is for these reasons that Castro is perceived by many observers to be hanging on. His future political survival would seem to depend upon very clever maneuvering indeed.

The Economics of Survival

If Fidel Castro and his followers formerly were unaware that good revolutionaries do not necessarily make good economists and administrators, they have painfully learned that lesson by now. Counterelites and revolutionaries, particularly, in less-developed states, are rarely experienced businessmen or politicians. Revolutionaries, for the most part, are blissfully ignorant of economic ties, interdependencies, and patterns of relationships between states that are the result of trial and error evolution over decades. Revolutionaries are apt to romanticize the range of real, future political options available to them once they have acquired power. However, they quickly discover that the acquisition of power is one thing; making the system work effectively in an interdependent world is quite another matter.

It is unlikely that Fidel Castro realized in 1960 the extent to which Cuba would be catapulted from one condition of economic dependency on a major power to another. The need for U.S. manufactured spare parts for Cuban industry, transportation, and communications; the comparative shipping cost of goods from the Western Hemisphere and from Eurasia; effective hemisphere-wide economic reprisal and isolation—all were contingencies the significance of which the members of the 26th of July Movement almost certainly were not fully aware. Their implications for Castro's political freedom of action is a central factor conditioning the Cuban situation.

Cuba's economic policies under the Castro regime have changed markedly since 1960. Industrialization, economic diversification, and agricultural collectivization have given way to a re-emphasis on sugar production and the agricultural sector in general, de-emphasis of industrialization, abandonment of economic diversification in favor of a niche in the world socialist division of labor, and the use of domestic forced labor and incentives to make collectivized agriculture work.

With accession to power in 1959, Cuba's revolutionary elite manifested the now familiar "industrialization and diversification of the economy" syndrome. Both "Che" Guevara and Fidel Castro viewed Cuba's one-crop agricultural economy as a major evil to be extirpated in favor of a more industrialized and balanced economy. As a result of their prognosis, scarce foreign exchange was expended in a helter-skelter fashion for various industrial plants and facilities with little or no thought given to sources of raw materials, markets, and transportation costs.

Foreign-owned and other private industries were nationalized, and agriculture was collectivized. According to Roger Berheim, a Swiss reporter on Latin American affairs and a recent visitor to Cuba, socialization of the economy was pushed further and more rapidly than in any other socialist country. The resulting disruption of economic ties and patterns and the reorientation of Cuba's trade to sources and markets some 6,000 nautical miles distant resulted in lowered productivity in all sectors of the economy and precipitous dependency on Soviet and East European trade and assistance (see Table 34).

In agriculture the by now familiar performance in other collectivized systems also developed in Cuba. By the end of 1965 only 30 per cent of the arable land remained in private hands. Yet during that same year private holdings supplied 46 per cent of the total grain produced, 56 per cent of the root vegetables, 70 per cent of the fruit and green vegetables, and about 90 per cent of the coffee, tea, and tobacco.[10]

Sugar

With Soviet urging, the Castro regime reversed its earlier policies and in 1963 re-emphasized sugar cane production. Constituting about 80 per cent of exports in value and about one third of Cuba's national income, sugar is vital to the economic health of the island and represents its most important source of foreign exchange. Because of fluctuations in sugar prices Cuba and the United States had long-standing agreements whereby the latter paid two cents per pound above the world market price for sugar coming under an established quota. The quota in 1960 had been set at just over three million tons, or about half of Cuba's production. This amounted to a subsidy of over $100 million per year. Other preferential trade arrangements brought the U.S. subsidy closer to $150 million.[11] Cuba's sugar economy and other ties with the United States provided the island nation with one of the highest standards of living in Latin America.

When Castro came to power in Cuba, relations with the U.S. deteriorated rapidly. In February 1960 U.S.S.R. First Deputy Premier Anastas Mikoyan signed the first of a series of trade and economic aid agreements with the Cuban government pledging to buy one million tons of sugar per year over the following five years and, in return, providing $100 million in credits for the purchase of equipment in the Soviet Union. By October 1960 the United States had eliminated Cuba's sugar quota entirely and placed an embargo on all exports to Cuba except for food and medicine.[12] Thus within a matter of months Cuba was forced to reorient its foreign trade. The U.S.S.R. and the East European states sought to provide for Cuba's minimal needs by absorbing and remarketing its sugar in exchange for industrial products.

In 1963 the Castro regime gave priority to increasing sugar cane production. Despite this, however, Cuba's sugar economy is beset with two serious problems: falling world market prices and decreased production, even with the allocation of more arable land to sugar cane.

World market prices for sugar, which averaged 8 cents a pound in 1963 and 12 cents in 1964, declined precipitously in 1965 and 1966 to between 1.5 and 2 cents, the lowest in over twenty years. The drop in price is the result of increased free-world sugar production. *Business Week* (June 25, 1966) reported that the Soviet Union and the East European states are buying Cuba's sugar for about 6 cents a pound. If this is the case, then they are paying a subsidy of about 4 cents, or twice as much as the United States paid under the pre-1960 arrangements. In addition to low prices sugar production in Cuba declined to the point where it is doubtful that the island met its 1966 barter-and-sales commitments. Of that year's sugar crop Cuba had commitments to sell 4.3 million tons to communist states, some 650,000 tons to Spain, Morocco, and Egypt, and to retain 450,000 tons for home consumption. However, the 1966 harvest only totaled 4.5 million tons, resulting in a shortage of some 800,000 tons to meet the outstanding obligations (see Table 31).

Cuba's poor showing on sugar production is due in small part to adverse weather conditions. Most observers would attribute dimished produc-

388 / ASPECTS OF MODERN COMMUNISM

TABLE 31

Cuba's Sugar Production (1958–70, Plan)

(millions of metric tons)

Year	1958	1959	1960	1961	1962	1963	1964	1965	1966	1967	1970
Actual production	5.8	6.0	5.9	6.8	4.8	3.8	4.4	6.1	4.5[a]	6.0[b]	—
Goal	—	—	—	—	—	—	—	—	6.5	7.5	10.0

[a]1966 data taken from *Business Week,* June 25, 1966, p. 58.
[b]Estimated in *ibid.*

SOURCE: *The New York Times,* Jan. 16, 1966, p. 4E.

tion mainly to the personnel and economic policies of the Cuban government.

Consumer goods

Other indicators that the Cuban economy is in real trouble appear in the sector of consumer goods. Queues and rationing are symbolic of prevailing conditions. Coffee, rice, beans, canned milk, meat, potatoes, bananas, and butter are among the important rationed food items. Rice, the dominant staple in the Cuban diet, has been cut through rationing to slightly more than two thirds of earlier consumption per capita. In the late 1950's consumption of rice per capita was ten pounds per month. In 1965 the rationed allowance of rice was six pounds per person per month. In 1966 the ration was reduced further to three pounds per person per month.[13] The 1966 shortage was attributed to the growing rift between Havana and Peking: the Chinese simply discontinued their shipments of rice to Cuba.

Concerted efforts and programmatic attention did lead to some successes in food production. There was a 300 per cent increase in the 1966 egg production over the 1965 level. Also milk production has remained at the fairly high level of 1959.

Industry, transportation and communications infrastructures

The U.S.-imposed embargo on exports to Havana combined with a shortage of foreign exchange has complicated Cuba's maintenance of its industrial, transportation, and communications infrastructures. These systems remain overwhelmingly dependent on the United States for replacement parts.[14] Plants are closed for lack of spare parts, and others are shut down to be cannibalized for the purpose of keeping the remaining ones operating. A September 1966 report by Carlos Rafael Rodriguez, former minister-president of the National Institute for Agrarian Reform, stated that between 40 and 60 per cent of Cuba's industrial capacity lay idle for lack of replacement parts, a deteriorating distribution and transportation system, and shortages of raw materials. In October 1964 it was reported by *Prensa Latina* that 600 buses of American manufacture had been withdrawn from service because they had no spare parts; many were to be cannibalized. Inadequate transportation and distribution capabilities hamper other facets of the economy: materials are not distributed to the proper place at the right time, and there has been a reported tendency for warehouse facilities to be loaded beyond capacity or to be nearly empty.

An attempt by the Castro government to overcome some of the internal transportation difficulties was undertaken through the purchase of trucks, buses, and other equipment from free-world states which chose to do business with Havana despite the U.S./O.A.S. boycott (see Table 32). Other noncommunist states which trade with Cuba include Mexico, Canada, Spain, Morocco, and Egypt. It should be noted that a portion of this trade involves barter arrangements to conserve scarce foreign exchange. Over-all, however, trade with noncommunist states is small. In 1965 imports from the free world amounted to $190 million in total value, or 22 per cent of Cuba's total imports. Table 33 shows comparative trade with the free world and the communist states.

TABLE 32
Major Noncommunist States Trading with Cuba (1964–5)

Exporting State	Type of Goods	Value
Britain (Leyland Motors)	Buses	——
France (Berliet)	Trucks	——
Japan	Textiles	$13,000,000
	Consumers goods	$12,000,000
	Electronics	$ 3,000,000

SOURCE: *Business Week,* June 25, 1966, p. 60.

TABLE 33
Free-World Trade with Communist Cuba (1960–5)
(millions of U.S. $)

	1960	1961	1962	1963	1964	1965
Imports from free world	430	209	107[a]	128[b]	321	190
(Percentage of total imports)	(78%)	(29%)	(14%)	(15%)	(29%)	(22%)
Exports to free world	467	166	119	210	291	150
(Percentage of total imports)	(75%)	(27%)	(23%)	(38%)	(40%)	(22%)

[a]Excludes U.S. ransom payment of $13 million.
[b]Excludes U.S. ransom payment of $50 million.

By itself the economic boycott of Cuba has not been completely successful. However, as a part of overall U.S./O.A.S. economic policy toward the Havana regime, the boycott has made a significant contribution toward the isolation of the island: Cuba's declining economic fortunes make it a poor business partner; depressed sugar prices in particular hamper the accumulation of foreign exchange and severely limit Castro's ability to pay for free-world goods; in this way poor domestic economic conditions and scarcity of foreign exchange tend to reinforce U.S./O.A.S. endeavors to isolate Cuba and thereby increase the costs to the Soviet Union.

While the economy of Cuba is in considerable difficulty, the U.S.S.R. has shown no intention of abandoning its Caribbean ally, despite the costs. Without Soviet credits to pay for its imports Cuba's economy would probably collapse. However, assistance from the communist states appears to be on the increase.[15] Such developmental and technical aid has been used to assist over 200 different projects, factories, and other installations. Of these the major endeavors being underwritten by the U.S.S.R. include a fishing port and processing facilities in or near Havana, a nickel plant, an oil refinery, an irrigation project, and the refurbishing of existing sugar processing facilities.[16]

TABLE 34

Estimated Communist Aid to Cuba (1960–5)
(millions of U.S. $)

Type	U.S.S.R.	Eastern Europe	China	Totals
Medium and long-term economic development credits	327	107	60	494
Military assistance	na.	na.	na.	600[a]
Balance of payments credits	na.	na.	na.	900
Grand total				1.994[b]

[a]Does not include the cost of military equipment removed by the Soviets following the Oct.–Nov. 1962 missile crisis.
[b]Other estimates place total Soviet assistance a $3 billion. (*U.S. News and World Report,* April 25, 1966, p. 57) and $2.1 billion (*Business Week,* June 25, 1966, p. 60).
SOURCE: Department of State data repr. U.S. Congress, House Subcommittee on Inter-American Affairs of the Committee on Foreign Affairs, "International Communism in the Western Hemisphere," 89th Cong., 1st Sess. (Washington, D.C., August 31, 1965), p. 7.

Representative of the problems and costs the Soviets find themselves bearing to maintain their Caribbean ally is supplying the island with oil. Prior to 1961 Cuba received its petroleum from sources in the Western

Hemisphere. It was a convenient stopping point for shipments from Aruba or the U.S. Gulf Coast. Havana, Cuba, is about 800 nautical miles from the farthest of these points. The U.S.S.R., on the other hand, must now supply Cuba with its own oil over a run of 6,500 nautical miles from Black Sea ports, for a 13,000 mile round trip.[17] Transportation costs per delivered barrel must be enormous. One measure of these costs may well involve the number of tankers permanently required to keep Cuba supplied, since at an average speed of fifteen knots it would take a tanker eighteen days one way. A model for estimating tanker requirements is developed below.

At an average 1964 consumption of 81,000 barrels of petroleum products per day Cuba was not and is not a prodigious user of oil. Puerto Rico, for example, had a similar consumption at 77,000 barrels per day, whereas Venezuela, at 181,000 barrels per day, used over twice as much, and Argentina, at 347,000 barrels, consumed over three times as much. Nevertheless, an average consumption of 81,000 barrels per day is about two thirds the capacity of a notional tanker equivalent to a T-2, which has a capacity of about 120,000 barrels of crude. By making the assumptions that the average tanker supplying Cuba has a capacity of 120,000 barrels, that it transits at an average speed of fifteen knots per hour, and has a turnaround time of three days at each of its terminal points, for a total of six days in ports, it can be calculated that twenty-eight tankers are continually required to maintain Cuba in oil.[18] This is about 14 per cent of the 1964 Soviet tanker fleet[19] (see Table 35).

TABLE 35

Comparative T-2 Tanker Requirements to Supply Cuba from the
Black Sea or Aruba
(based on a notional tanker of 120,000 bbls. capacity)

Source	RT Distance (nautical miles)	Total Tanker Cycle Time[a]	Number Required at Various Average Daily Consumption Levels (barrels)		
			81,000	100,000	60,000
Black Sea	13,000	42 days	28	35	21
Aruba	1,600	10 days	7	9	5

[a]Includes fifteen knots average speed and three days in-port time at each terminal.

The above model says nothing about the requirement for dry-cargo ships. If it is assumed that only three dry-cargo ships call at Cuban ports for each tanker, then there may be as many as 112 ships, both tankers and dry-cargo types, every forty-two days just to maintain the Cuban economic system. Under the assumptions of the model an annual total of 1,008 ship sorties (tanker and dry-cargo) would be required to maintain Cuba. Free-world shipping calling at Cuban ports was as follows: 1963 (370), 1964 (394), 1965 (290), 1966 (276).

Fairly gross calculations of this kind support the inference that possible Cuban alignment and dependency on the Chinese People's Republic (C.P.R.) is more of a conceptual possibility than a real possibility. It should be noted in this regard that the estimated January 1965 merchant fleet of the C.P.R. totalled only 166 vessels. Only 19 of these were tankers. Therefore, without extensive and costly chartering of other flag ships it is very doubtful that the Chinese communists have the capability to maintain Cuba, even if they so desired. These considerations and costs would change markedly, of course, if the U.S./O.A.S. boycott ended or suffered a diminution in effectiveness.

Just how burdensome the Soviet leadership regards Cuba is unknown. Certainly, it can be expected to take every action to reduce costs. Short of abandoning the island, this could be done by making the economic system more efficient and effective and by fashioning and implementing diplomatic and political measures which would erode the economic boycott and end the isolation of Cuba within the Western Hemisphere. Also the burden of cost might become more palatable to the Kremlin if Havana could be made to serve Soviet interests more effectively in Latin America without triggering a nuclear confrontation with the United States. Apparently it is in anticipation of present and future benefits accruing to U.S.S.R. interests that the Kremlin leadership has reconciled itself to maintaining its Caribbean ally. A range of these possible uses and benefits will be examined next.

Cuba, the Soviet Union, and the United States

As a small, insular state Cuba has little or no capability to affect significantly the external environment within the Western Hemisphere or elsewhere.[20] Even its symbolic value as a communist outpost is apparently unproductive for revolutionary causes in Latin America. However, Cuba as a base for the projection of Soviet capabilities and interests is another matter entirely. The use of the island as an instrument of U.S.S.R. policy is what constitutes the threat to the United States and other noncommunist states. In this sense Cuba's power in external affairs is "other-supplied" and "other-directed."

It has been argued in this paper that Soviet policy is more likely to follow a course involving a less overt use of violence. It has been argued further that Fidel Castro really has no choice but to accept growing U.S.S.R. hegemony under prevailing conditions. However, this still leaves the problem originally posed regarding the likely uses and benefits which the Soviets may derive from Cuba. The problem from the U.S.S.R. point of view is far more difficult, given the U.S./O.A.S. ban on strategic weapons and the use of Cuba as a base for overt aggression in the Western Hemisphere. Still, there are a number of actual and potential uses, some of which will be identified and treated briefly as follows: (1) Cuba as a base for training and equipping communist subversive efforts directed at governments in Latin America, Africa, and Asia; (2) the use of Cuban soil as a politically reliable base to support a range of expanding Soviet intelligence, maritime, and naval activities and other interests; (3) the long-term possibility of developing Cuba into a communist model for the undeveloped, agriculturally oriented small state.

Cuba as a Base for Subversion

The fact that the Soviets are not stressing violent revolution and guerrilla wars of national liberation does not mean that they have eschewed violence as an instrument of policy. The concept of peaceful coexistence, as interpreted by the contemporary Moscow leadership, does not exclude armed struggle from its arsenal. It simply seeks to use it more effectively and in those places where the forces of "counterrevolution" are not so well organized. In Latin America the emerging Soviet technique appears to emphasize more a broad united front. Following the acquisition of power by "progressive" democratic elements, the communists hope to undermine the new leadership and direct the revolution. On the other hand, if a rural-based guerrilla movement seemed promising, there is nothing in U.S.S.R. pronouncements or practices that would preclude support for such a movement. In short, Moscow appears to be pursuing a flexible policy with respect to methods for furthering communist take-overs. In any case, the Kremlin does not wish to be committed to guerrilla-type violence, regardless of conditions.

Reportedly, this is one of the messages which Premier Aleksei Kosygin personally delivered to Fidel Castro at their June 1967 meeting in Havana. In this connection the outcome of the Arab-Israeli conflict was expected to reinforce the Kremlin's caution in the use of violence to further communist causes.

This more flexible approach to the acquisition of power seems to explain what often appears to be a contradictory policy on the part of the Soviet Union. A recent example was the January 1966 Tricontinental Conference (the Afro-Asian-Latin-American People's Solidarity Conference) held in Havana. A high Party official from the U.S.S.R. signed the resolution of the conference calling for the rendering of "economic, financial, and other assistance, including arms and ammunition to countries engaged in armed struggle and liberation"[21] at the same time that Kremlin diplomats were informing Latin American governments that Moscow had no intention of overthrowing them.

While the Soviets appear to have de-emphasized revolutionary violence and are certainly less overtly militant than Castro would like them to be, there is evidence that Moscow intends to maintain a capability to use Cuba as an outpost for subversive purposes. The U.S.S.R. has participated in and supported the major communist-sponsored meetings held at Havana, of which the above-mentioned January 1966 Tricontinental Conference was an example. This represented an attempt to unify dissident and subversive elements throughout the world and to develop a global strategy. The conference resulted in the establishment of organizational bodies for the purpose of setting priorities and coordinating policies.[22] A permanent executive secretariat is located in Havana with Captain Osmany Cienfuegos as secretary-general.

In addition to coordinating subversive elements throughout Latin America, potential guerrillas and revolutionaries are brought into Cuba for training. A report by John A. McCone, former director of the Central Intelligence Agency, stated that at least 1,000 to 1,500 persons from other Latin American countries had traveled to the island during 1962 for ideological indoctrination or guerrilla training or both.[23] Since then the reported number of guerrilla training and indoctrination centers in Cuba has increased fourfold, from 10 in 1963 to 43 in 1966.[24] Some of the old-time Spanish, communist-guerrilla experts are reportedly in Cuba to help run the various training programs. Two such experts have been identified in the persons of General Enrique Lister and Colonel Alberto Bayo, the latter being the author of an early work on guerrilla warfare from which "Che" Guevara reportedly borrowed liberally for his much publicized book *La Guerra de Guerrilla*. Finally, promising students may be sent to the Soviet Union for lengthy training in sabotage, intelligence, and other related arts. U.S.S.R. training programs have been reported by Cuban defectors.

Trained Cuban paramilitary personnel are reportedly active in various West African states. In October 1966 there were an estimated 500 to 1,000 Cubans in the Congo (Brazzaville) alone. Additional Cubans operate in Guinea and other areas as well. The purpose of these forces is believed to include the training and staffing of guerrilla groups to support dissident and subversive elements in other African states, and training and equipping a Congolese militia to support leftist-leaning President Alphonse Massamba-Debat against his own more conservative army. These Cuban efforts allegedly are being undertaken with Soviet financial support and equipment.[25]

Cuba as a Base in Support of Direct Soviet Maritime, Naval and Other Activities

The U.S.S.R. failed in 1962 to use Cuba as a base for offensive strategic missile systems. It remains under notice that the U.S./O.A.S. will not permit the basing of such systems on the island. Nevertheless, there are a number of possibilities for using Cuba in ways that would enhance the effectiveness of certain Soviet strategic systems or permit a reduction in their cost. Strategic systems based on Cuba could look sufficiently ambiguous as to make a response by United States difficult. Some possibilities along this line include land and ocean-based electronic and hydroacoustic intelligence facilities, and the direct or indirect basing of Soviet submarines.

The U.S.S.R. has the largest and most modern, ocean-going fishing fleet in the world. Cuban basing is a great convenience and an economy for the Soviet fishing fleet. It allows for a more efficient use of the fleet by decreasing the amount of time necessary to shuttle between the Soviet Union and South Atlantic fishing grounds. Cuba also provides a place for crew rest. Plans call for the development of a large fish processing plant and for the expansion of facilities to repair and home-port a large fishing fleet in Cuba.

Finally, it should be noted that in addition to some limited intelligence gathering capabilities, a fishing fleet could be used to transport a sizable number of men and supplies to remote areas. It might be applied directly in support of guerrilla or other subversive-insurrectionary activities.

Cuba is an island which is some 780 miles long. Portions of its land area overlook the U.S. Gulf Coast, the Eastern seaboard, parts of the Atlantic sea lanes, Central America including the eastern approaches to the Panama Canal, and the northern coast of South America. It may be possible that intelligence facilities, based on Cuban soil, could monitor part, if not all, of the maritime and naval traffic along these littorals as well as some of the space activities of the United States. Such systems as long-range radars, radio-direction finders, and hydroacoustic facilities based on Cuba may come to make a significant contribution to Soviet surveillance activities.

It is possible that the Soviets might try to base strategic, missile-firing submarines in Cuba despite the ban against offensive weapons.[26] It would be of considerable advantage for them to do so, given their apparent desire to attain a reasonably reliable and invulnerable nuclear force. For the U.S.S.R. to operate missile-firing submarines from the Kola Peninsula to a station, say, 100 miles off the coast of New York would be enormously expensive. Submarines are crew-endurance limited, if not always fuel-endurance restricted. Since it is 4,000 miles one way, or 8,000 miles round trip from Kola, several weeks would be spent in transiting to and from the deployment station. Depending upon operating doctrine, transit speeds, crew and fuel endurance limitations, it would require five or more submarines just to keep one on station (that is, four or more back somewhere in the pipeline and one forward). Whereas basing submarines in Cuba would gain a 75 per cent reduction in distance and would allow deployments on a one-for-one basis, i.e., one back and one forward. For submarine stations in the Gulf of Mexico the requirements to operate from Kola become even more formidable, while Cuba basing could be carried out on a one-for-one basis.

Since direct support of submarines from Cuba might trigger a U.S.–Soviet confrontation, the U.S.S.R. might very well consider the contingency of indirect basing for its submarines. Assuming the submarines are always crew-endurance limited and, if nonnuclear, then also fuel-endurance limited, Soviet submarines could operate directly from their bases in the U.S.S.R. to stations off the coasts of the United States. They could be met then, somewhere at sea, and supported by tenders or other types of ships that base in Cuba. Submarines could be refuelled and replenished from fishing-fleet support vessels, and entire crews could be exchanged and taken by surface vessel to Cuba for rest. In this way, or some variant of it, the Soviets could maintain the fiction that no strategic weapons were based on Cuban soil, since no submarine need actually approach or directly use Cuban ports. Yet the U.S.S.R. could gain significant benefits from Cuba basing and enjoy a reduction in operating costs for a sea-based missile system. On-station time per submarine might be doubled or tripled, and thus submarines in the pipeline shuttling to and from Soviet ports could be reduced to a less costly ratio to maintain one on forward station.[27]

The U.S.S.R. reportedly has embarked upon a program to build up its merchant marine. Cuba could play an important role in support of Soviet long-time maritime aspirations. As a politically reliable base it could serve as an entrepôt, a transshipment facility, and as a repair, bunkering, and crew-rest facility. Furthermore, as a Western Hemisphere base supporting U.S.S.R. trade with Latin America, the diplomatic positions of both Cuba and the Soviet Union would be strengthened for a larger voice in any proposed schemes for international control of a future canal across the isthmus of Central America. If not the Soviets, then Cuba could make a strong demand for access to any canal-control schemes, based upon a regional international organization or upon actual or potential traffic through a canal.

Cuba as a Showcase Model

Given the stringent economic conditions in present-day Cuba, it is somewhat paradoxical to treat the island as a prospective socialist economic success worthy of showing off. While it is not a likely contingency, it is possible that the situation might develop very well for the Soviets and the Cuban communists in the future: the economic boycott could falter or end; Cuba might solve its domestic economic and managerial problems; it conceivably could gain access to Venezuelan or other nearby oil sources; and the Soviet Union might more easily supply Cuba through its projected merchant fleet of the 1970's. If these transformations were to occur, the symbolic importance of Cuba for the undeveloped world would become very greatly enhanced.

The fact that Cuba had been a relatively well-developed economic system at the time of the communist take-over would be suppressed. Instead, Cuba's identification as a member of the Afro-Asian grouping of less-developed and "exploited" states would continue to be stressed. For the benefit of target audiences throughout the undeveloped world, communist propaganda could be expected to make a great deal of publicity out of a Cuba which successfully had sundered its "imperialist shackels" and, by following the socialist political and economic model, emerged a success.

Conclusions

Whatever aspirations the leaders of the 26th of July Movement might have held for Cuba's greater international autonomy have foundered on the rock-hard lessons of twentieth-century international power relationships. Cuba probably has less autonomy now than in the years prior to Castro. In effect, Cuba is a satellite of the Soviet Union.

For Fidel Castro there does not seem to be any real option that would permit the survival of his person and regime other than close accommodation with the Soviet Union. The pressures of this association on the (Cuban) regime are in the direction of greater bureaucratization and more pervasive totalitarian controls. Castro's charisma seems to have passed its peak and probably will continue to diminish with time, bureaucratization, and Soviet hegemony.

This is not to say that Cuba does all of the accommodating. The Soviets do some and probably suffer a good deal from some of Castro's actions. However, from the point of view of the U.S.S.R., continuing to support and to encourage Fidel Castro's hold over the Cuban people is probably seen as the cheapest and least risky form of communist rule, at least for the time being.

Despite the high costs of maintaining Cuba the Soviets are likely to retain their Caribbean outpost. They will seek to reduce their costs and to increase their benefits. In this connection they probably will try to dispel the image of Cuba as a threat to other Latin American states in order to gain greater diplomatic and economic acceptance within the Western Hemisphere. However, Cuba will continue to serve, with some U.S.S.R. backing, as a base for furthering revolutionary interests. The precise tactics will depend upon prevailing conditions within the Hemisphere. Cuba probably fits nicely into long-range Soviet ambitions to realize the maritime and naval capabilities of a great power. It can serve as a base for both U.S.S.R. and Cuban fishing fleets, for merchant shipping, and in support of strategic systems of direct military value to the Soviet Union.

The relationship between the Caribbean charismatic leader and the U.S.S.R. appears to be unstable under the geographic conditions and prevailing political and economic conditions and constraints. The possibilities for conflict, not directly precipitated by U.S. policy, are numerous. For example, Castro, in a sort of suicide move, could embroil the United States and the Soviet Union by attacking the U.S. naval base at Guantanamo. The U.S.S.R., under pressure to translate its Caribbean liability into an asset, may precipitate another crisis like that in October 1962 by pursuing policies unacceptable to the United States. An insurrection could possibly occur within Cuba despite the totalitarian controls. In this regard the experiences in Poland, East Germany, and Hungary cannot be a comfort to either the Castro regime or to the Soviets. This is particularly the case since Cuba not only lacks geographic contiguity with another communist state but also is several thousand miles from the U.S.S.R. Finally, U.S. policy with respect to Cuba cannot be of comfort to Fidel Castro or to the Soviet leadership. Stated American policy seeks to bring about those conditions which will encourage the Cuban people to eliminate communism from Cuba. This along with the reality of Cuba's geographic location is another important factor which distinguishes Cuba from the other communist-ruled states.

Notes to Chapter 14

1. U.S. Congress, House Subcommittee on Inter-American Affairs of the Committee on Foreign Affairs, 88th Cong., 1st Sess., *Castro-Communist Subversion in the Western Hemisphere: Hearings* (Washington, D.C., Feb. 1963), p. 257.

2. The February 1966 trade agreement will raise the exchange of goods between the U.S.S.R. and Cuba from $747 million to $914 million, a 22 per cent increase over the previous year. This means that the Soviet Union will absorb more of Cuba's subsidized sugar, paying possibly as much as 6 cents per pound, while the world market price is currently less than 2 cents. SOURCE: Brig. Gen Edwin F. Black, Director, Western Hemispheric Region, Office of the Secretary of Defense (ISA), *Washington Report,* WR 66-30 (Aug. 8, 1966), p. 3.

3. Roger Bernheim, "Cuba's Permanent Revolution—II," *Swiss Review of World Affairs* (Nov. 1966), p. 10.

4. U.S. Department of State, Bureau of Intelligence and Research, "The Communist Economic Offensive Through 1964," Research Memorandum RSB-65 (Aug. 4, 1965), p. 6.

5. José Manuel Fortuny, "Has the Revolution Become More Difficult in Latin America?" *World Marxist Review* (Aug. 1965), p. 39.

6. Robert M. Sayre, Deputy Assistant Secretary for Inter-American Affairs, "Review of Movement of Cuban Refugees and Hemisphere Policy

Toward Cuba," *The Department of State Bulletin* (May 2, 1966), p. 709.

7. See David D. Burks, "Cuba: Seven Years After," *Current History* (June 1966), p. 38.

8. Quoted from "Atlantic Report: Cuba," *The Atlantic* (Nov. 1966), p. 28.

9. One of Theodore Draper's major points deals with the necessity for Castro to maintain his identity within the communist world. Failure to do so, Draper believes, will result in the disappearance of Castro and Castroism. See his *Castroism: Theory and Practice* (New York, 1965).

10. *Prensa Latina,* Sep. 23, 1966.

11. Leland L. Johnson, "U.S. Business Interests in Cuba and the Rise of Castro," *World Politics* (Apr. 1965), p. 445.

12. *The Cuban Crisis of 1962: Selected Documents and Chronology* ed. David L. Larson (Boston, 1963), p. 297.

13. *U.S. News and World Report,* Apr. 25, 1966, p. 56.

14. Sayre, *op. cit.,* p. 710.

15. Black, *op. cit.,* p. 3.

16. "International Communism in the Western Hemisphere," *op. cit.,* p. 7.

17. See the interview with the U.S.S.R. merchant marine minister in *Soviet Life,* XI:6 (June 1967), 4–5.

18. According to the model it requires 42 days for the first tanker to complete the cycle. Since two tankers must unload every 3 days, two thirds of 42 tankers, or 28 tankers, is the minimum required.

19. U.S. Department of Commerce, Maritime Commission, *Merchant Fleets of the World,* Report Number MAR-560-20 (Apr. 16, 1965), pp. 4–5.

20. The Institute for Strategic Studies, *The Military Balance, 1966–67,* (London, 1966), p. 11, contains data on the Cuban armed forces.

21. For the wording of the resolution, signed by Soviet delegate Sharif Rashidov, member of the Central Committee of the Party and candidate member of this Politburo, see Sayre, *op. cit.,* p. 711.

22. Black, *op. cit.,* p. 1.

23. U.S. Congress, House Subcommittee on Inter-American Affairs of the Committee on Foreign Affairs, 88th Cong., 1st Sess., *op. cit.,* p. 256.

24. Black, *op. cit.* p. 3.

25. *The New York Times,* Oct. 23, 1966, p. 20.

26. An investigation by this writer of the publicly available literature on the 1962 crisis turned up nothing specifically banning foreign submarines from Cuba. It should be noted that U.S./O.A.S. governments appear concerned with the possibility of Soviet submarines, since they are reportedly cooperating to develop antisubmarine warfare capabilities off the Central and South American coasts. See statement by Congressman Daniel J. Flood, House Subcommittee on Inter-American Affairs, 89th Cong., 1st Sess., *International Communism in the Western Hemisphere* (Washington, D.C.: Sep. 1, 1965), p. 31.

27. While the above discussion is concerned with strategic missile-firing submarines, the same deployment cost and basing considerations apply to other types of submarines as well, such as the antishipping attack type used in a more traditional interdiction role.

Discussion

HENRY H. KEITH

The foregoing paper is of interest regarding what it covers as well as what it does not. These comments will be directed at the two categories, beginning with the material discussed. They will center chiefly on exceptions which should be taken and with questions concerning the evidence presented and the interpretation rendered. Later remarks will concentrate on items omitted, which are essential to an understanding of the *castrismo* phenomenon.

Professor Wilson indicates in his paper that there appears to be a growing disenchantment and exasperation on the part of the Soviet personnel presently working in Cuba, and he infers that this can be taken as an indication of a stiffening of trade terms which the U.S.S.R. offers Cuba. It is unfortunate that the nature and quality of evidence to support this contention cannot be described as conclusive. One Soviet engineer's criticism in Cuba and even many East European communist opinions that Castro is a "buffoon" can hardly qualify as indicators that the U.S.S.R. leadership would be willing or able to alter its policy of aid to Cuba unless other factors came into play.

One can only sympathize with the writer when he points out the difficulty of measuring what Cuban aid costs the Soviet Union. Therefore, to characterize the cost as "substantial" places an undue burden upon Professor Wilson's initial point that such matters are difficult to ascertain. In spite of the obstacles inherent in assessing Soviet expenditures, perhaps one might suggest that new ways of analyzing publicly available U.S.S.R. statistics be considered. For example, it is possible to calculate a series of items which could reflect the type of enterprises that must be foregone by the Soviet Union (such as manufacturing installations) with a resultant deprivation of urgently desirable programs to stimulate further economic growth. The point is that there should be concrete ways in which one can measure the sacrifice which Cuban aid represents to the U.S.S.R. In the United States many observers seem quite certain that the escalating involvement in Vietnam means cutbacks in domestic programs previously introduced by the present Administration, such as the "War on Poverty." What programs must the Soviets defer in order to continue aid at present levels to Cuba? This would seem to offer possibilities for fruitful analysis. The order of priority for Cuban aid must be very high indeed. What one needs is some attempt at determining the level of that priority on a comparative basis.

Professor Wilson sets forth alternatives open to the U.S.S.R., but he does not suggest the alternative of retaining Soviet interests in Cuba without expansionism. From his own comments it seems clear that Moscow has been pragmatic in the kind of alternatives adopted (and adapted) for different places at different times. The possibility could be raised that the U.S. and U.S.S.R. might negotiate an agreement providing, in return for an American rapprochement with Cuba (leaving the Castro regime intact, of course) and including restoration of normal trade relations, that the Soviet Union would discontinue use of Cuba as a base for undermining U.S. influence in Latin America and elsewhere. It would seem, incidentally, that U.S.S.R. use of Cuba as a base for subversion is very much conditioned by what Fidel Castro may wish to do at any given time. It is conceivable (and indeed probable) that the nature and type of subversion as well as the timing depends far more upon Fidel Castro's judgment than upon that of the Kremlin leadership. Professor Wilson could have gone into a consideration of the possibility that it might be in the Soviet interest to keep Castro "reined" as much as possible (when his goals differ from those of the U.S.S.R.) and to await or perhaps to work for his demise in the hope that a more malleable and reliable regime might follow.

A strong exception must be entered here to Professor Wilson's assertion that the Soviet Union scored a "near success" in the Dominican Republic during the recent civil war. Unless he is privy to information which has not been made available to the public, there appears to be little reason to draw the inference that the U.S.S.R. directed the rebel movement. Indeed, there is no convincing evidence upon which to base the conclusion that the communists, regardless of orientation, whether Soviet, Castroite, or Chinese, were really in control of the Dominican rebellion. Perhaps it should be stressed that most nonofficial sources, such as Tad Szule's *Dominican Diary,* make the point that the extent of communist control over the Dominican rebellion was far from clear to everyone concerned, including the communists themselves.

Regarding the degree of predominance of the U.S.S.R. in Cuba, some doubts must be expressed and questions raised. The fact that "Che" Guevara disappeared from Cuba does not necessarily mean that the Soviets are responsible for his removal (although this may well have been the case). What is the proof of this? Secondly, the happy fact that Fidel Castro's speeches last only two hours instead of five does not allow the inference that the U.S.S.R. exercises a restraining hand on the Cuban premier's oratorical powers and speechwriting. One might be closer to the truth in speculating on the possibility that Castro feels more confidence and does not need to harangue his followers so interminably. The *Christian Science Monitor* (January 6, 1967) has indicated that Castro is speaking from positions of increased strength as a result of his firm command over the regime in Cuba. One should not forget that Fidel Castro is in his ninth year of control and that he is beginning to gain a significant measure of respectability in Europe. The Cuban leader's style is obviously changing, and this is probably predicated upon his successful control of the island and its people.

This leads to a consideration of Castro's political future. Professor Wilson would have one believe that the Cuban dictator "may be in a corner" because of the extension of totalitarian controls over his people, not to mention repeated economic failure. The crucial point is, not whether Castro is popular, but how well he personally manages to control his regime and people. Popularity and communist regimes are hardly compatible, although there is no communist regime which does not take into account political and economic groups in building and maintaining its support. Purges, shake-ups, political imprisonments, etc., are endemic to communist systems, particularly in the initial period of their existence. The important point is that various institutional controls (and they may assume myriad forms) are evolved to ensure the permanence of the regimes. In the case of Castro controls have developed along strongly personalist lines. His own political "life expectancy" has probably never really depended upon popularity, except perhaps in the first days following the events which brought him to power. At any rate, Castro's popularity has never been tested, since no free elections have been held in Cuba (or in any other communist state), and there is no likelihood of them in the future. The central issue at stake here is that Castro remains bent on retaining *personal* control. As Ernst Halperin states in *Current History* (December 1966): "Love of absolute power is his controlling passion. He will not share power or permanently delegate it even to close companions. In 1959, he could easily have had himself elected president of a democratic Cuban republic. But he would inevitably have had to share and delegate power, and he would have been restricted by constitutional provisions and legislative and judiciary institutions. By continuing the revolution he prevented establishment of institutional controls. As in most such regimes, there is much private gambling and circulation of anti-regime jokes. But the dictator's decisions are never publicly challenged or even mildly criticized, and all attempts at organized opposition are immediately suppressed."

With reference to Castro's charisma and its practical effect Halperin states that it is operative to the extent of commanding 5 to 10 per cent of the active population (about 100,000 fanatics). In Halperin's words this represents "more than enough to control a country of seven million in which there are no elections and any organized opposition or even public dissent is punished as a crime." Halperin concludes by making the essential point that institutionalization of totalitarian dictatorship may carry in it the seeds of potential discord. "It thus appears that institutionalization, which is so often regarded as a prerequisite to totalitarian dictatorship, is actually a long-term threat to its existence."

Fidel Castro's interest may not be efficiency at all, but even the reverse. Since the industrialization program failed, he has turned to the traditional monocultural alternative, which also has meant increased dependence on the Soviet Union. The permanence of the Castro regime has indeed been built upon the foundations of dependence, primarily upon the U.S.S.R. and secondarily upon other communist states. In perspective Cuba's customary dependence upon the United States has been shifted to the Soviet Union. It is noteworthy that the role of Cuba as a dependent has not altered, only the object of that dependence. It was not clear to Castro that the pattern of dependence would be of the traditional monocultural type until after the experiment in industrialization had failed (1963), a failure largely brought about by the departure of technically skilled personnel. But by this time Castro had convinced the U.S.S.R. (and the rest of the world) that he was a bona fide communist and that Cuba was a full-fledged member of the communist family. Castro has been able to bring about greater involvement with and dependence upon the Soviet Union as the means to prevent American intervention.

At the risk of belaboring a point, the problem of Fidel Castro's charisma is mentioned and its possible attenuation due to the "threat" posed by bureaucratization of the Cuban regime. Professor Wilson is in agreement with Theodore Draper when he says that "Castro's charisma seems to have passed its peak and probably will continue to diminish with time, bureaucratization, and Soviet hegemony." This evaluation can be questioned; for example, the above-cited Ernst Halperin has done so effectively: "Castro is an innovator in the art of totalitarian control. His charisma enables him to rule by not allowing organizations and institutions to take a definite shape. One might call this the principle of permanent revolution through incessant disorganization. To phrase it thus at least shows up the innate instability of the system: as long as there is no institutionalization, the fate of the regime hangs on one thread—the life of the charismatic dictator."

Professor Wilson makes an essential point when he states that the one important factor which distinguishes communist Cuba from the other communist-ruled states is the avowed U.S. policy to encourage the Cuban people to eliminate communism. He might also have mentioned that this American objective probably has had the net effect of reinforcing Castro's regime within Cuba by promoting national unity under the dictator's personal leadership.

This leads to a consideration of the fundamental goals of Soviet policy vis-à-vis Latin America and the degree to which these objectives may be in agreement with the Castro regime's objectives. Professor Wilson's paper does not enter into a full discussion of this subject, but it may be of interest to provide a brief consideration of it here. One highly reliable source (which cannot, unfortunately, be quoted) indicates that as early as May 1963 U.S.S.R. policy in Latin America was guided by two basic principles: (1) to unify all left-wing and nationalist (i.e., anti-American) forces in an effort to promote a "nationalist and bourgeois democratic" revolution; and (2) at a later stage to encourage a socialist (i.e., communist-controlled) upheaval to follow the bourgeois revolution. It does not appear that these basic objectives have altered in any significant way. The Soviet Union's problem in the Western Hemisphere may be characterized as three-fold: (1) how and when to promote the kind of revolutions in Latin America which it wishes to occur; (2) how to keep the Castro regime in line with these objectives; and (3) how to prevent the tension between Washington and Havana from exploding, which might have a deleterious effect upon over-all planning and timing for U.S.S.R.-oriented revolutions in Latin America. The Soviets have been able up to the present to keep tensions between Cuba and the U.S. from reaching the danger point, but they have had their problems in restraining Fidel Castro in his training of revolutionaries from other parts of Latin America. The main reason Moscow would like to see Cuba drop its support of armed violence in Latin America is that the more Castro meddles in the affairs of other Latin American countries, the less the U.S. will allow Cuba to build its own socialism in peace and quiet.

It should be made clear that Fidel Castro's success in securing a definite commitment by the U.S.S.R. to support his personalist regime was undoubtedly bought at the price of having Cuban–U.S. relations very largely under the control of Moscow. This is not to suggest that Fidel Castro is a "puppet" of the Soviet Union in its dealings with other countries, communist-ruled or not. The Havana regime has shown increasing independence in the area of its foreign relations (except for the U.S.), particularly in regard to trade agreements, which are often negotiated on an *ad hoc* basis. In this respect Cuba reflects the growing tendency among communist-ruled states toward polycentrism.

Professor Wilson's paper might have been enriched by the inclusion of comments on the recent interview with Fidel Castro which appeared in the January 1967 issue of that venerable scholarly journal *Playboy*. Perhaps the most revealing statement is Castro's assertion that the U.S. had made a noninvasion pledge to the Soviet Union and to Cuba during the missile crisis. Castro was asked if the agreement was still in effect, and his reply included the following:

> This is indisputable. The agreement is a matter of both fact and legality. The United States has since alleged that because we haven't permitted inspection, there is no such agreement: but *de facto*, they accept it. They acknowledge that the Soviet Union has fulfilled its part of the bargain. Thus, they are required to fulfill theirs. On more than one occasion they

have made declarations that the agreement doesn't exist. But that agreement, as I said, exists *de facto,* and I can say to you that even *more* agreements exist besides, about which not a word has ever been said. However, I don't think this is the occasion to speak about them. I am not writing my memoirs; I am a prime minister in active service. One day, perhaps, it will be known that the United States made some other concessions in relation to the October crisis besides those that were made public.

Another matter of interest in the interview was Castro's comments on Cuba's shift-over to agriculture, the traditional monoculture of sugar as the mainstay of the Cuban economy. As Professor Wilson rightly points out, the U.S.S.R is willing to pay a much higher price than that of the world market for Cuban sugar, thus conferring a sizable subsidy on the Castro regime while allowing it to make dollar purchases in Europe, such as the recently announced British fertilizer plant. What does this policy actually mean in terms of Soviet strategy? Perhaps it means that the Kremlin has decided that it is a good deal less costly to subsidize Cuba this way than it is to try helping massively with industrialization. At least this has been the case since "Che" Guevara's disappearance.

One last point of interest in the Castro interview is the role which he envisages for himself in the future. He lays stress on two things: eternal youth and his commitment to agriculture. The latter one might call the "Father Earth" image. This is the way Castro phrases it:

> It is more difficult for me to imagine myself as an old man than as a retired statesman, because of the hardship it will be for me not to be able to climb mountains, to swim, to go spear-fishing and to engage in all the other pastimes that I enjoy. But there is one thing to which I am very much attracted that old age will not deter me from: studying, experimenting, and working in agriculture. When I retire, I will be able to devote all my working time to that. So I don't think I will be bored. But perhaps I will fall into that habit that comes to all of us, of thinking that the younger generation is bungling everything. That is a mania characteristic of all old people—but I'm going to try to remain alert against it.

A last comment applies to the interdependence of charisma, *caudillismo,* and communism in Fidel Castro. The fascinating thing for the historian of Latin America is that the indigenous plant of *caudillismo,* with a Castro twist, has managed to survive and even thrive in Cuba while under the greatest pressure from international communist leadership, not to mention that from the United States. Professor Wilson's study would have benefitted from some attention to this phenomenon, which is truly *sui generis.*

Finally, there is ample evidence to lead one to conclude that as long as there is a Fidel Castro, Castroism, the Cuban "variant" in the "communist family of revolutions," as Theodore Draper calls it, will survive. Professor

Wilson is correct when he states that Castro will need to do fancy footwork, but he has provided a convincing demonstration of his technique in the past. There does not seem to be any reason to believe that he has forgotten any of the old steps or cannot invent many more complex ones in the intricate choreography of the world power conflict.

notes on contributors

BALLIS, WILLIAM B. Professor of Political Science, University of Michigan. Author of *The Legal Position of War* (1937); *The Mongolian People's Republic* (1957).

BILINSKY, YAROSLAV Associate Professor of Political Science, University of Delaware. Author of *Perspectives on Soviet Youth* (1960); *The Second Soviet Republic: The Ukraine After World War II* (1964).

CHEN, ARTHUR SHU-YUAN Research Social Scientist (South & Southeast Asia), Aerospace Studies Institute, Air University, Maxwell AFB, Alabama. Author of many USAF publications; *Military Aspects of World Political Geography* (co-author).

CHENG, CHU-YUAN Research Economist, Center for Chinese Studies, University of Michigan. Author of *Communist China's Economy: 1949–1962* (1963); *Economic Relations Between Peking and Moscow* (1964); *Scientific and Engineering Manpower in Communist China, 1949–1963* (1966).

DOMES, JUERGEN Academic Counsellor (Associate Professor) and Head, Research Unit on Chinese and East-Asian Politics, Otto-Suhr-Institute, Free University of Berlin; member, Academic Advisory Council, German Association for East-Asian Studies. Author of *Mehrheitsfraktion und Bundesregierung* (1964); *Von der Volkskommune zur Krise in China* (1964); *Politik und Herrschaft in Rotchina* (1965); *Entwicklungsländer zwischen nationaler und kommunisticher Revolution* (1965, co-author); *Der chinesische Kommunismus—Zur Geistes- und politischen Geschichte* (1966).

DRAGNICH, ALEX N. Professor of Political Science, Vanderbilt University. Author of *Tito's Promised Land* (1954); *Yugoslavia* (1949), *The Fate of East Central Europe* (1956) co-author; *Government and Politics: An Introduction to Political Science* (1966, editor and co-author).

GROSS, HERMANN Professor of Economics and Director of the Institute for Economy and Sociology of Southeastern Europe, University of Munich; co-editor *Osteuropa-Wirtschaft* (Stuttgart) and *East European Quarterly* (University of Colorado). Co-author of *Wirtschaft und Gesellschaft Südosteuropas* (1961); *Berlin and the Future of Eastern Europe*

(1966); *Jahrbuch der internationalen Politik 1963; Grosse und Gros-senstruktur der Unternehmen* (1964); *Südosteuropa-Jahrbuch (*1957, 1959, 1960, 1966).

HARVEY, MOSE L.   Director, Institute for Advanced International Studies, University of Miami. Author of *The Development of Russian Commerce on the Black Sea and Its Significance* (1938); *War as a Social Institution* (1941, co-author); *The Threat of Soviet Imperialism* (1954, co-author); *Focus on the Soviet Challenge* (1963); *East-West Trade and United States Policy* (1966).

HAUPTMANN, JERZY   Professor and Chairman, Department of Political Science, Park College, Missouri; editor, *The Midwest Review of Public Administration* and *The Lutheran Scholar.* Author of *The Dilemmas of Politics* (1958); *Problems in Political Theory* (1961, co-author); *Berlin and the Future of Eastern Europe* (1966, co-author); *Western Policy and Eastern Europe* (1966, co-author).

HOANG, VAN CHI   Vietnamese writer and lecturer on Vietnam. Author of *The Fate of the Last Viets* (1956); *The New Class in North Vietnam* (1958); *From Colonialism to Communism: A Case History of North Vietnam* (1963); *Vietnam: Seen From East and West* (1966, co-author).

KEITH, HENRY H.   Instructor, Department of History, University of South Carolina.

KINTNER, WILLIAM R.   Deputy Director, Foreign Policy Research Institute, University of Pennsylvania; Professor of Political Science, Wharton School, University of Pennsylvania. Author of *The Front is Everywhere* (1950); *Atomic Weapons in Land Combat* (1953, co-author); *Forging a New Sword* (1958); *Protracted Conflict* (1959); *The Haphazard Years* (1960); *A Forward Strategy for America* (1961); *The New Frontier of War* (1962); *Building the Atlantic World* (1963); *Peace and the Strategy Conflict* (1967).

KULSKI, WLADYSLAW W.   James B. Duke Professor, Department of Political Science, Duke University. Author of *Germany from Defeat to Conquest: 1913–1933* (1945, under the pseudonym W. M. Knight-Patterson); *The Soviet Regime: Communism in Practice* (1954, 1956, 1959, 1964); *Peaceful Co-existence: An Analysis of Soviet Foreign Policy (*1959); *International Politics in a Revolutionary Age* (1964); *De Gaulle and the World: The Foreign Policy of the Fifth French Republic* (1966).

LEE, YOUNG HO   Assistant Professor, Department of Political Science, University of Georgia.

McCONNELL, JAMES M.   Professional Staff Member, Center for Naval Analyses of the University of Rochester, Arlington, Virginia.

SOKOL, EDWARD D.   Professor of History, University of Georgia. Author of *The Revolt of 1916 in Russian Central Asia* (1954).

STAAR, RICHARD F.   Professor of Foreign Affairs, The National War College, on leave-of-absence from position as Professor and Chairman, Department of Political Science, Emory University. Author of *Poland, 1944–1962: The Sovietization of a Captive People* (1962); *The Communist Regimes in Eastern Europe: An Introduction* (1967).

SUH, DAE-SOOK   Assistant Professor of Political Science, University of Houston. Author of *The Korean Communist Movement, 1918–1949* (1967).

TURNER, CARL B.   Associate Professor of Economics, North Carolina State University. Author of *An Analysis of Soviet Views on John Maynard Keynes* (1968).

WALKER, RICHARD L.   Director, Institute of International Studies, University of South Carolina. Author of *Western Language Periodicals on China* (1949); *Multi-State System of Ancient China* (1954); *China under Communism: The First Five Years* (1955); *China and the West: Cultural Collision* (1956); *The Continuing Struggle: Communist China and the Free World* (1958); *Democracy Confronts Communism in World Affairs* (1965, editor); *The China Danger* (1966).

WEATHERBEE, DONALD E.   Assistant Professor of International Studies, University of South Carolina. Author of *Ideology in Indonesia: Sukarno's Indonesian Revolution* (1966).

WHITING, KENNETH R.   Professor of Eurasian History, Air University, Maxwell AFB, Alabama. Author of *Ideologies in Conflict* (1960); *The Soviet Union Today* (1962; rev. ed, 1966); *The Development of the Soviet Armed Forces, 1917–1966* (1966).

WILSON, DESMOND P., JR.   Professional Staff Member, Center for Naval Analyses of the University of Rochester, Arlington, Virginia. Co-author of study for the Chief of Naval Operations on U. S. Navy overseas base requirements in the 1970's (1965).

ZYZNIEWSKI, STANLEY JOHN   Associate Professor of History and Chairman, Russian Area Studies Program, University of Kentucky. *Russian Thought and Politics* (1957, co-author); *Eastern Europe in the Sixties* (1963, co-author); *Yearbook of the American Philosophical Society* (1963, co-author); *Russia and the Polish Question after 1863* (forthcoming). Now deceased.

index

Albania, xi, xii, 17 (chart I), 18 (table 1), 120 (table 3), 124 (table 4), 135 (table 6), 157 (table 9), 380, 384
Almeida, Juan, 384 (table 30)
Antiballistic missile system, 13, 58, 100, 188
Apparatchik, 30, 32
Apra Harbor, Guam, 105
Argentina, 391
Army of the Rhine, British, 180
Aruba, Netherlands Antilles, 391
Australia, 350
Autarchy, in China, 227; COMECON, 171; North Vietnam, 372; Soviet Union, 60, 62, 64, 67, 79

B

Bacilek, Karol, 129
Bad Schreiberhau. *See* Szklarska Poreba
Bandung, Indonesia, 211
Bayo, Colonel Alberto, 394
Belgium, 359
Belgrade, Yugoslavia, 117
Beria, Lavrenty P., 28, 38, 53
Berlin, blockade of, 27, 76; East sector, 130, 146; ultimatum, 29, 58, 99, 112, 173; wall, 134, 377
Bessarabia. *See* Moldavia
Bilinsky, Dr. Andreas, 56
Bita, Piro, 124 (table 4)
Blagojević, Dušan, 125
Bogdo-Gegen, 291, 292
Brazil, xvii
Brezhnev, Leonid I., at Bialowieza conference, 125; at Bucharest, 184; bureaucratic past, 4; domestic policy, 55; ideology, 95; influence of, 30, 53, 122; in Mongolia, 308; secretary-general, 30; on Warsaw Pact, 183; on world conference, xix
Britain, 389 (table 32)
Bucharest, Romania, as Cominform center, 117; COMECON center, 146; Declaration of, 182–87; Warsaw Pact meeting, 126
Budapest, Hungary, as COMECON cen-

ter, 146; Cominform meeting, 117; party congress, 133; preliminary world conference, xix, 121; revolt at, 130
Bukovina (Northern), U.S.S.R., 128
Bulganin, Nikolai N., 303
Bulgaria, 17 (chart I), 18 (table 1), 120 (table 3), 124 (table 4), 127 (table 5), 135 (table 6), 155 (table 7), 157 (table 9), 159 (table 10), 161 (table 11), 165 (table 12)
Burma, neutrality of, 362; trade with North Vietnam, 350, 358

C

Cambodia, xvi, 358, 369
Canada, 389
Capitalism, xix, 69
Castro, Fidel, as buffoon, 378–79, 400; *caudillismo* of, 12, 382, 405; charisma of, 4, 382, 397, 402–3; controls by, 385, 403; economic policies, 385–92; First Secretary, 384 (table 30); future, 384–85, 402; loyalty to, 382–83; as Marxist-Leninist, 381–82; missile crisis, 380, 404–5; relations with China, xvii, 216–17; with United States, 392–93, 398; with U.S.S.R., xvii, xviii, 377 ff.; respectability in Europe, 401–2; subversive policies of, 393–94, 404
Castro, Raul, 384 (table 30)
Caudillismo. See Castro, Fidel
Ceauşescu, Nicolae, biography of, 120, 121 (table 2); relations with China, 133; with U.S.S.R., x, 183–85, 191
Ceylon, 358
Ch'en Yi, Marshal, 268, 273, 307
Ch'en Yün, 273
Chervenkov, Vulko, 120
Chiang Kai-shek, Generalissimo, 260, 284, 285
China, People's Republic of, 3, 17 (chart I), 18 (table 1); economy in, 233 (table 13), 234 (table 14), 235 (table 15), 237 (table 16), 238 (table